L.A. Baseball

From the Pacific Coast League to the Major Leagues

PHOTOGRAPHS FROM
the Los Angeles Public Library Photo Collection

ESSAYS BY
Tomas J. Benitez, Greg Burk, Glen Creason, David Davis, Lynell George, Emily Green, Amy Inouye, Glynn Martin, Stuart Rapeport, Bob Timmermann, Tom Zimmerman

EDITED BY
David Davis

Photographs from the Collection of

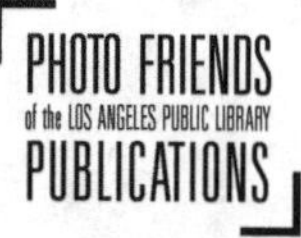

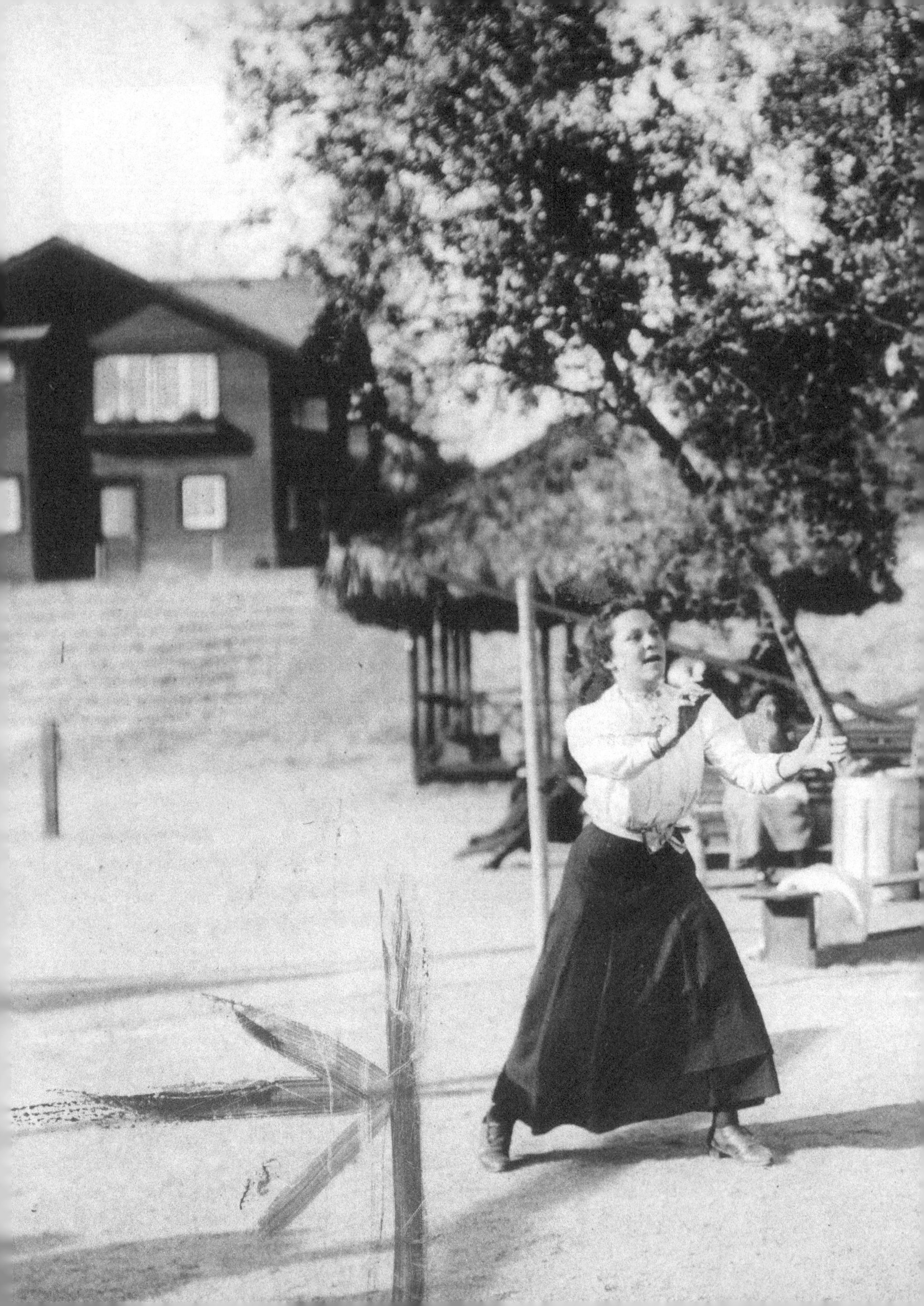

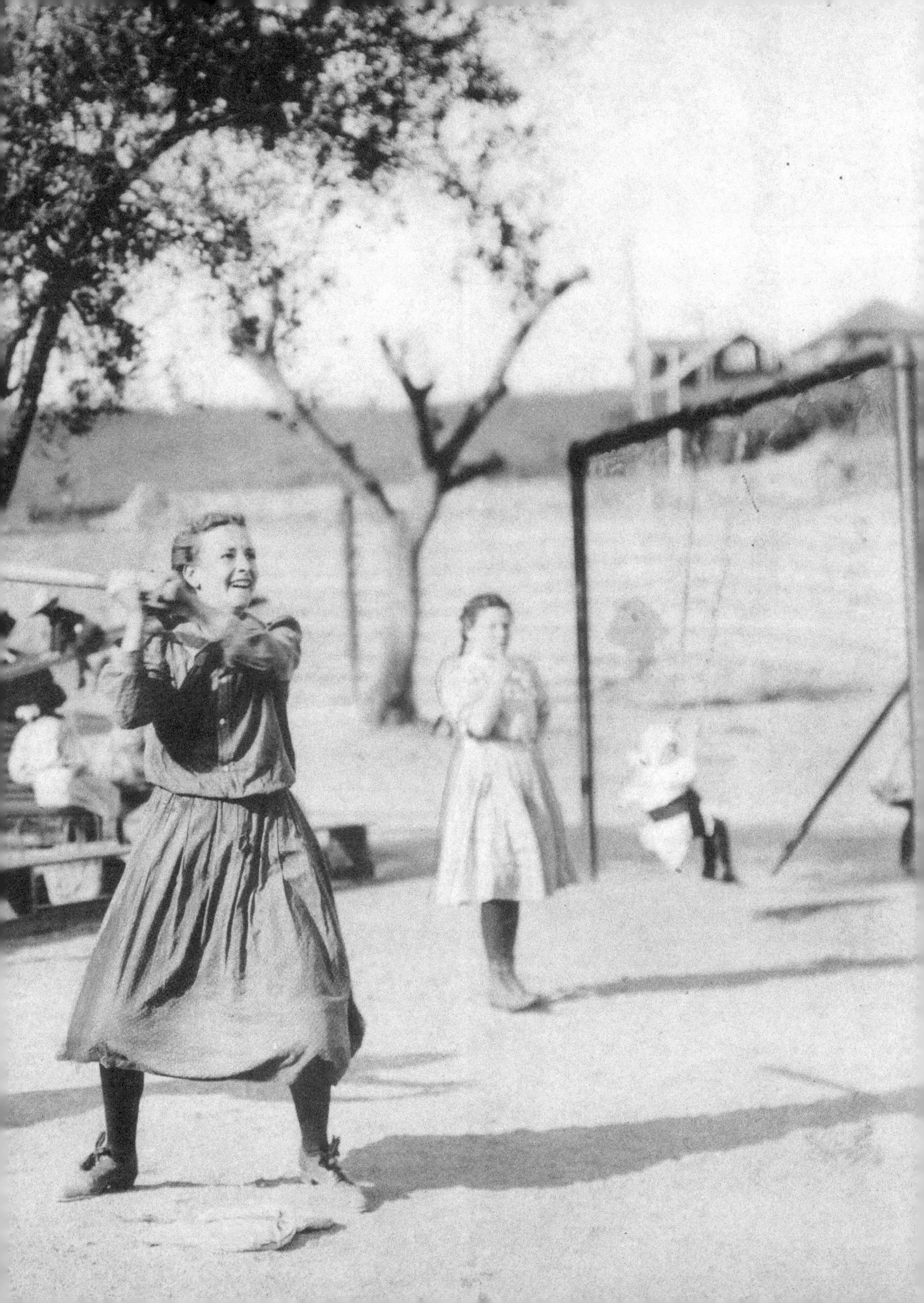

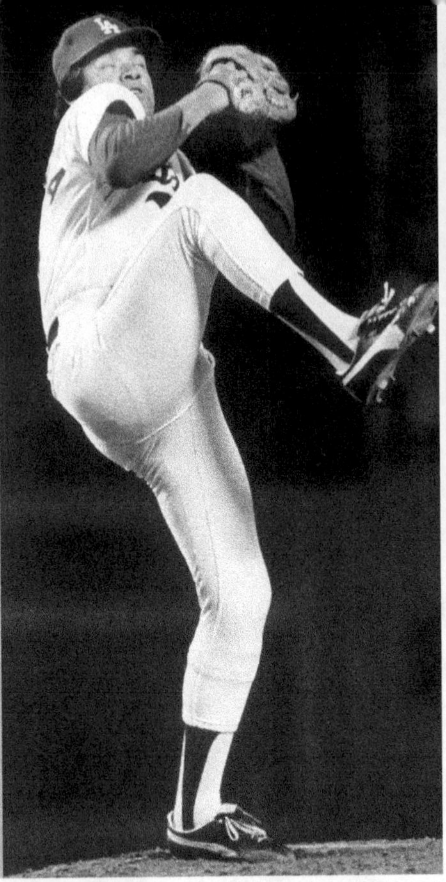

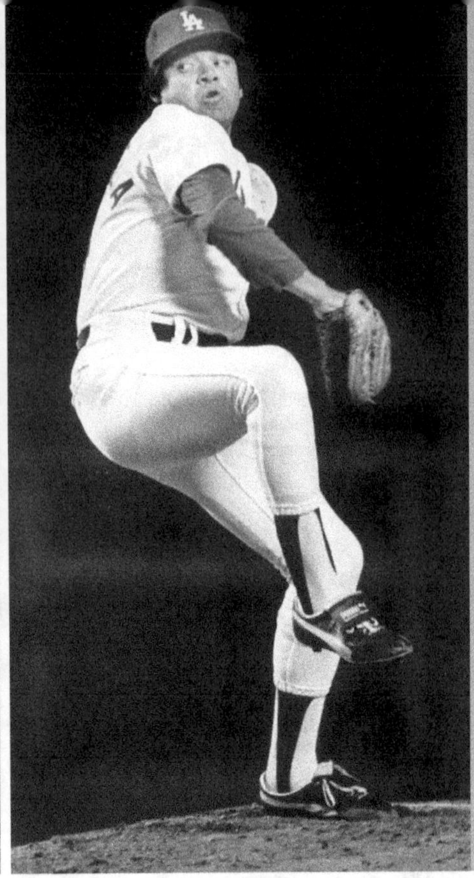

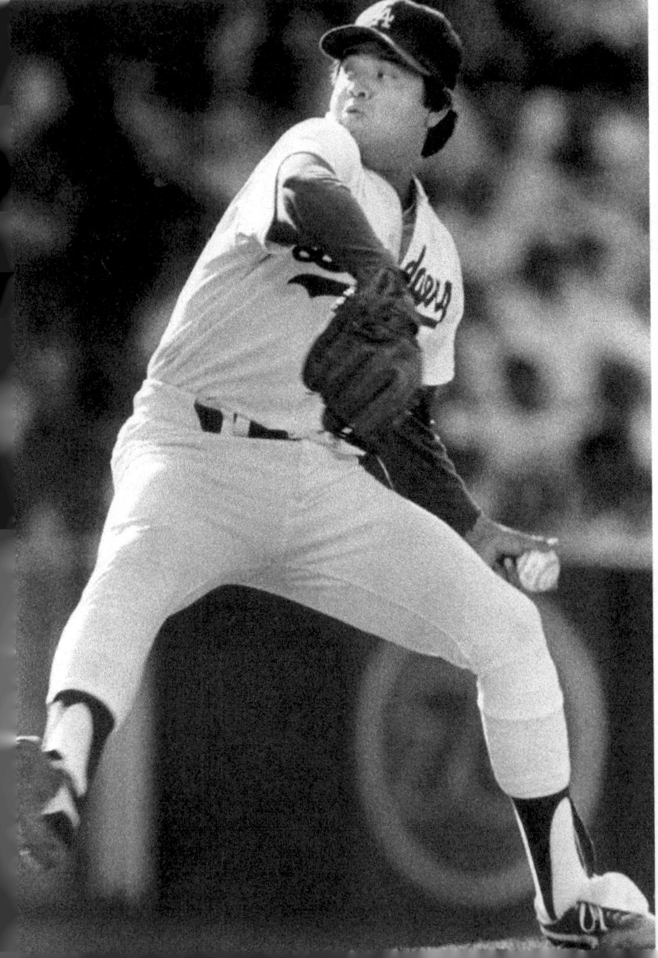

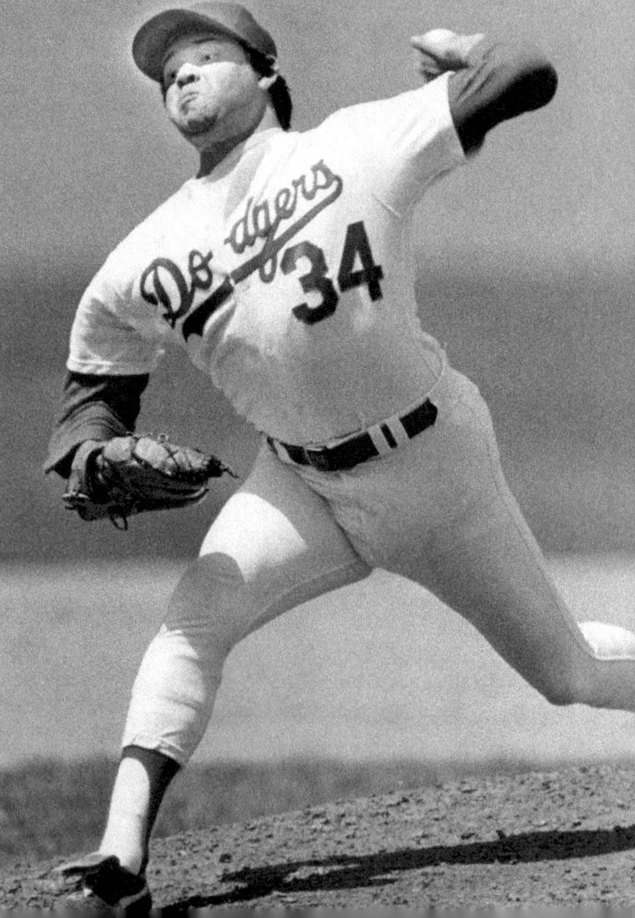
Dodgers
34

Contents

OPPOSITE, TOP LEFT & RIGHT, BOTTOM RIGHT: Fernando Valenzuela (James Ruebsamen/Herald-Examiner Collection)

OPPOSITE, BOTTOM LEFT: (Paul Chinn/Herald-Examiner Collection)

PAGES 2-3: "Bloomer girls" playing baseball in Echo Park. (Herald-Examiner Collection)

Leading Off

Like all of America, Southern California caught baseball fever in the 19th Century. The sport that writers dubbed the national pastime spread to every part of the Southland, from Santa Monica to Long Beach to Pasadena and beyond. Members of Riverside's Cahuilla Indian tribe played ball, *Issei* immigrants from Japan played *besuboru*, Mexican American kids played *béisbol.*

Schools, colleges, businesses, and towns fielded their own teams. Semi-pro and club teams proliferated, as did so-called industrial leagues. African American players from the Negro Leagues gathered for wintertime training, while talented local ballplayers stocked the rosters of Major League teams: Fred Snodgrass, Walter Johnson, John "Chief" Meyers, Gavvy Cravath.

L.A.'s inaugural Minor League team formed in 1892 as part of the four-team California League. The short-lived Los Angeles Seraphs played their home games at Athletic Park on Seventh Street, where the first night game in California is believed to have taken place. In 1901, a second effort to base an L.A. team in the California League took hold. These L.A. Angels (also known as the Looloos) played at the diamond located on the northern end of Chutes Park along Washington Boulevard. Future Hall of Famer Rube Waddell pitched briefly for the club.

Two years later, the Angels moved to the newly organized Pacific Coast League. They played first at Chutes Park and then beginning in 1925 at Wrigley Field, located at 42nd Place and Avalon Boulevard. Team owner and chewing-gum magnate William Wrigley also owned the Chicago Cubs of the National League; Wrigley's players used his resort on Catalina Island for spring training and exhibition games.

The Angels were joined in the PCL by the Vernon Tigers (a team that spent two years as the Venice Tigers). The Tigers left for San Francisco in 1926, only to return to Southern California in 1938 as the Hollywood Stars. The Stars and the Angels enjoyed a fierce rivalry, especially after the Stars moved into intimate Gilmore Field, located east of Fairfax Avenue between Beverly Boulevard and 3rd Street.

The post-war years heralded change. On April 15, 1947, Jackie Robinson broke Major League Baseball's "color line" when he began playing for the Brooklyn Dodgers. By the early 1950s, MLB owners were seeking opportunities outside the established (and crowded) East Coast market. The Boston Braves moved to Milwaukee in 1953, and the Philadelphia Athletics relocated to Kansas City the next year. That set the stage for the Dodgers to come to L.A. in 1958, while their rivals, the New York Giants, uprooted for San Francisco. Three years later came the expansion Los Angeles Angels in the American League. Baseball in

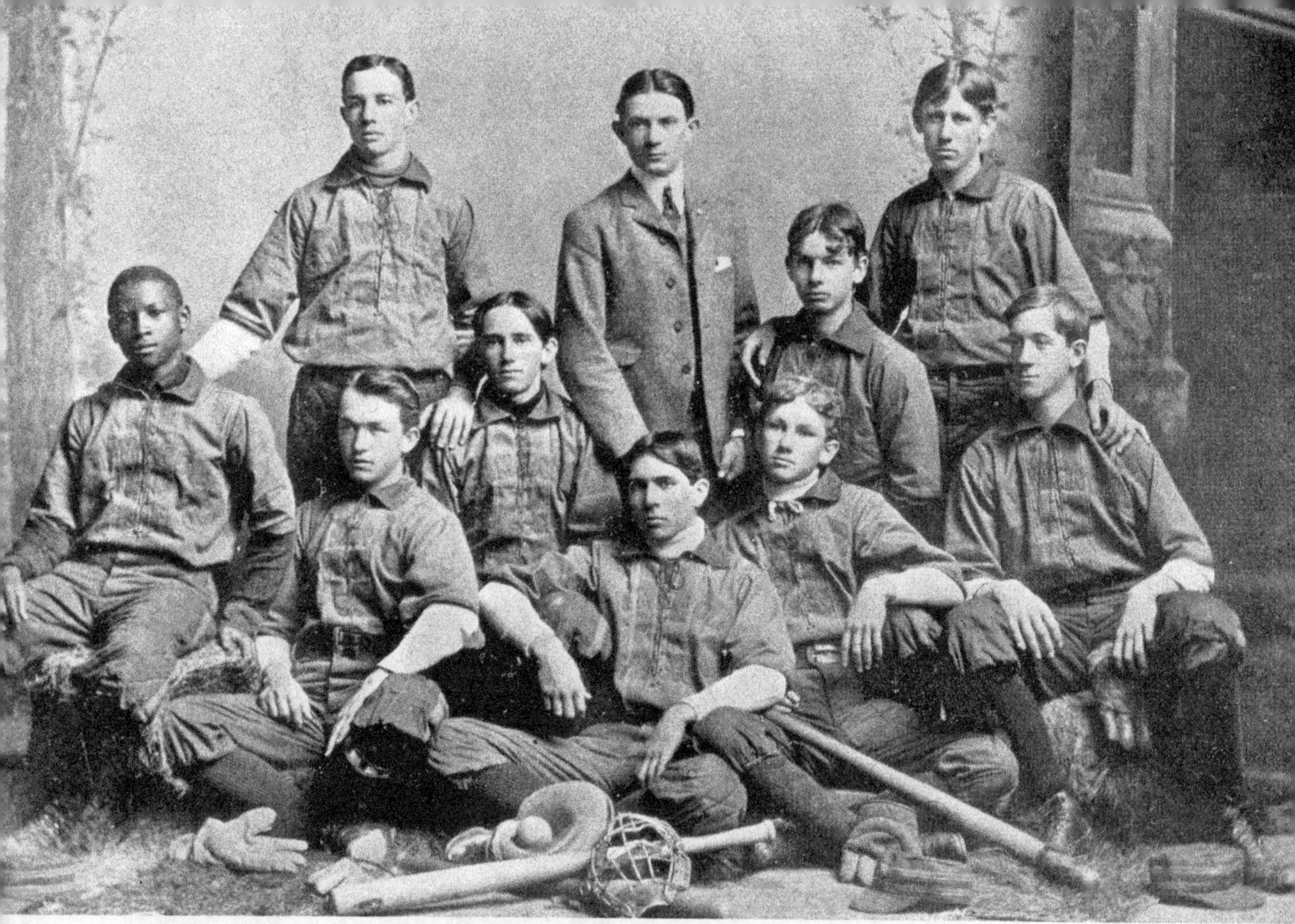

The Commercial High baseball team, circa 1900.
(Security Pacific National Bank Collection)

Southern California would never be the same.

Photography and baseball have been inextricably linked since the invention of the daguerreotype process in 1839. Professional baseball players were among the first athletes to be photographed extensively (usually in studio portraits). Gradually, as innovations in camera, lens, flash, and film technology caught up to the speed of athletes in motion, photographers produced black-and-white and then color action shots of baseball's most exciting and memorable moments on the field.

The Los Angeles Public Library's vast photo collection supplied the images for this book and the accompanying exhibit. Many of the pictures seen here were originally published in the *Valley Times* and *Herald-Examiner* newspapers. Others came from the groundbreaking "Shades of L.A." project of family photographs. Together, they capture every aspect of our national pastime up until 1989, when the *Herald-Examiner* was shuttered: famous players and anonymous weekend warriors; changes in uniform style and ballpark architecture; and the timeless essence of a game roiled by social change. Play Ball!

—David Davis

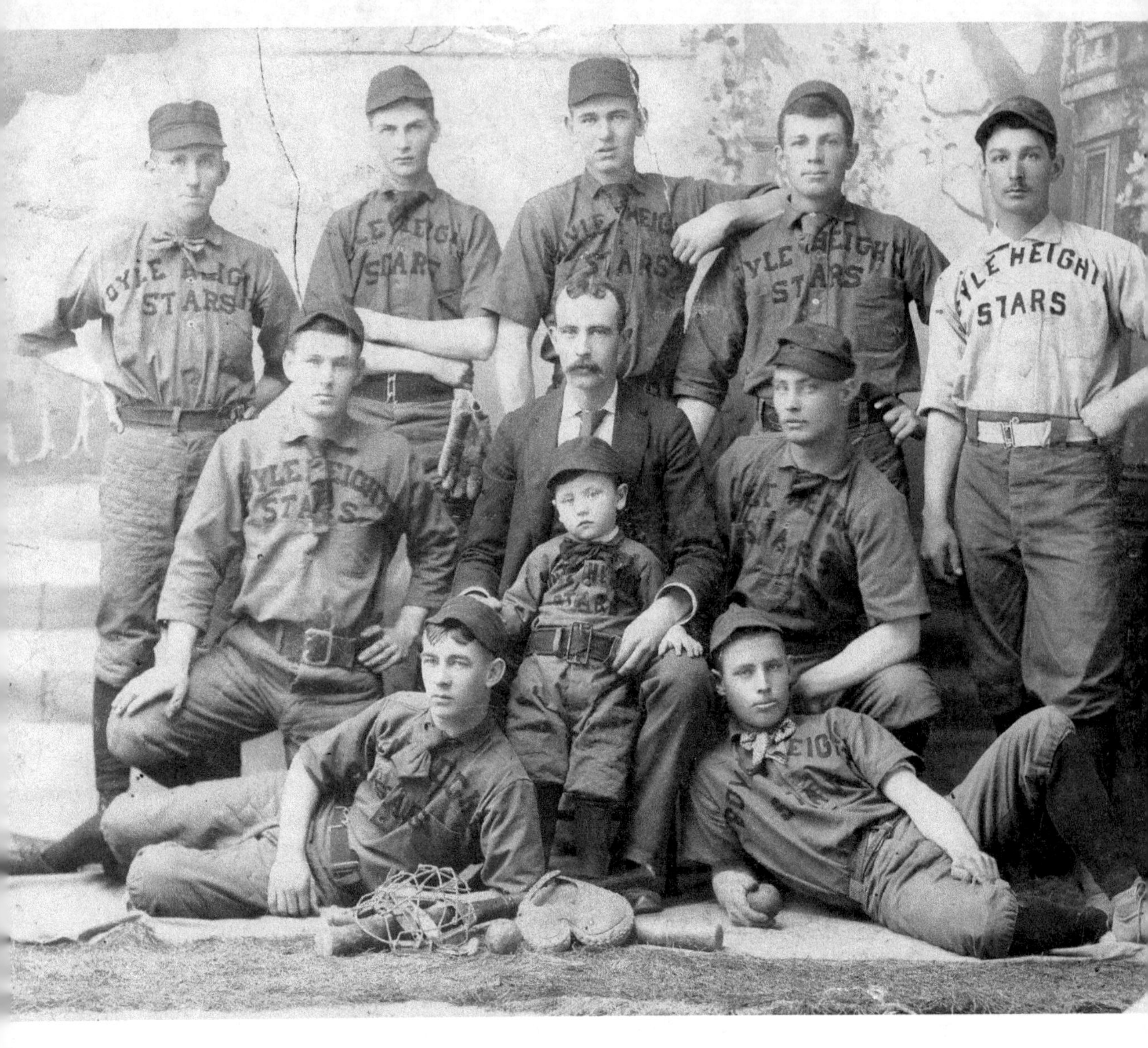

The Boyle Heights Stars, an early neighborhood team.
(Herald-Examiner Collection)

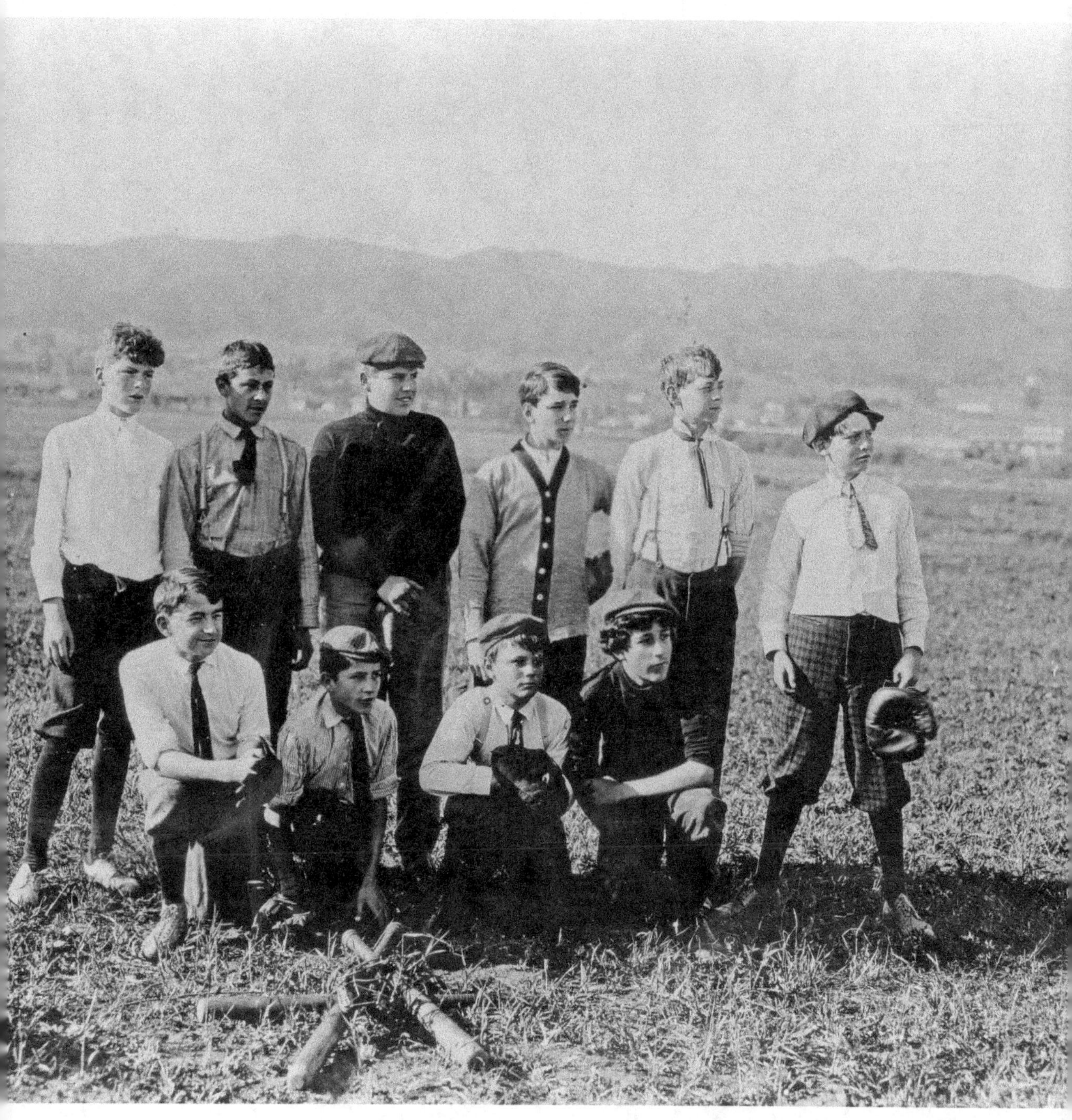

The Hollywood High baseball team, circa 1900.
(Security Pacific National Bank Collection)

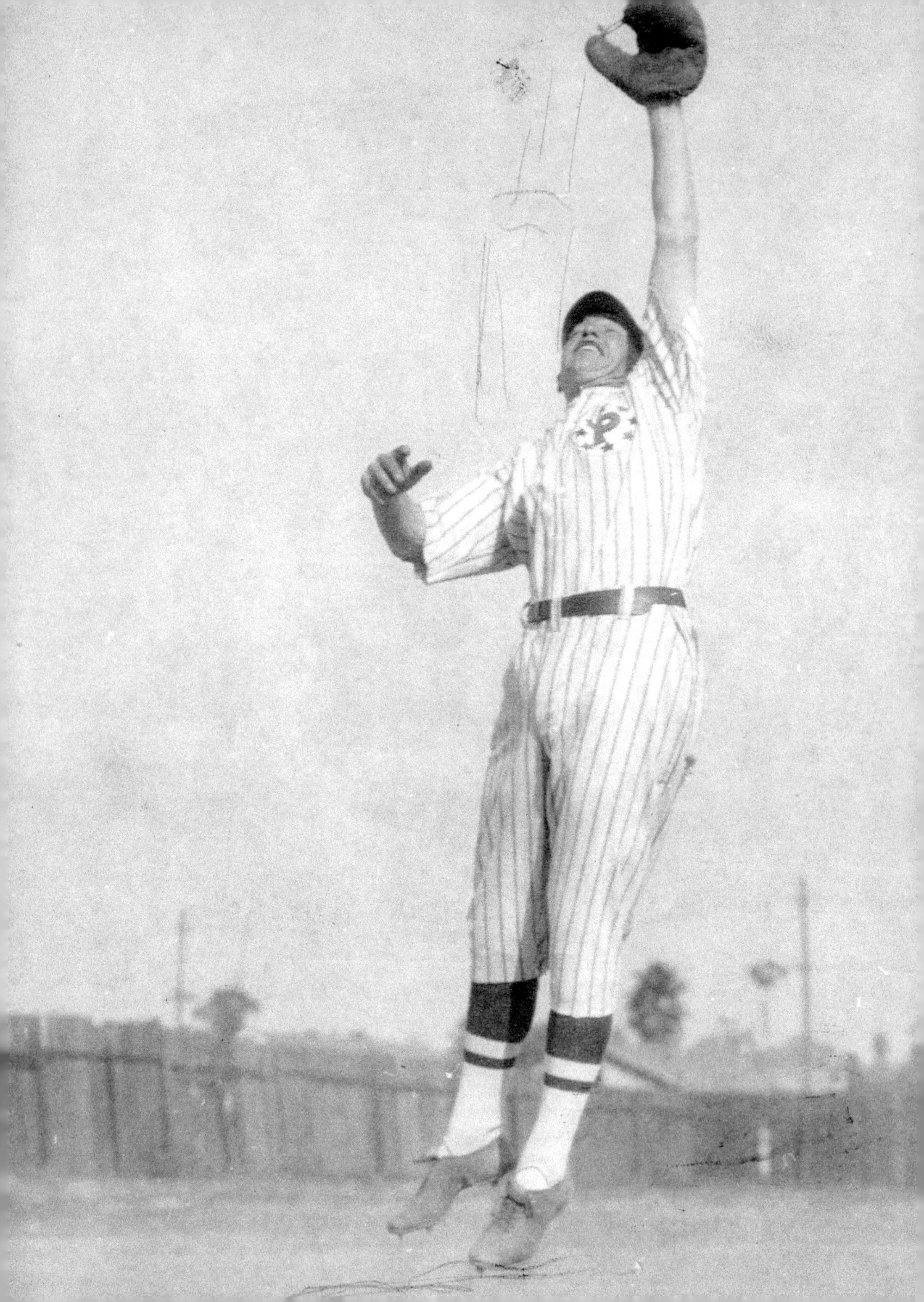

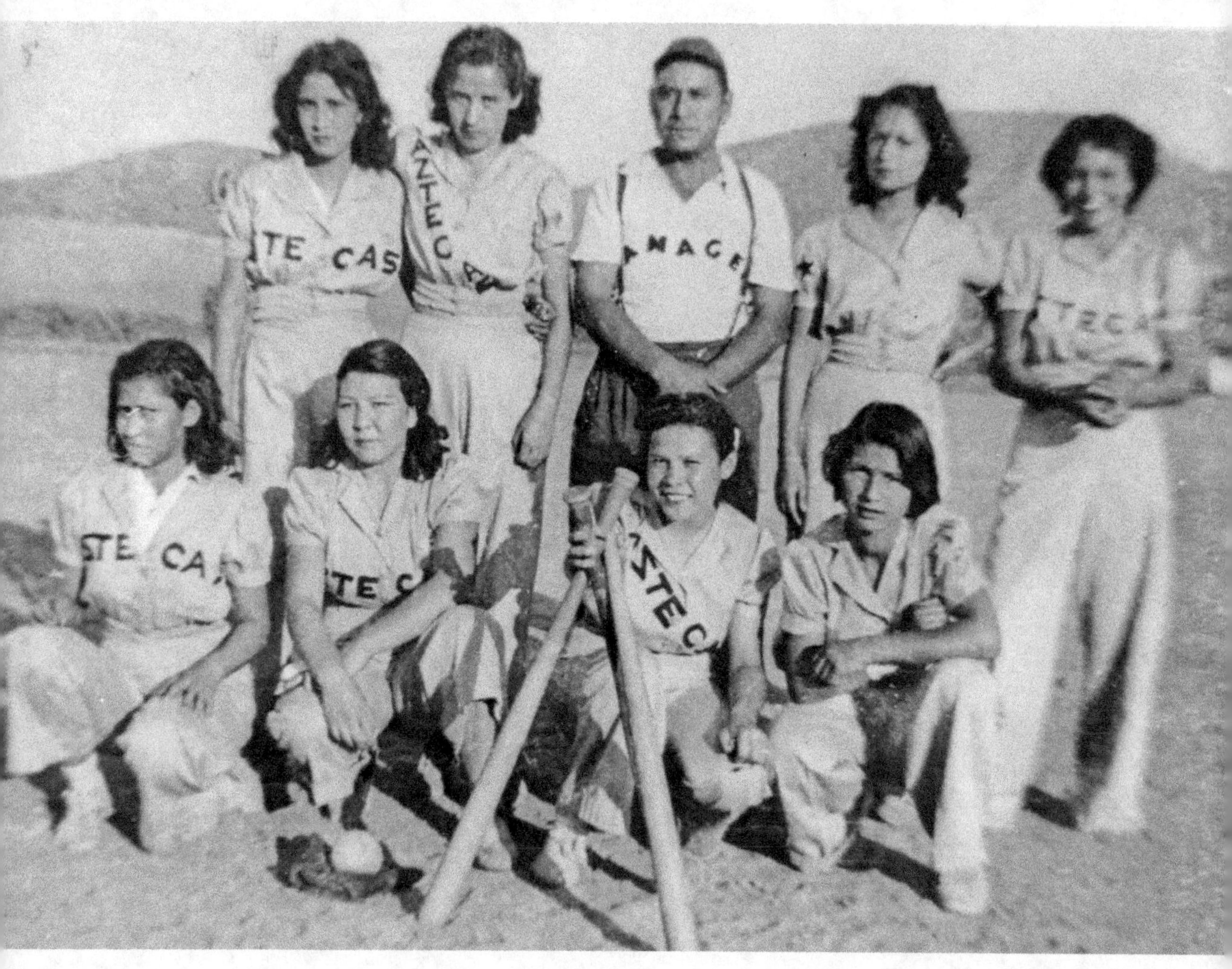

Group portrait of the Aztecas, from Pacoima, circa 1935.
(Delta (Fonseca) Ortega/Shades of LA)

OPPOSITE: Jim Thorpe became famous for winning gold medals in track at the 1912 Olympics; he also played baseball in the Pacific Coast League.
(Herald-Examiner Collection)

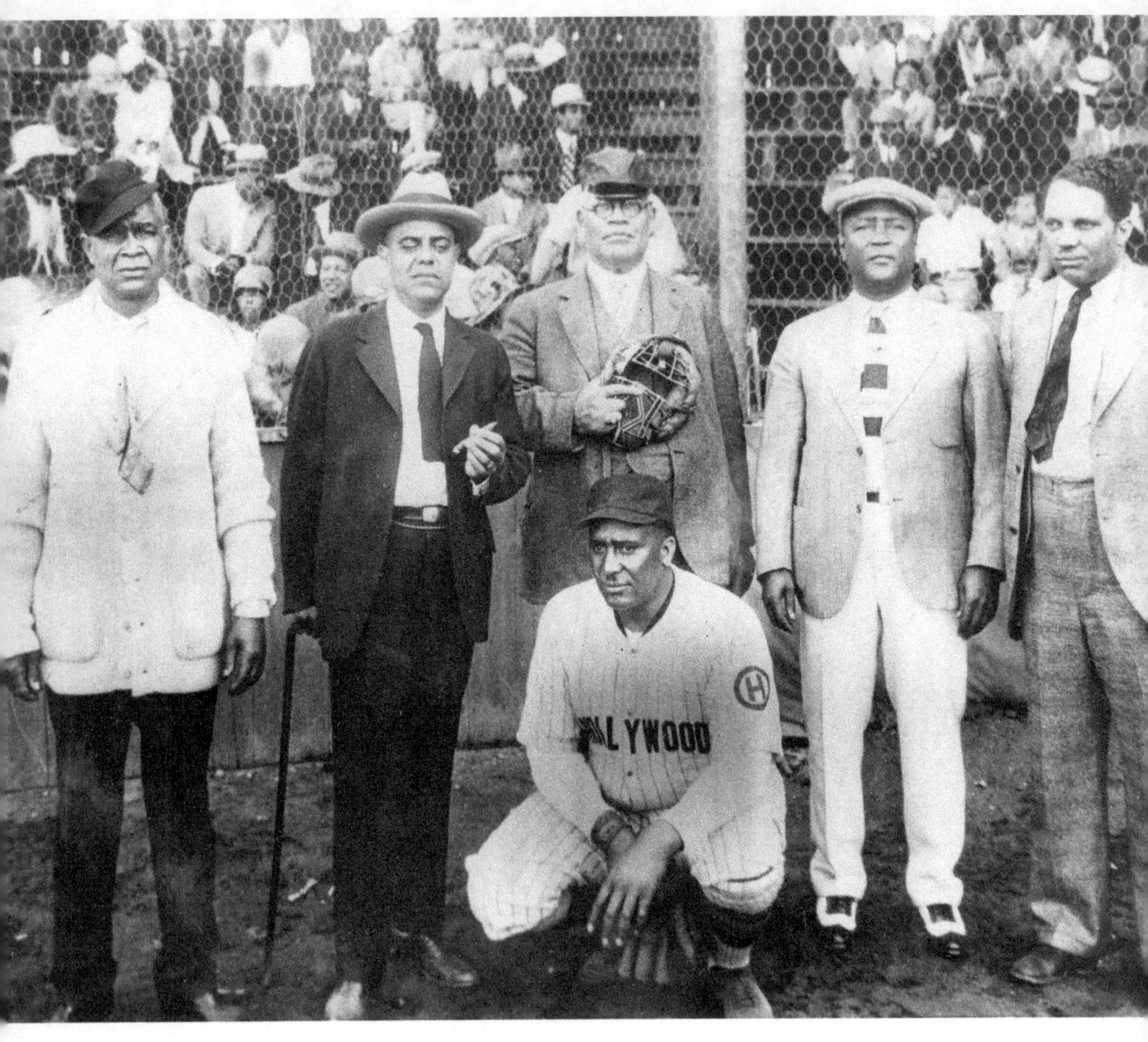

Pre-game meeting at White Sox Park, home of the California Winter League, featuring pitcher and Negro League executive Andrew "Rube" Foster (*second from right*). (Shades of L.A.)

OPPOSITE: Pitching ace Leroy "Satchel" Paige, before a game at White Sox Park, at 38th Street and Compton Avenue. (Herald-Examiner Collection)

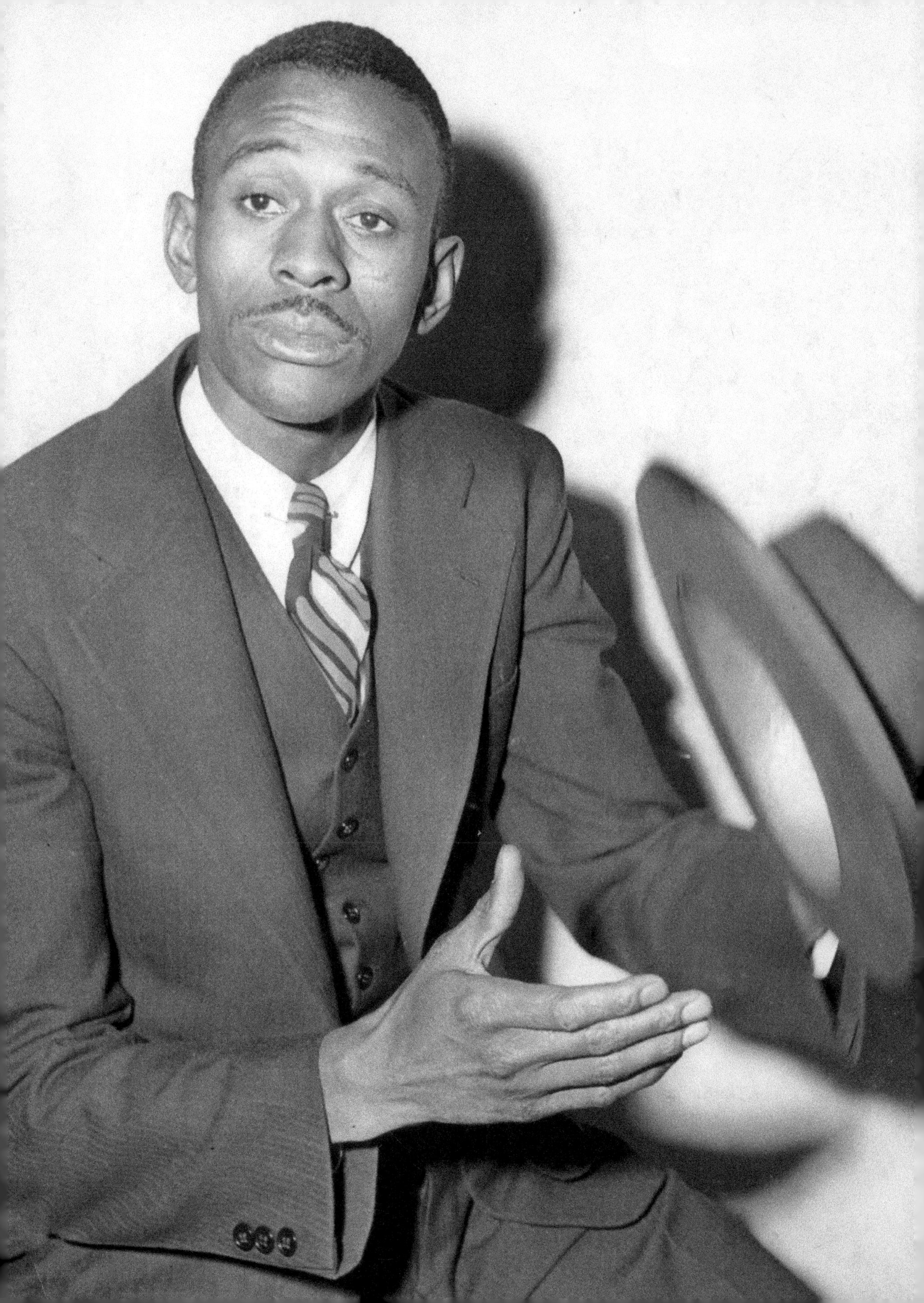

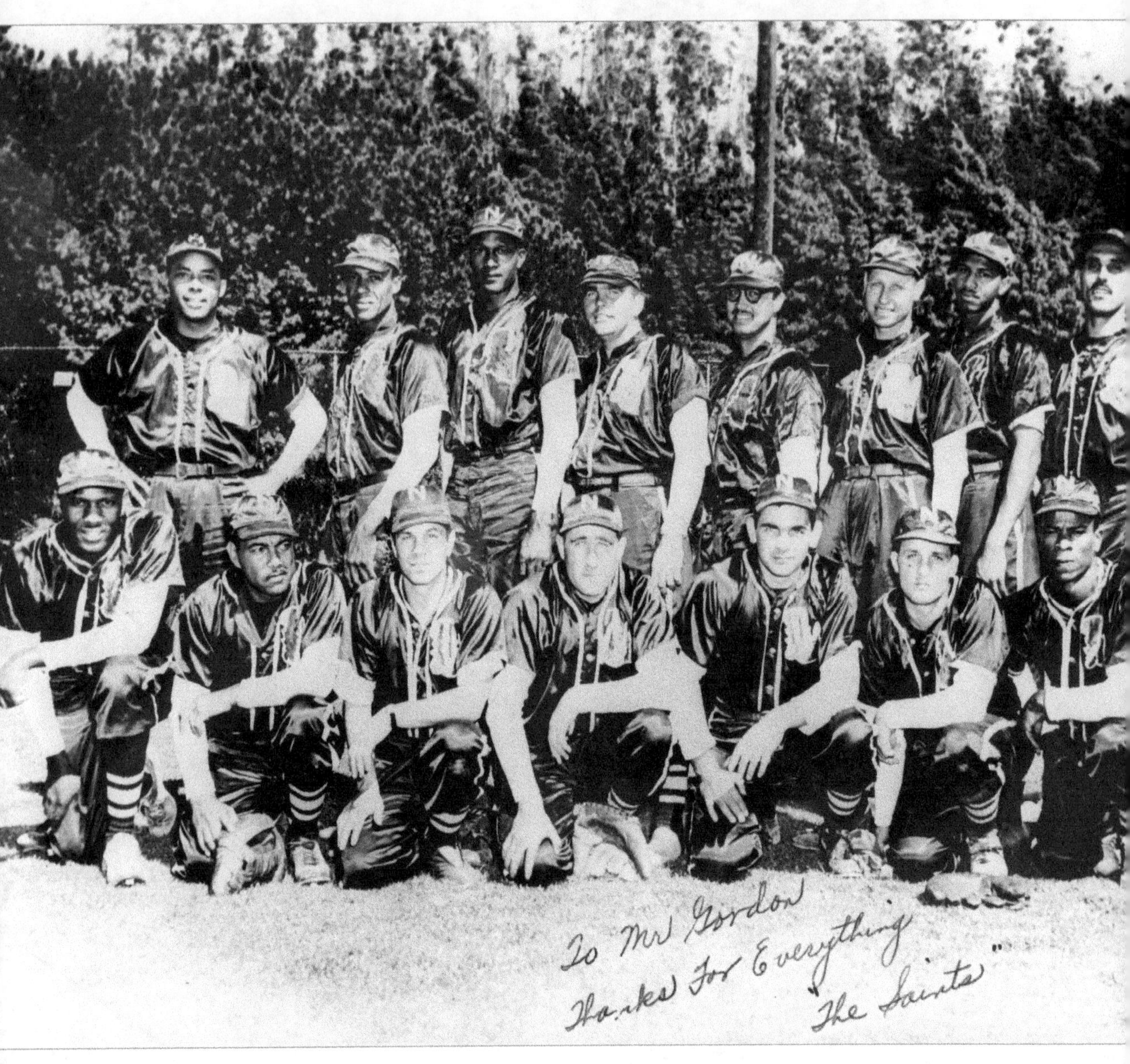

The Saints baseball team made up of police officers from the Newton Street station, featuring Tom Bradley (*standing, third from left*), circa 1943. (Shades of L.A.)

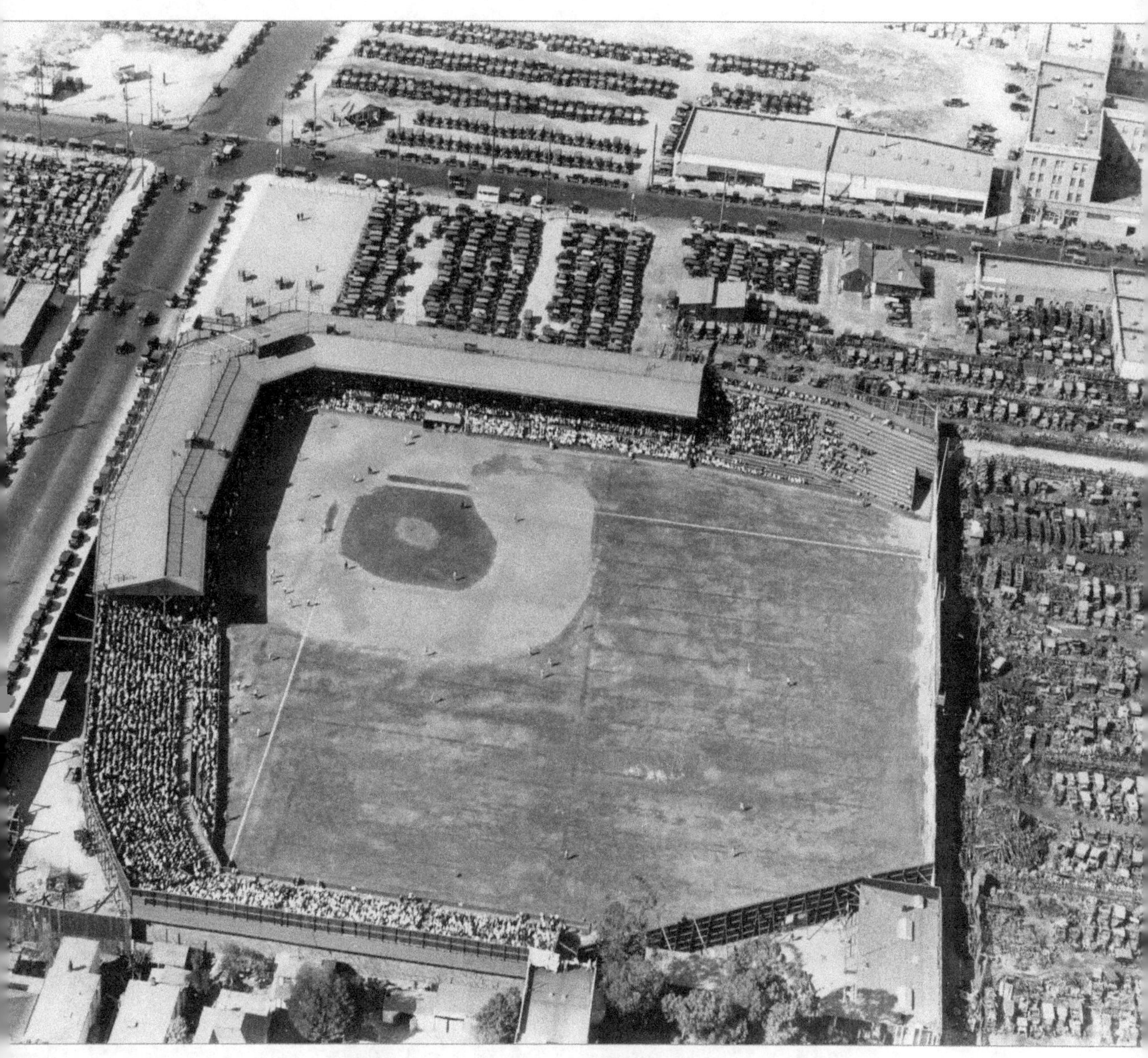

Aerial view of Washington Park in downtown L.A.,
home to the Los Angeles Angels, circa 1920.
(Security Pacific National Bank Collection)

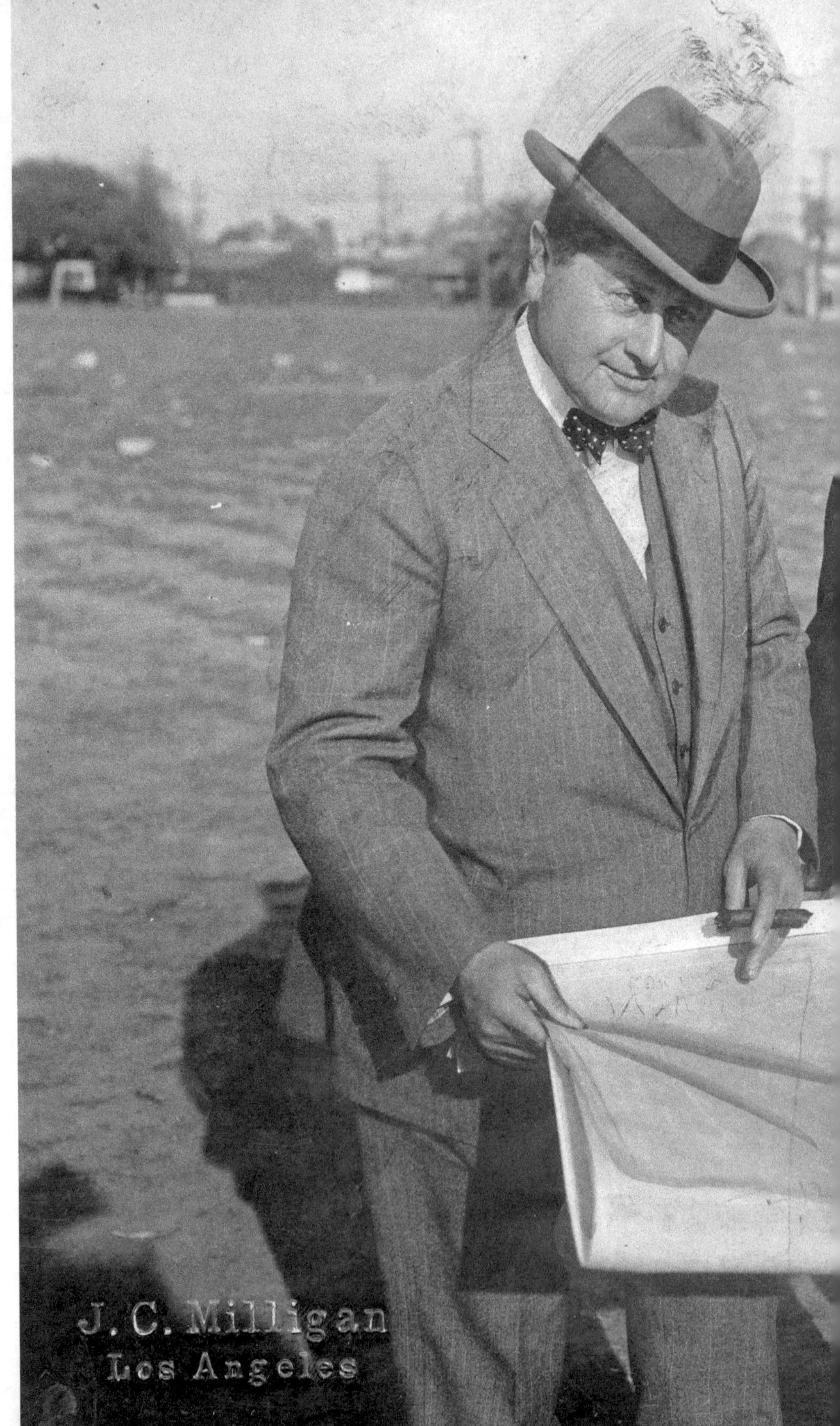

Chewing-gum magnate William Wrigley (*left*) looks over blueprints for Wrigley Field, circa 1924. (J.C. Milligan/ Herald-Examiner Collection)

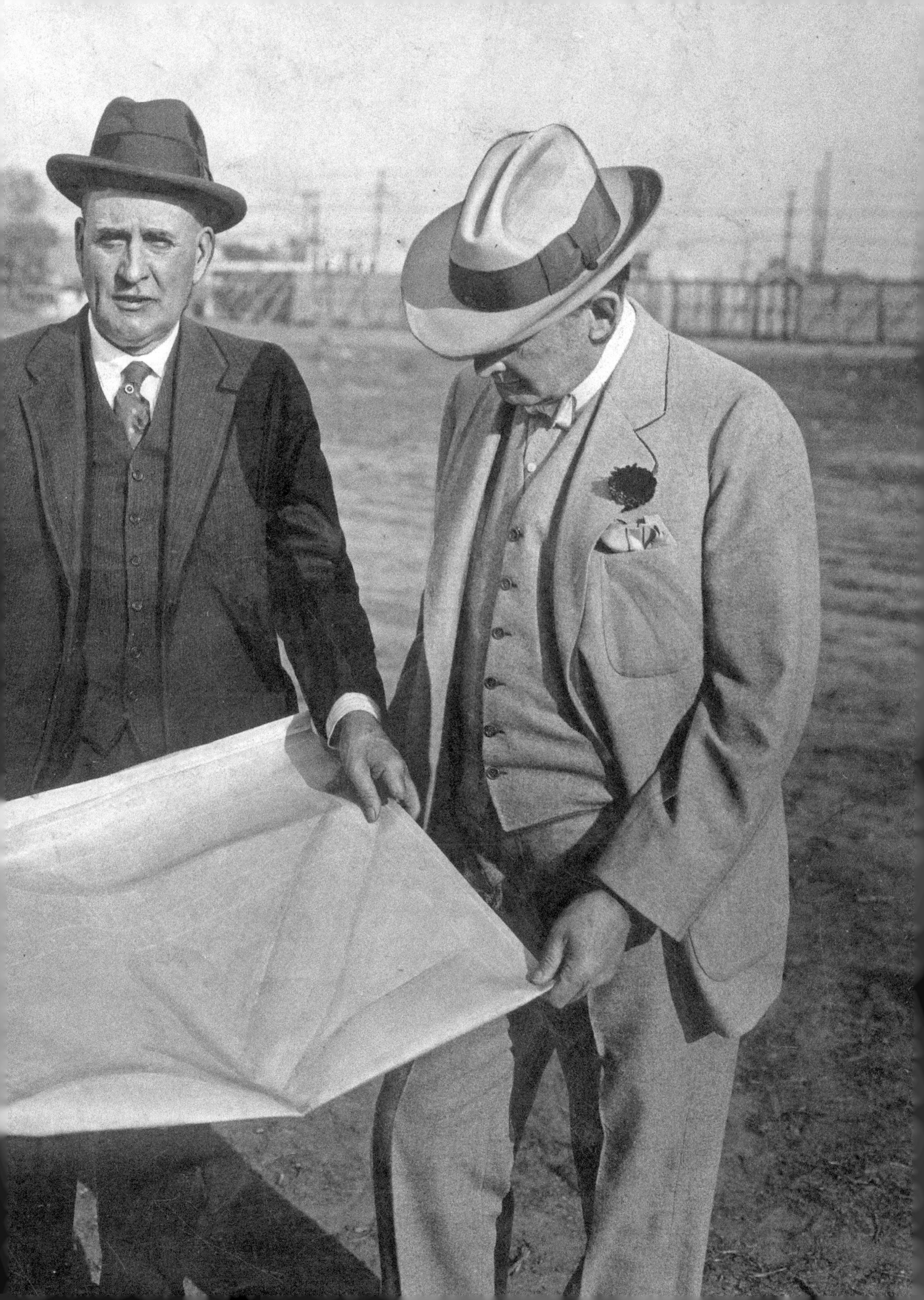

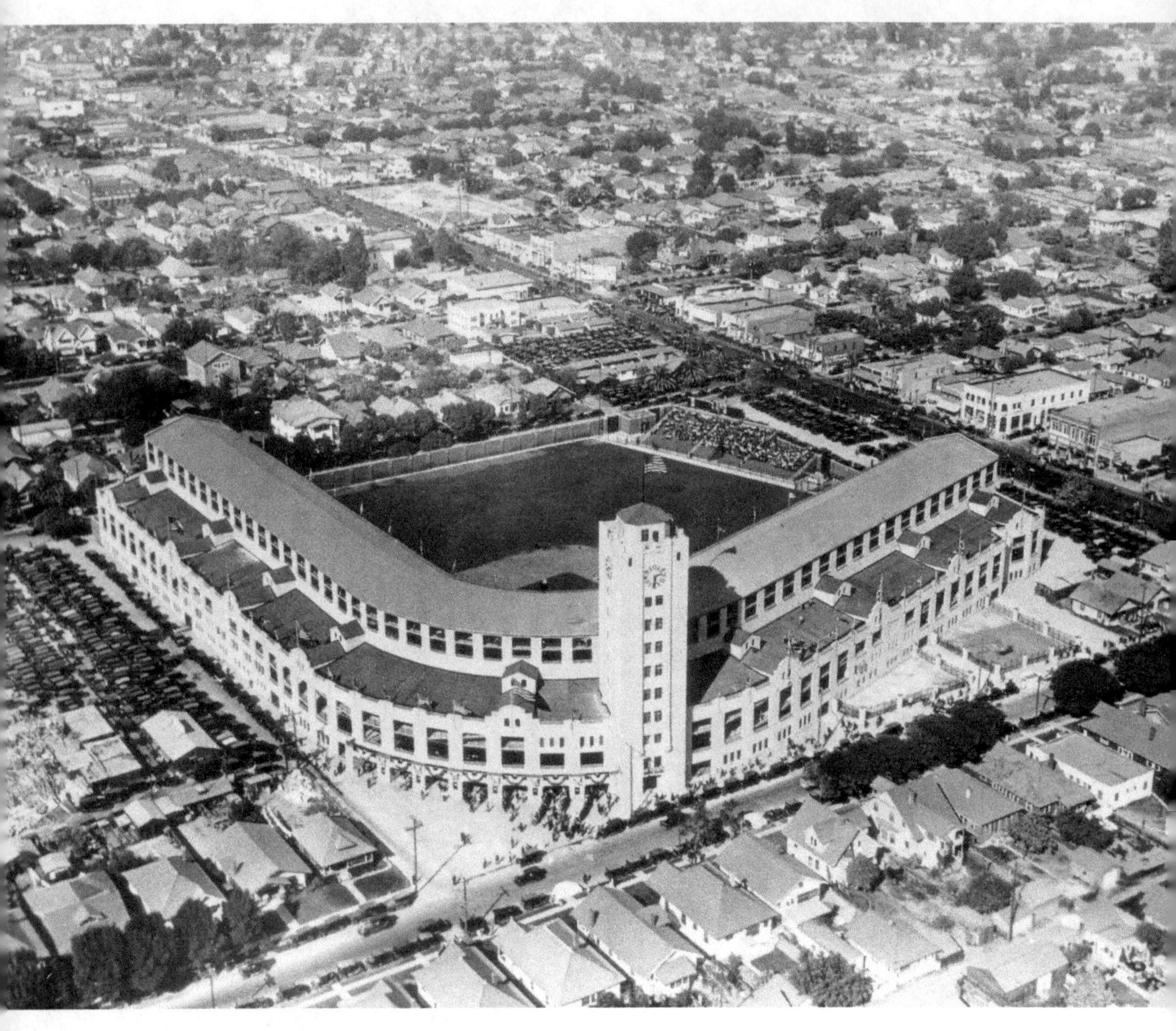

Opening Day at Wrigley Field, 1925.
(Security Pacific National Bank Collection)

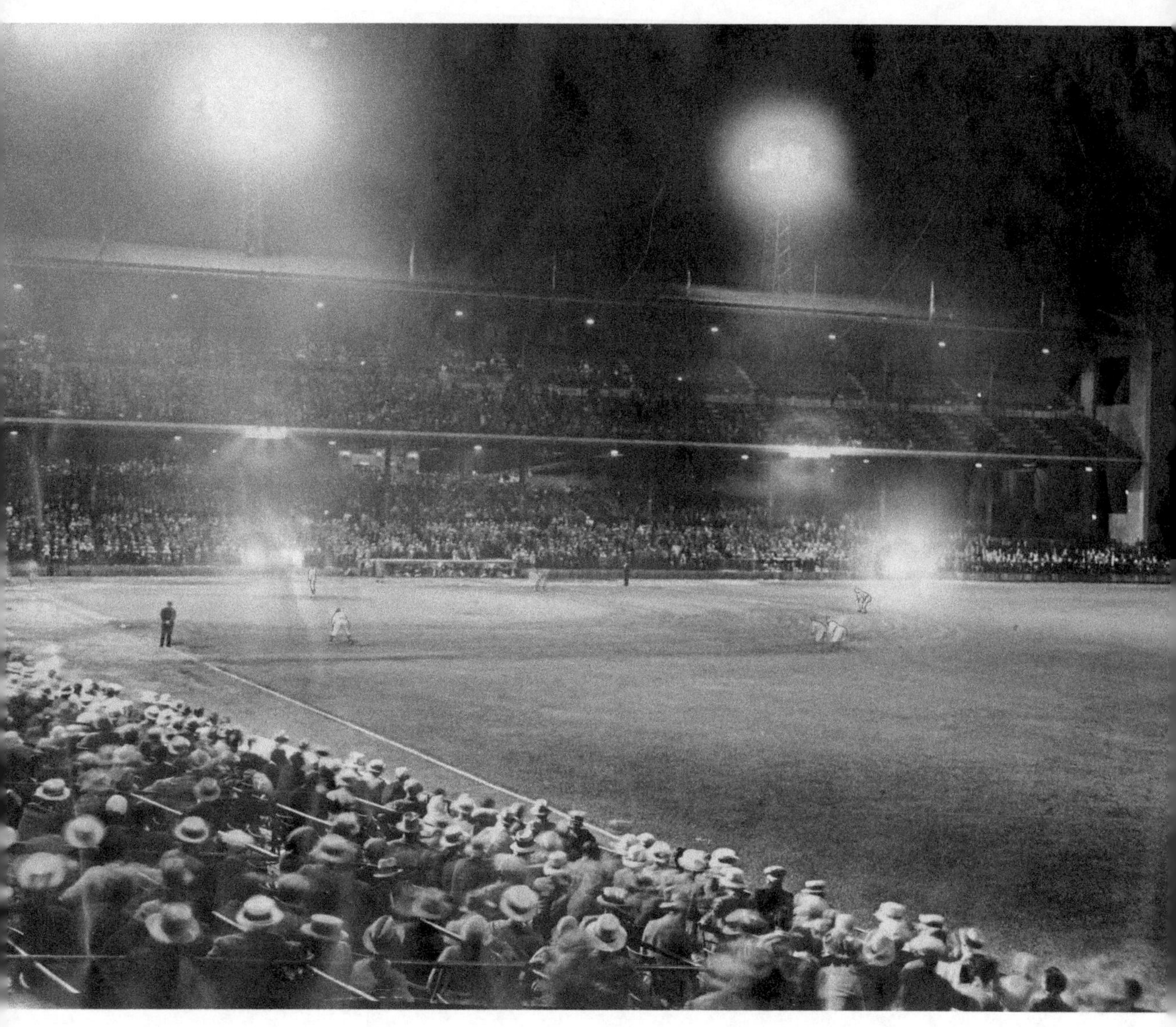

First night game at Wrigley Field, July 22, 1930.
(Herald-Examiner Collection)

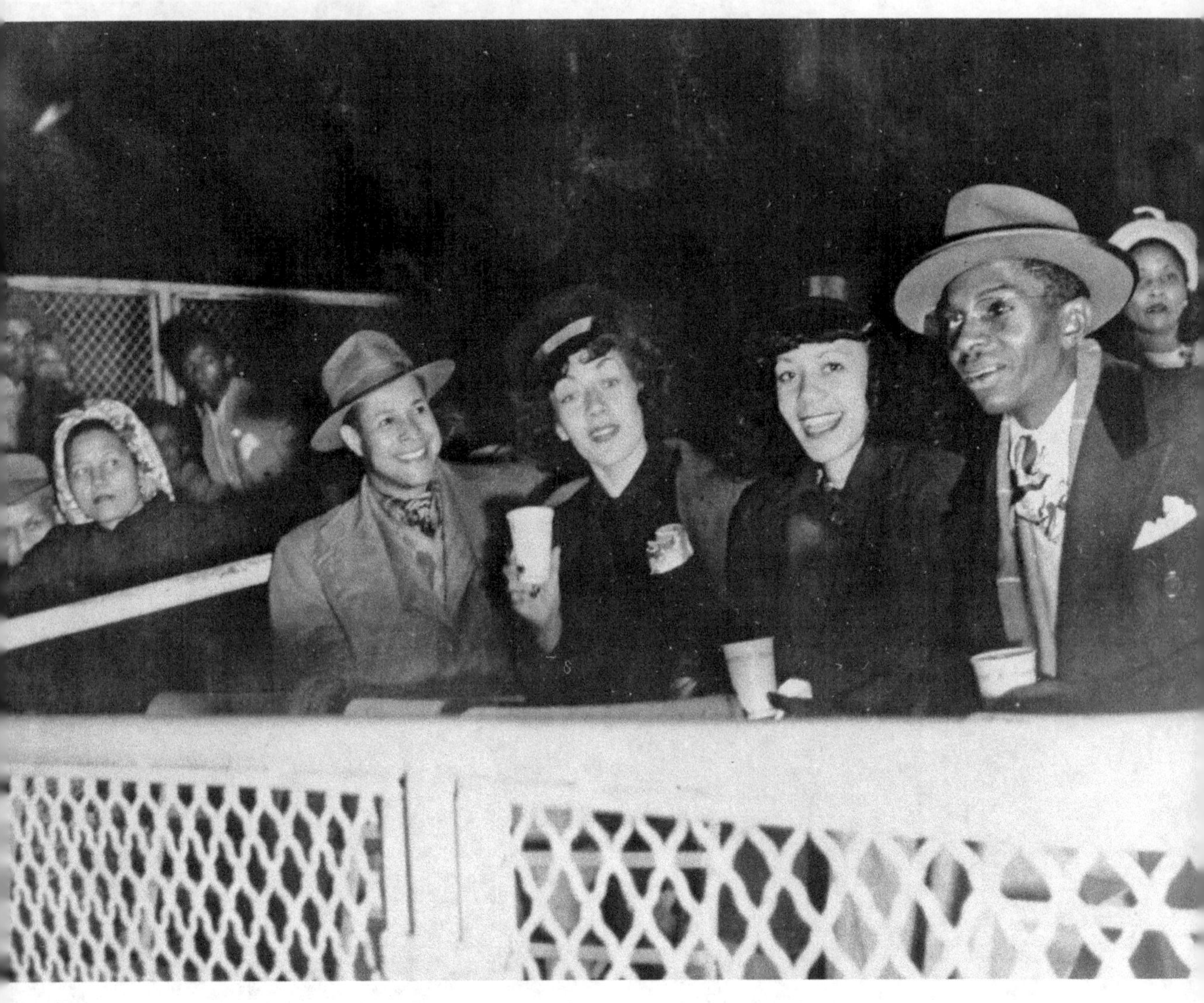

Fans watching a game at Wrigley Field.
(Shades of L.A.)

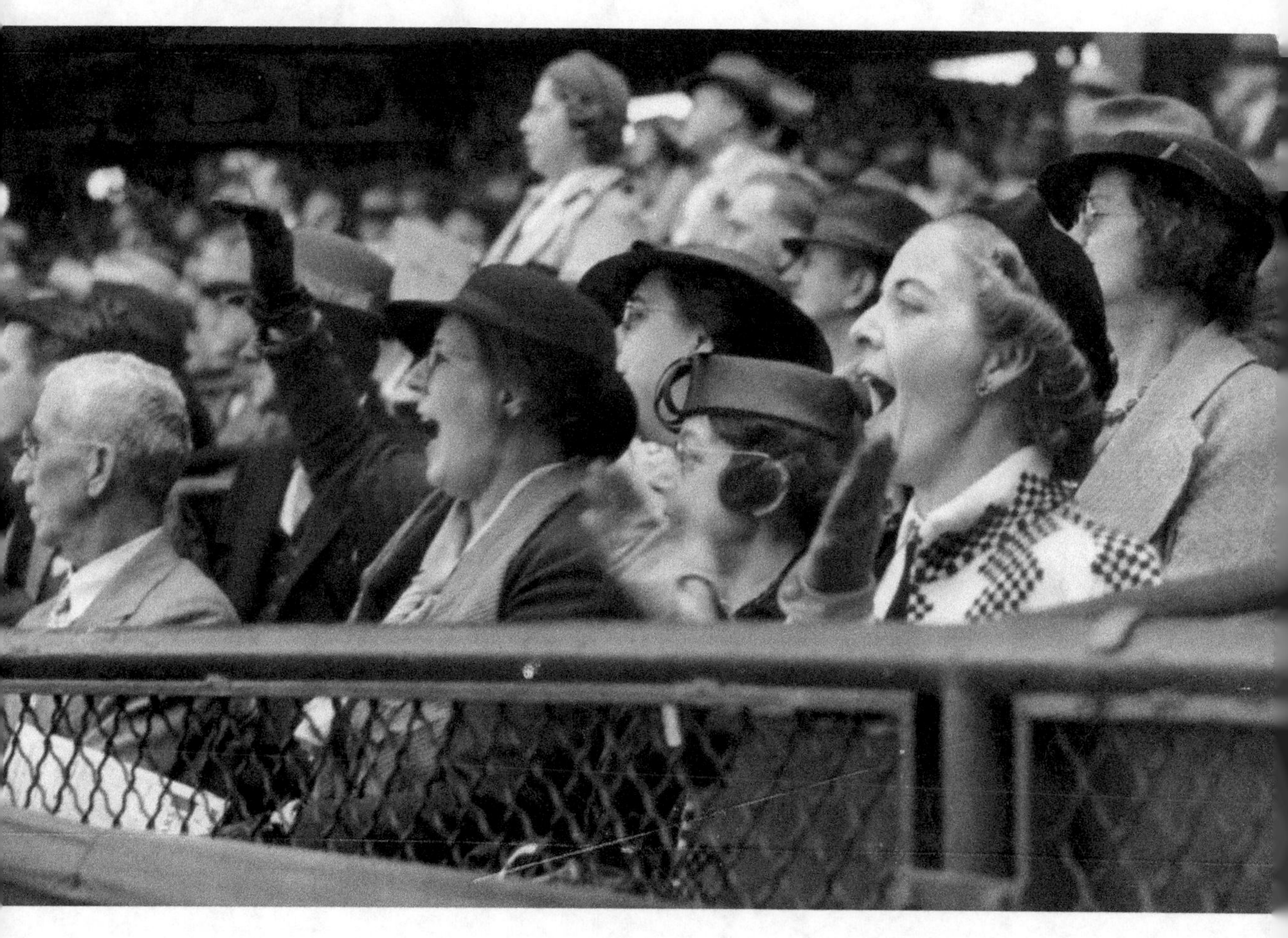

Fans cheer on the Angels at Wrigley Field.
(Herald-Examiner Collection)

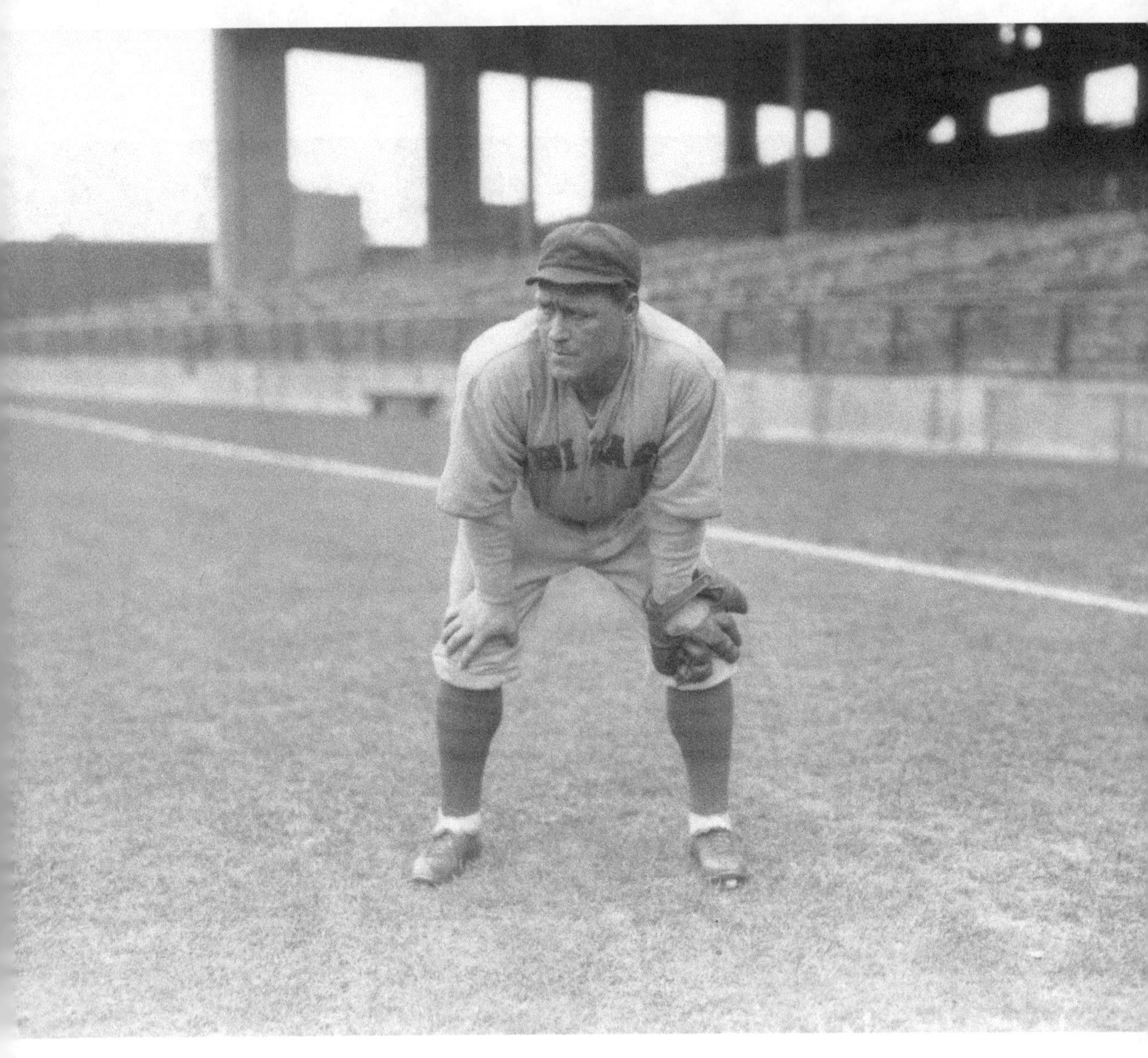

Chicago Cubs great Hack Wilson, circa 1930,
when the Cubs used to hold spring training on Catalina Island.
(Security Pacific National Bank Collection)

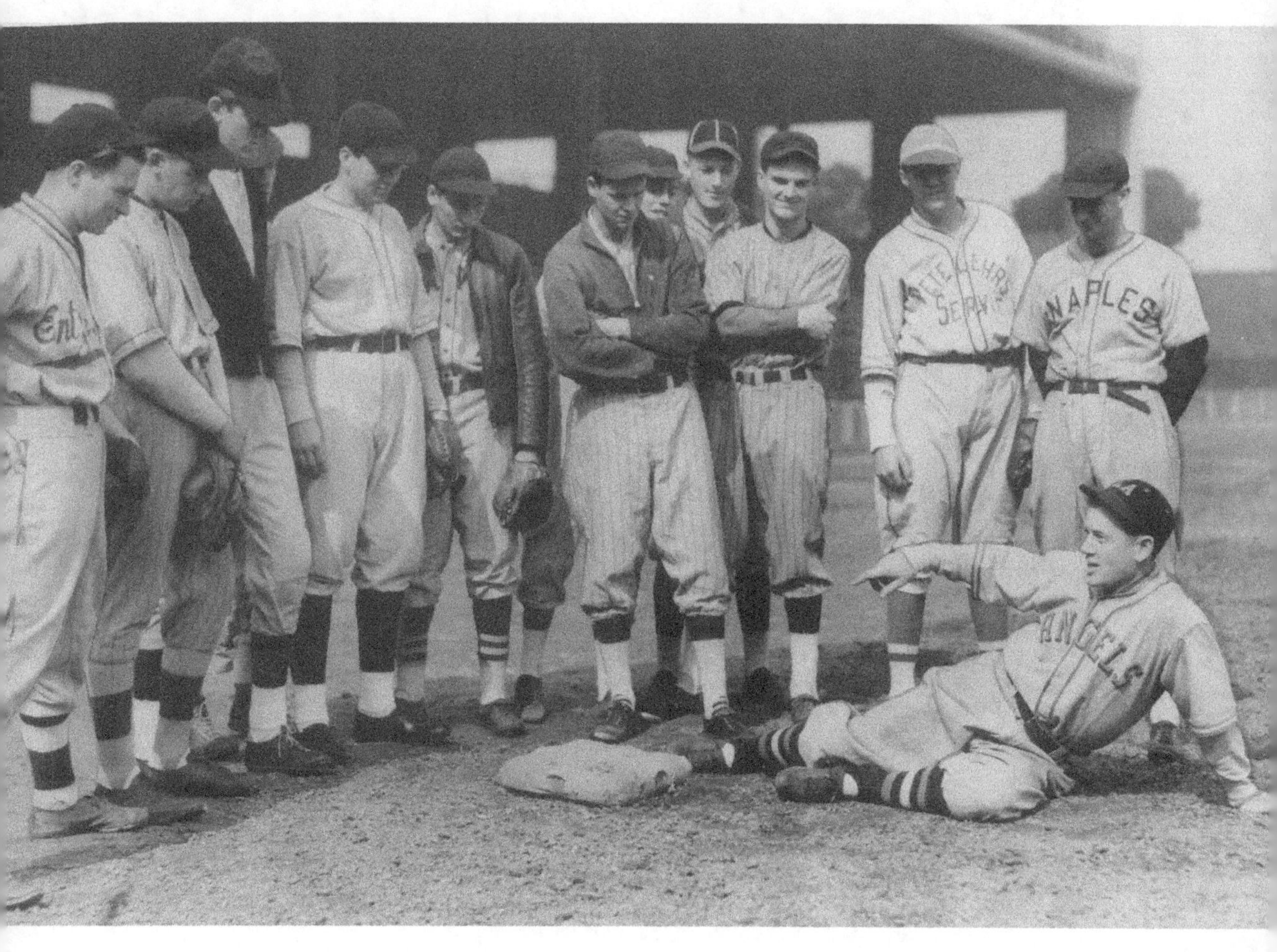

Angels star Arnold "Jigger" Statz demonstrates sliding technique at a local clinic.
(Carroll Photo Service/Herald-Examiner Collection)

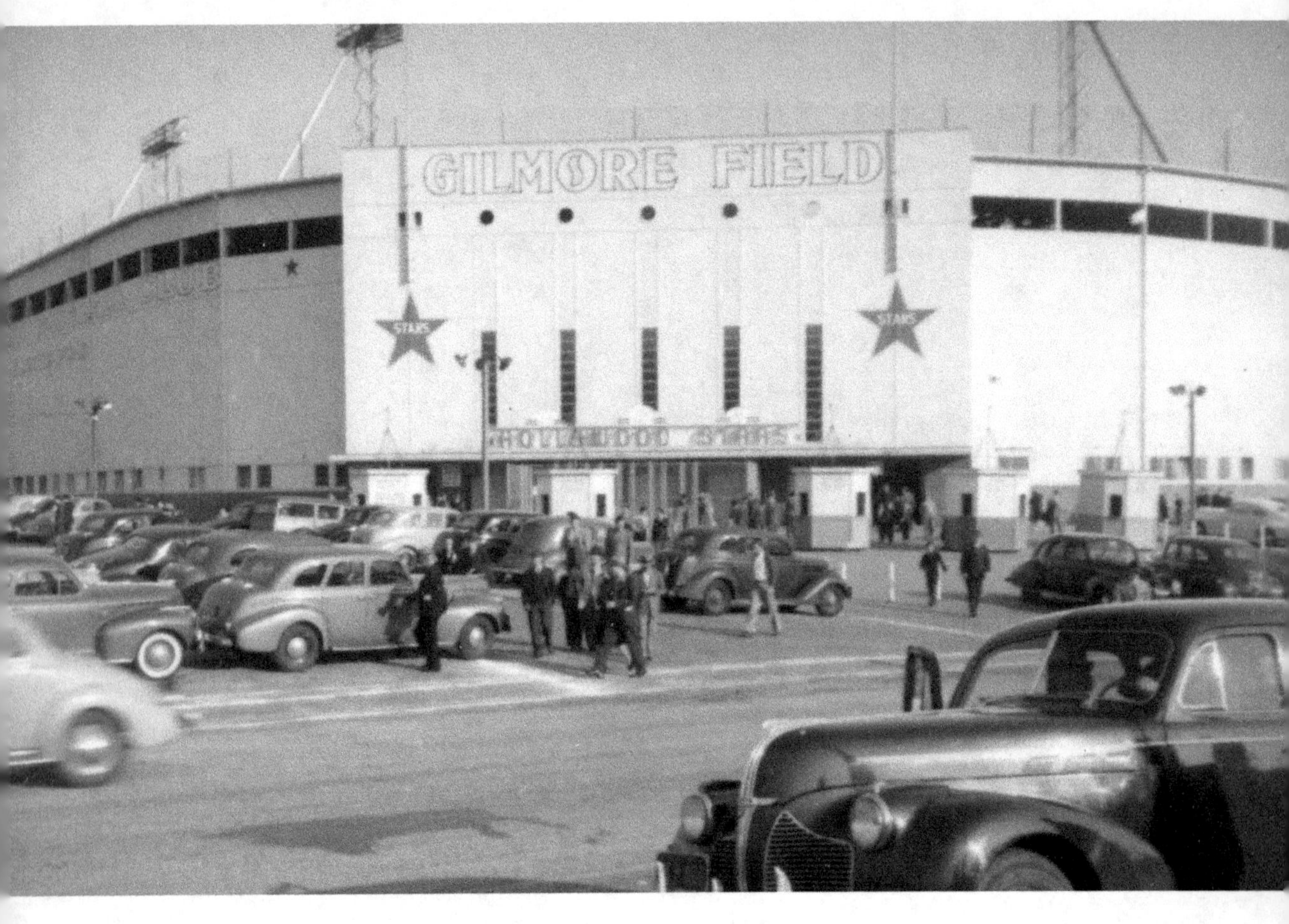

Exterior view of Gilmore Field, home to the Hollywood Stars.
(Herman Schultheis)

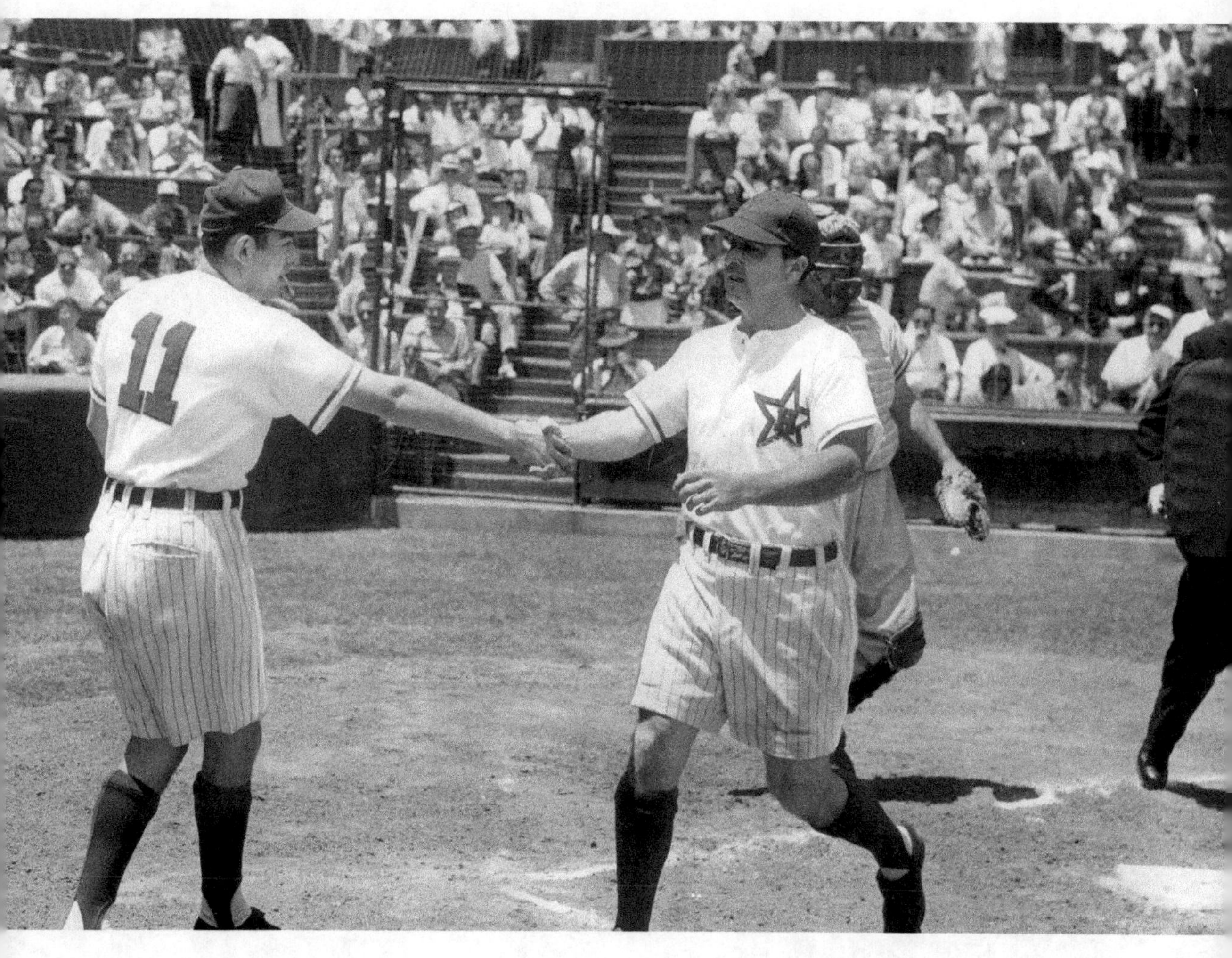

Stars slugger Frank Kelleher is congratulated after hitting a home run.
The stylish but impractical shorts lasted only a few seasons.
(De Wan Studios/ Herald-Examiner Collection)

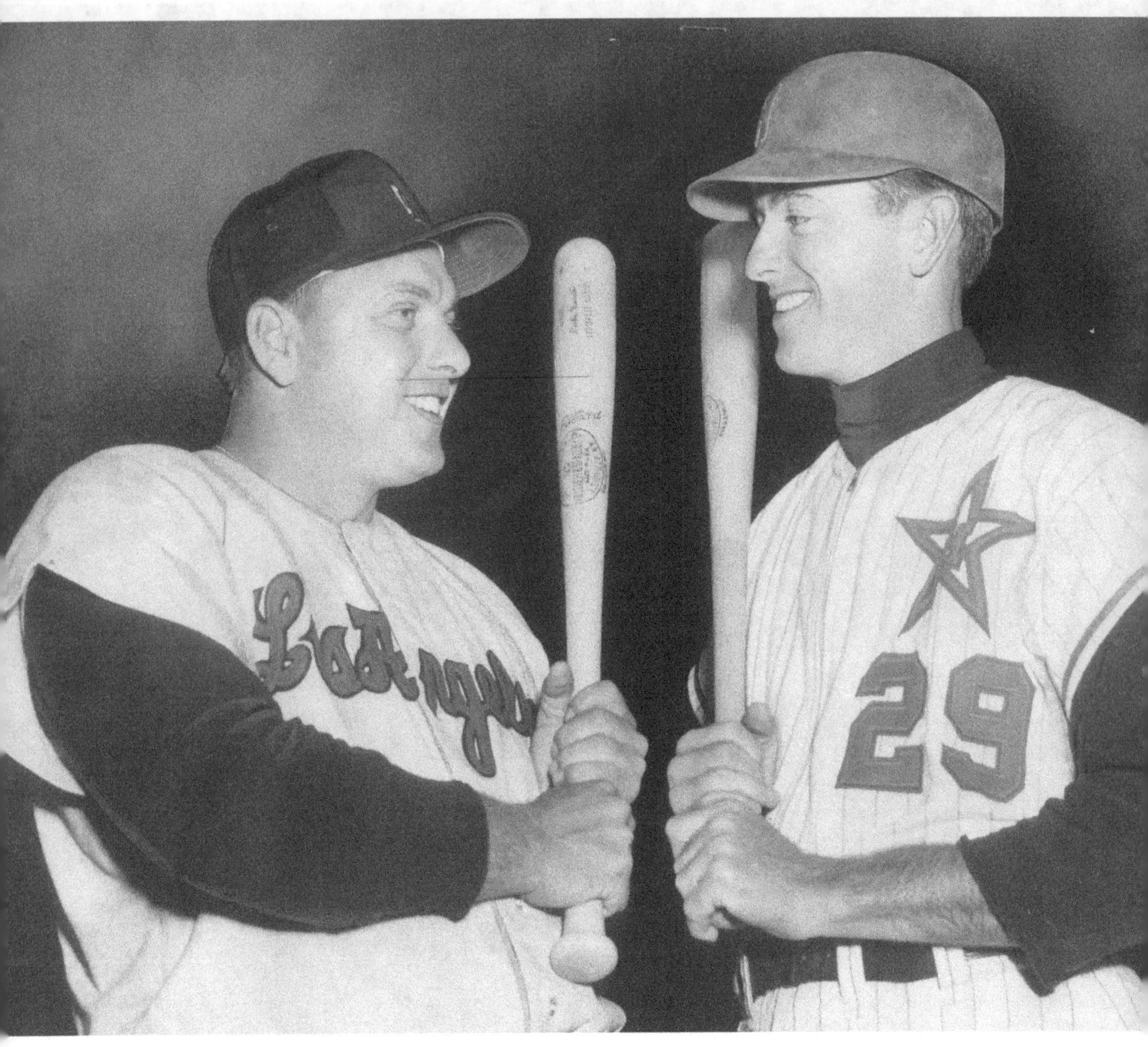

Rival sluggers Steve Bilko of the Angels (*left*) and Dick Stuart of the Stars.
(Howard Ballew/Herald-Examiner Collection)

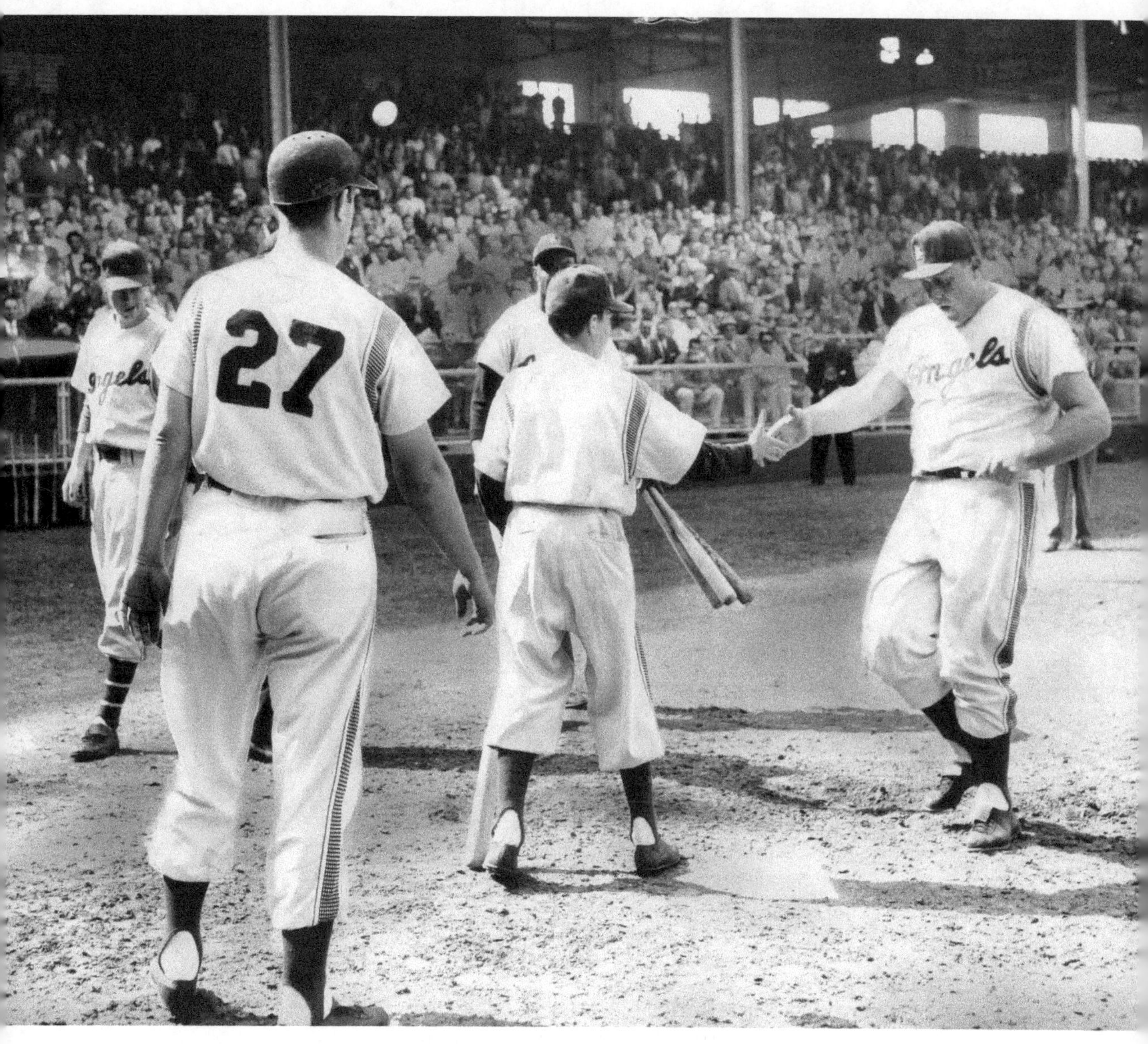

Mighty Steve Bilko after hitting yet another home run for the Angels.
(Bill Walker/Herald-Examiner Collection)

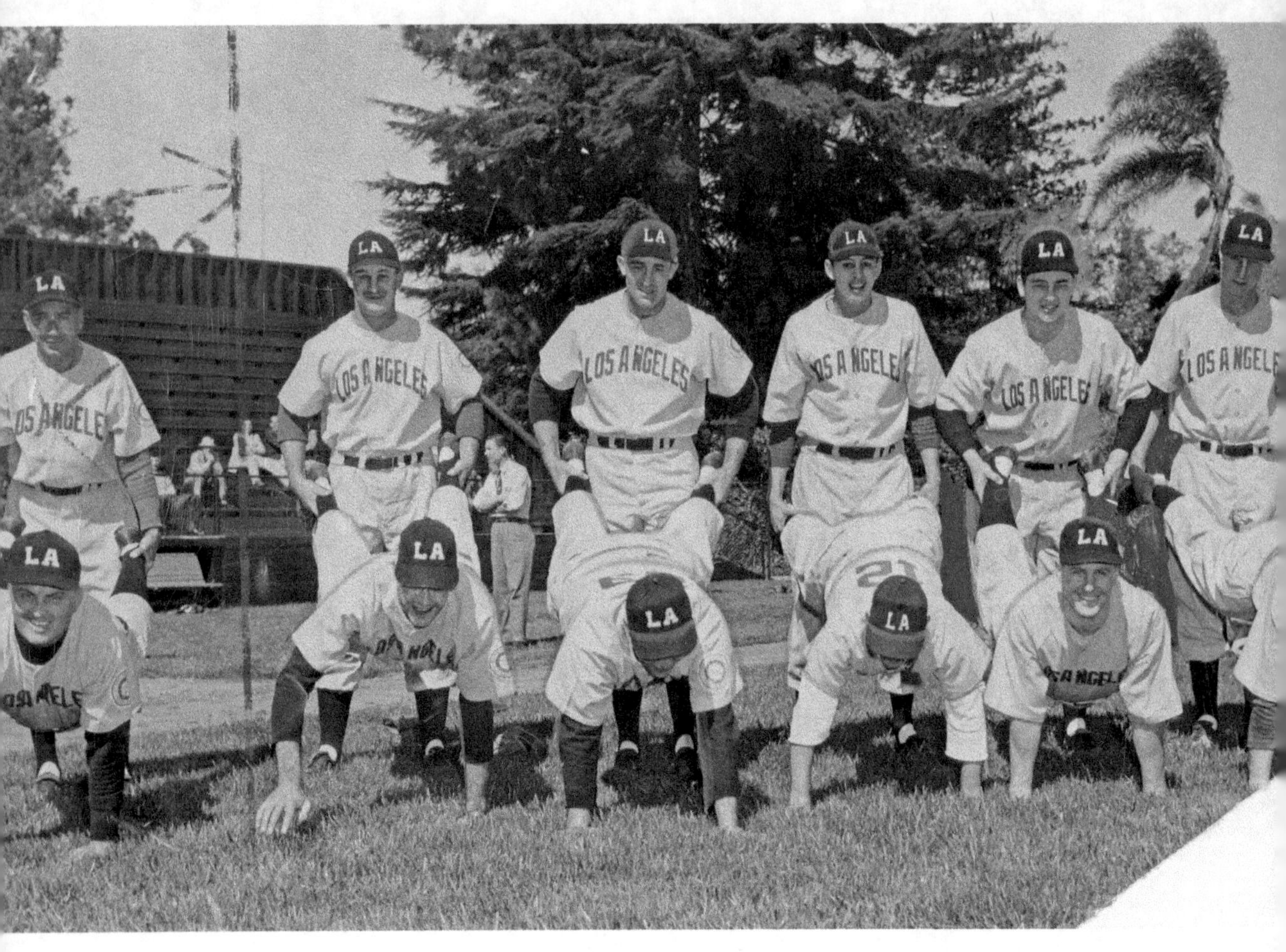

Wheelbarrow exercises during L.A. Angels spring training in Fullerton, 1952. (Herald-Examiner Collection)

OPPOSITE: Bert Shepard and manager Ted Hamilton of Clay's Garage semi-pro team inspect the pitcher's artificial leg. Shepard's right leg was amputated after he was wounded during World War II; he returned to pitch in one game for the Washington Senators. (Valley Times Collection)

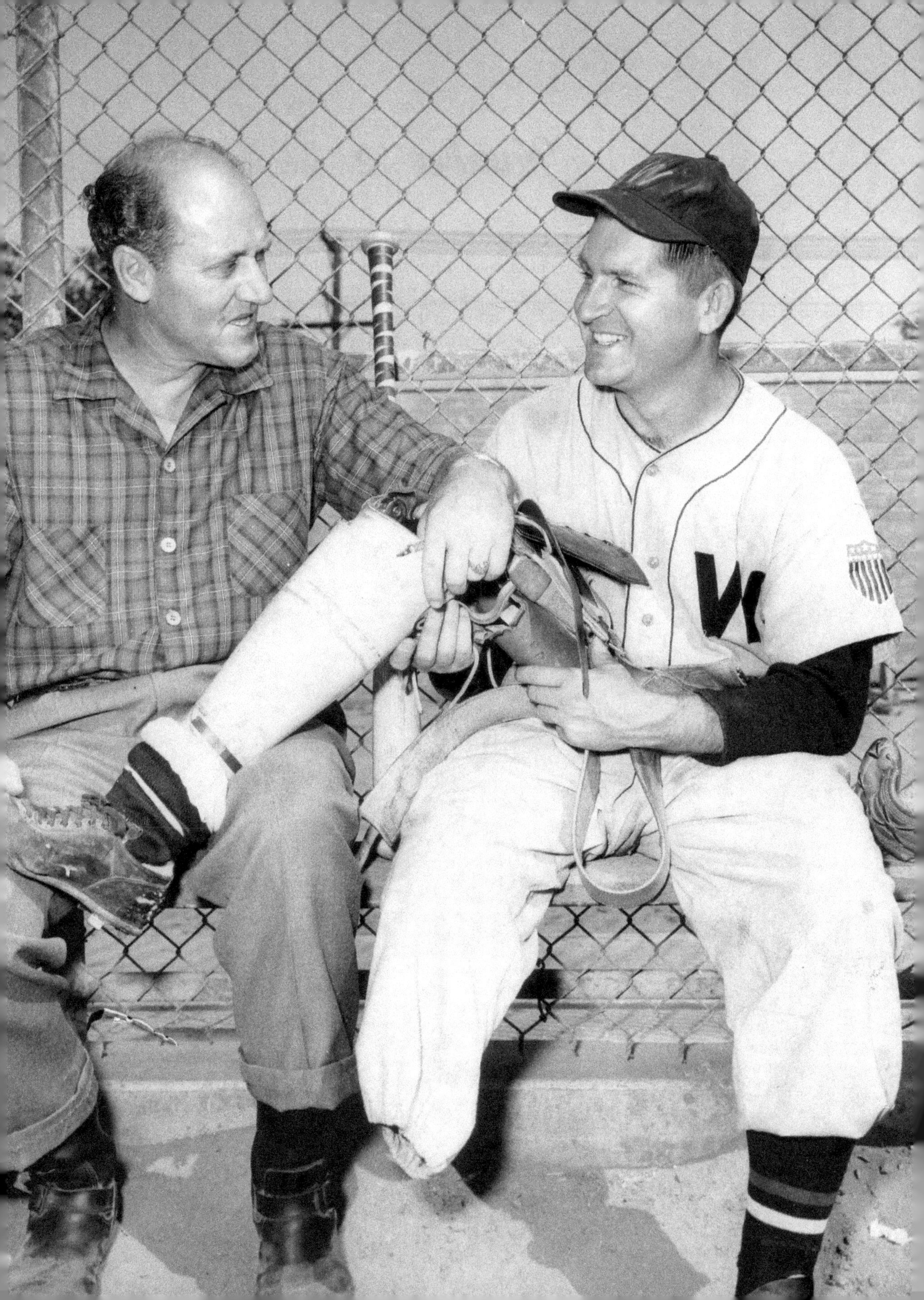

Number 42

Long before he broke baseball's color barrier with the Brooklyn Dodgers in April of 1947, Jackie Robinson was a multi-sport athlete who excelled in football, basketball, track and field, and baseball, of course, at Pasadena's John Muir High School, Pasadena Junior College, and UCLA. A fiery ballplayer who won the N.L. MVP in 1949, Robinson led Brooklyn to their first World Series title (1955). His uniform number (42) is retired throughout Major League Baseball.

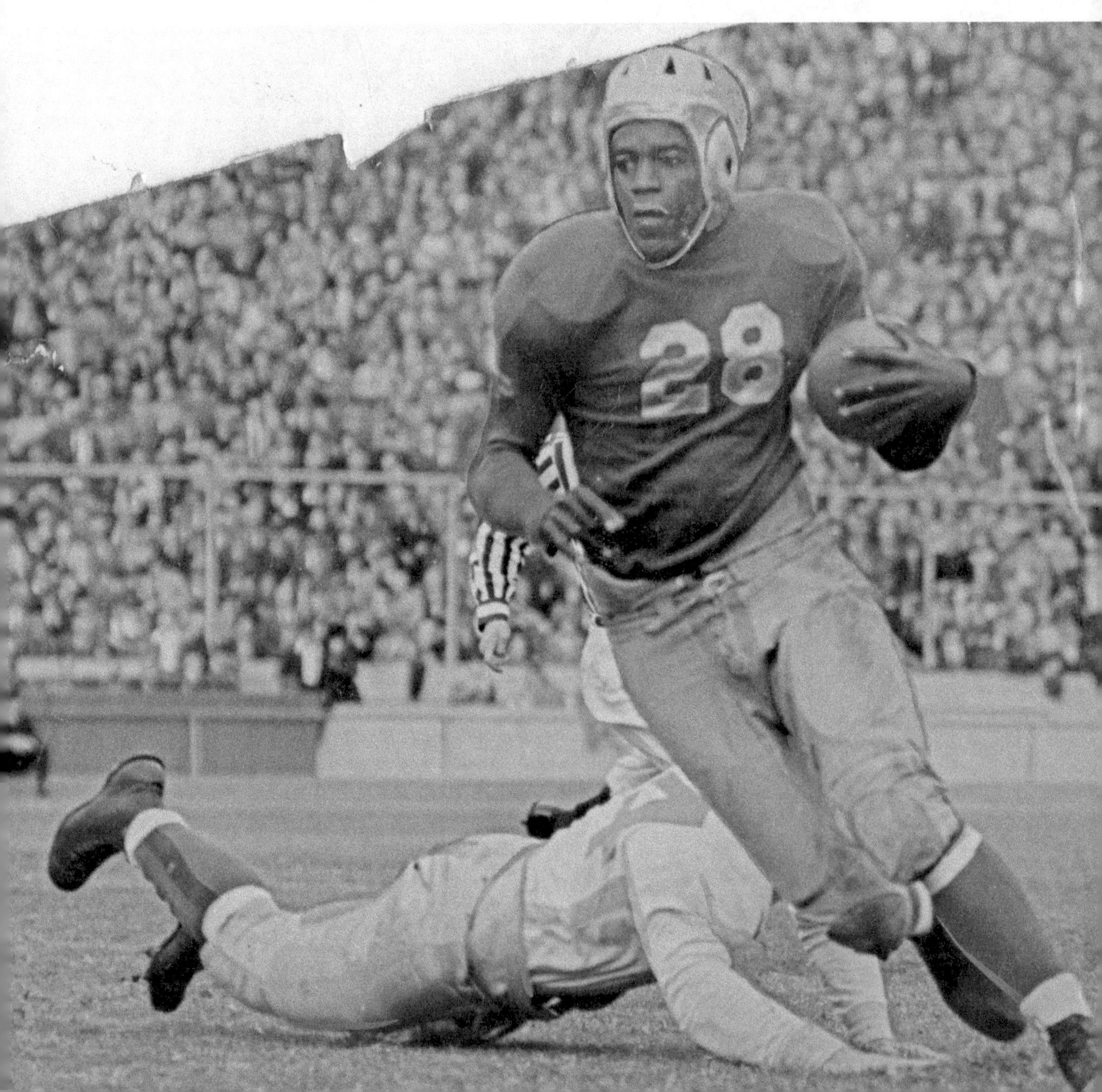

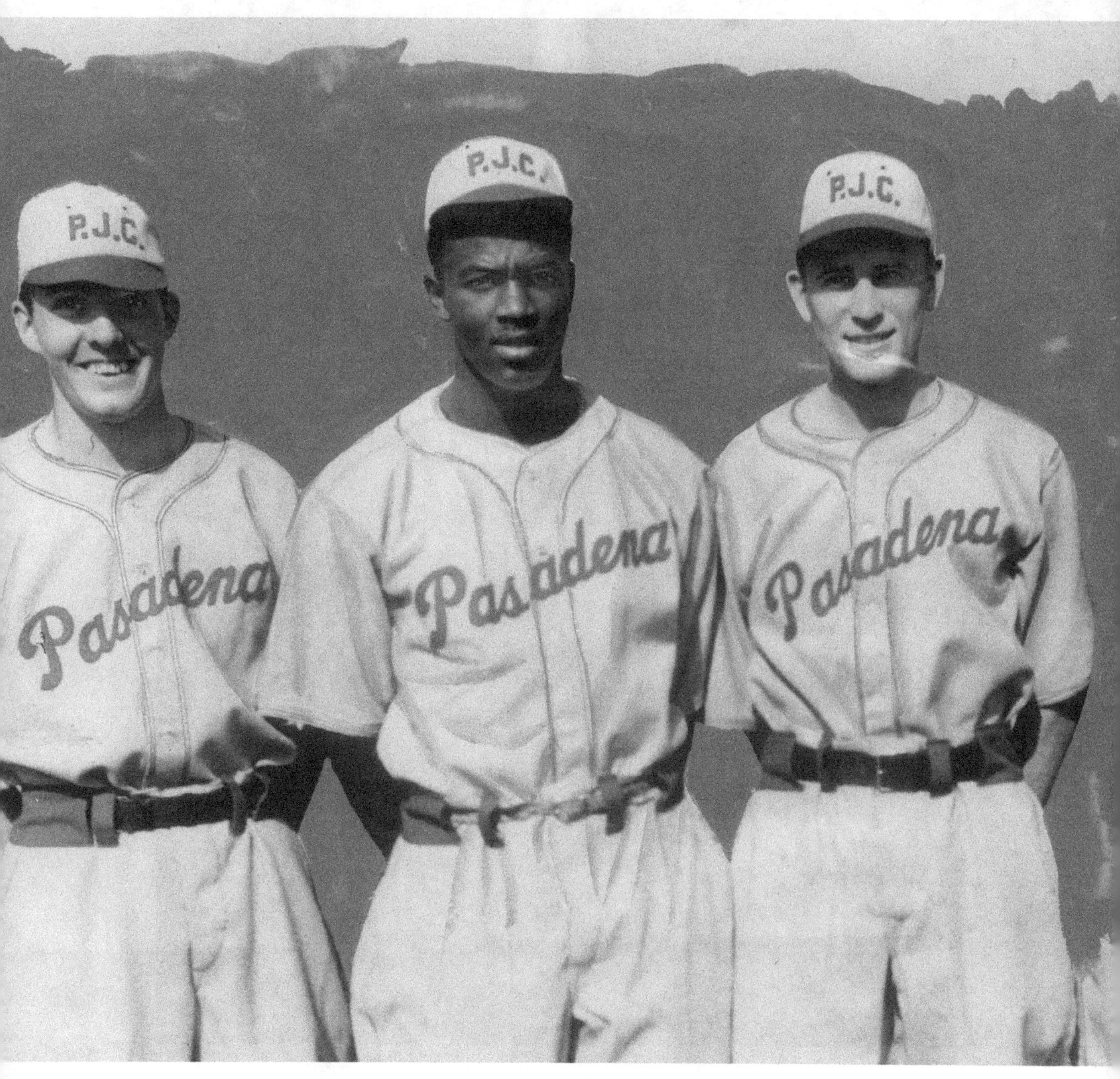

ABOVE: (Herald-Examiner Collection)

OPPOSITE: (Jack Burrud/Herald-Examiner Collection)

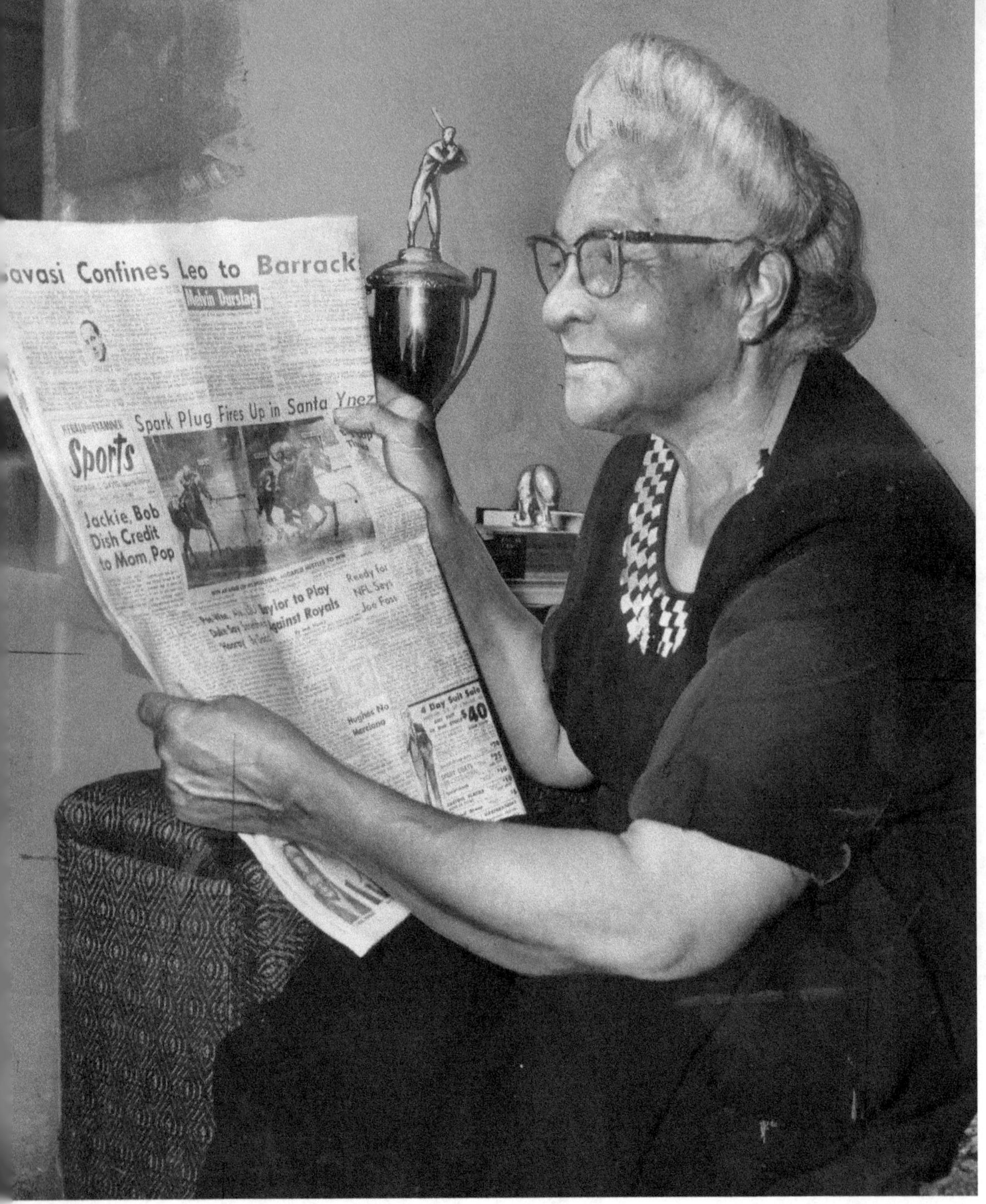

Mallie Robinson reads the news that her son has been elected to the Baseball Hall of Fame in 1962. (Terry Sullivan/Herald-Examiner Collection)

OPPOSITE: In one of the last public appearances before his death, Robinson signs an autograph for a fan at Dodger Stadium in 1972. (Sergio Ortiz/ Herald-Examiner Collection)

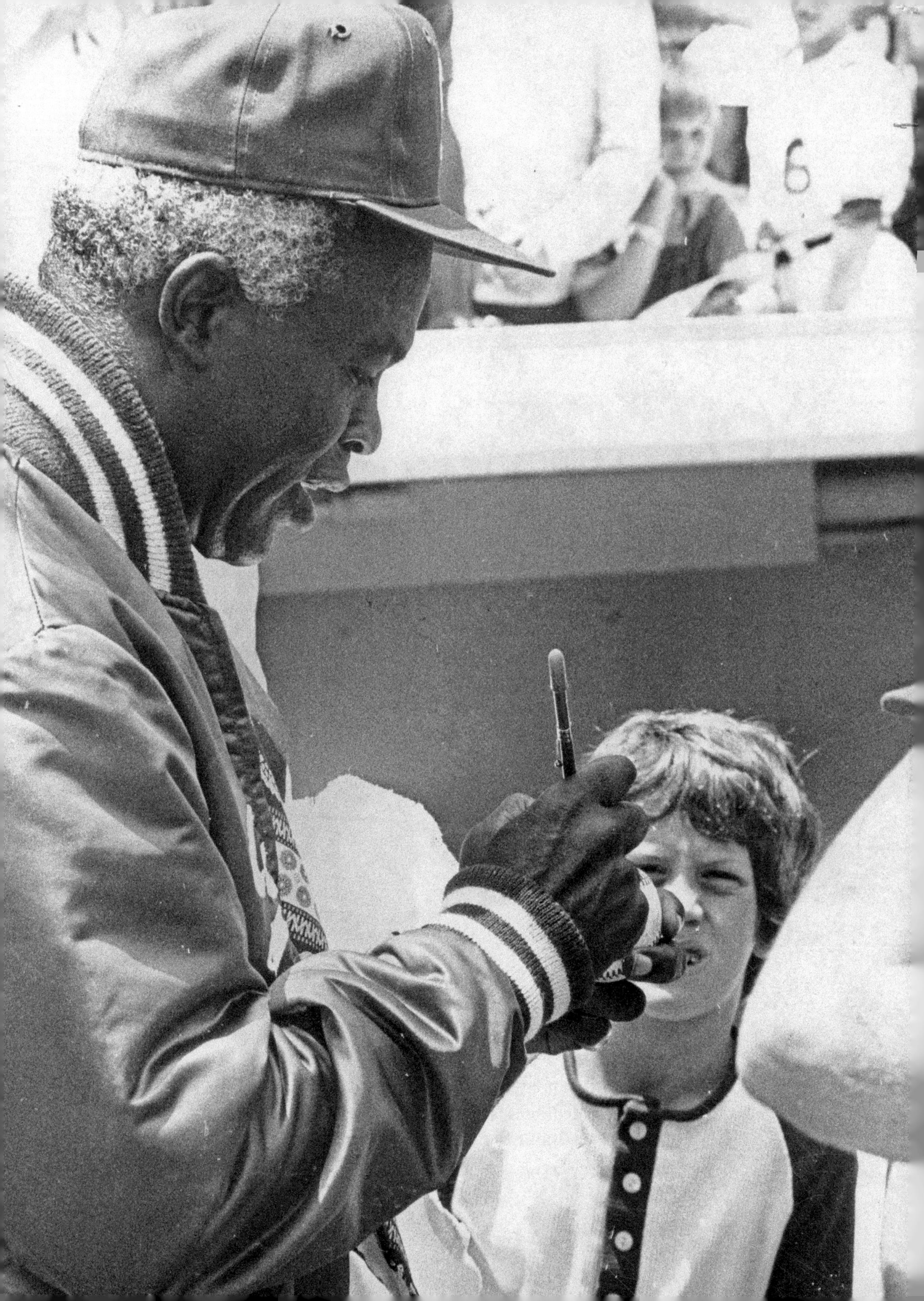

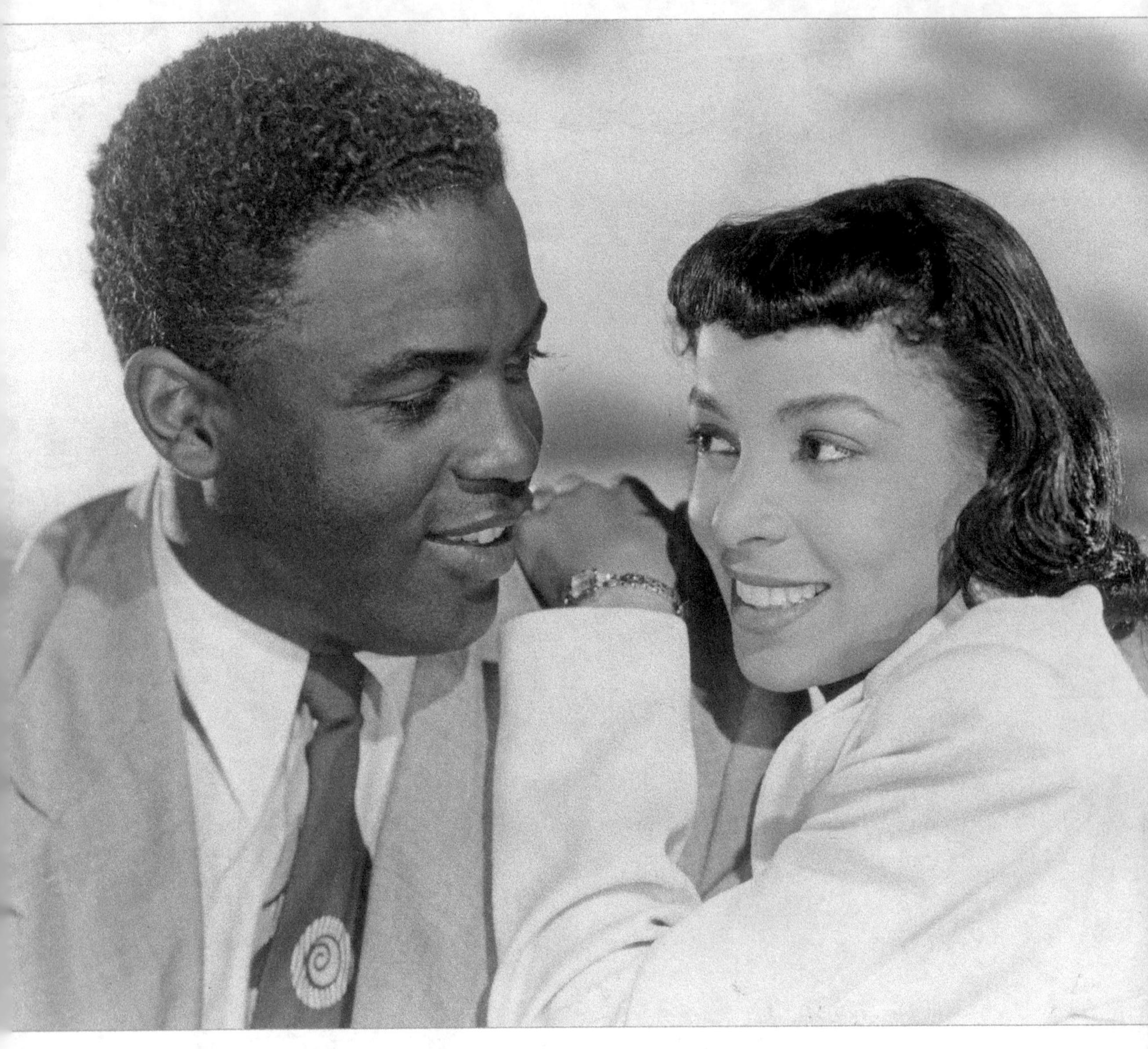

Robinson portrayed himself in *The Jackie Robinson Story,* with actress Ruby Dee as his wife Rachel. (Herald-Examiner Collection)

OPPOSITE: Rachel Robinson throws out the ceremonial first pitch as UCLA dedicates Jackie Robinson Stadium in 1981. (Paul Chinn/Herald-Examiner Collection)

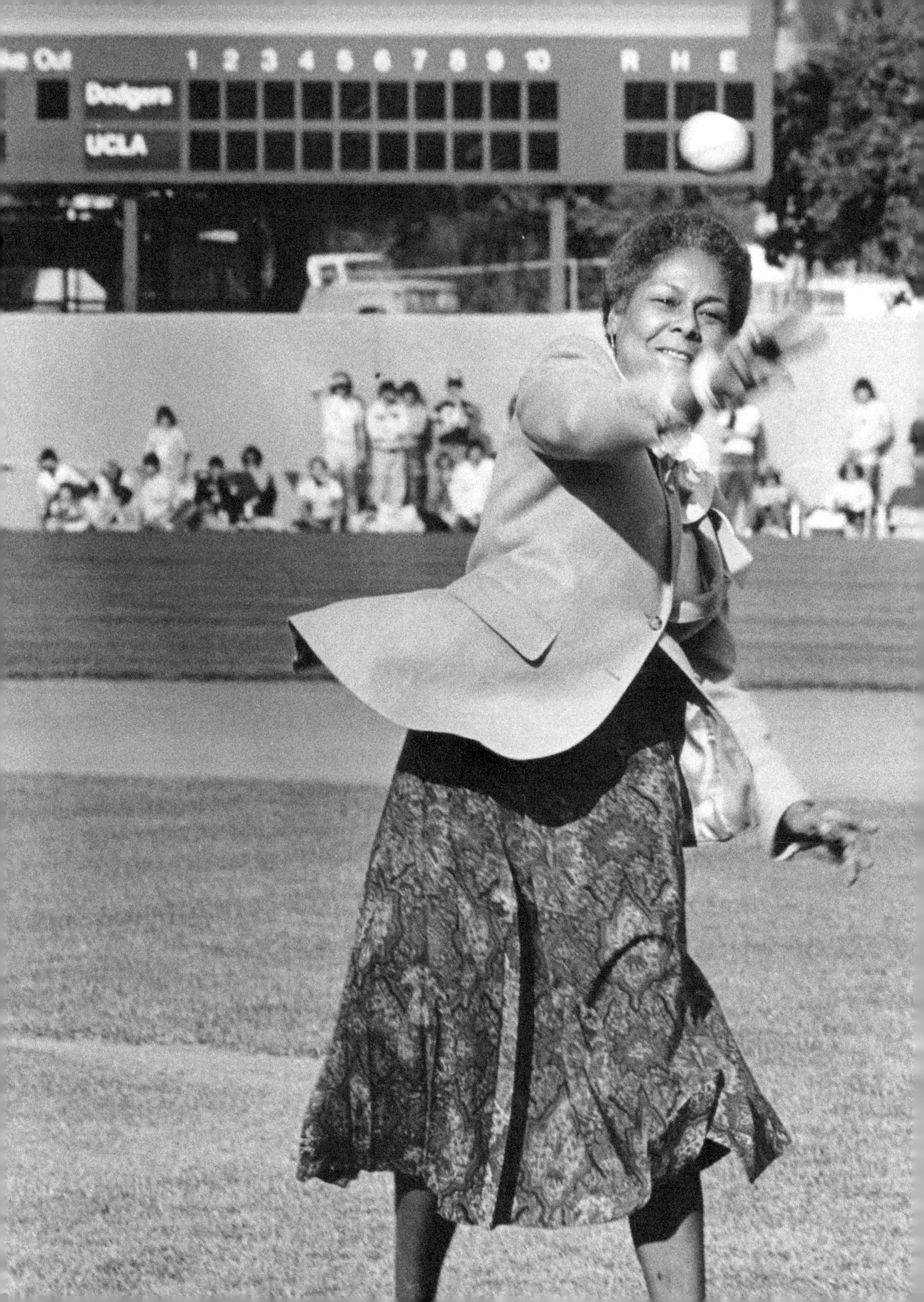
1 2 3 4 5 6 7 8 9 10
R H E
Dodgers
UCLA

HOUSING AUTHORITY OF THE CITY OF LOS ANGELES

1401 EAST FIRST STREET
TELEPHONE ANGELUS 2-2121

COMMISSIONERS
NICOLA GIULII, CHAIRMAN
LLOYD A. MASHBURN
VICE-CHAIRMAN
J. E. FISHBURN, JR.
MAURICE SAETA
GEORGE A. BEAVERS, JR.

EXECUTIVE DIRECTOR
HOWARD L. HOLTZENDORFF

BOX 2316 TERMINAL ANNEX
LOS ANGELES 54, CALIFORNIA

To The Families of The Palo Verde and Chavez Ravine Areas:

This letter is to inform you that a public housing development will be built on this location for families of low income. The attached map shows the property that is going to be used. The house you are living in is included.

Within a short time surveyors will be working in your neighborhood. Later you will be visited by representatives of the Housing Authority, who will ask you to allow them to inspect your house in order to estimate its value. Title investigators will also visit you. You should be sure that any person who comes to your house has proper identification.

It will be several months at least before your property is purchased. After the property is bought, the Housing Authority will give you all [illegible] development.

Three offices are being opened in this area to give you information and answers to your questions. They are located as follows:

Santo Nino Parochial Hall at 1034 Effie St., (rear of Church)
San Conrado Mission at 1809 Bouett, (near Amador St.)
Tony Visco's old grocery store at 1035 Lilac Terrace

You are welcome to come in at any time. We will be open day and night this week, July 24 through July 28, and during the day Saturday, July 29. Next week we will be open during the day and in the evenings by appointment. Telephone ANgelus 2-1963 for any information.

We want to assure you that it is our intention to help you and work with you in every way possible.

Yours very truly,

Sidney Green

Sidney Green
Management Supervisor

(Herald-Examiner Collection)

Chavez Ravine

In 1949, photographer Don Normark decided to explore the communities of La Loma, Bishop, and Palo Verde (known collectively as Chavez Ravine), just north of downtown L.A. There he discovered a tight-knit community set amidst wild roses, dirt roads, wandering goats, and tin-roofed bungalows.

Even as Normark photographed the predominantly Spanish-speaking residents of Chavez Ravine, the place he called a "poor man's Shangri-la" was doomed. The following year, the Los Angeles City Housing Authority announced plans to build approximately 10,000 public housing units for low-income families, using the power of eminent domain to buy up property and bulldoze homes to make way for the Elysian Park Heights project.

L.A.'s pro-business powerbrokers rallied to block the project, and the proposed housing was never built. The nearly 200 acres of land that the Housing Authority had acquired was sold to the city of L.A., with the stipulation that the property be reserved for public use. By the mid-1950s, with the area essentially vacant and only a few holdout families remaining, the fate of Chavez Ravine was in limbo.

Meanwhile, Brooklyn Dodgers owner Walter O'Malley was stymied in his efforts to build a new baseball stadium to replace aging Ebbets Field. As O'Malley explored options beyond New York, he attracted the attention of L.A. politicians eager to woo a Major League Baseball team to the West Coast. O'Malley dipped his toe in the untapped market by buying Wrigley Field and the Angels of the PCL in early 1957.

Later that year, O'Malley and the city of Los Angeles struck a controversial deal. The city council voted to overturn the land-use restriction for Chavez Ravine and hand over the property (now totaling over 300 acres) to O'Malley. L.A. also agreed to pay for grading and road improvements in the area. In exchange, the owner agreed to build a privately financed stadium on the site and transfer Wrigley Field to the city.

Critics decried the "sweetheart deal" involving land originally set aside for public use, and O'Malley had to overcome other hurdles, including several lawsuits. Voter approval of the land swap was also required; the pro-stadium referendum barely passed in the summer of 1958. Finally, after several longtime residents of Chavez Ravine refused to leave their homes, law enforcement forcibly evicted them so that construction on the new ballpark could begin.

The "poor man's Shangri-La" would soon be re-shaped into a stadium that *Los Angeles Times* columnist Jim Murray called "the Taj Mahal, the Parthenon, and Westminster Abbey of baseball."

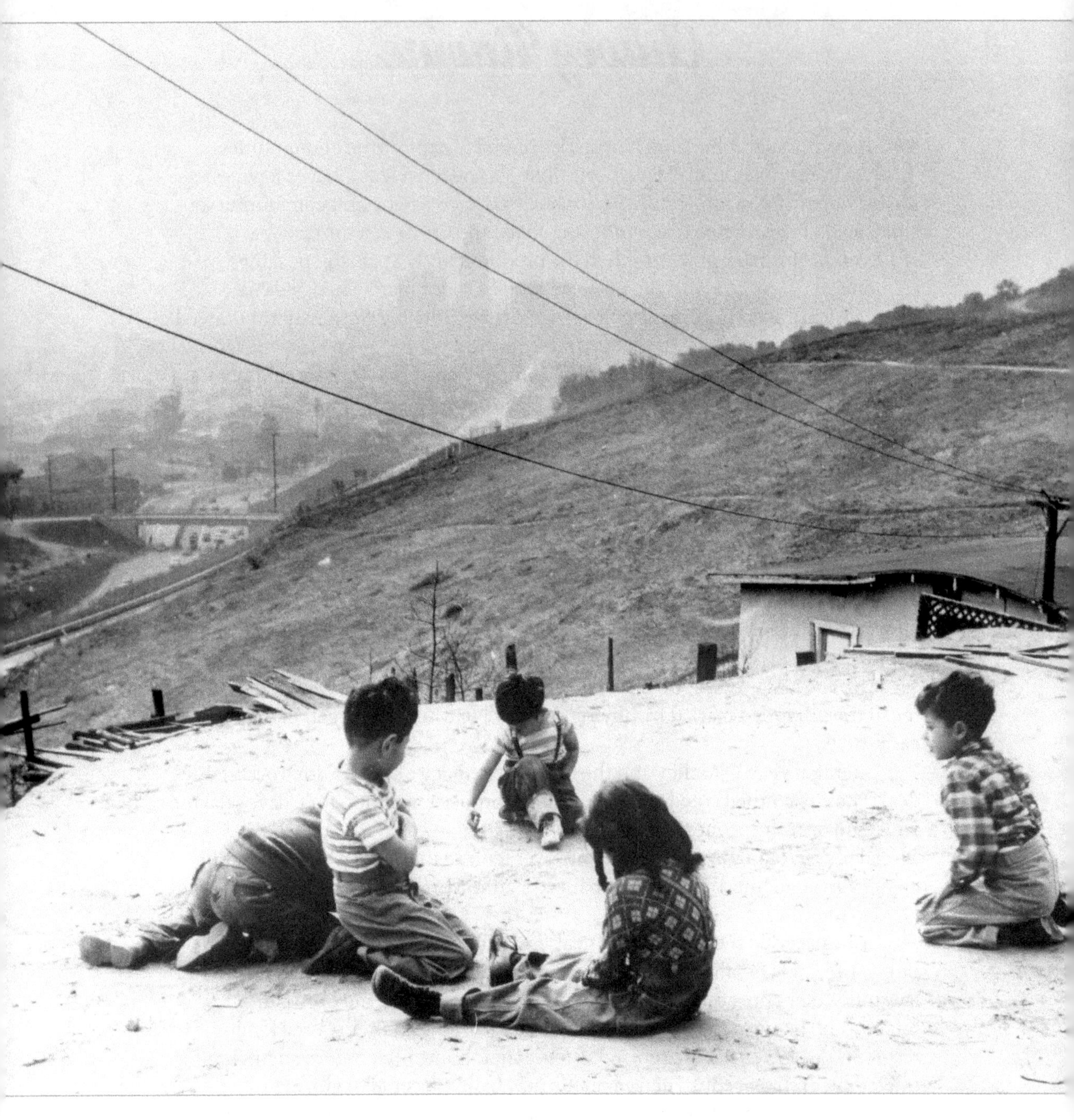

(Don Normark/Housing Authority Collection)

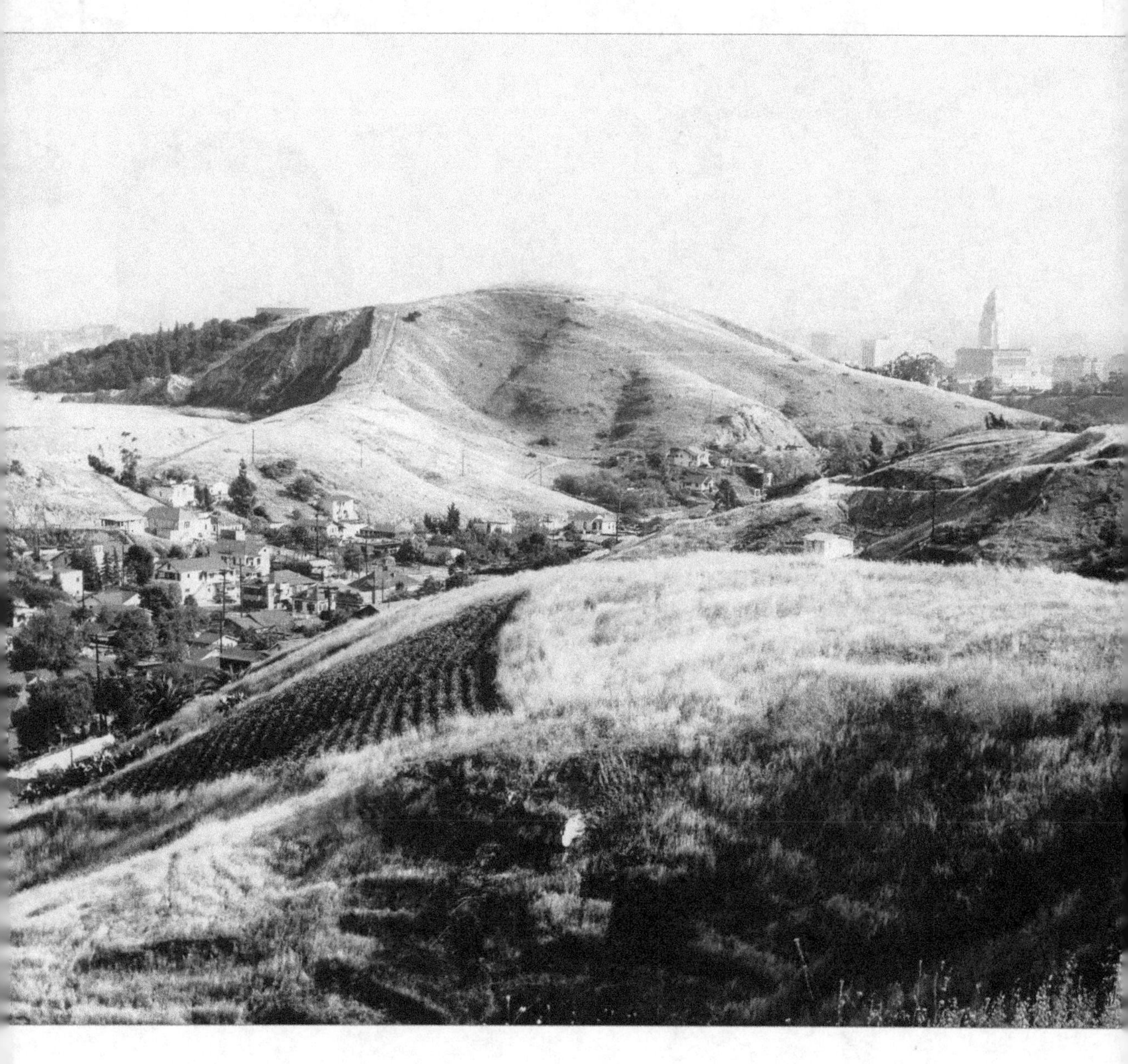

(Housing Authority Collection)

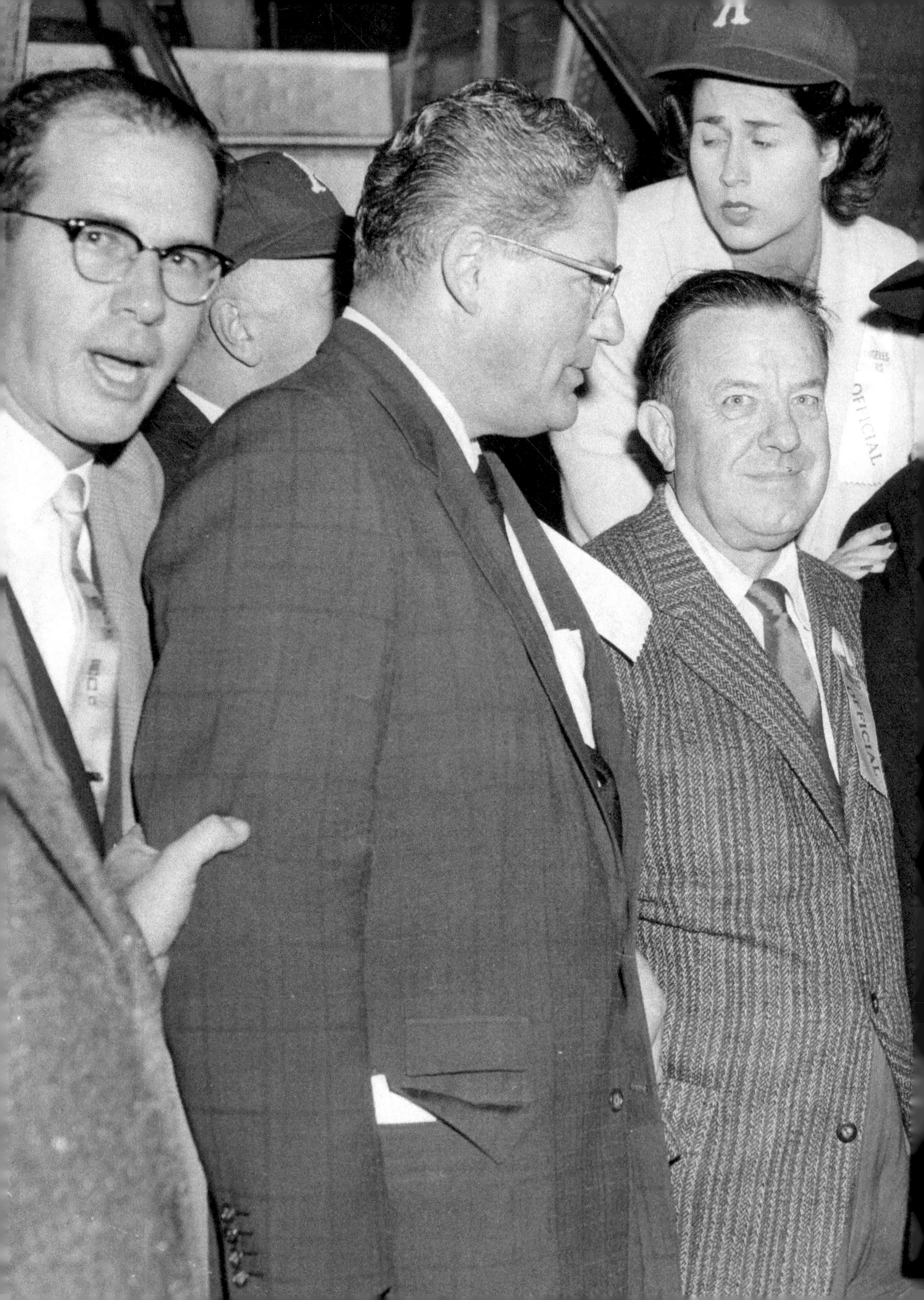
OFFICIAL
OFFICIAL

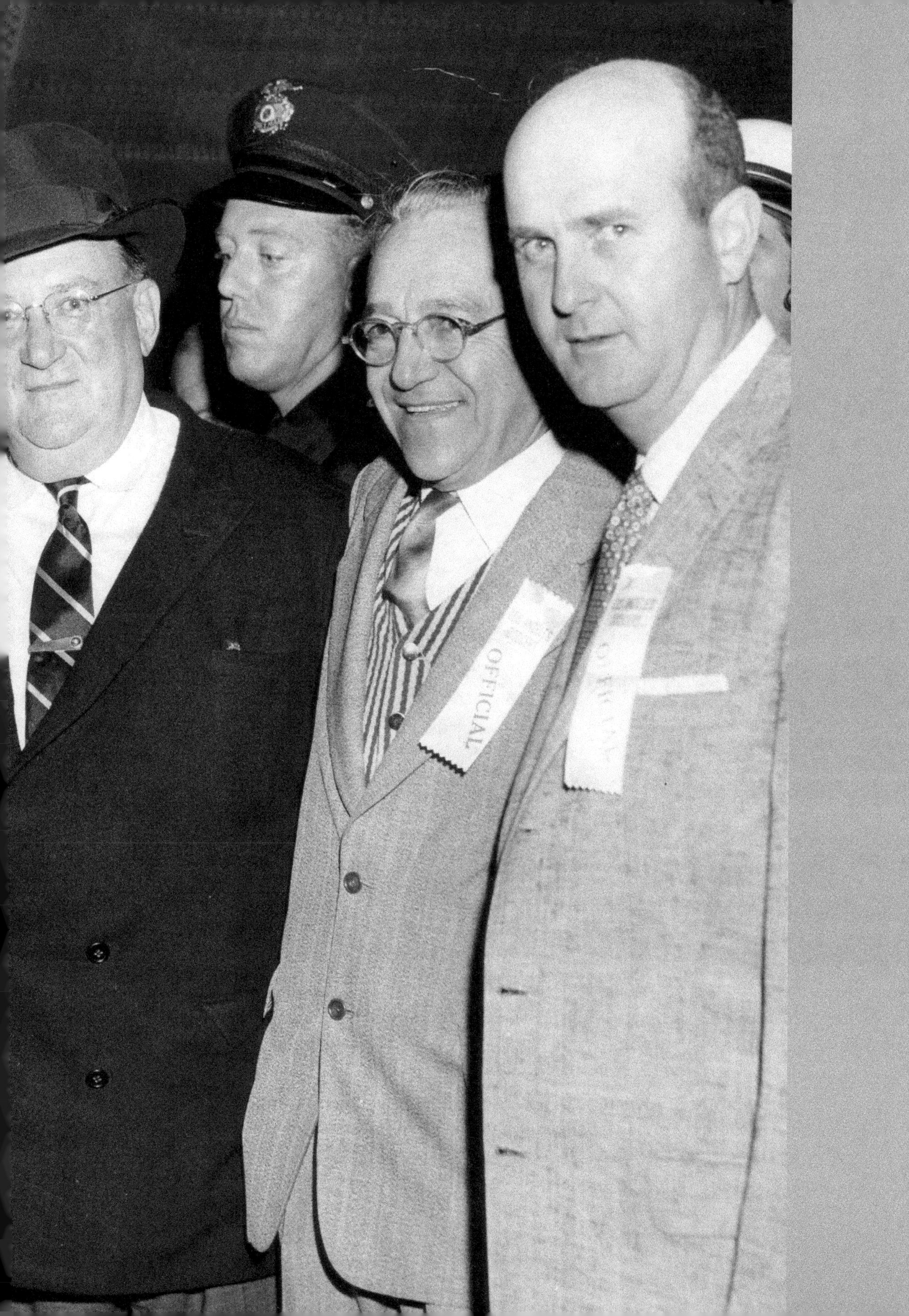
OFFICIAL

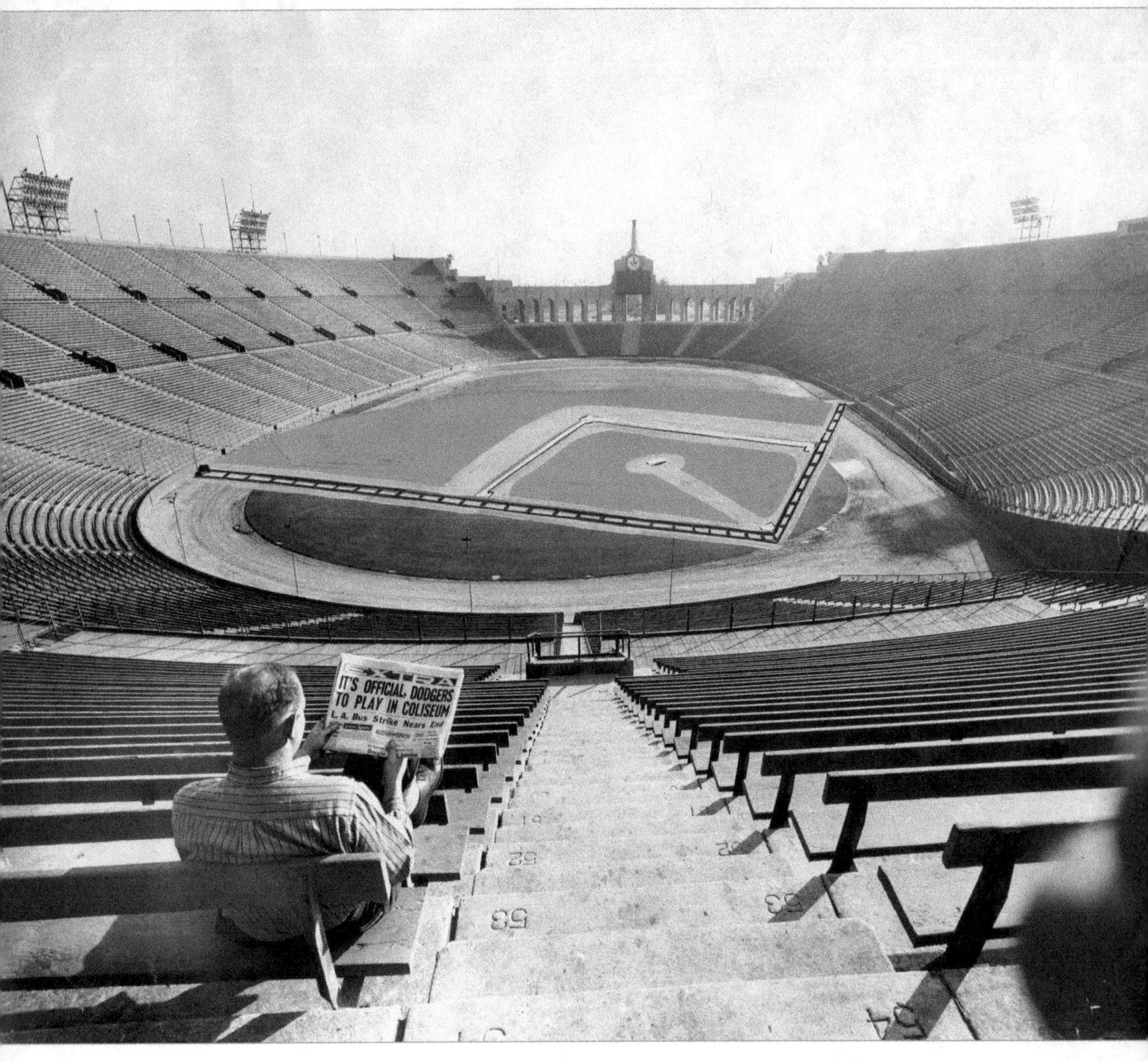

ABOVE & OPPOSITE: When the Dodgers announced plans to move to L.A., it was unclear whether they would initially play at Wrigley Field or the L.A. Coliseum. (Herald-Examiner Collection)

OVERLEAF: Local officials, including city councilwoman Rosalind Wyman (*top*) and county supervisor Kenneth Hahn (*left*), greet Dodgers owner Walter O'Malley (*center*) on his arrival in L.A. in 1957. (Herald-Examiner Collection)

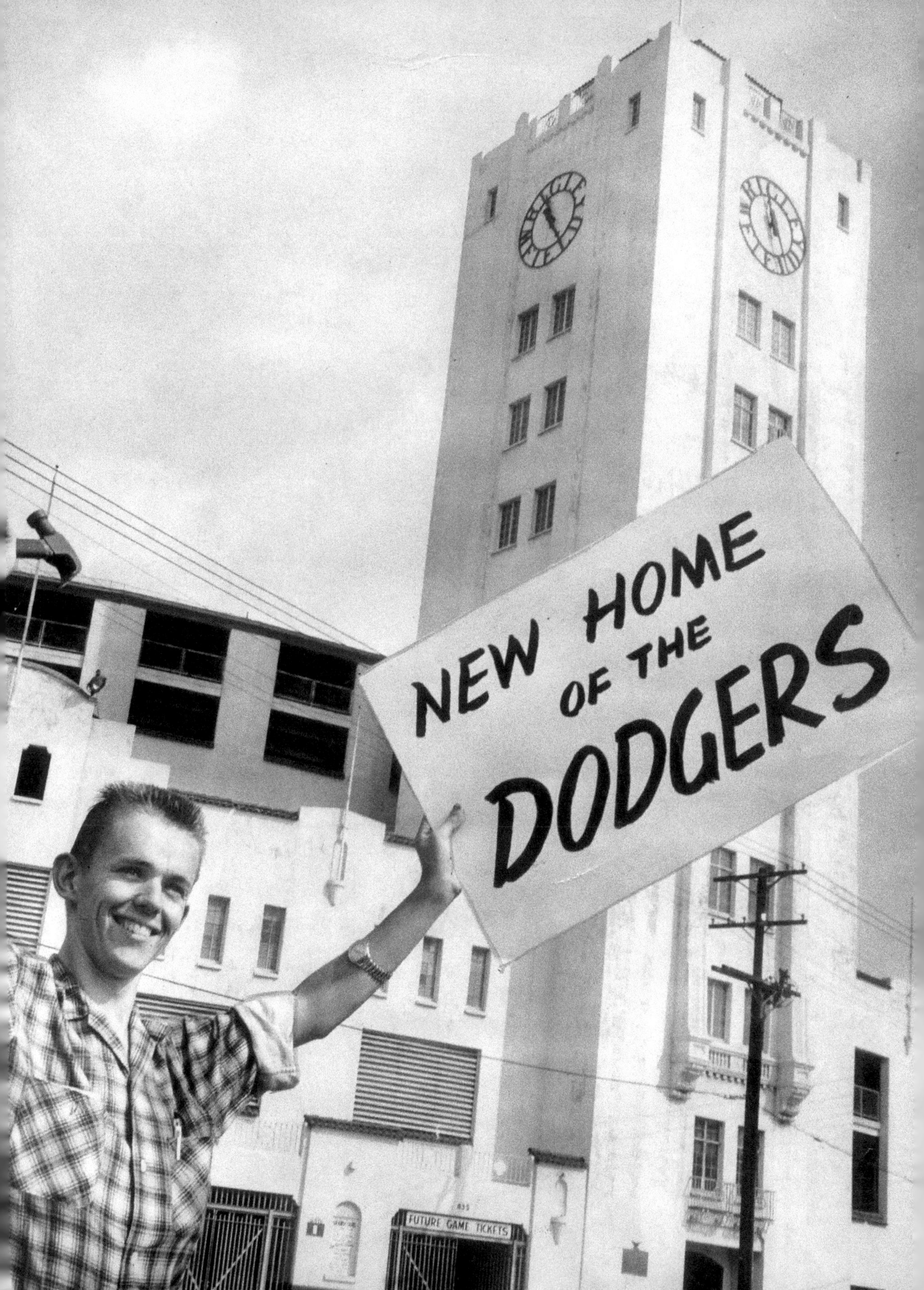
NEW HOME
OF THE
DODGERS
FUTURE GAME TICKETS

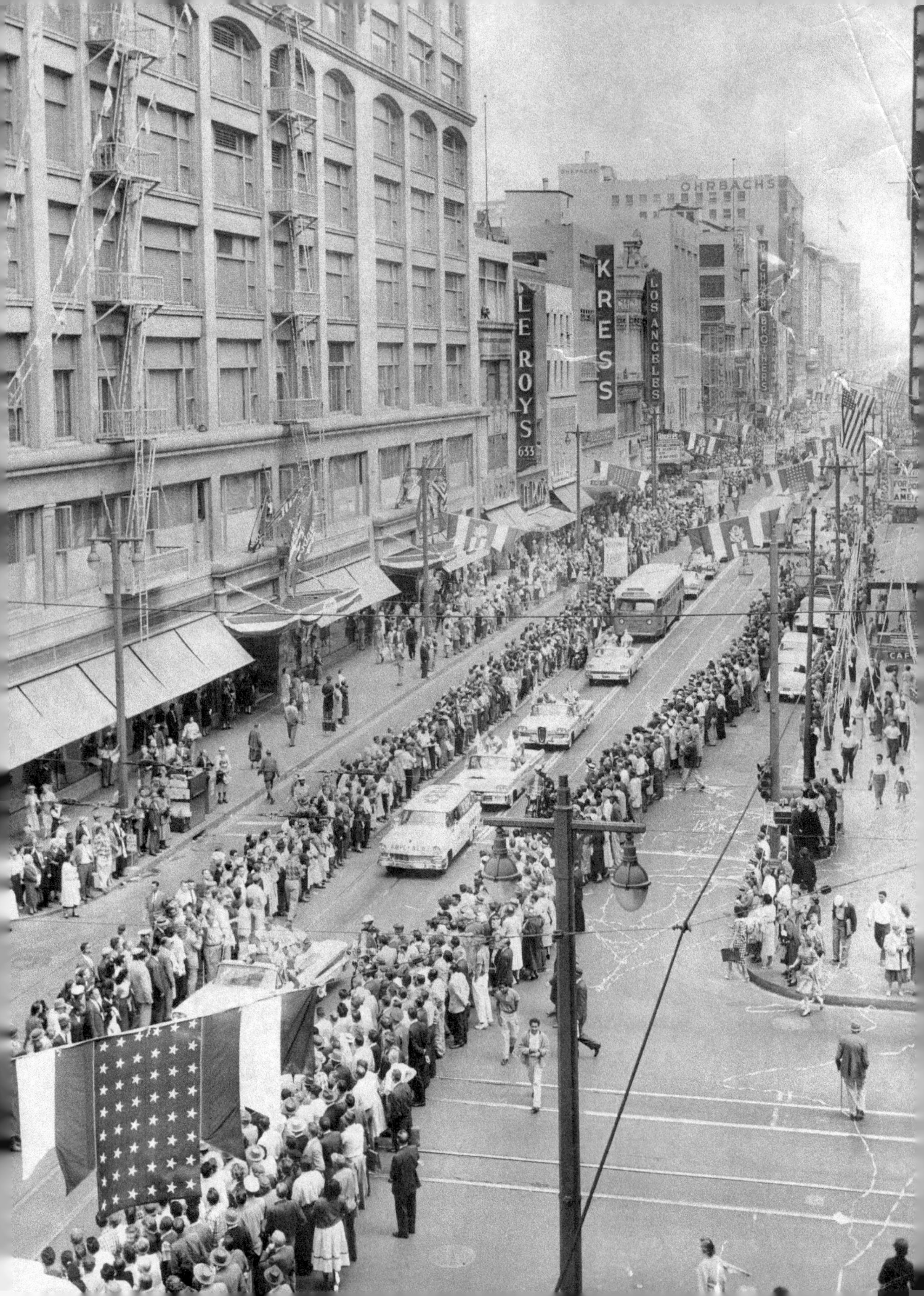
OHRBACHS
LE ROYS
633
KRESS
LOS ANGELES
BROTHERS

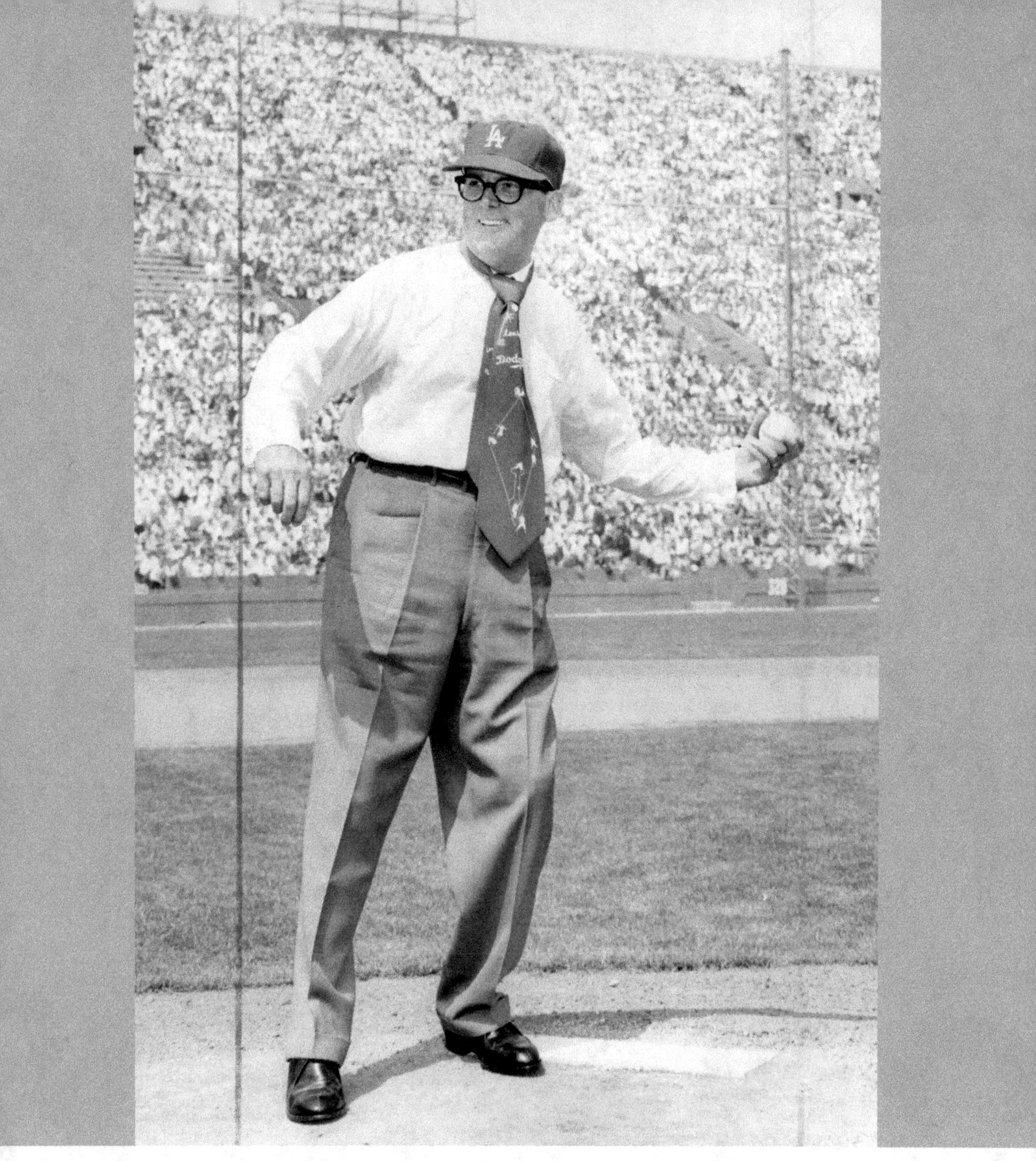

L.A. Mayor Norris Poulson threw out the ceremonial first pitch. (Valley Times Collection)

OPPOSITE: Opening Day began with a welcome rally at City Hall, followed by a parade through downtown L.A. (Herald-Examiner Collection)

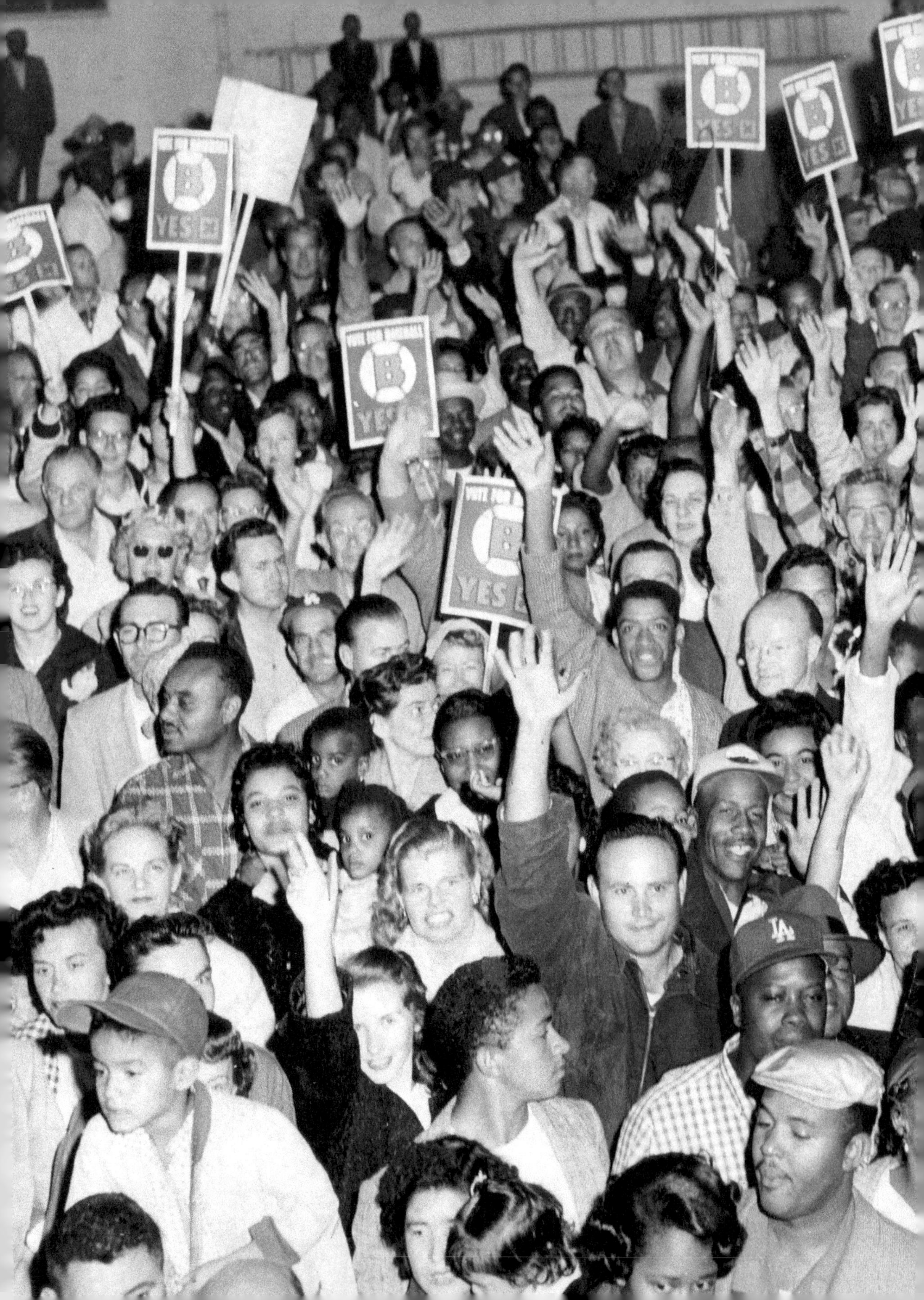
VOTE FOR BASEBALL
B
YES

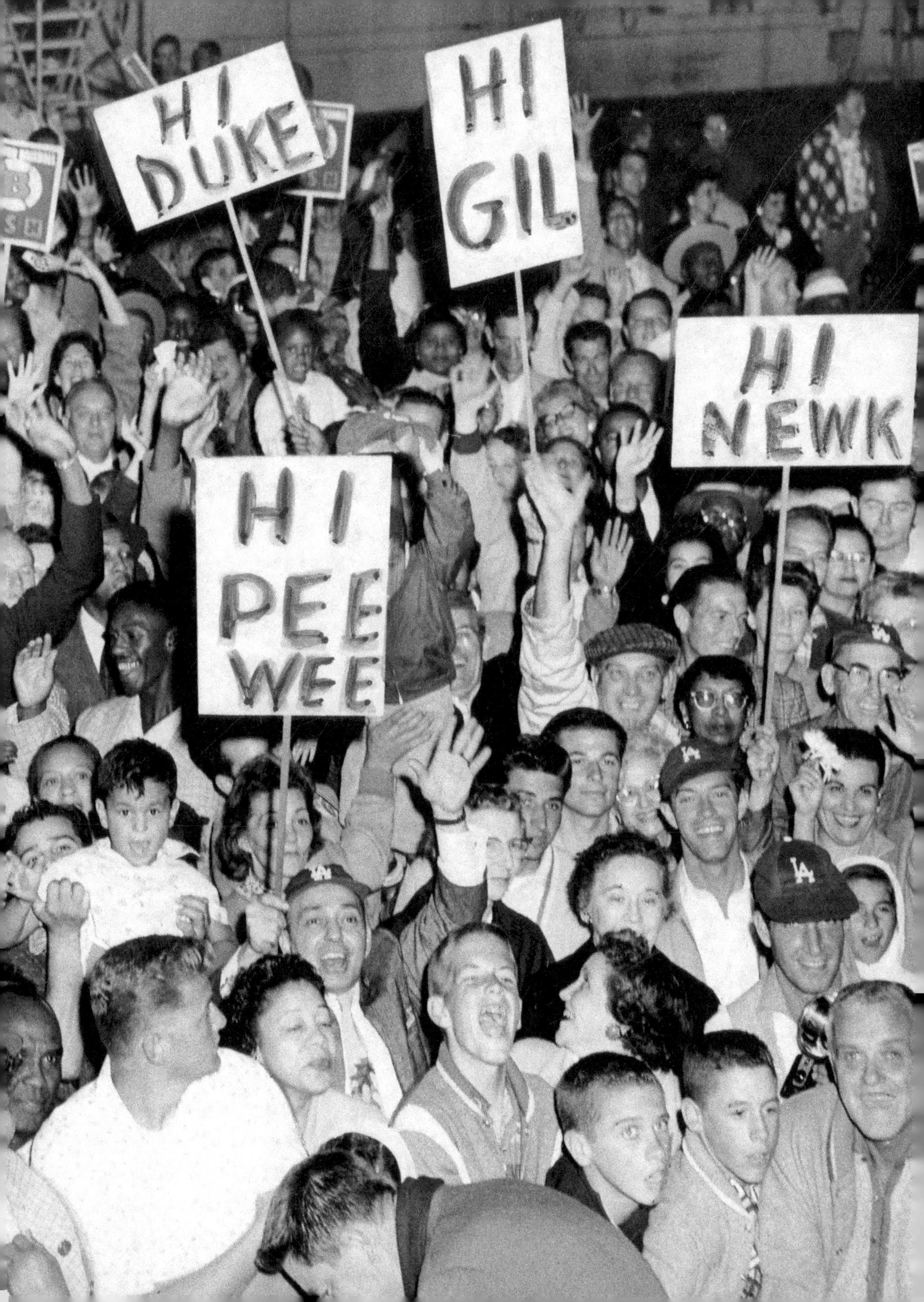
HI DUKE
HI GIL
HI NEWK
HI PEE WEE

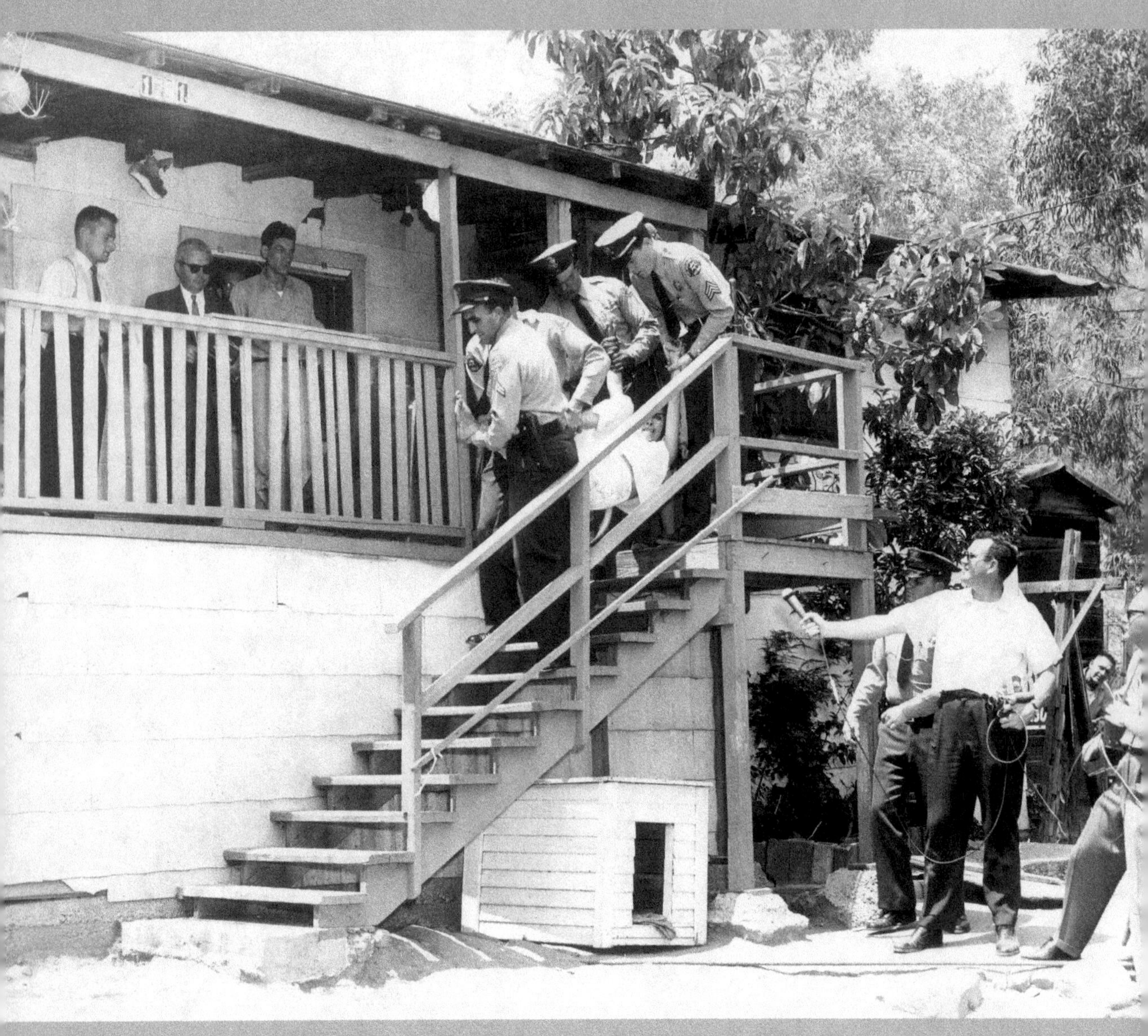

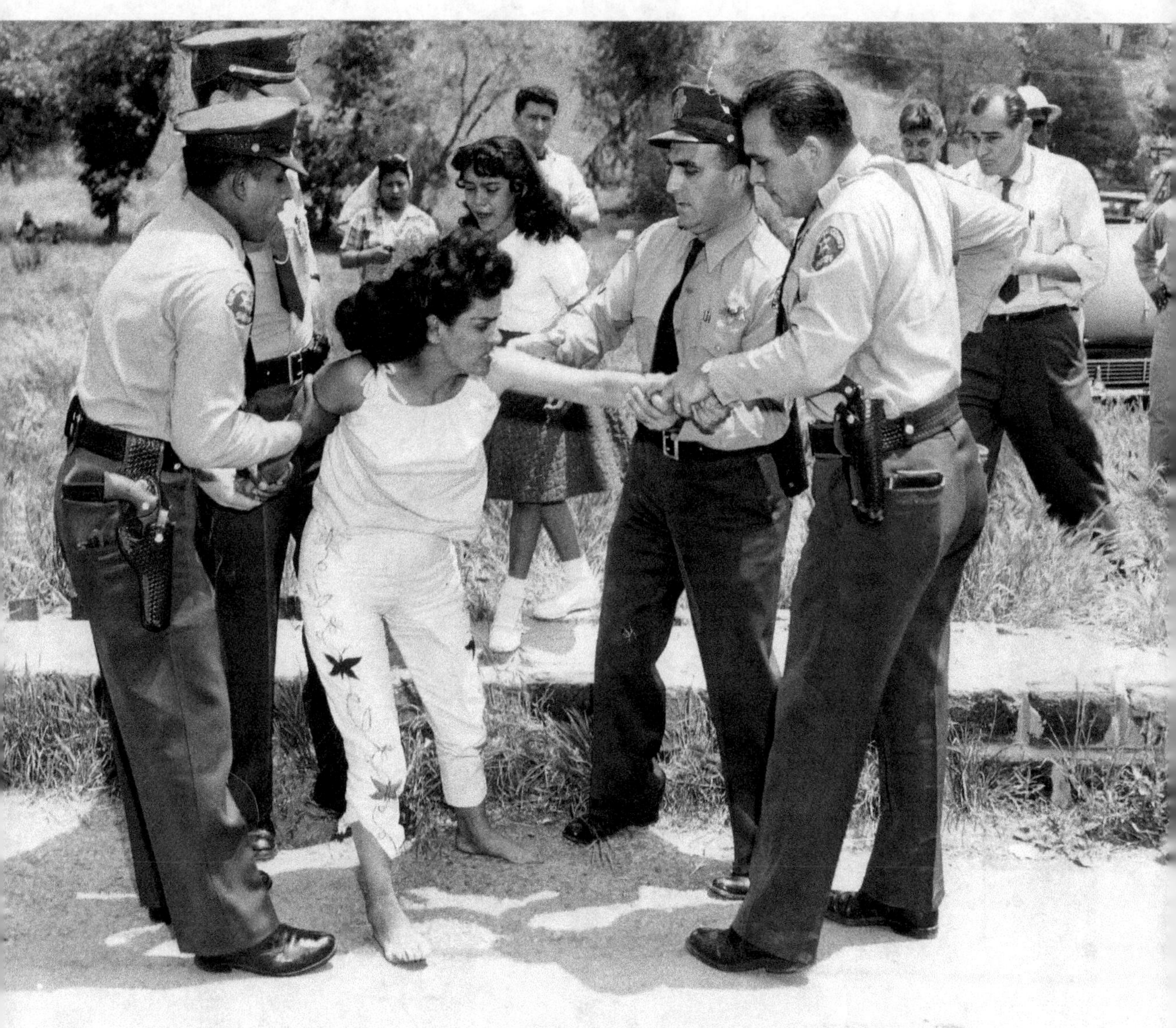

Last holdouts: Sheriffs evict Aurora Vargas from her family's property in Chavez Ravine. (Herald-Examiner Collection)

OPPOSITE: (Herald-Examiner Collection)

PAGES 46-47: Rally for Proposition B: L.A. voters narrowly approved the deal between Walter O'Malley and the City Council for Dodger Stadium to be built in Chavez Ravine. (Cliff Brown/Herald-Examiner Collection)

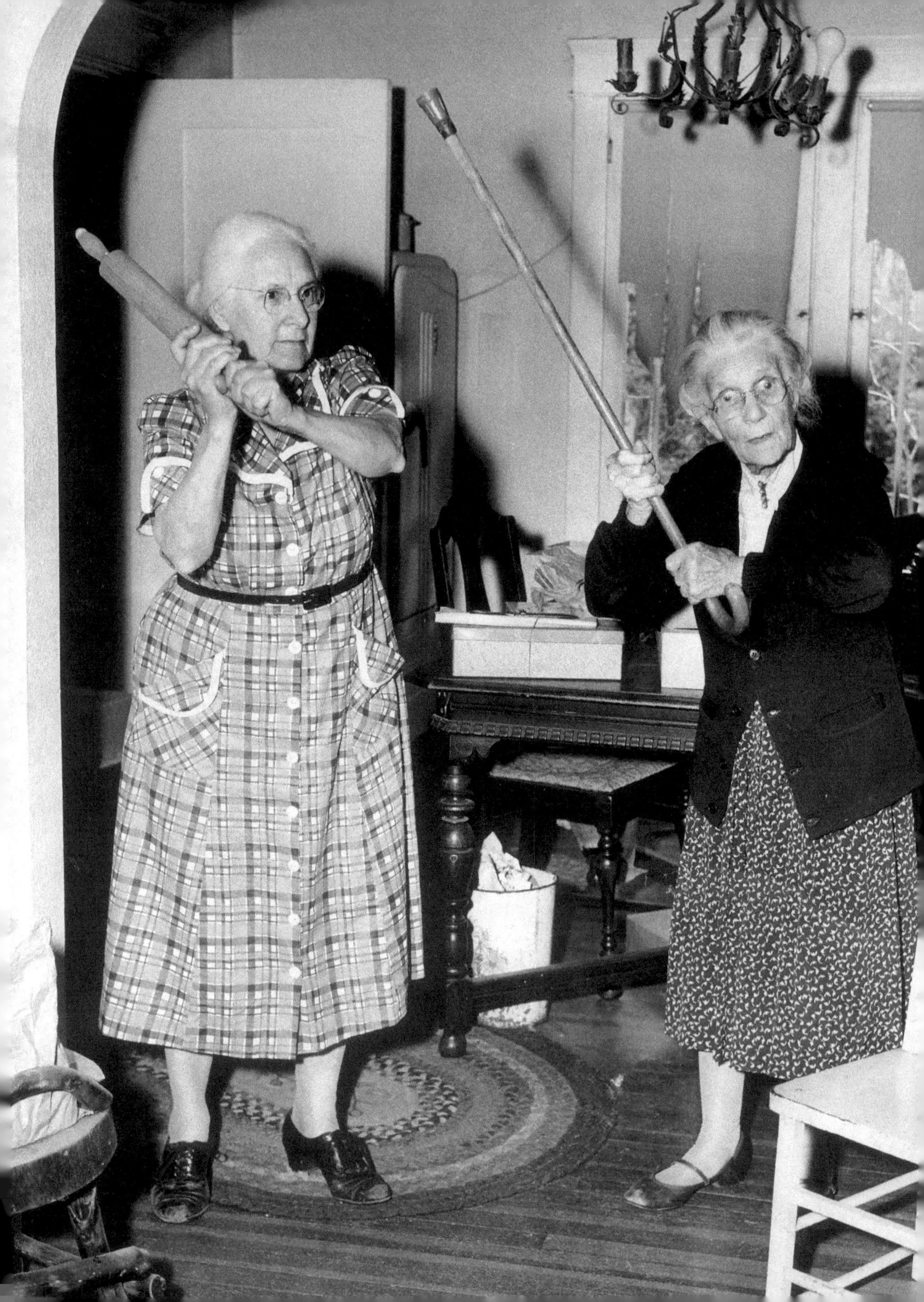

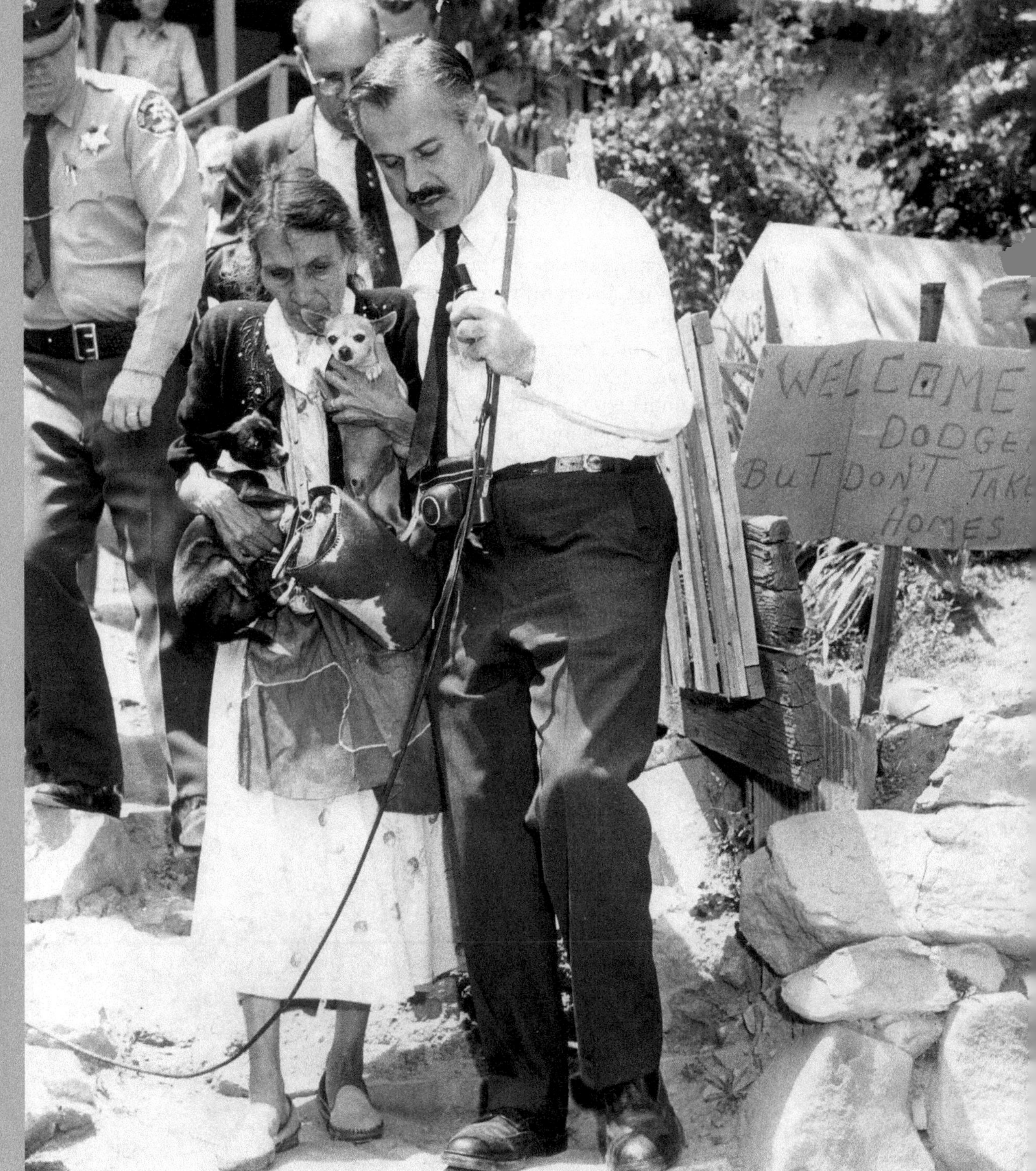

ABOVE: The Vargas family eviction. (Herald-Examiner Collection)

OPPOSITE: Chavez Ravine residents Alice Martin and Ruth Rayford prepare to fight their eviction. (Herald-Examiner Collection)

“It’s Time for Dodger Baseball!”

No player, manager, or executive in the Dodgers organization has connected more intimately with Angelenos than Vin Scully. Called the “Fordham Thrush with the .400 larynx” by sportswriter Jim Murray, Scully began his Hall of Fame career with Brooklyn in 1950, moved with the club to L.A. in 1958, and entertained and educated generations of fans about the nuances of the game until his retirement in 2016. Scully’s story-telling skills and soothing tones resonated throughout the Southland; many fans brought their transistor radios to the stadium so as not to miss a word of Vin’s hardball poetry.

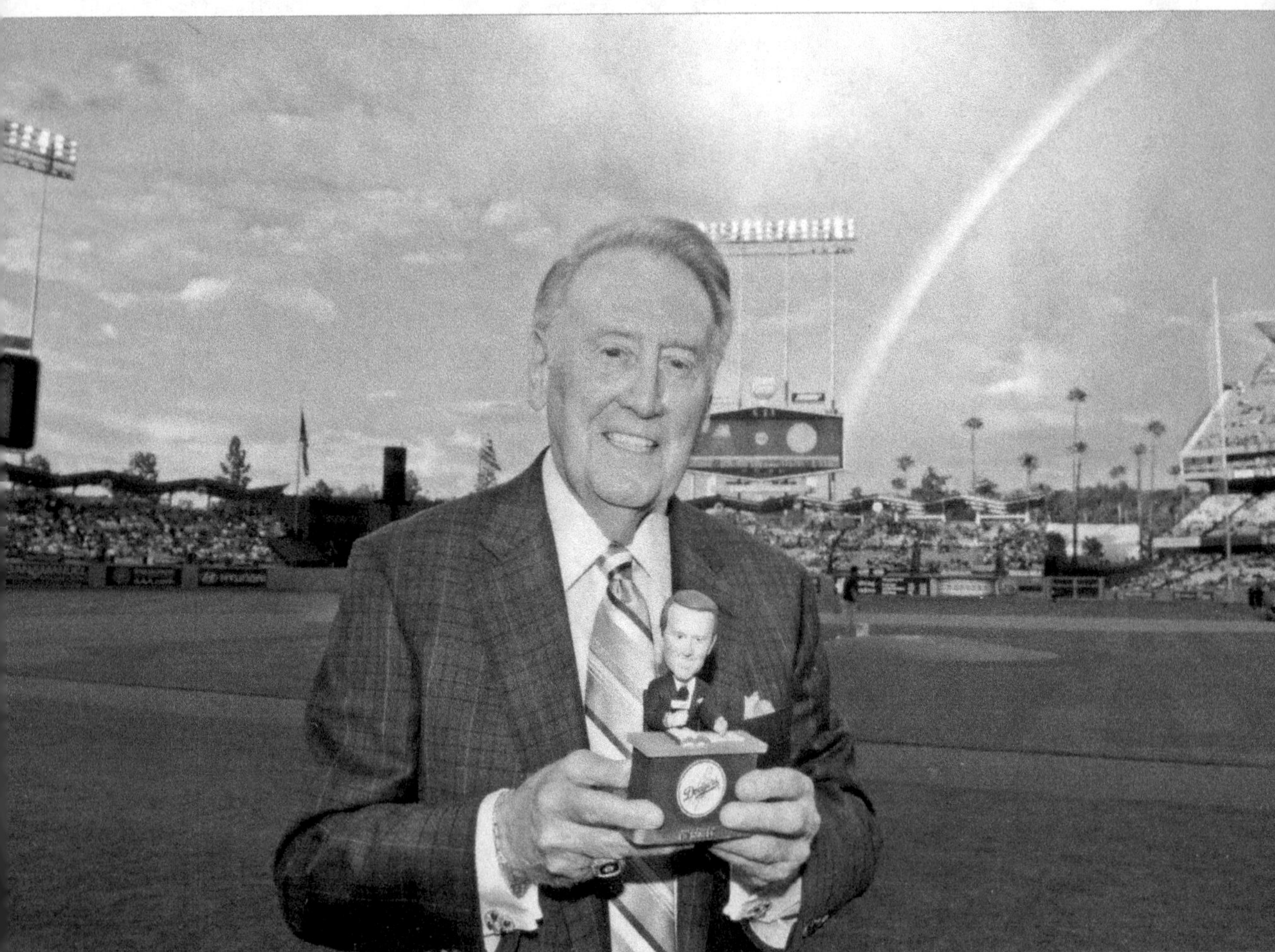

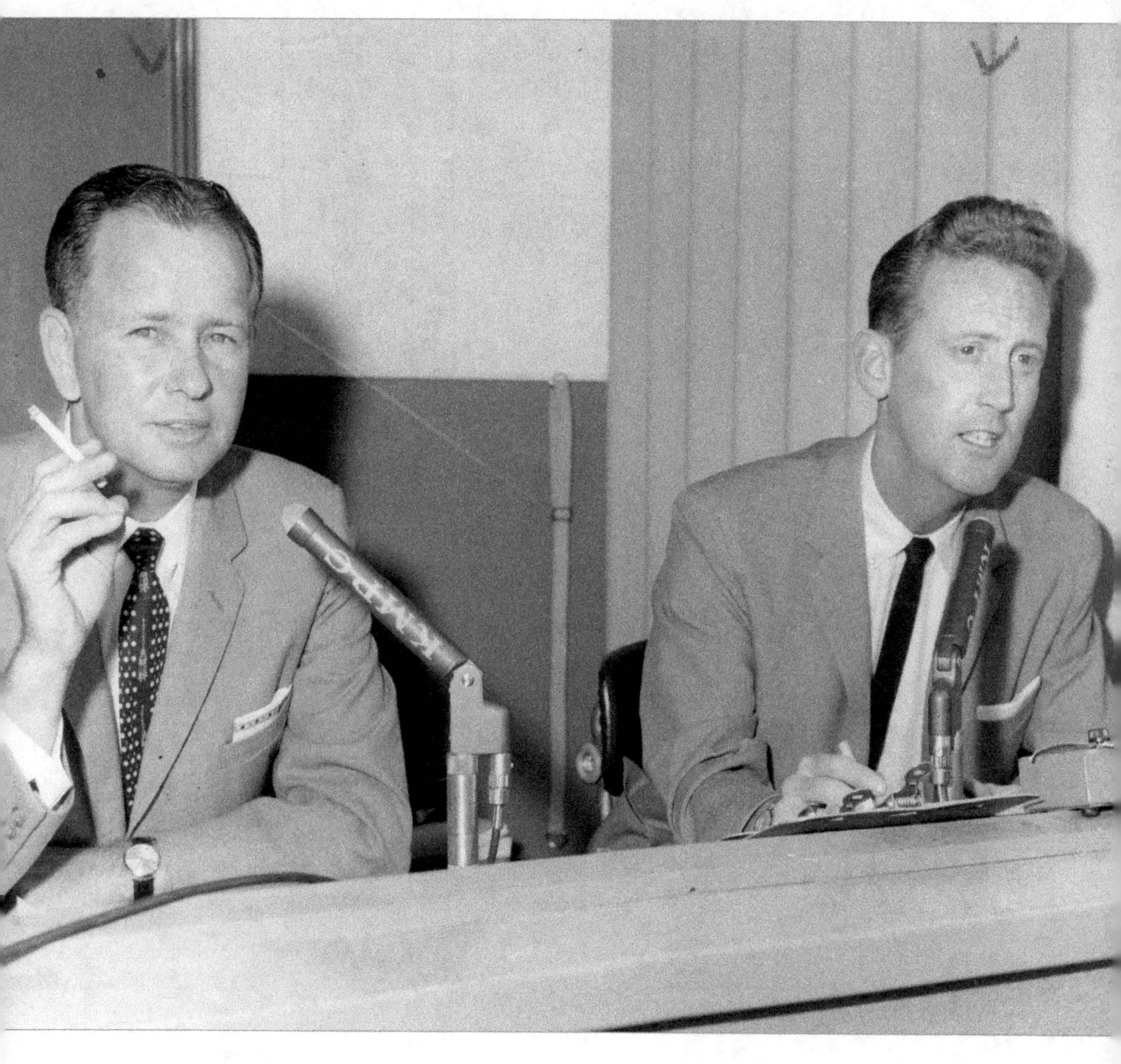

With longtime partner Jerry Doggett. (Herald-Examiner Collection)

OPPOSITE: Vin Scully bobblehead night, August 30, 2012. (Gary Leonard)

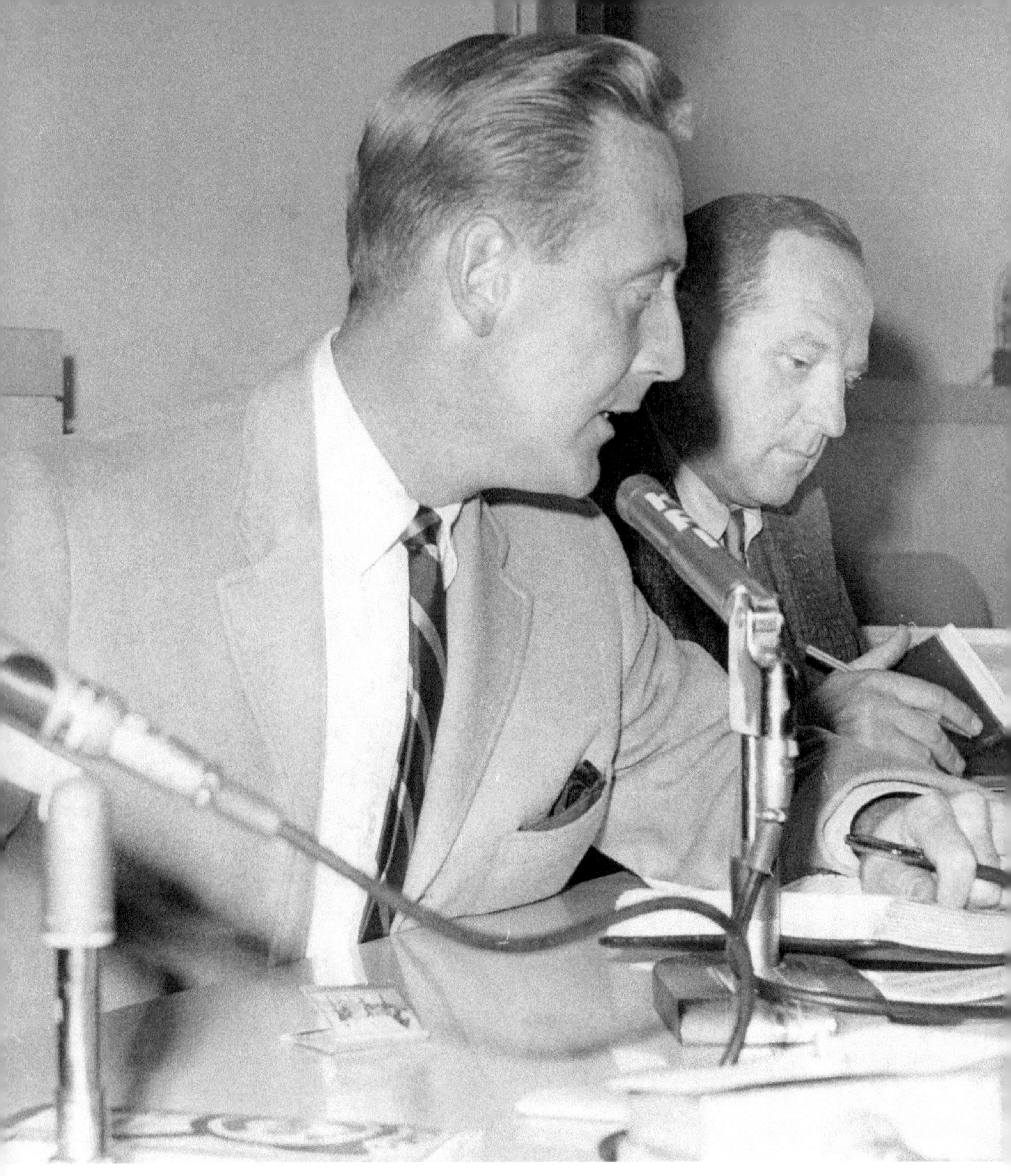

With statistician Allan Roth in the press box. (Herald-Examiner Collection)

OPPOSITE: As a TV game-show host. (Herald-Examiner Collection)

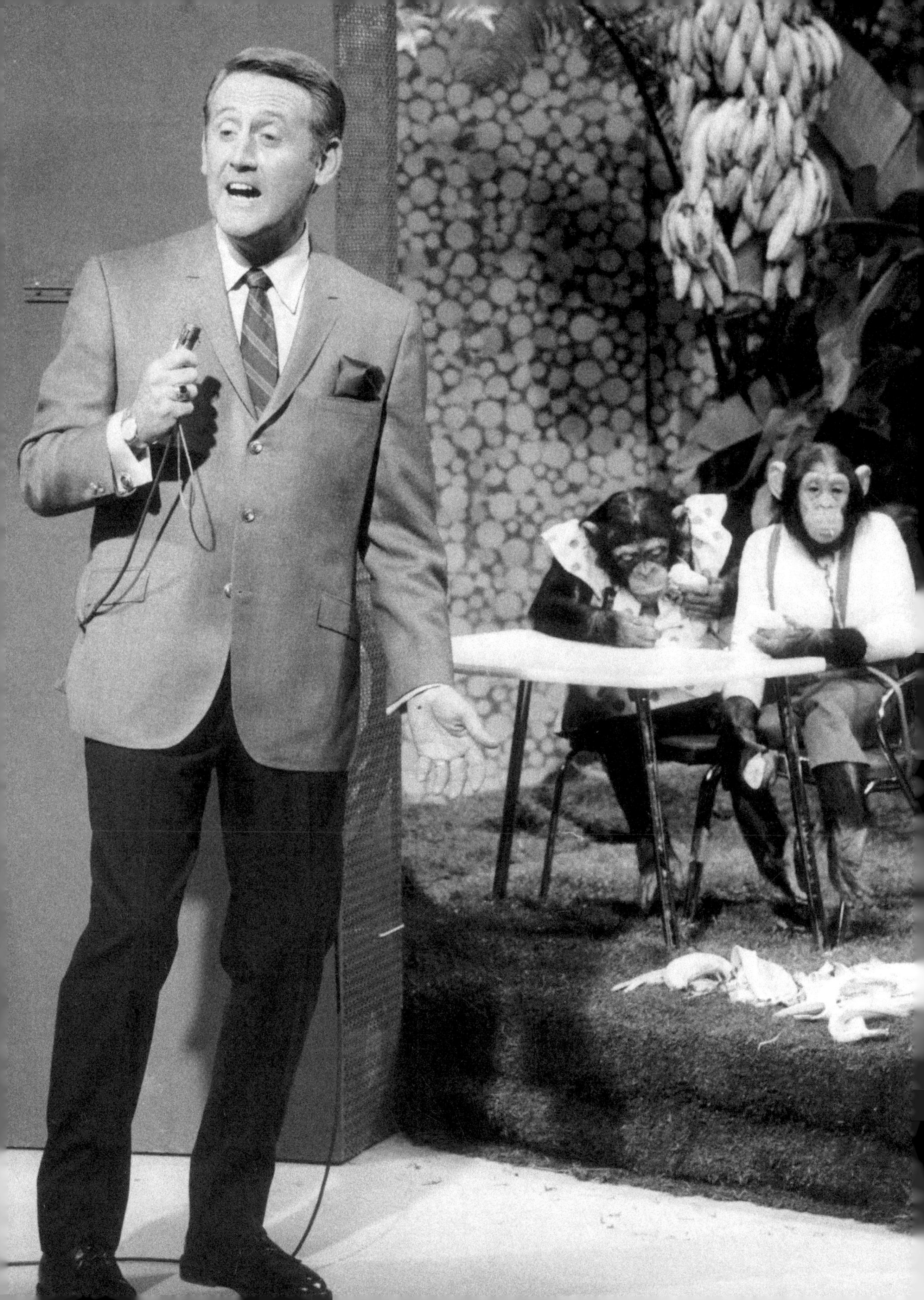

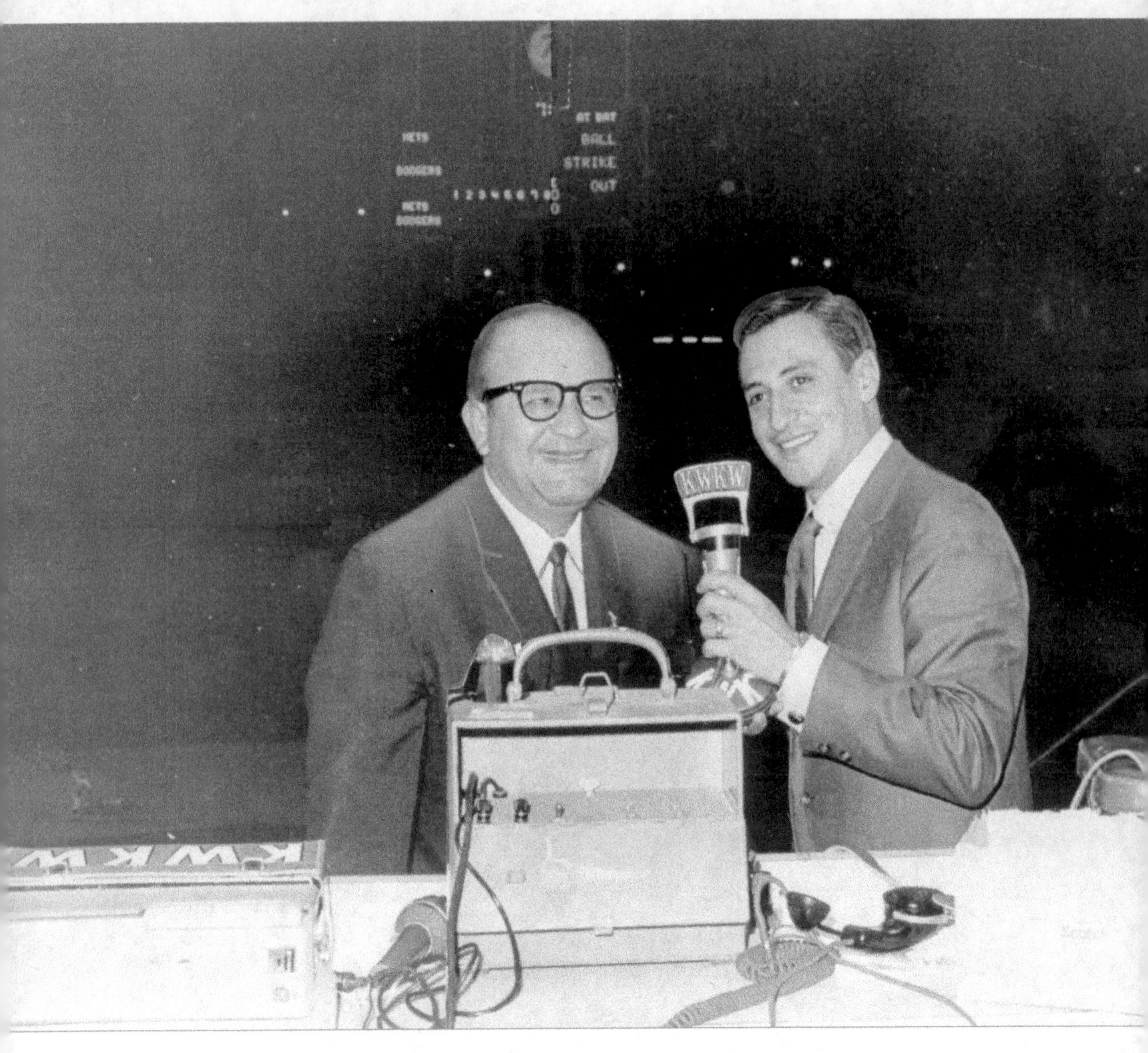

Hall of Fame announcer Jaime Jarrin (*right*), with former partner Jose Garcia, credited Scully with an assist when he began broadcasting Dodger games in Spanish in 1959.
(Y. Callagher/Herald-Examiner Collection)

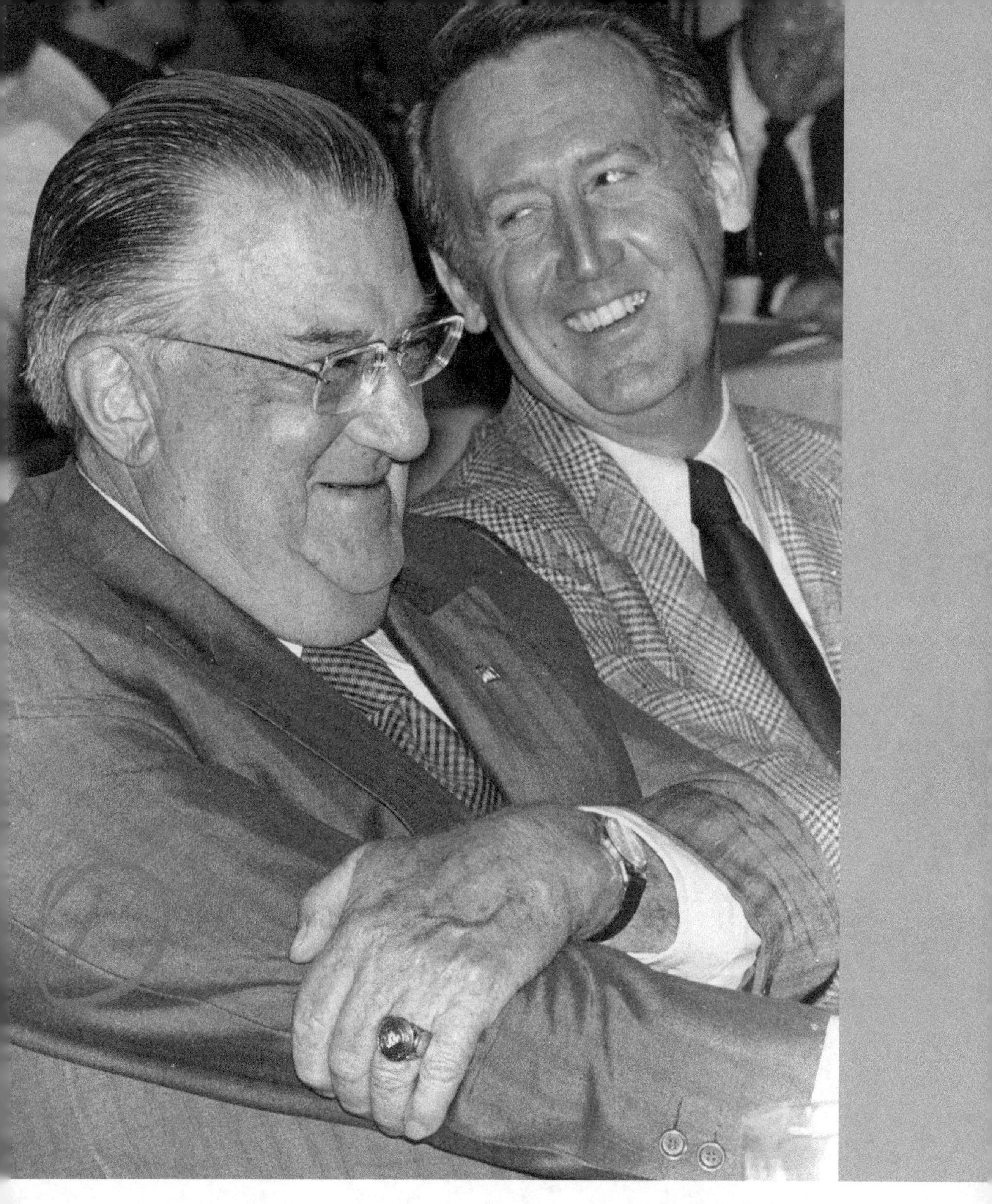

With Dodgers owner Walter O'Malley. (Herald-Examiner Collection)

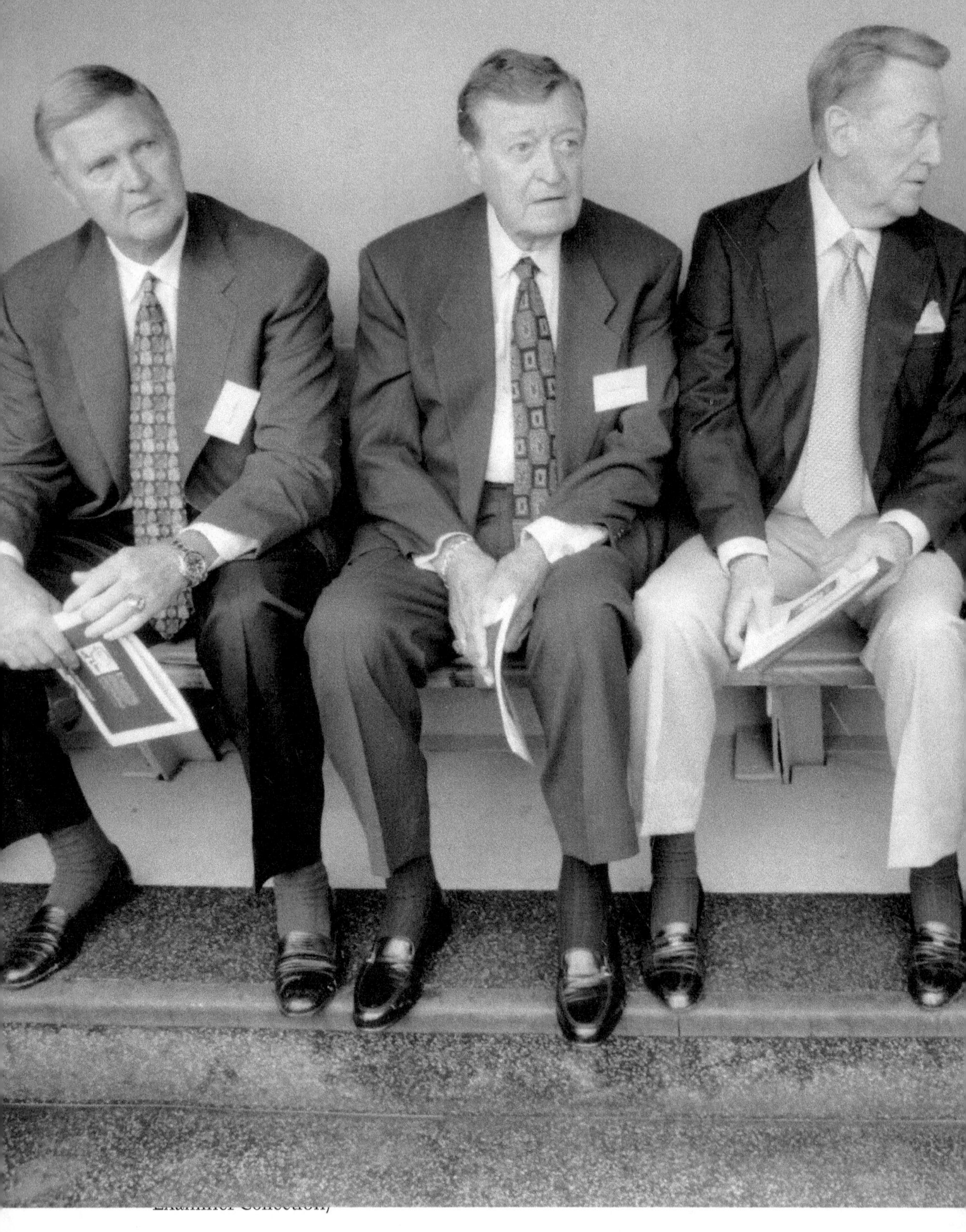

Examiner Collection)

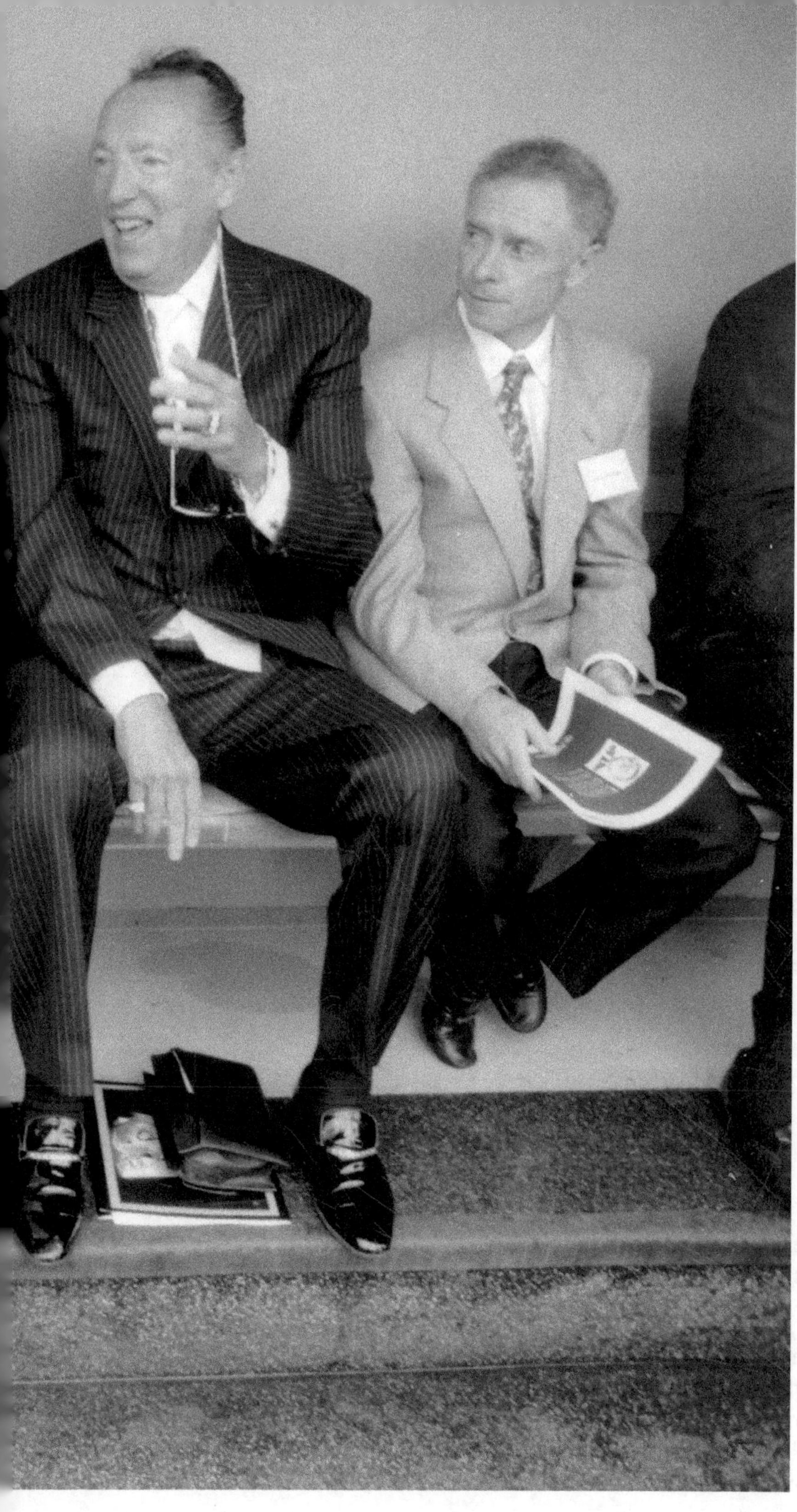

Sitting with (*from left*) Jerry West, Chick Hearn, Al Davis, and jockey Chris McCarron at the memorial service for Jim Murray. (Gary Leonard)

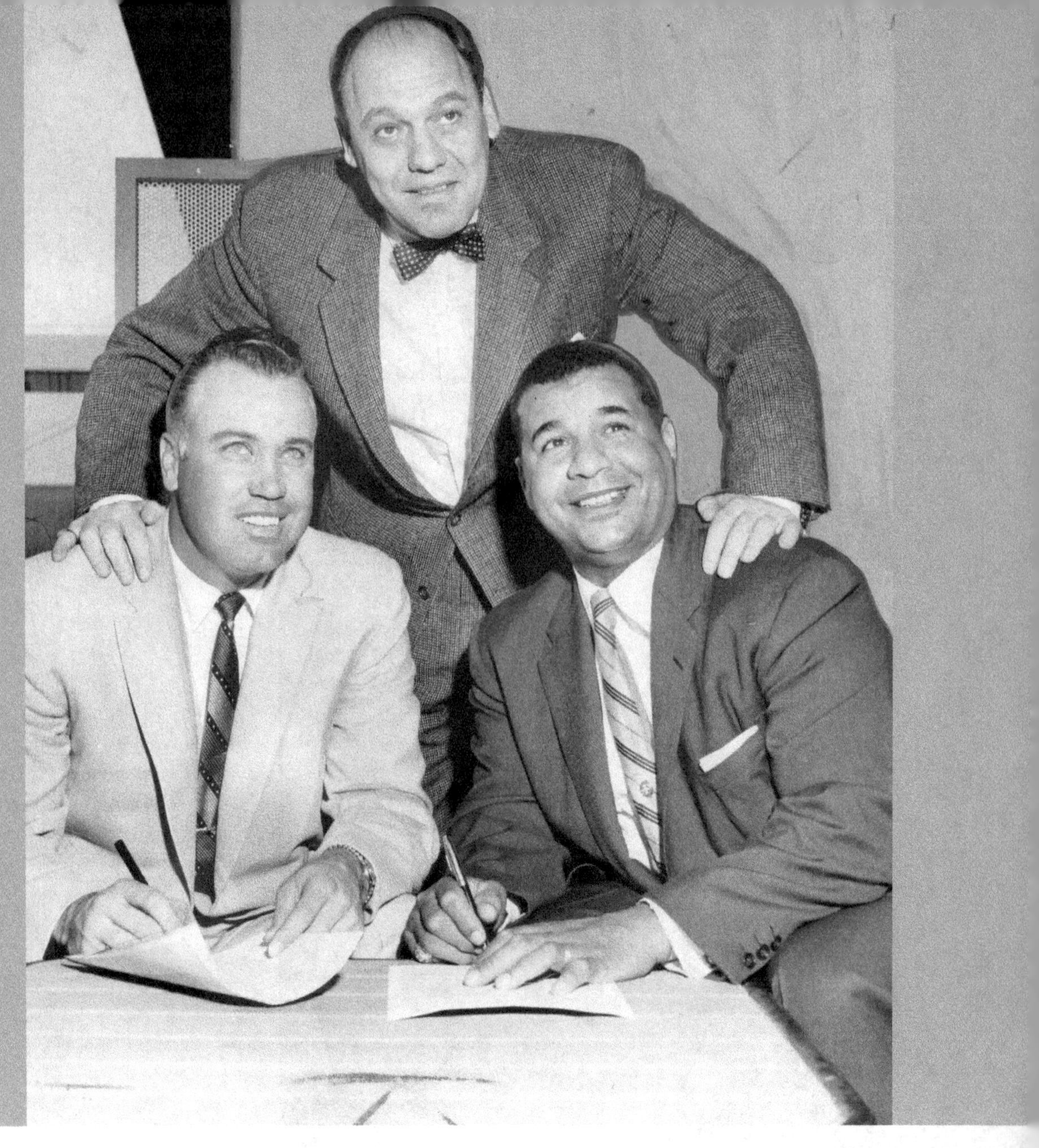

Outfielder Duke Snider (*left*) and catcher Roy Campanella sign their contracts for the 1958 season as general manager Buzzy Bavasi looks on. (Herald-Examiner Collection)

OPPOSITE: After Campanella was paralyzed in a car accident, the Dodgers staged "Roy Campanella Night" at the Coliseum on May 7. 1959. Here, Dodgers manager Walter Alston and New York Yankees manager Casey Stengel flank the Hall of Fame catcher as he acknowledges the record crowd of 93,103 fans. (Tom Courtney/Herald-Examiner Collection)

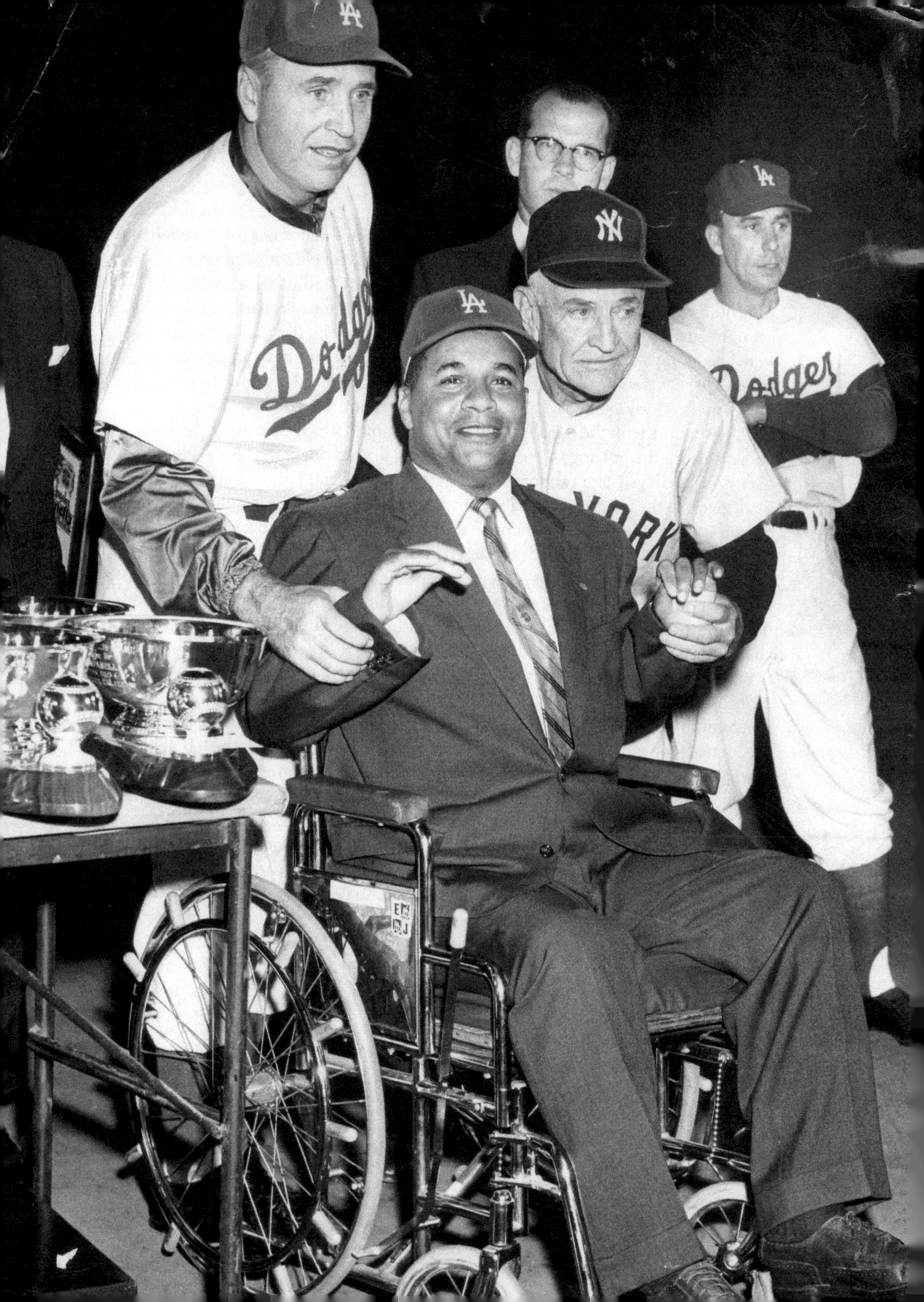
Dodgers
YORK
Dodgers

Hit and Run

For reasons unknown to me, on Saturday mornings Major League Baseball was broadcast on a TV station in San Diego. Los Angeles didn't receive the broadcasts, but if you twisted the antenna and fiddled with the knobs, you could watch the games. It was before the Dodgers came to town, but we were already Dodger fans. Pee Wee Reese, Duke Snider, and Roy Campanella were becoming recognizable names to 8-year-olds. They may have played some preseason games at the old Wrigley Field in 1955 or 1956, and my father and uncles took us kids to one. What I remember most about Wrigley Field was seeing hot dog vendors with the big aluminum steamer boxes strapped around their bodies to keep the hot dogs warm as they walked up and down the aisles yelling, "Get your hot dogs!" The vendors would slather mustard and pile onions on the food, give it to the person on the aisle, then everyone would pass it along, bucket-brigade style, to the customer, then the money would get passed back to the vendor, then any change would get passed back to the fan. When I was nine years old, the Dodgers arrived in Los Angeles for good, and it was more exciting than Christmas to go to a game. We drove to the Coliseum from Mar Vista. There was no freeway yet, and we drove through neighborhoods I had never seen, probably going east along Exposition Blvd. The parking lot was full, so Uncle Danny had to find street parking. Residents were offering spots on their front lawns for fifty cents. We found a space and walked to the Coliseum. It was overwhelming inside the stadium—people were so excited, yelling and cheering. The Dodgers played the Pirates—Joe Pignatano caught, Duke Snider hit a home run over the left field fence, Don Zimmer and Charlie Neal played infield. I'm not sure who played first base, maybe Norm Larker. We were disappointed that Wally Moon didn't hit a Moon Shot. The Dodgers lost 5 to 3. We were sad as we walked back to the car, trying to remember where it was parked. As we walked along, maybe 39th Street near Hoover, somebody smashed their car into another car, then sped off, hit and run. My dad and uncles rushed us along to Uncle Danny's '57 Chevy station wagon and we drove home in silence. But the game was fun, even though we lost. We ate hot dogs, peanuts, and Crackerjacks, frozen Carnation chocolate malts. I still have my souvenir pennant.

—Stuart Rapeport

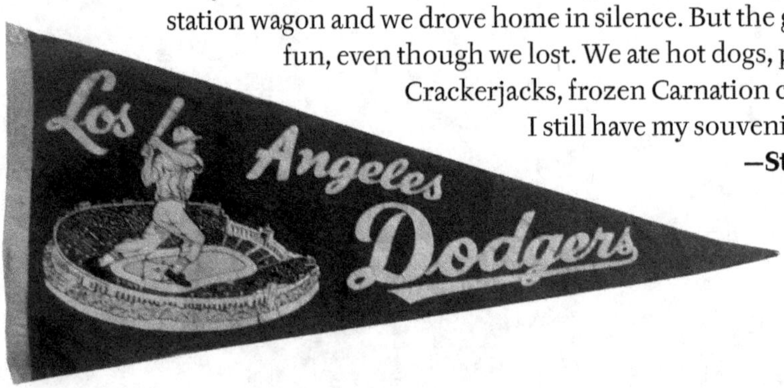

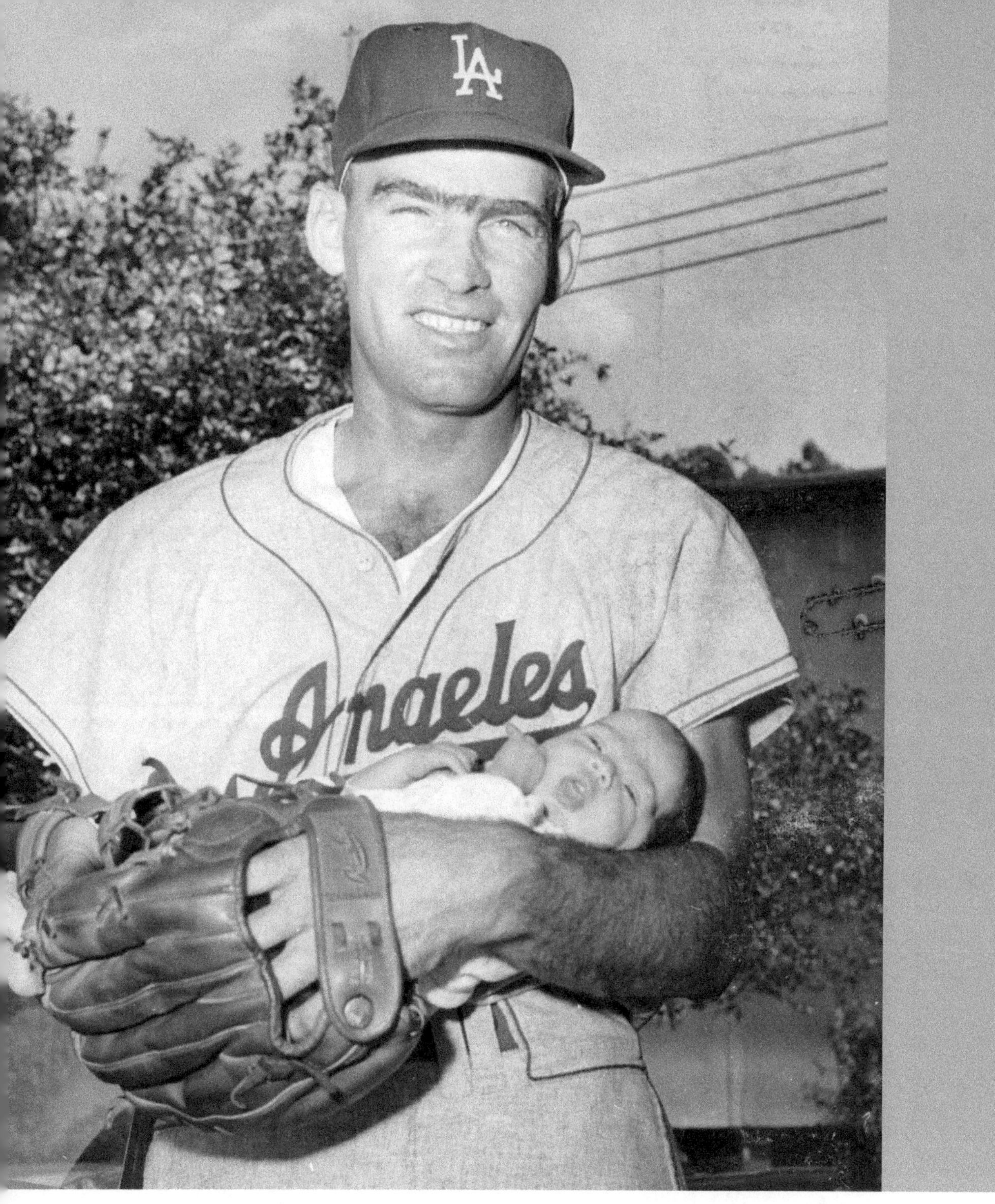

Known for his "Moon Shots" over the leftfield screen at the Coliseum and for his unique unibrow, outfielder Wally Moon beams while holding his daughter Mary. (Valley Times Collection)

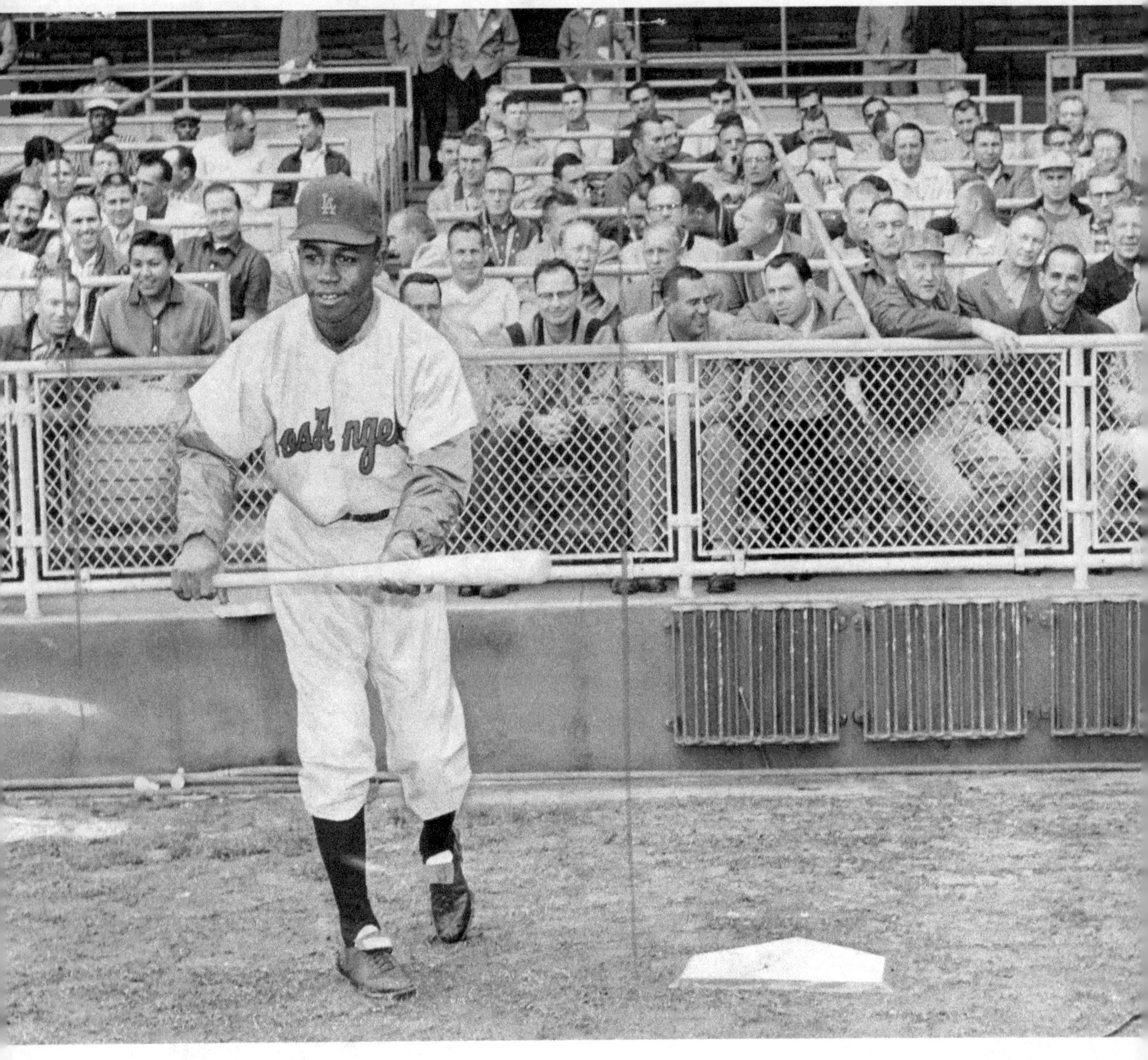

Infielder Jim "Junior" Gilliam demonstrates
proper bunting technique at the Big Baseball School.
(Herald-Examiner Collection)

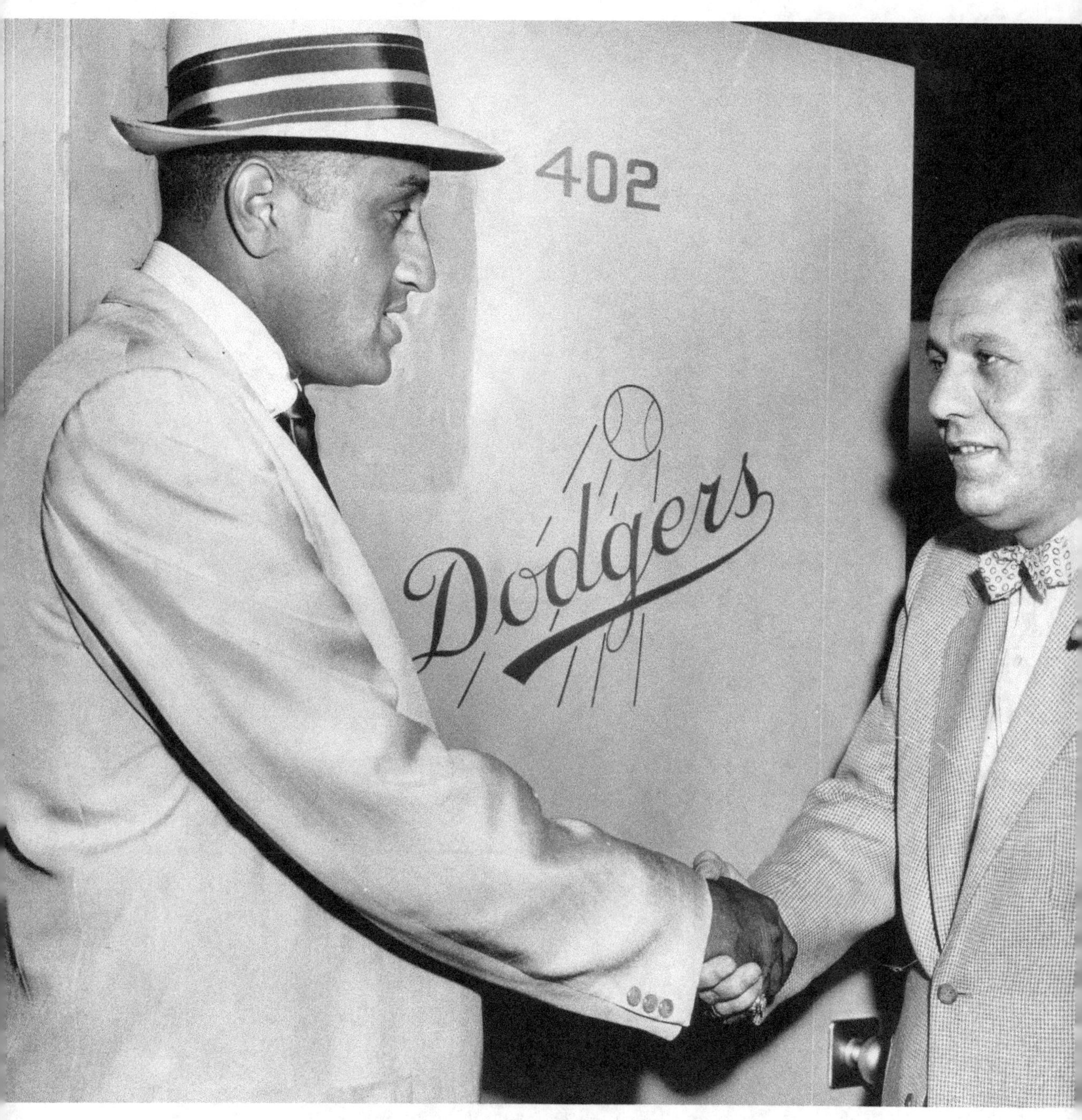

Pitcher Don Newcombe shakes hands with general manager Buzzy Bavasi
after he was traded to the Cincinnati Reds.
(Herald-Examiner Collection)

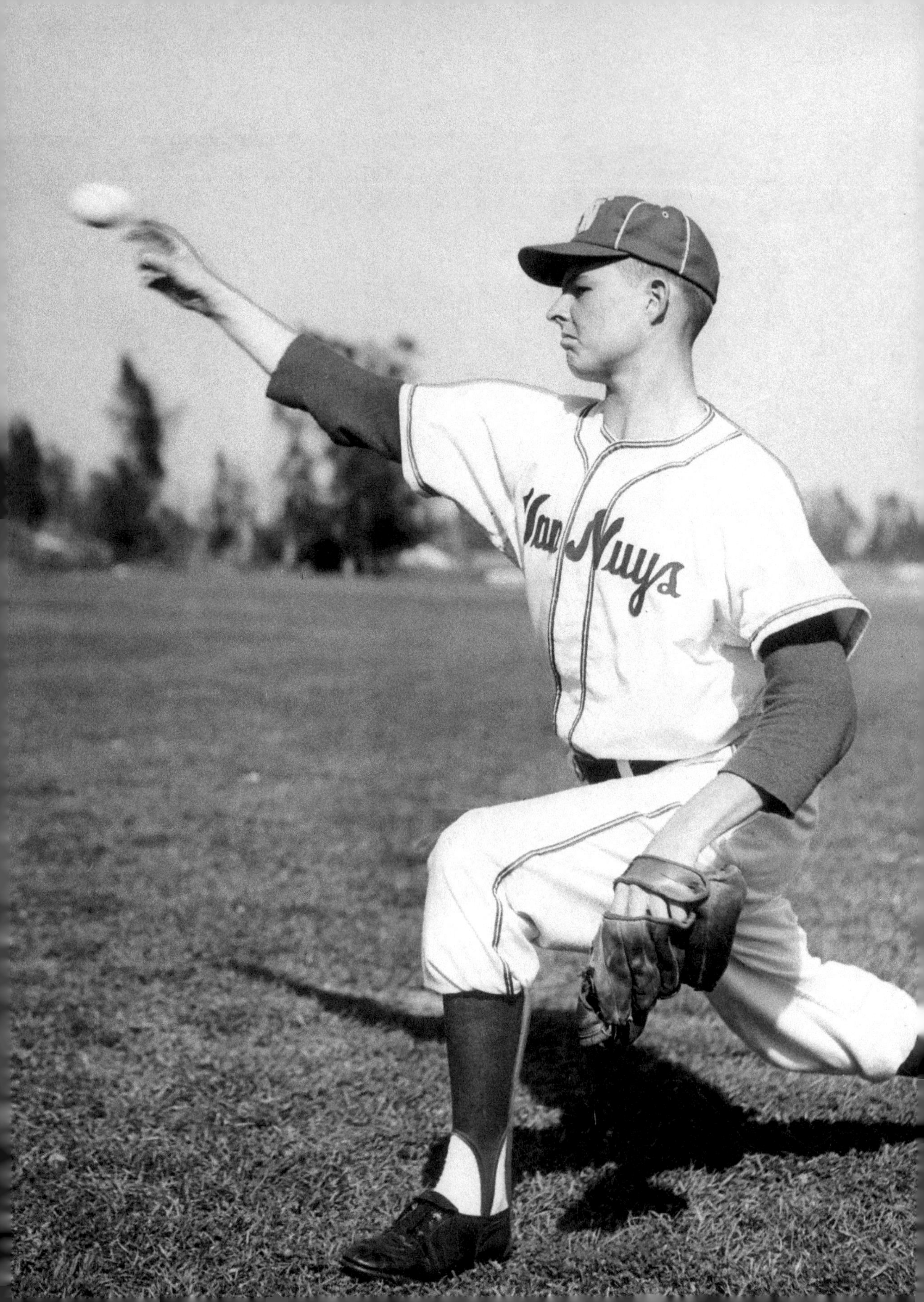
Van Nuys

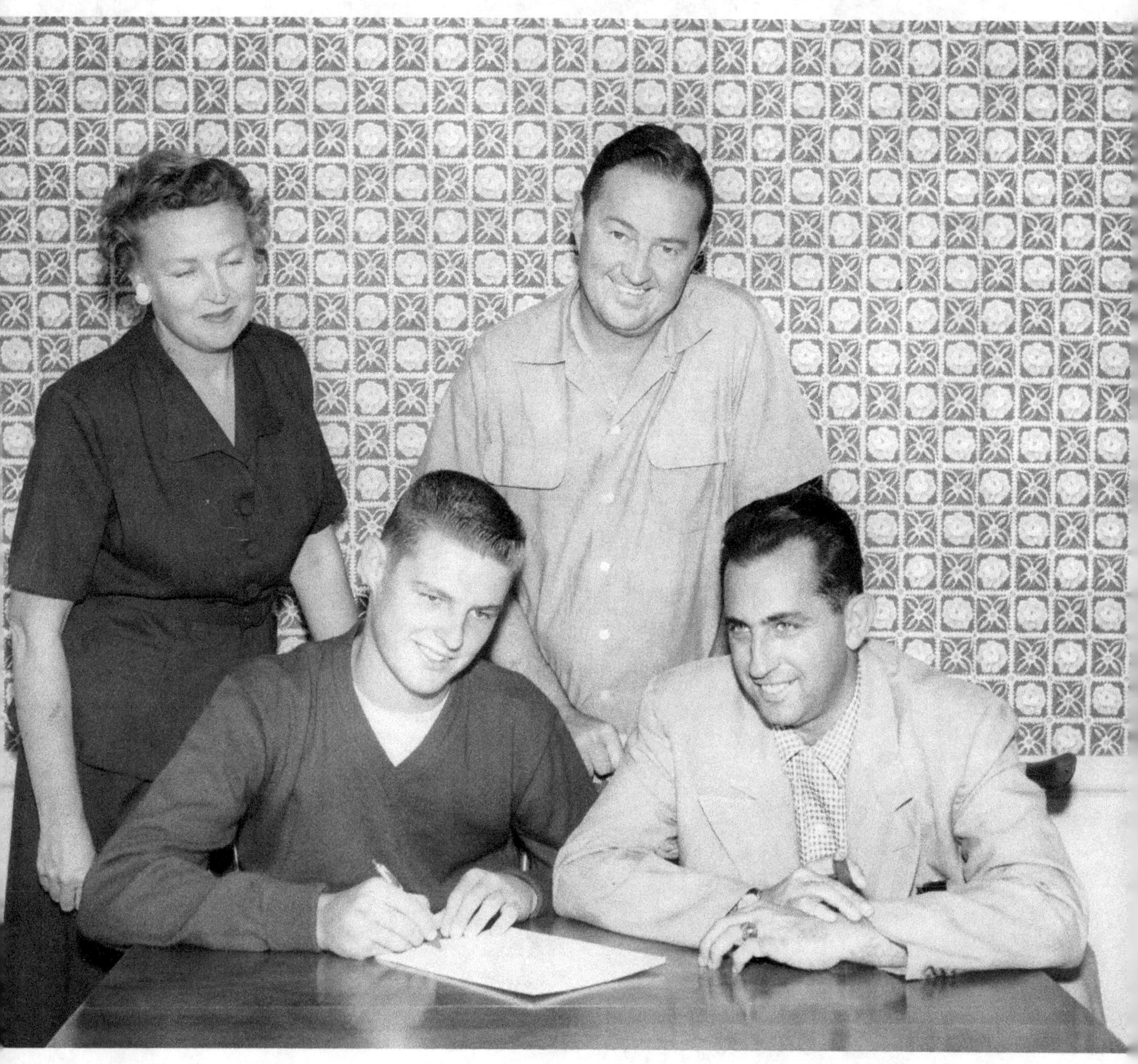

Don Drysdale was a star pitcher for Van Nuys High School
before he signed his first professional contract with the Dodgers.
(Valley Times Collection)

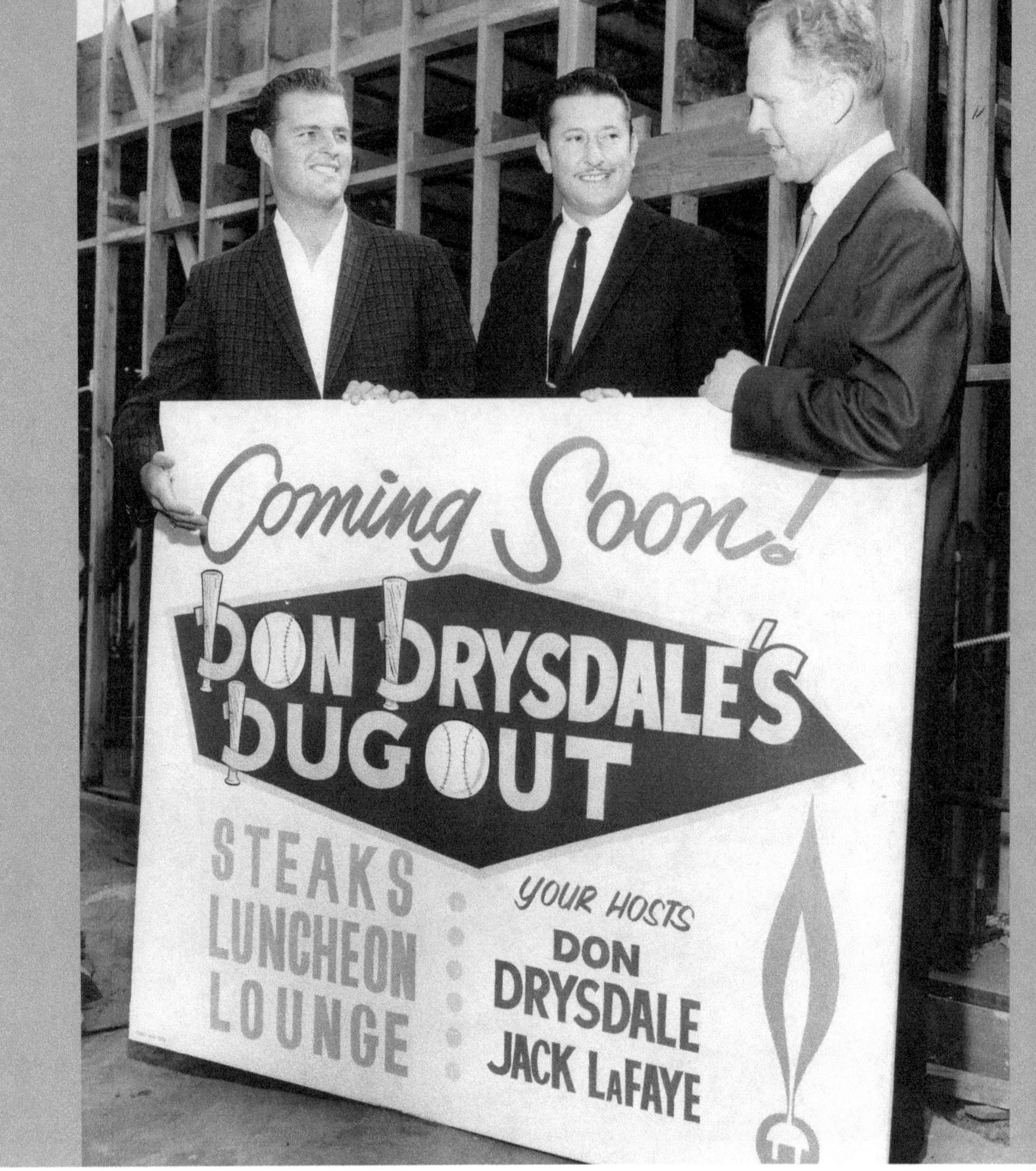

Drysdale's Dugout lounge was located near his childhood home in Van Nuys. (Vanguard Photography/Valley Times Collection)

OPPOSITE: "Big D" was an intimidating force on the mound; he was enshrined in the Baseball Hall of Fame in 1984. (Gordon Dean/Valley Times Collection)

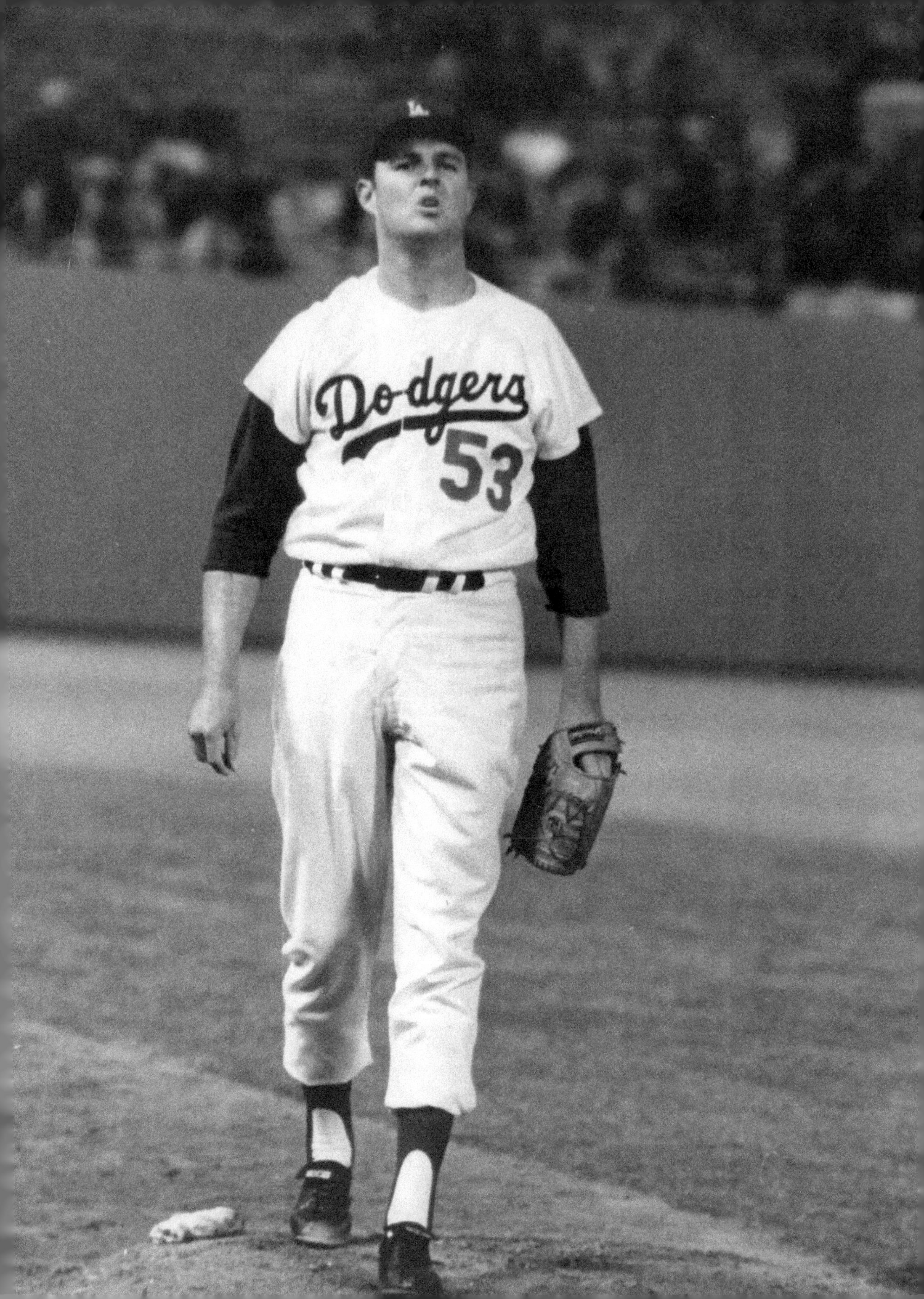
Dodgers
53

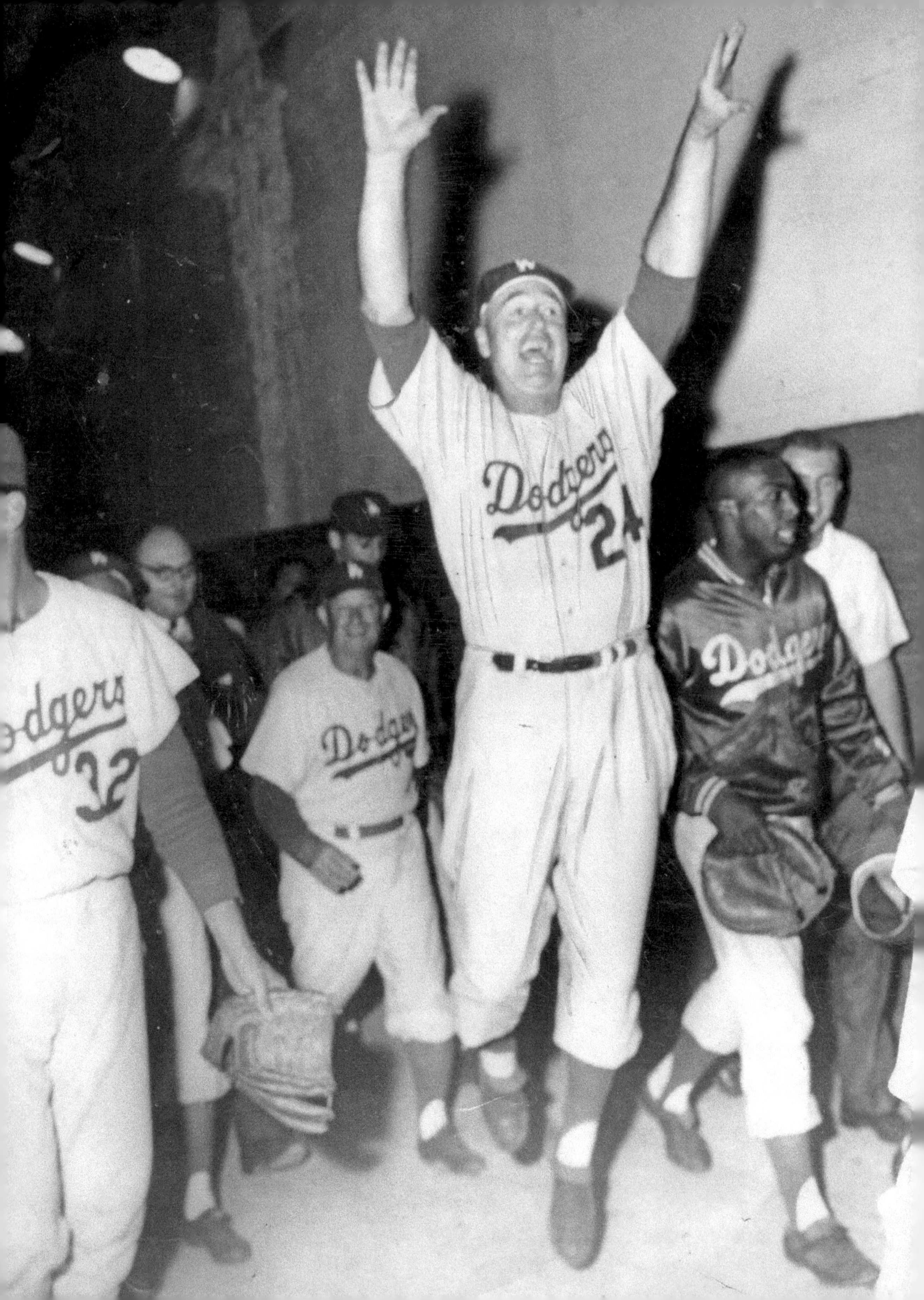
Dodgers
24
32
Dodgers

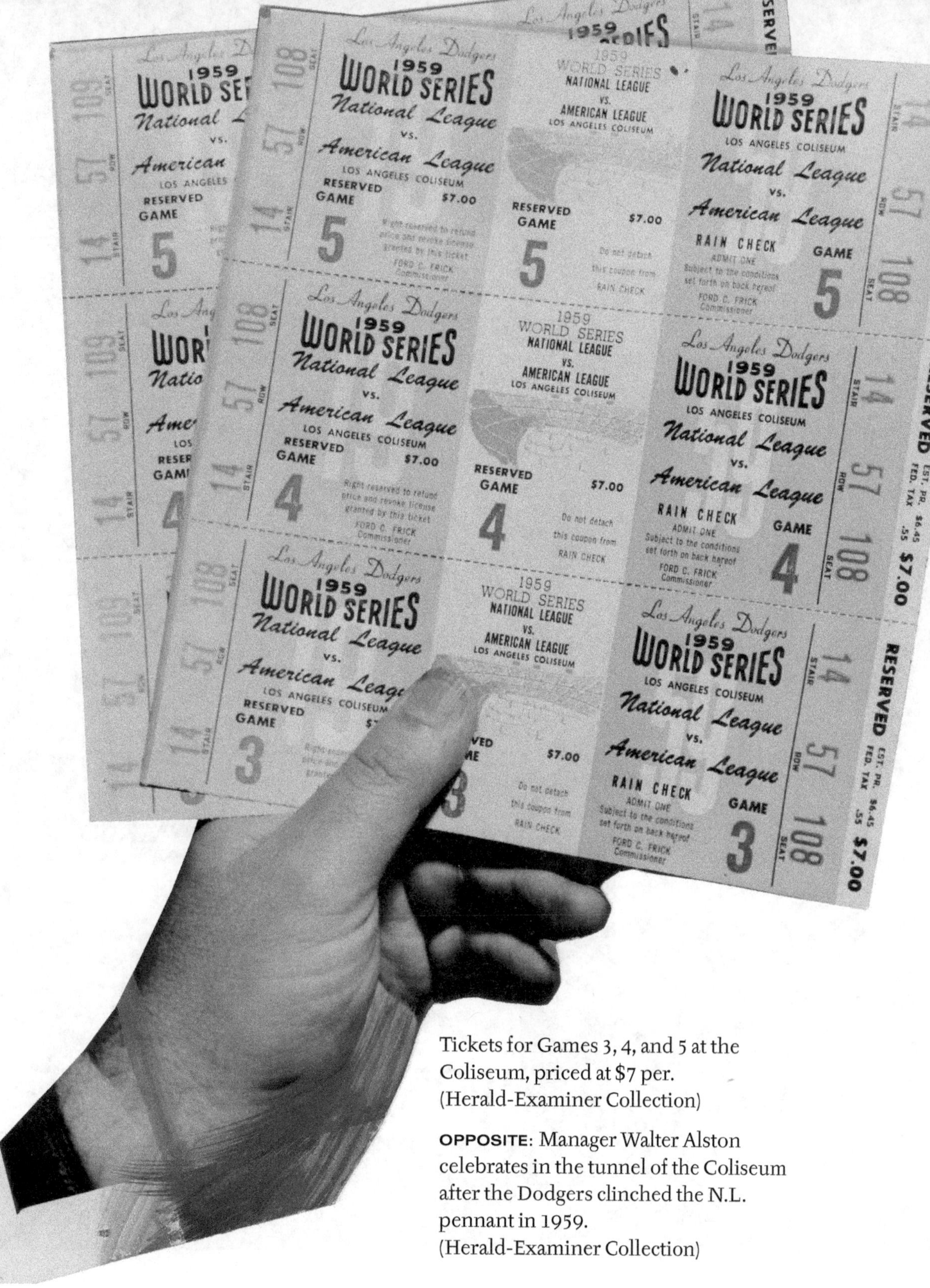

Tickets for Games 3, 4, and 5 at the Coliseum, priced at $7 per. (Herald-Examiner Collection)

OPPOSITE: Manager Walter Alston celebrates in the tunnel of the Coliseum after the Dodgers clinched the N.L. pennant in 1959. (Herald-Examiner Collection)

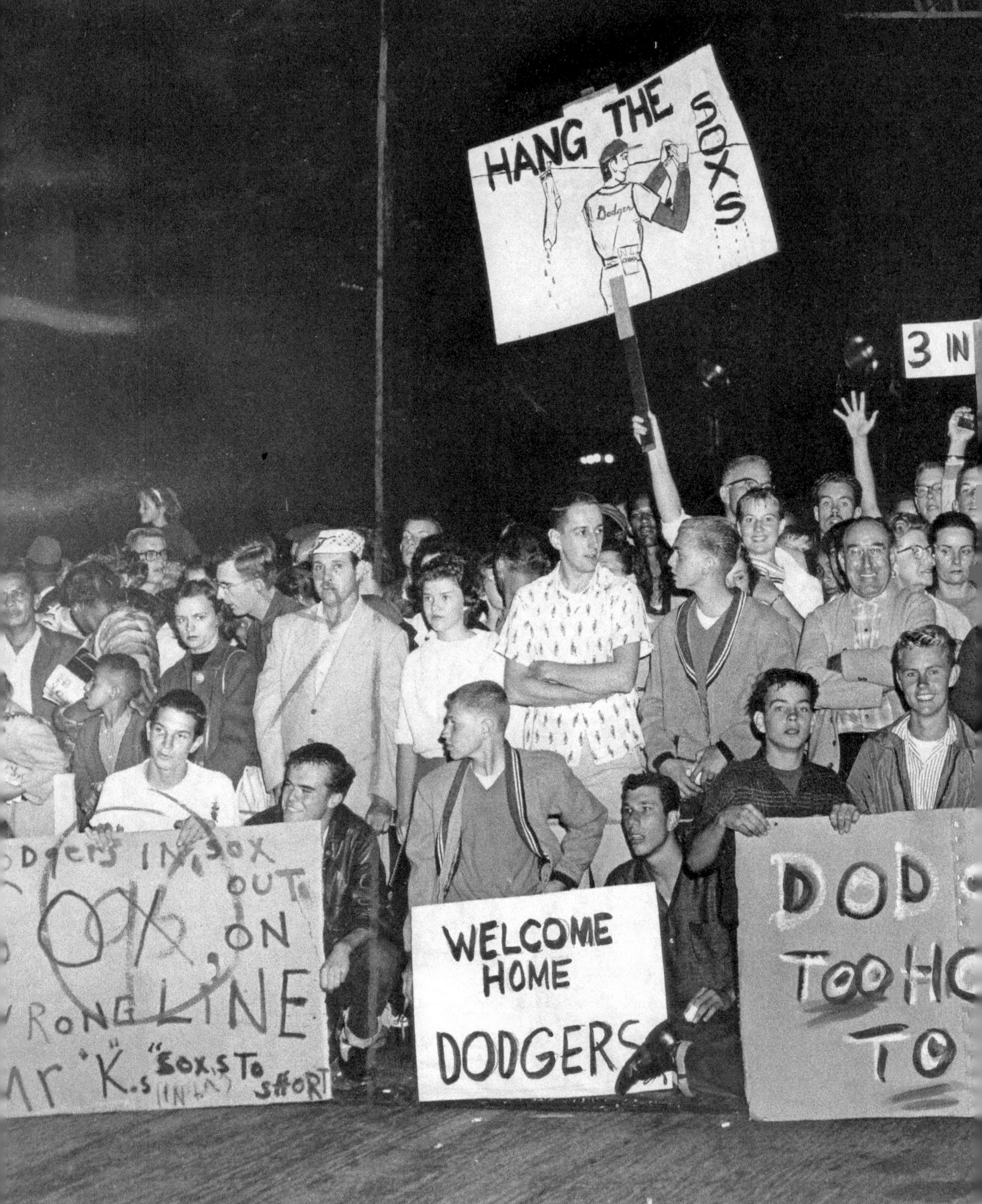
HANG THE SOXS
Dodgers
3 IN
WELCOME
HOME
DODGERS
TOO
TO

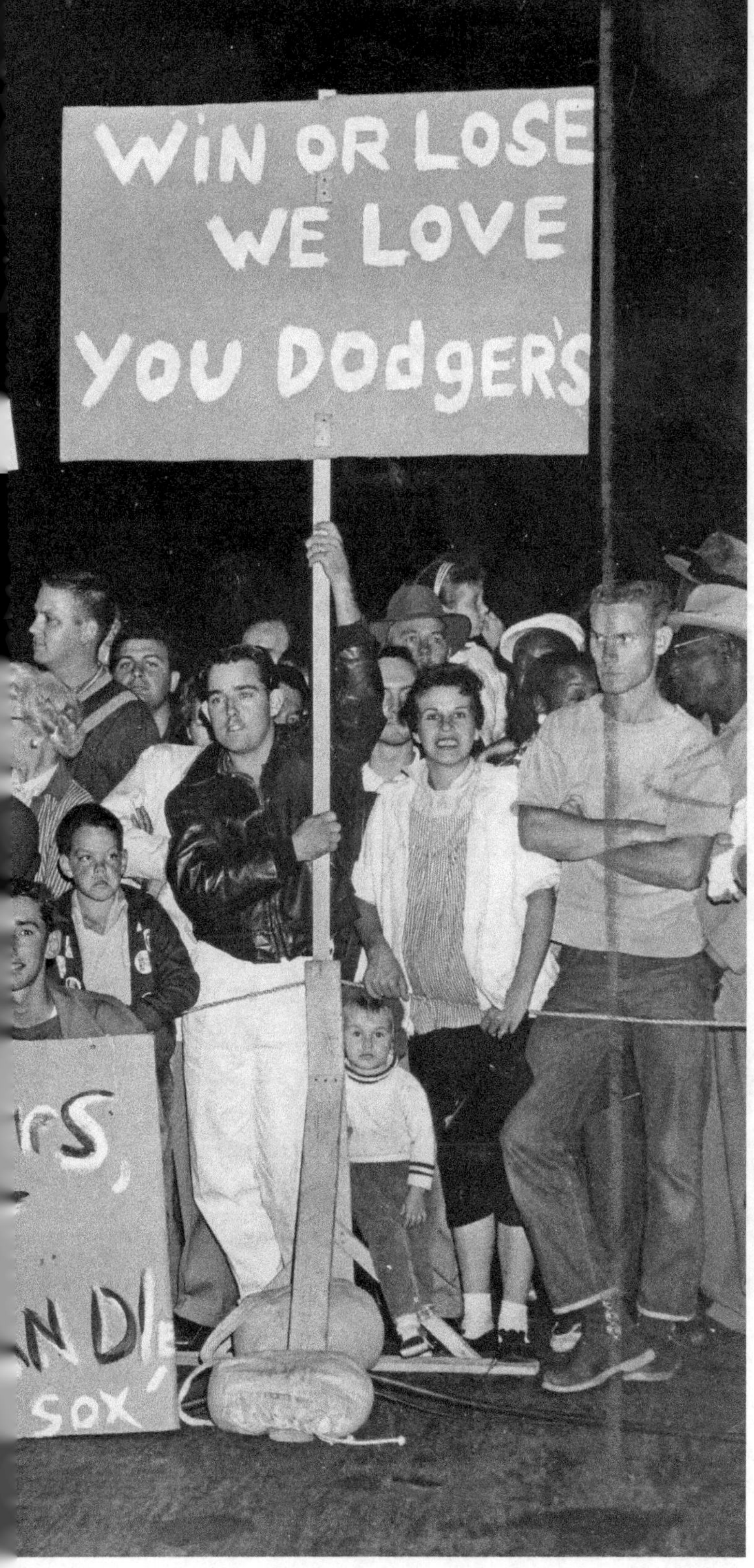

Fans greet the Dodgers at the airport after L.A. and the White Sox split the first two games of the 1959 World Series in Chicago. (Herald-Examiner Collection)

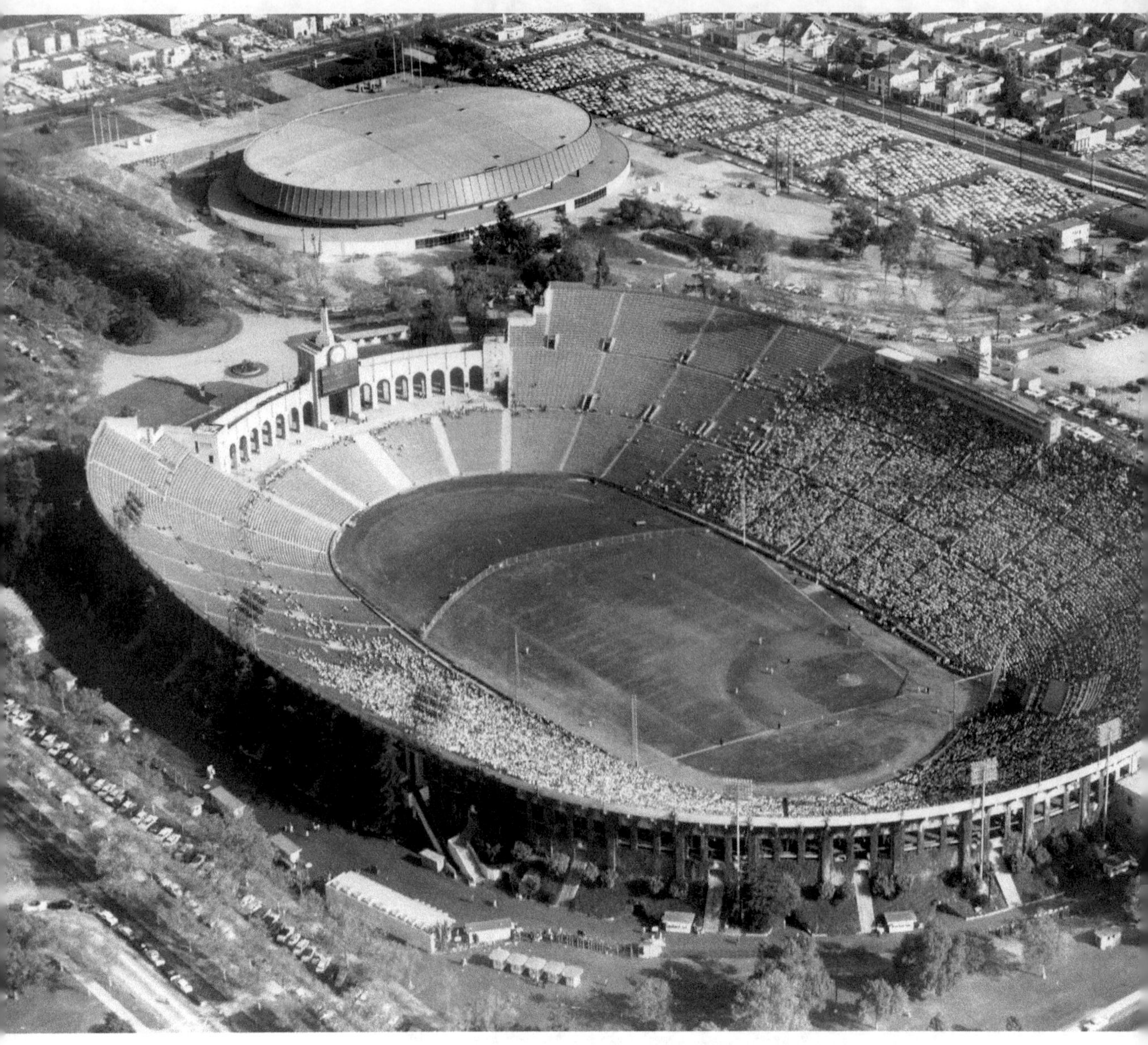

Aerial view of the action during Game 3 of the 1959 World Series, the Dodgers' first World Series game in L.A. (Herald-Examiner Collection)

OPPOSITE: Outfielder Carl Furillo was the hero of Game 3, with a key pinch-hit that helped starting pitcher Don Drysdale (*right*) get the victory over the White Sox. (Milton Martinez/Herald-Examiner Collection)

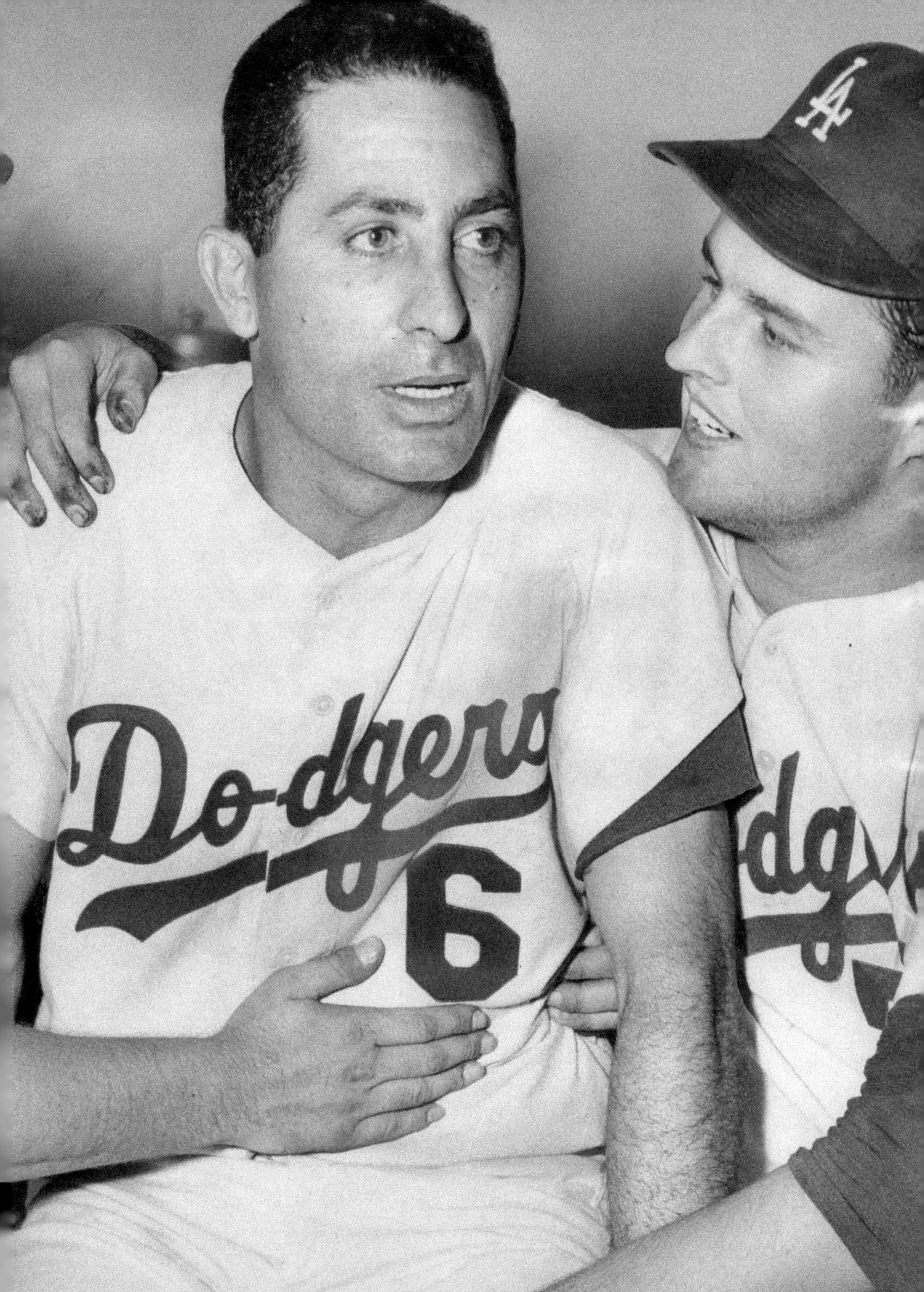
LA
Dodgers
6

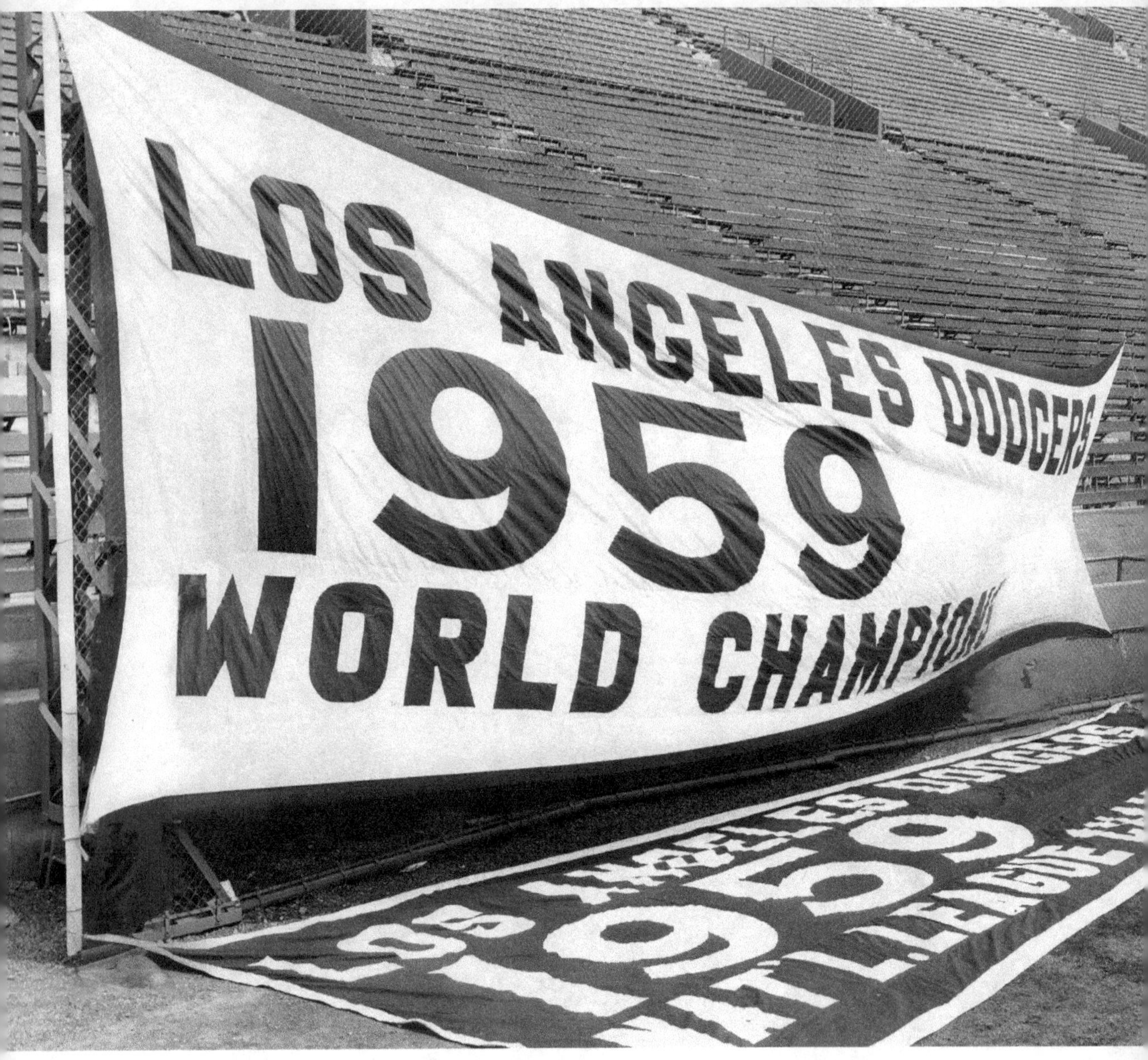

World Champions banner unveiled, 1959.
(George O'Day/Herald-Examiner Collection)

OPPOSITE: This ticket scalper was convicted of selling a $3.50 box seat for $5 before a Dodgers-Giants game at the Coliseum.
(Herald-Examiner Collection)

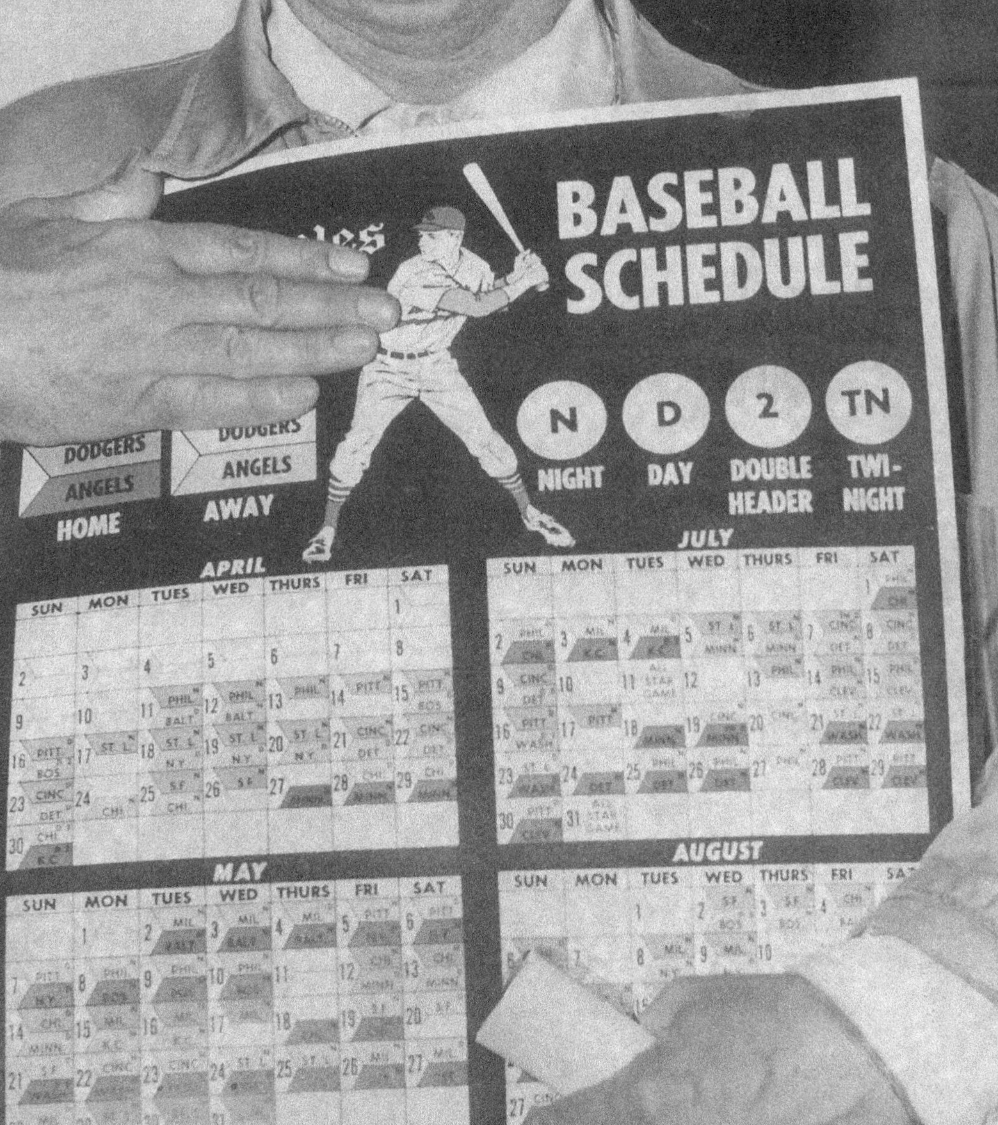
BASEBALL
SCHEDULE
DODGERS
ANGELS
HOME
DODGERS
ANGELS
AWAY
N
D
2
TN
NIGHT
DAY
DOUBLE HEADER
TWI-NIGHT
APRIL
MAY
JUNE
JULY
AUGUST

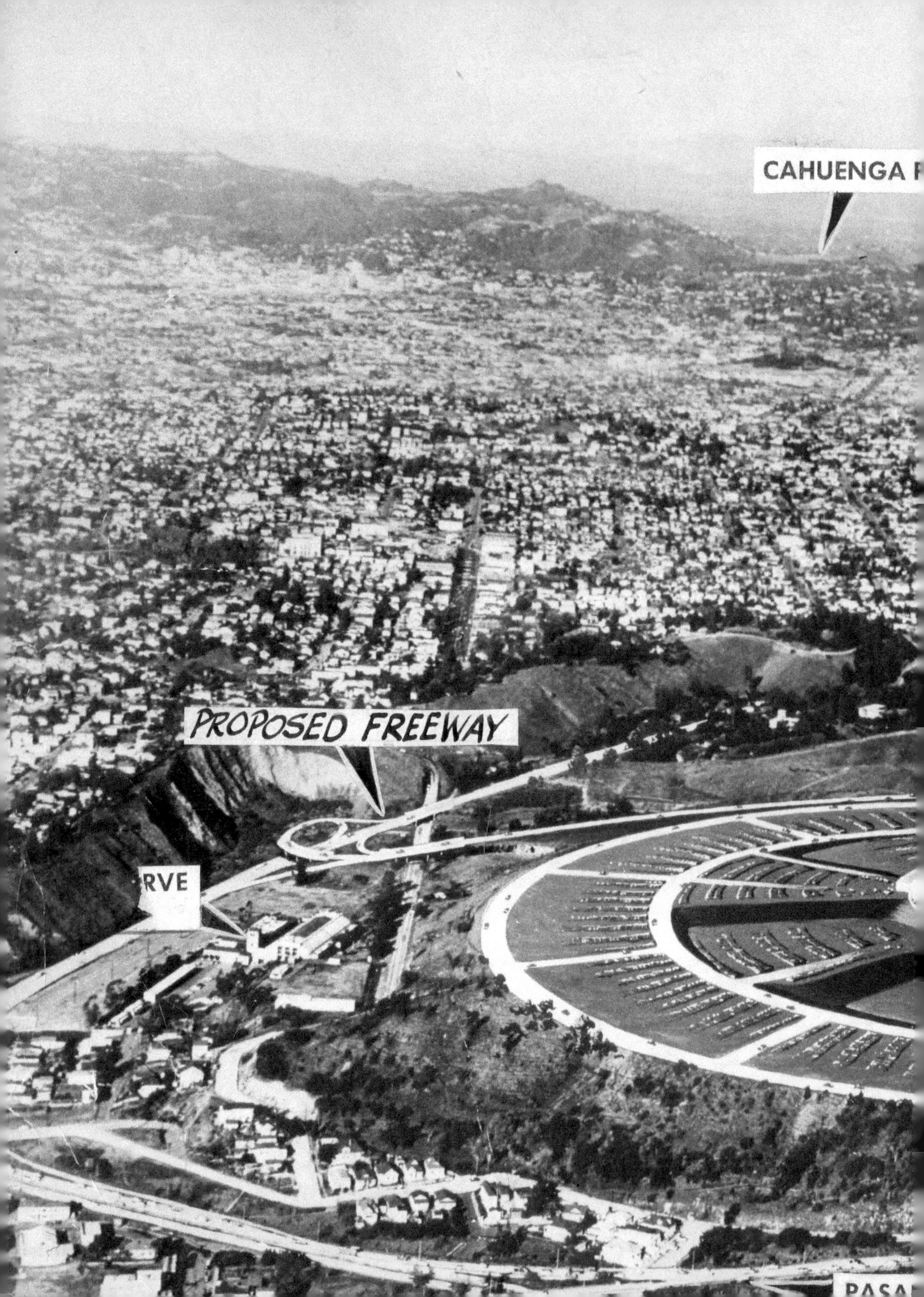
CAHUENGA P
PROPOSED FREEWAY
RVE
PASA

The Building of Dodger Stadium

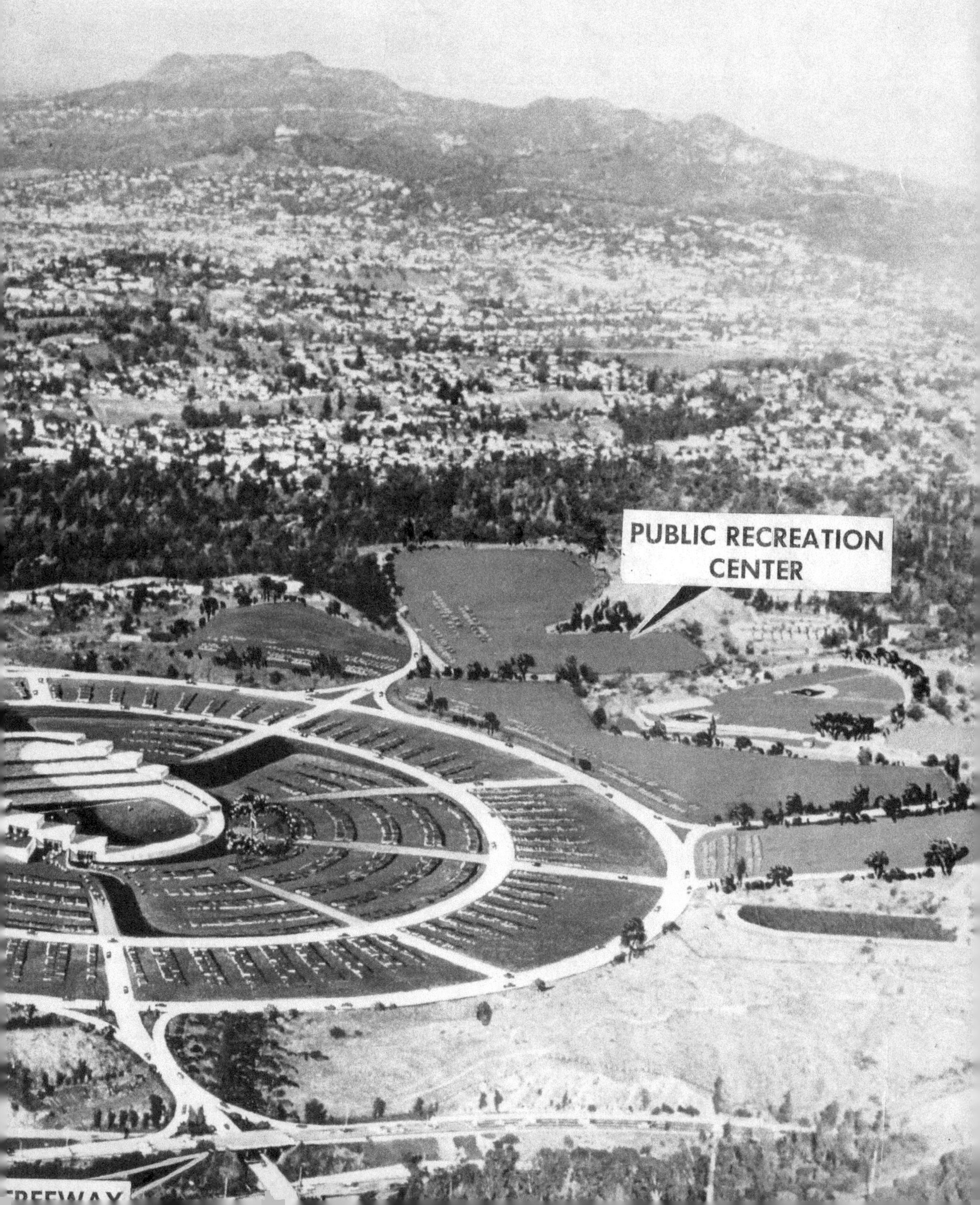

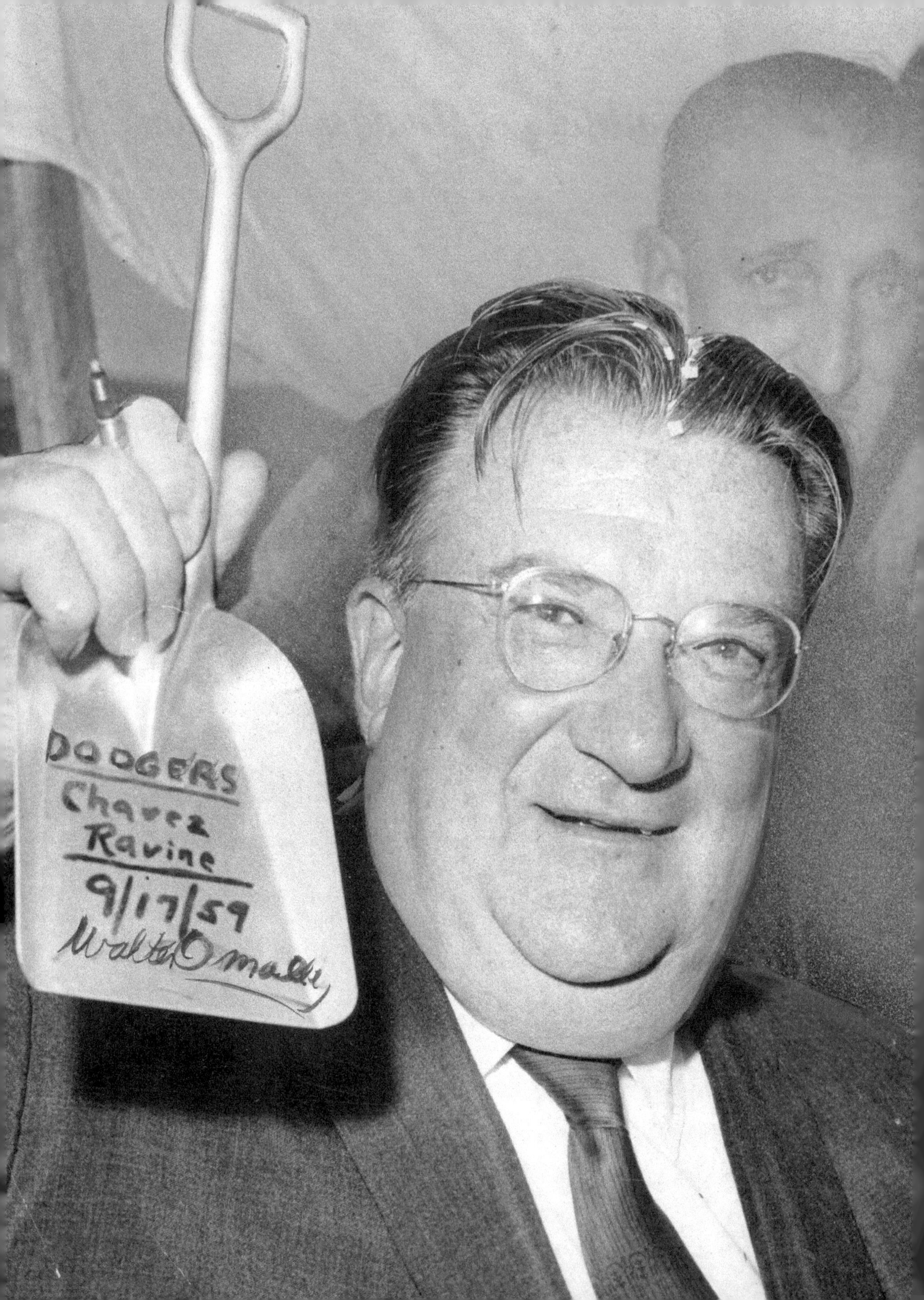
DODGERS
Chavez
Ravine
9/17/59
Walter O'Malley

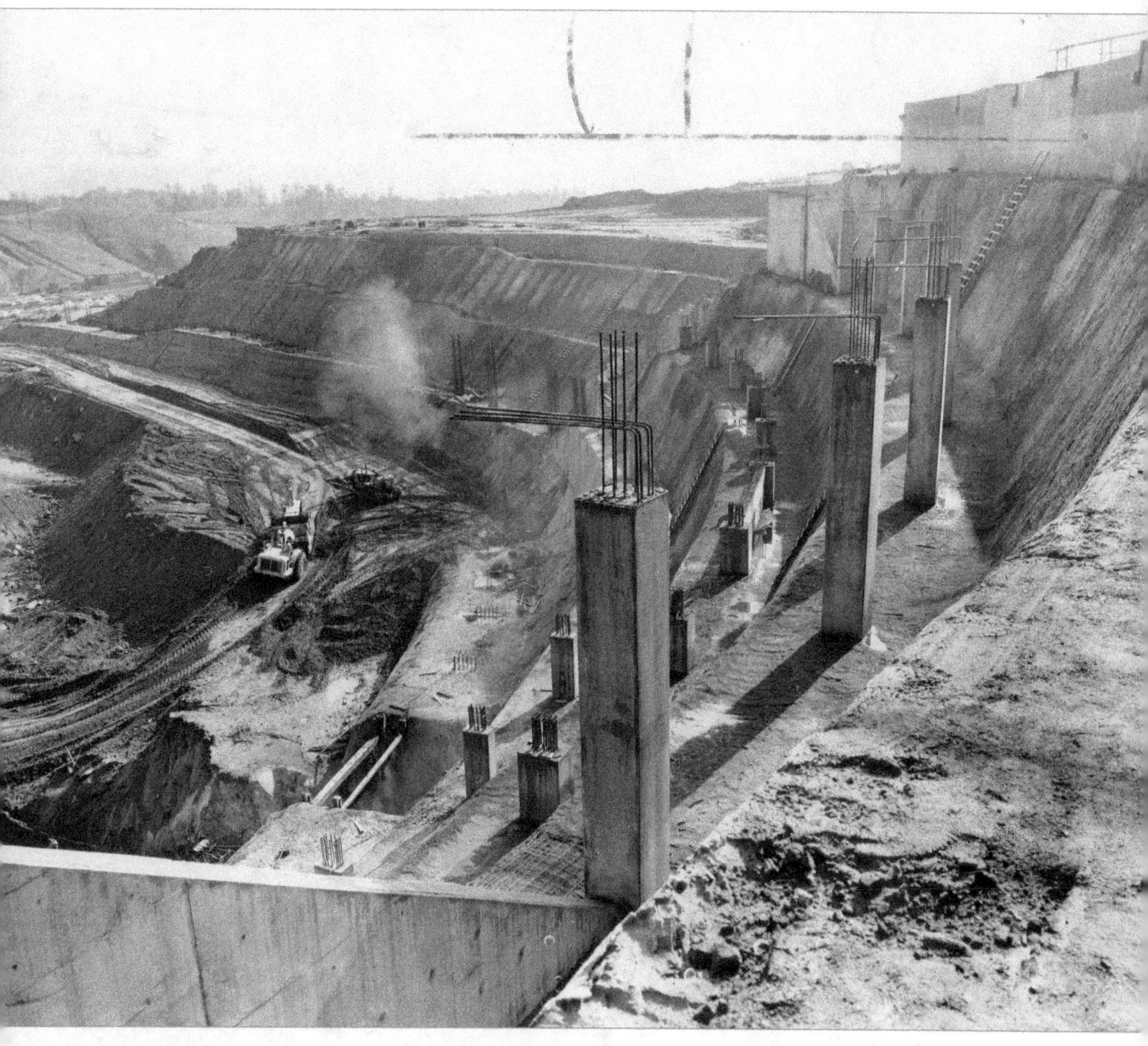

ABOVE: The stadium takes shape. (Herald-Examiner Collection)

OPPOSITE: Dodgers owner Walter O'Malley after the groundbreaking ceremony. (Herald-Examiner Collection)

PAGES 78-79: First proposed rendering of the new stadium. (Herald-Examiner Collection)

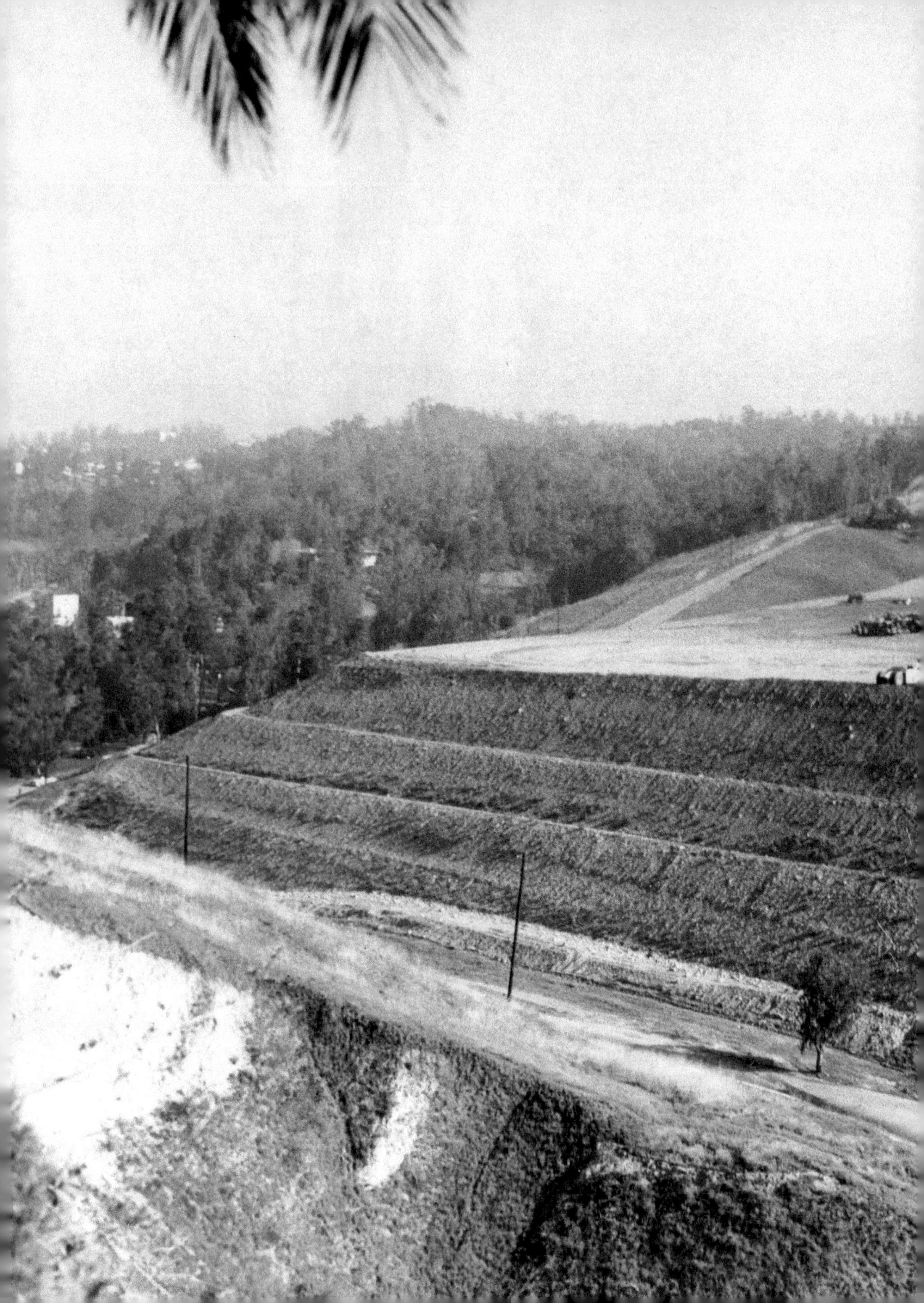

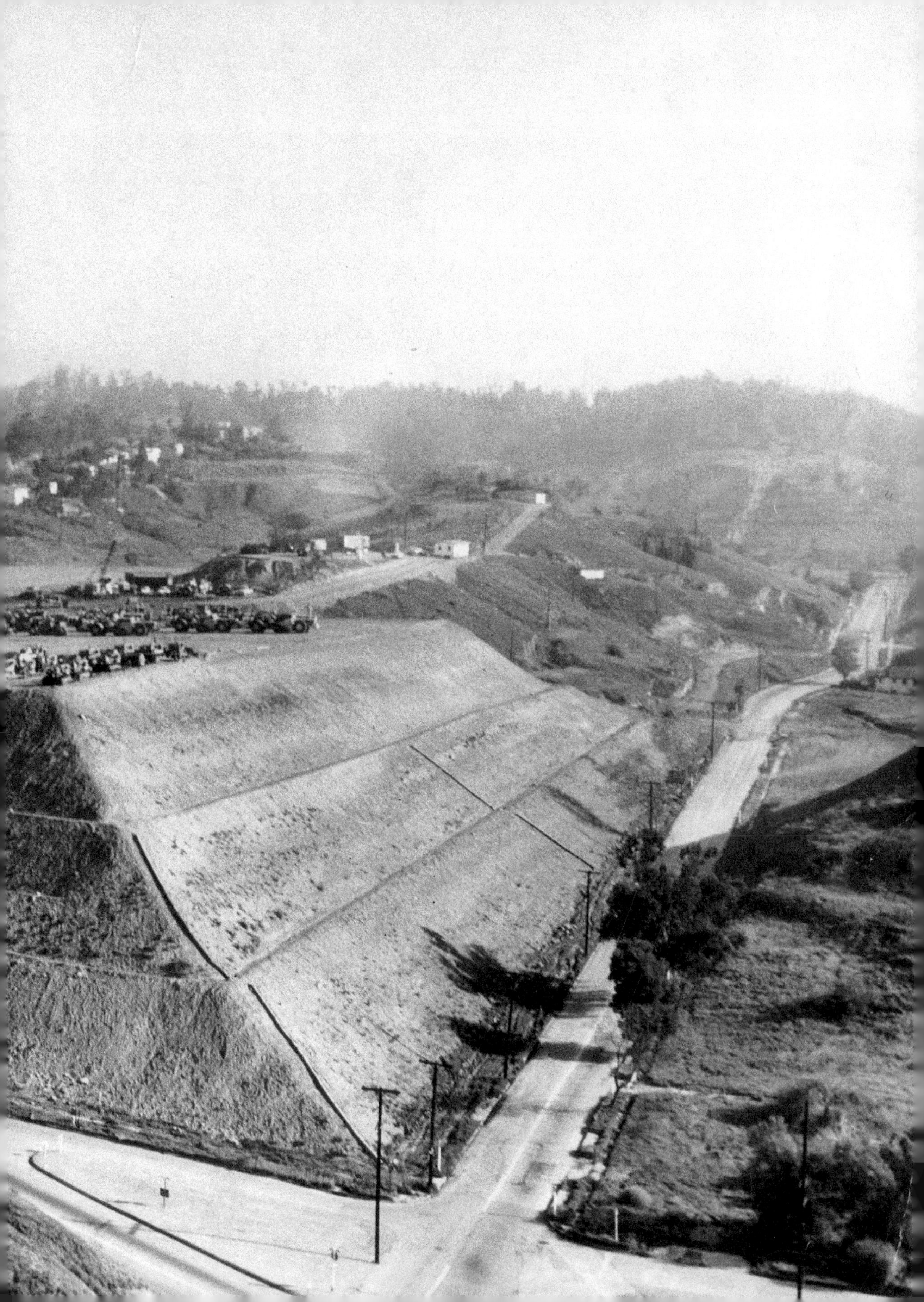

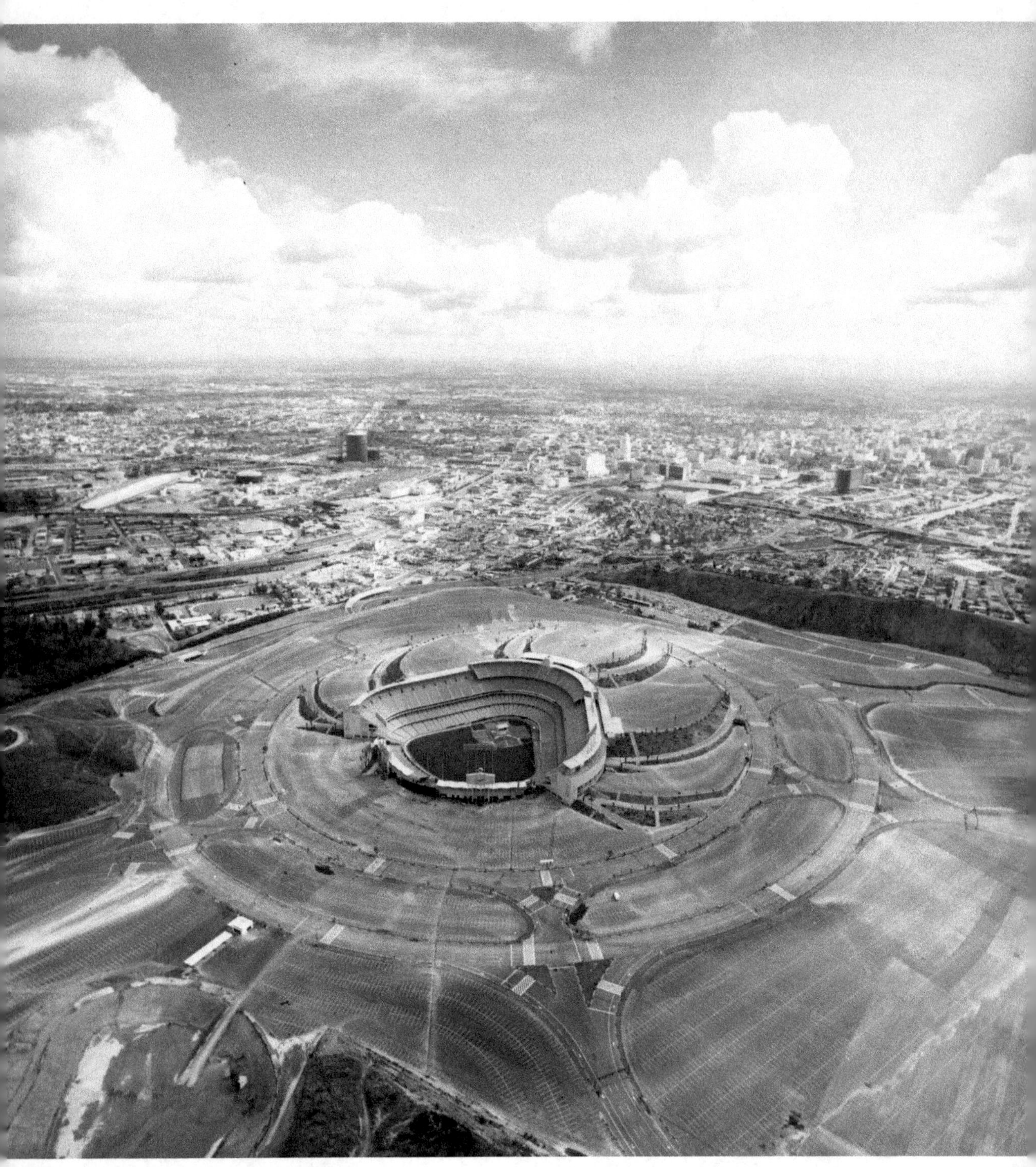

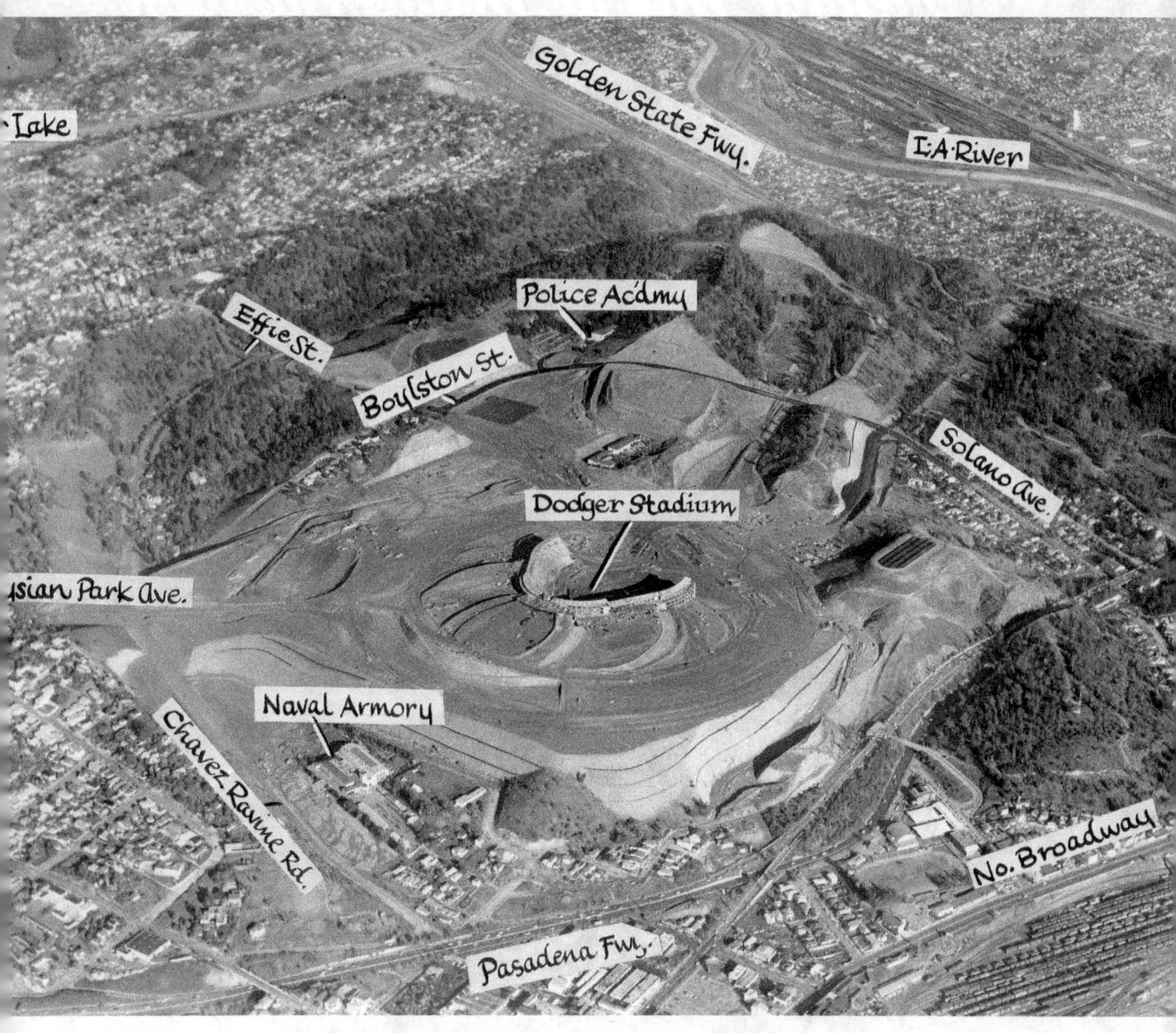

ABOVE: (Harold Morby/Herald-Examiner Collection)

OPPOSITE: (Modernage Photo Service/Security Pacific National Bank Collection)

PAGES 82-83: (Herald-Examiner Collection)

Opening Day at Dodger Stadium April 10, 1962

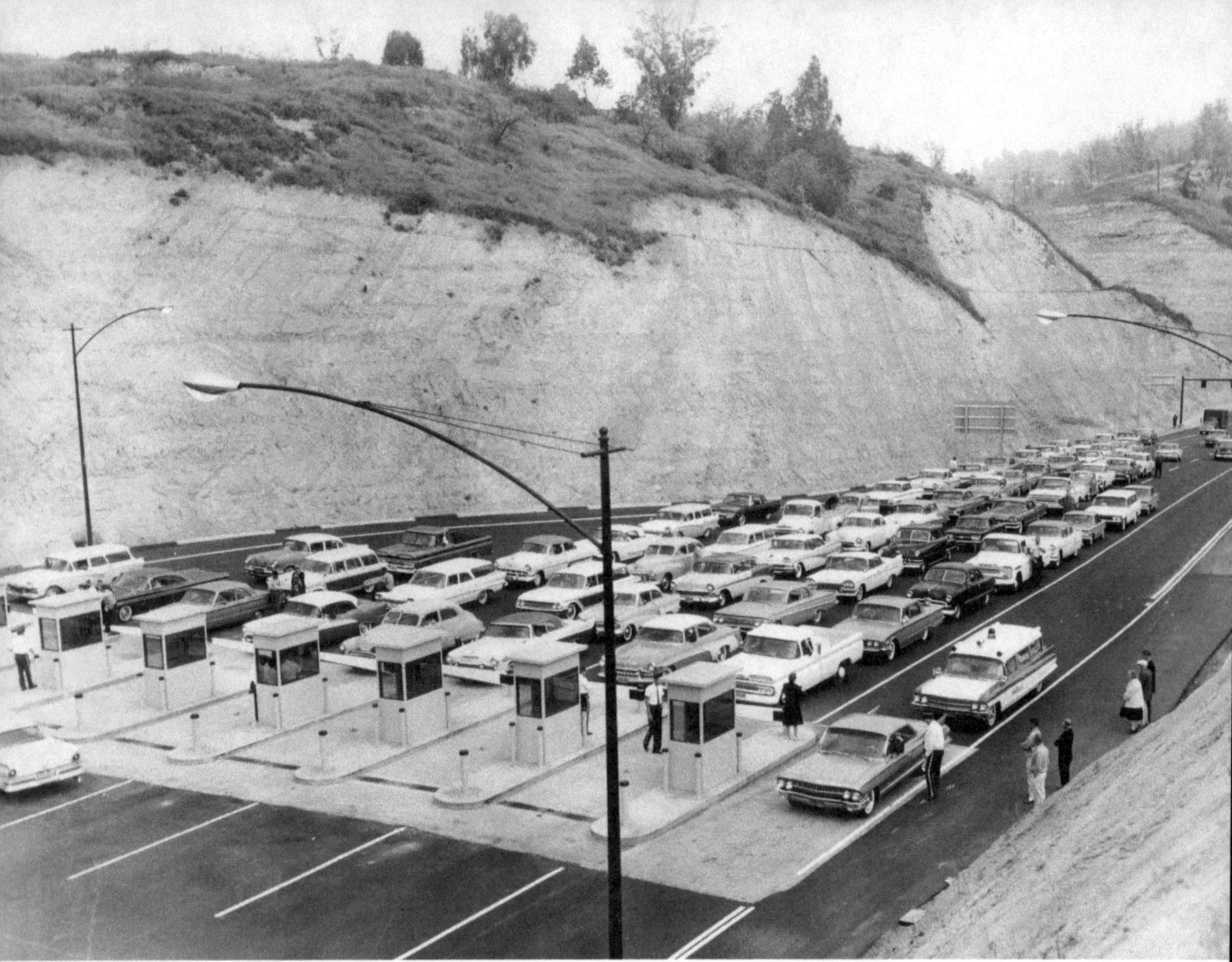

Cars at the Solano Street entrance line up to enter the stadium. (Herald-Examiner Collection)

OPPOSITE: The "key" to Dodger Stadium, presented to Walter O'Malley by Baseball Commissioner Ford Frick (*left*) and N.L. President Warren Giles. (Herald-Examiner Collection)

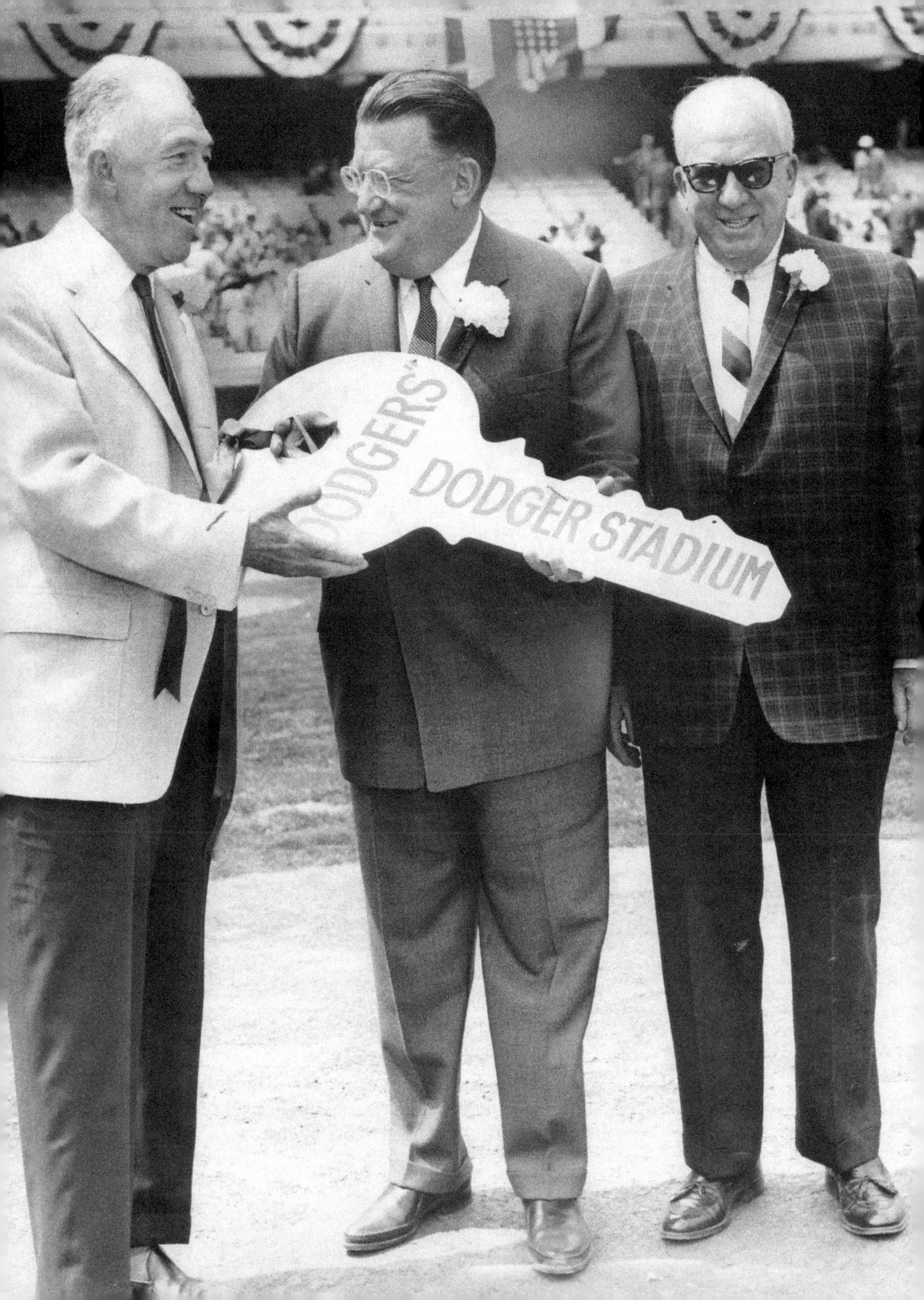
DODGERS'
DODGER STADIUM

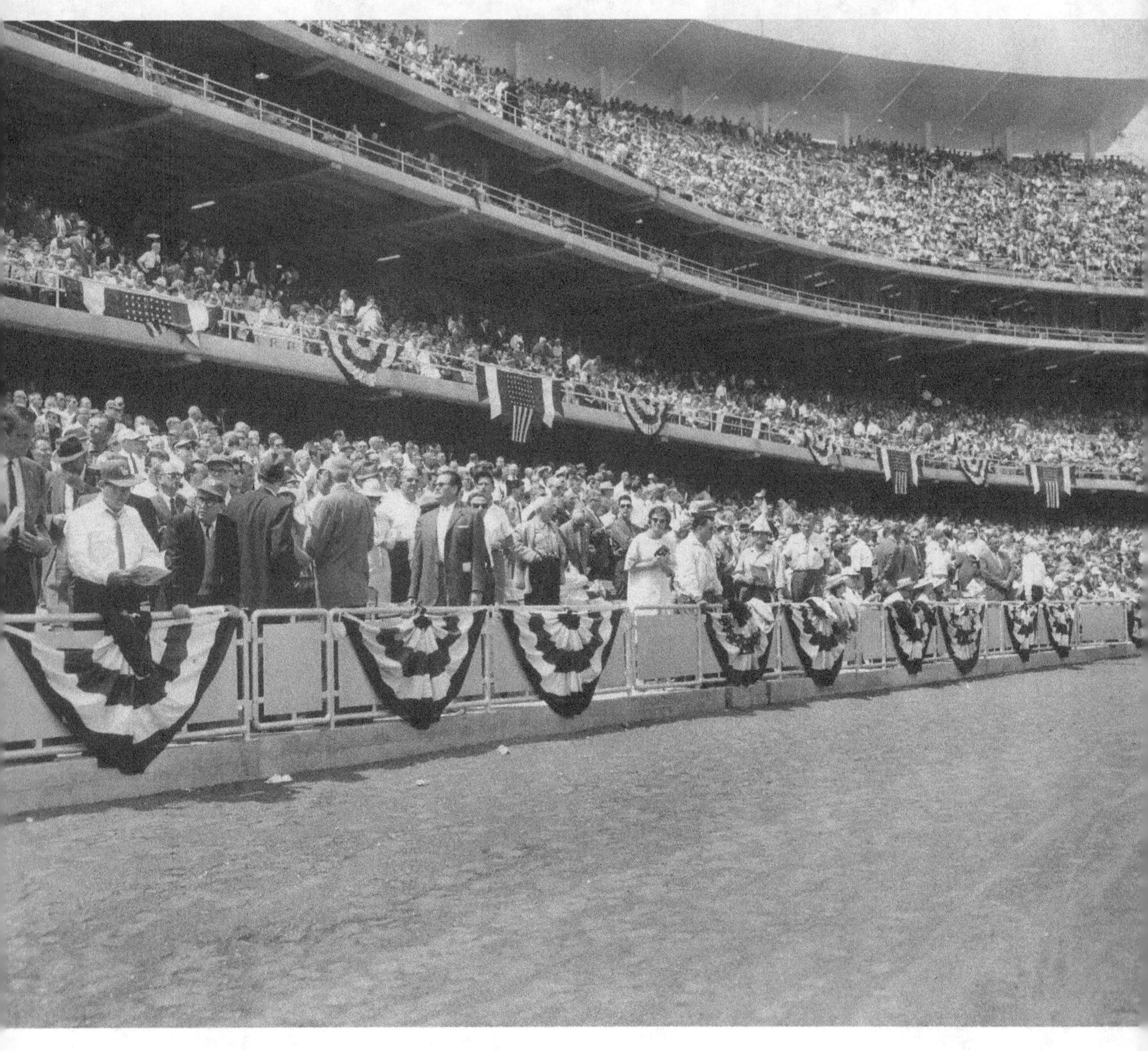

Fans ready for the first game.
(Herald-Examiner Collection)

OPPOSITE: No public drinking fountains were initially installed inside the new stadium, and so fans resorted to using bathroom faucets to quench their thirst (Tom Courtney/Herald-Examiner Collection)

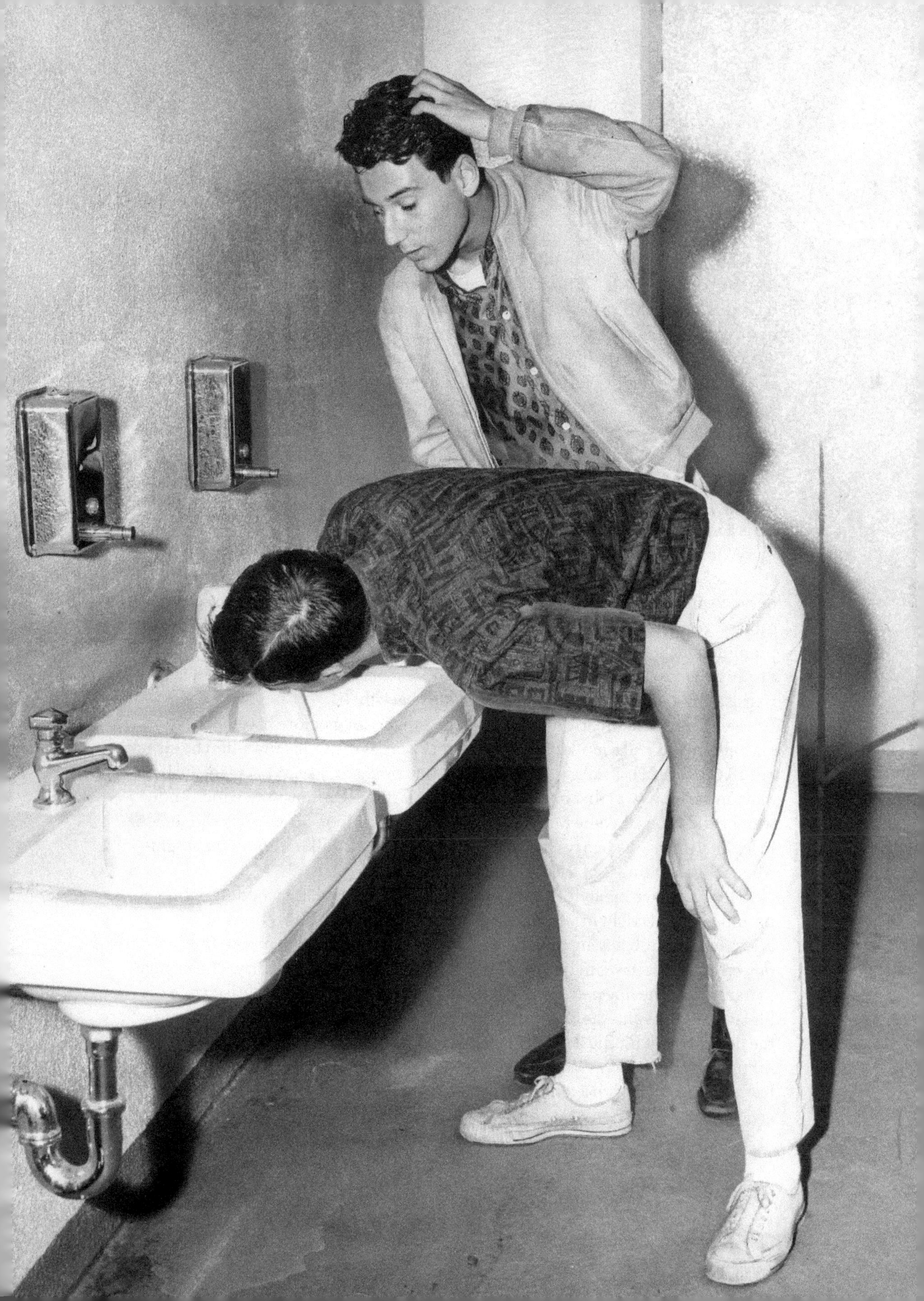

Sandy's Magic

I need only say "Sandy," and every baseball-wise friend knows of whom I speak. There are but a handful of Los Angeles sports icons who have achieved this kind of status: Vin. Fernando. Magic. Kareem. No one speaks ill of Sandy out here and he never disappoints in his rare public appearances, always looking fit, healthy, and ridiculously handsome in his 80s. If I had a dollar every time I heard someone say, "He looks like he could pitch a few innings today," I would be able to afford World Series tickets. When I peruse historic photos of my favorite athlete of all-time having a beer and a smoke after another pitching gem, I feel even more love for the guy Georgie Jessel called "the greatest Jewish athlete since Samson." He was a ladies' man without being a heel, and he was patient and cool when being interviewed ad nauseam by the scribes. He never wavered from the gold standard of class even in his foray into Hollywood, when he played himself on "Mister Ed." He is a municipal treasure.

When I was a kid we took him for granted and referred to him merely as "Koufax," which often went hand in hand with "Drysdale," forming the greatest one-two punch in pitching history (for us). In those years we only got to see nine games a year on TV. I saw maybe a dozen more in person since my dad was a prominent ticket-broker in town during Sandy's big years. Thanks to the great Scully we were able to feel like we were at the rest of the games while glued to a transistor radio, the essential tool of L.A. kids back then.

Sandy was erratic early in his career. One night, long before his golden seasons, myself and a few kids from my street were at the Coliseum when he struck out 18 Giants in a crucial game during the 1959 pennant race. What made it all the more miraculous was that he got a base hit to start the winning rally, which ended with beetle-browed Wally Moon sending one of his "Moon Shots" over the screen in left field for a 5-2 victory. Six decades later we are still talking about that night—when we got a glimpse of the greatness to come.

He had a pitching style that kids all over L.A. emulated. He stood straight up and raised his right leg, bowing his strong back, then pushing down in a devastating arc, bringing his blessed left arm over the top in a smooth but powerful thrust. It was in his hands that his super-human powers lay. Those huge mitts and lengthy fingers could hold five baseballs, and when he released one of his fastballs the spin was uncanny, with the ball actually rising in flight, making the possibility of hitting it solidly pretty slim. His curve ball was ridiculous. It dropped off the table, as Vinny used to say, in a quick downward dip that would have made contact with a tennis racket difficult. Those two pitches made him great.

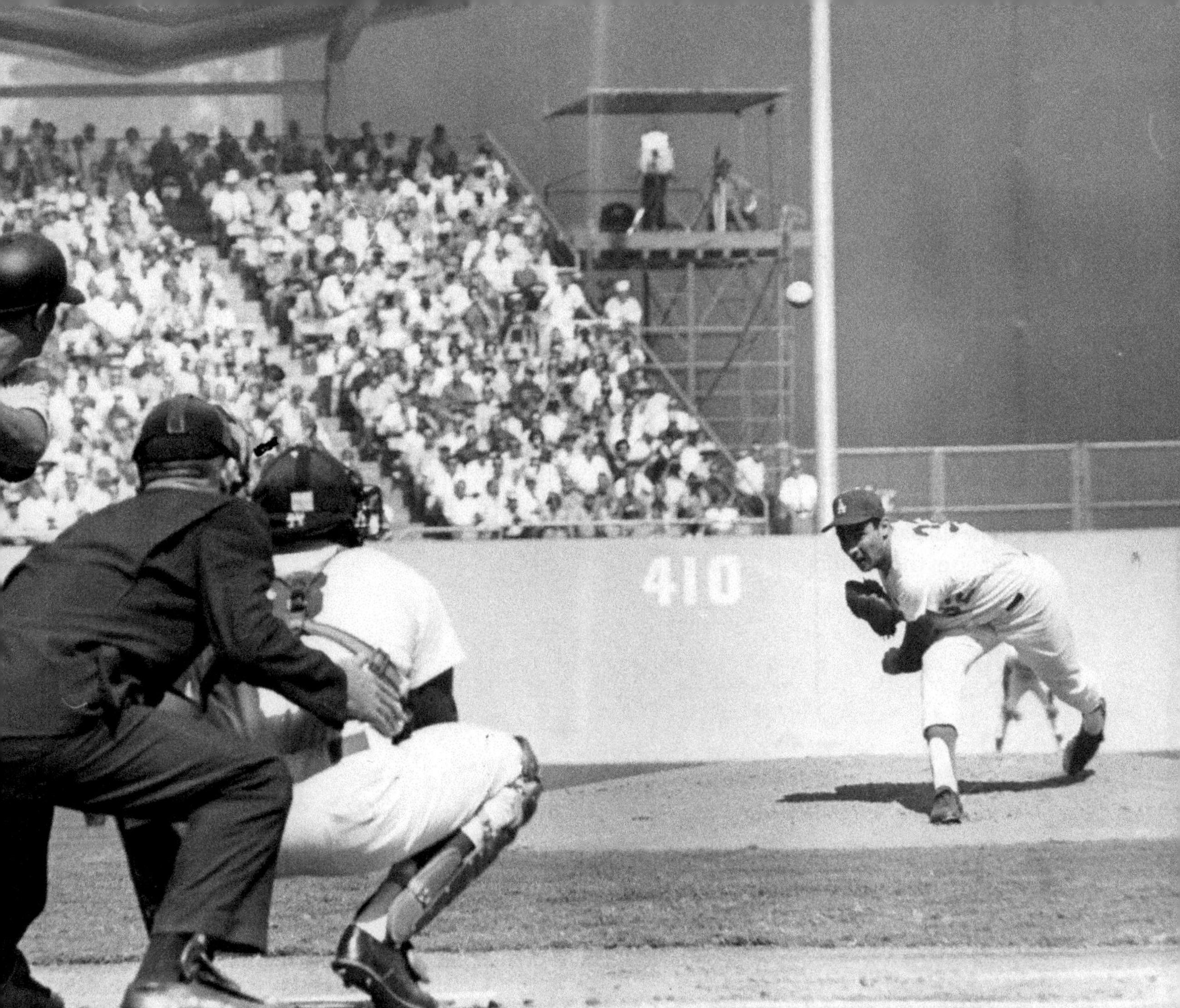

Pitching the Dodgers to a four-game sweep of the New York Yankees in the 1963 World Series. (Gordon Dean/Valley Times Collection)

By 1962 his control was masterful and the wins piled up. During his magical four-season run, from 1963-1966, when you saw the name "Koufax" slated as that night's starting pitcher in the morning paper you were filled with confidence. He was virtually unhittable, winning countless big games with his aching left arm, throwing a mind-boggling 27 complete games two seasons in a row! Anyone wondering why Sandy retired in 1966 after the greatest run in pitching history need only note the number of innings he logged in 1965: 335. By sheer will he pitched another 300-plus innings in 1966 and won 27 games with pain that would have kept most mortals on the disabled list. It was his commitment to pitching that destroyed his elbow.

There was another night, lost in the mists of baseball time, when my dad dragged me out to the stadium when Koufax was on the mound. He'd bought seats in the upper deck and performed the ultimate feat of bluff and bravado by talking his way, level by level, into the dugout boxes. He flashed a fake press pass slipped to him by famed *Her-Ex* columnist Bob "The Chopper" Hunter and used his silver tongue to push past stiff-backed ushers until we sat (uncomfortably for me) next to Doris Day at field level.

On the night a half century ago, I saw the Koufax that was legend. He mowed down the Phillies with surgical precision. I distinctly recall the mismatch with light-hitting Clayton Dalrymple, who took a quick strike three and walked back to the dugout like a man returning from a root canal. What struck me that night was how tall Sandy looked on the mound, like Zeus at Olympus hurling thunderbolts, some of them falling off the table.

—Glen Creason

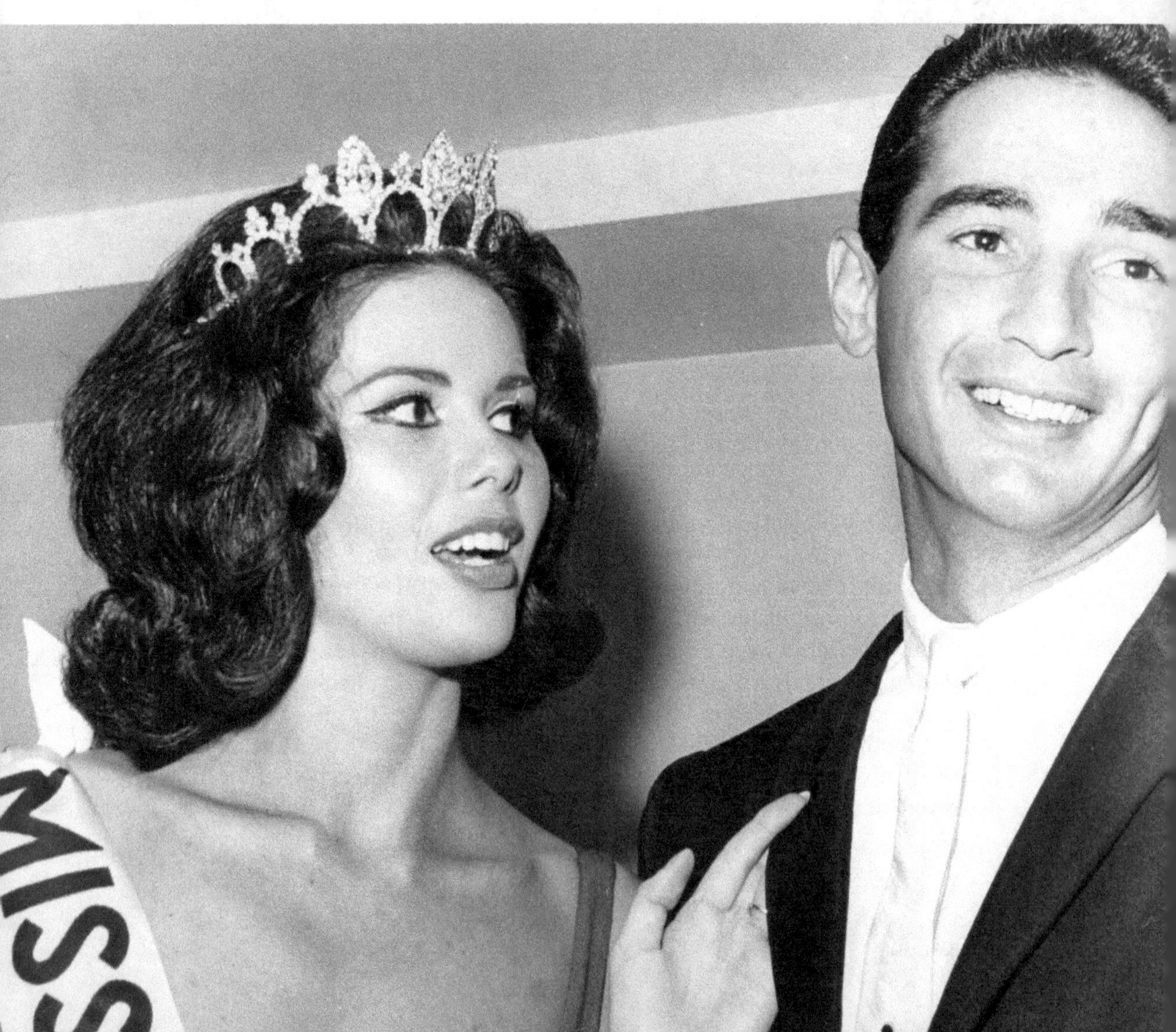

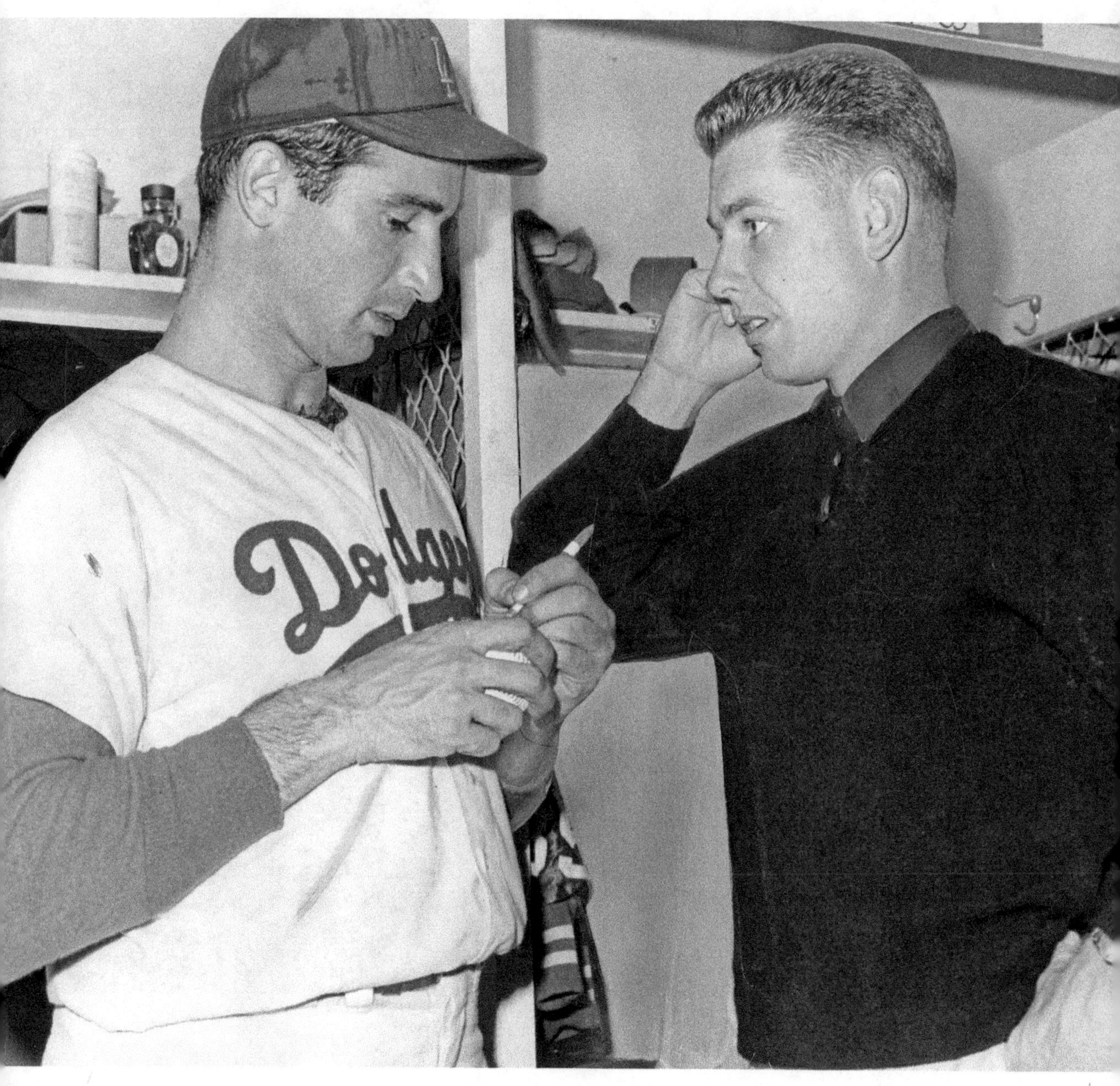

Autographing a ball for catcher Jeff Torborg after pitching his fourth career no-hitter. (Howard Ballew/Herald-Examiner Collection)

OPPOSITE: With Linda Kennon, also known as Miss Los Angeles. (Herald-Examiner Collection)

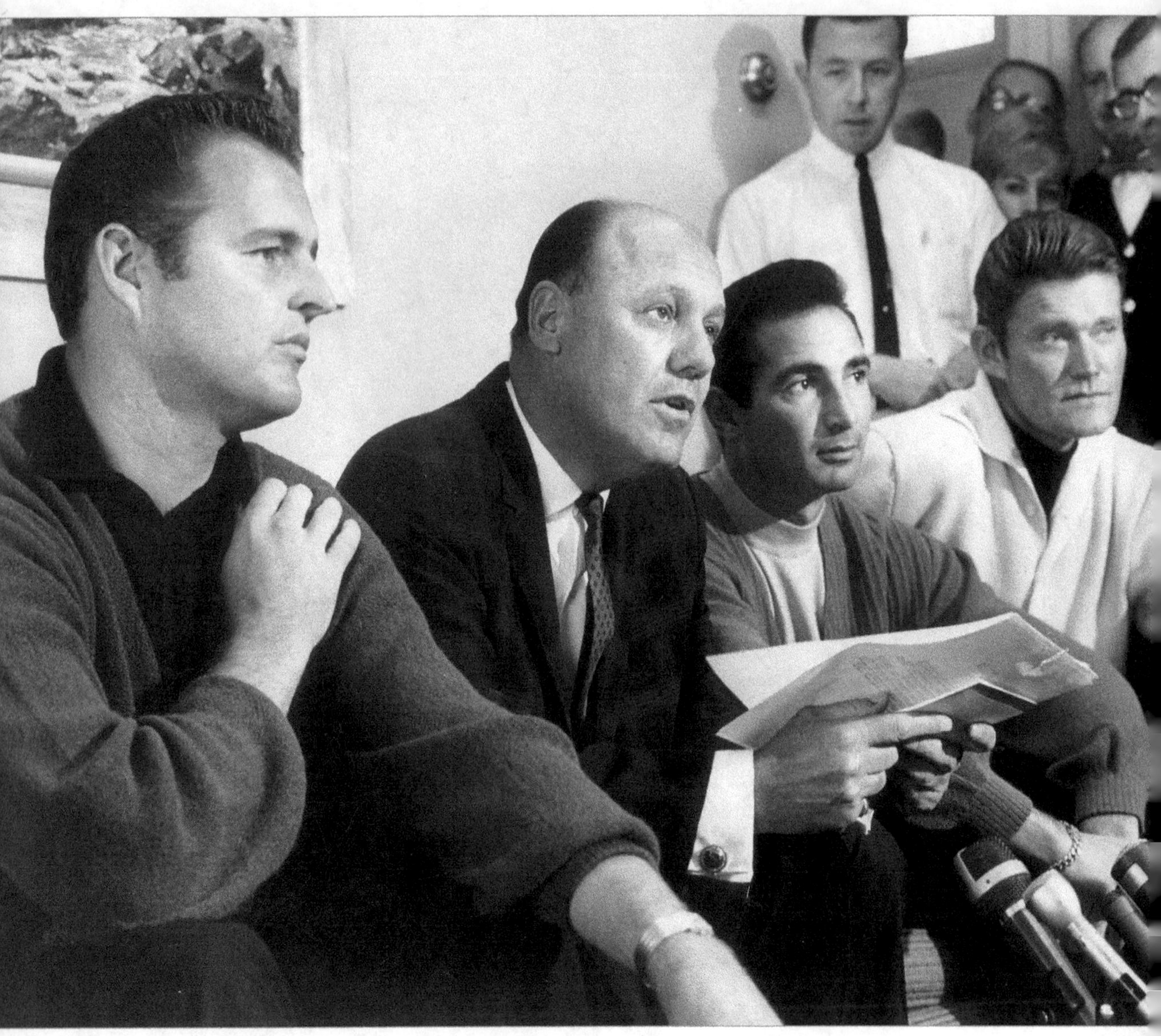

At a press conference with (from left) Don Drysdale, Buzzy Bavasi, and Chuck Connors, after the two pitchers ended their contract holdout. (Joe Rustan/Herald-Examiner Collection)

OPPOSITE: Icing his arm after pitching another gem. (Herald-Examiner Collection)

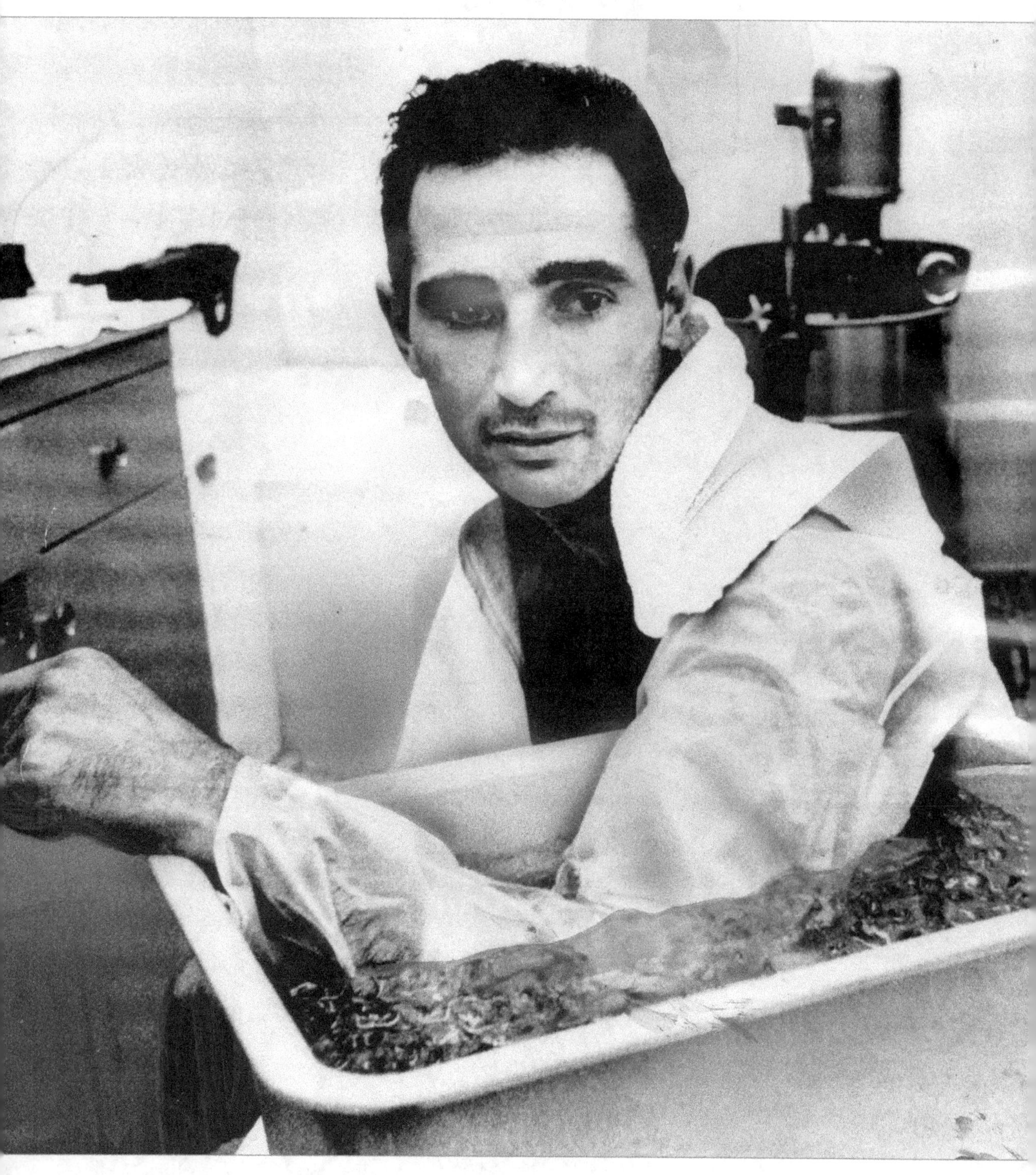

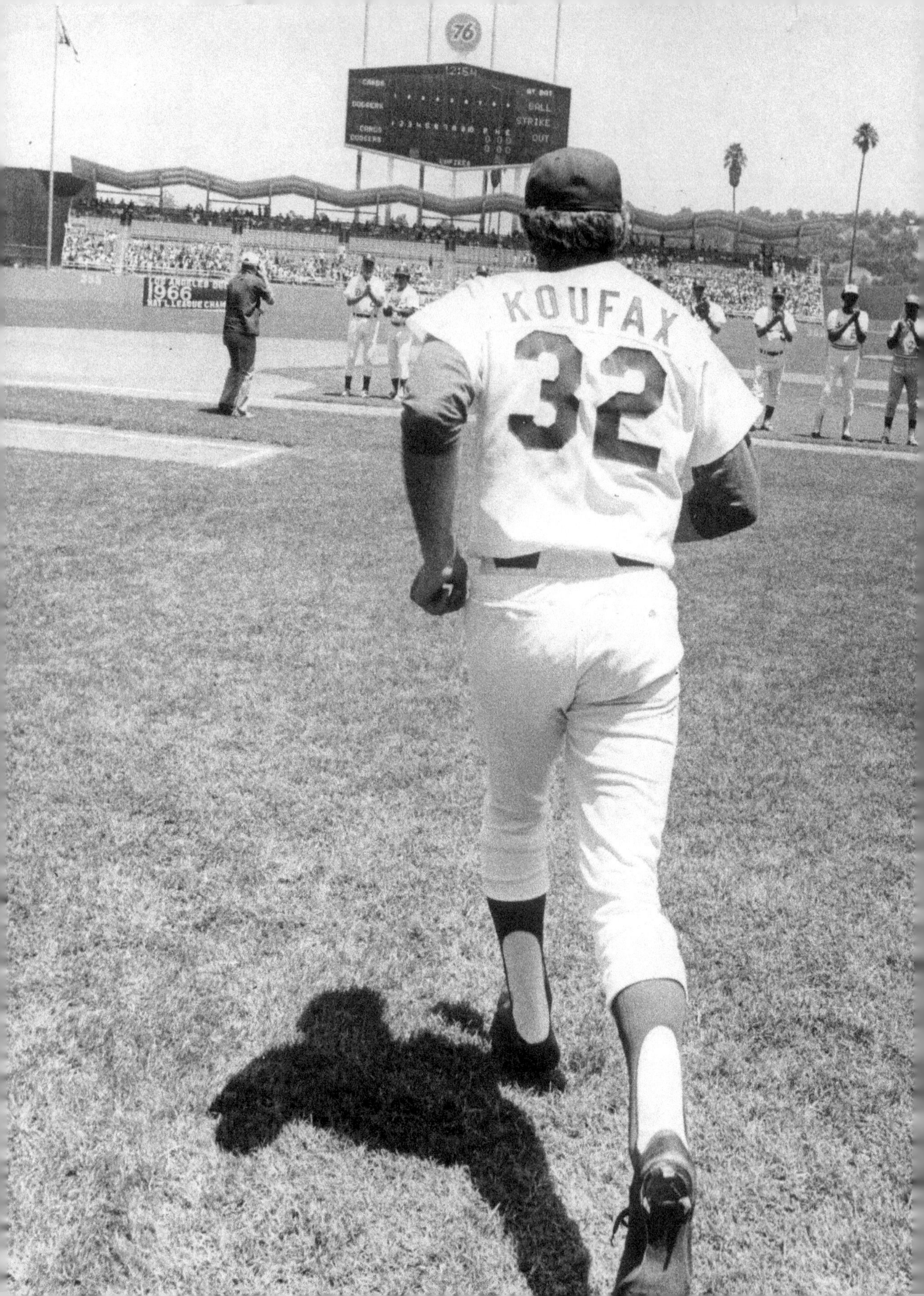
76
BALL
STRIKE
OUT
1966
KOUFAX
32

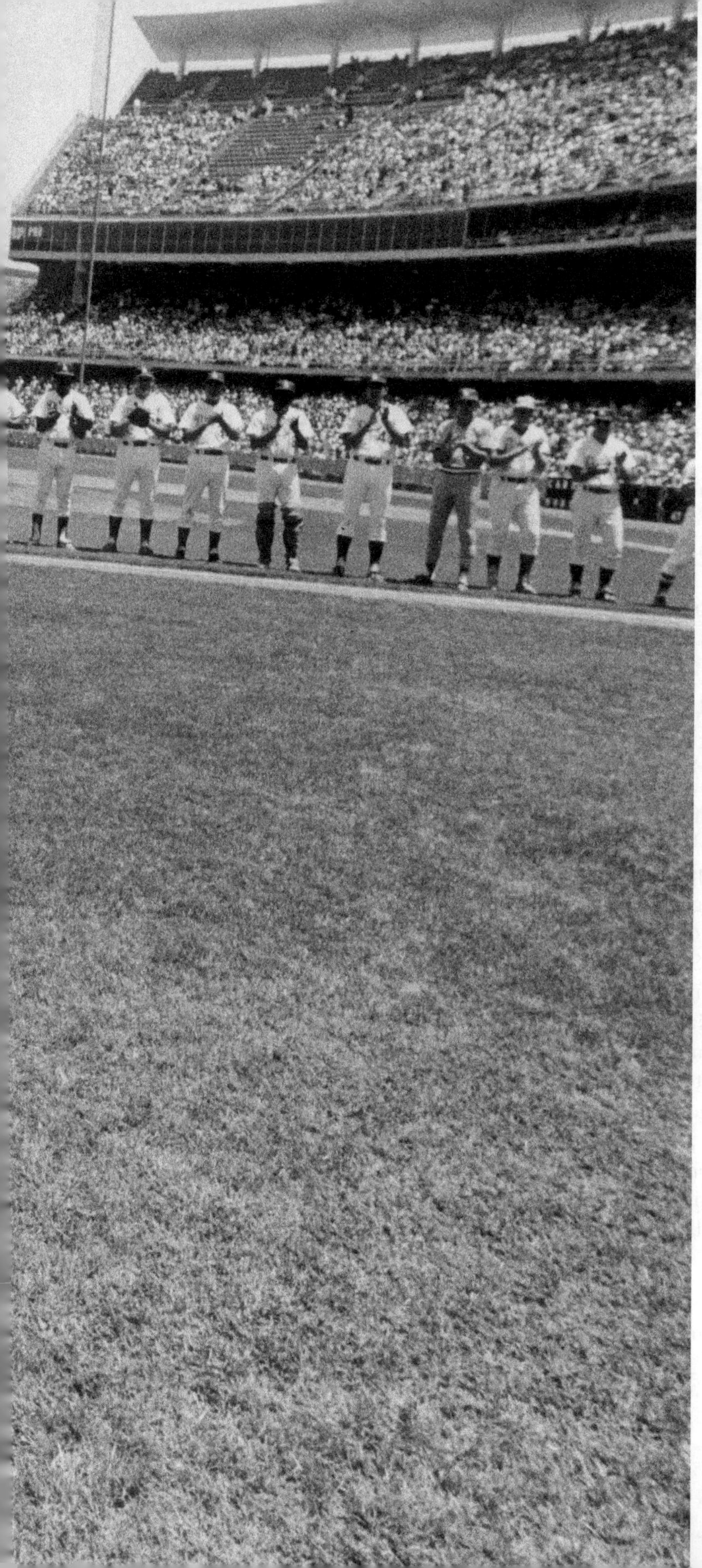

Saving the best for last: Koufax being introduced at an old-timers' game in 1978. (James Roark/ Herald-Examiner Collection)

I Heart Baseball

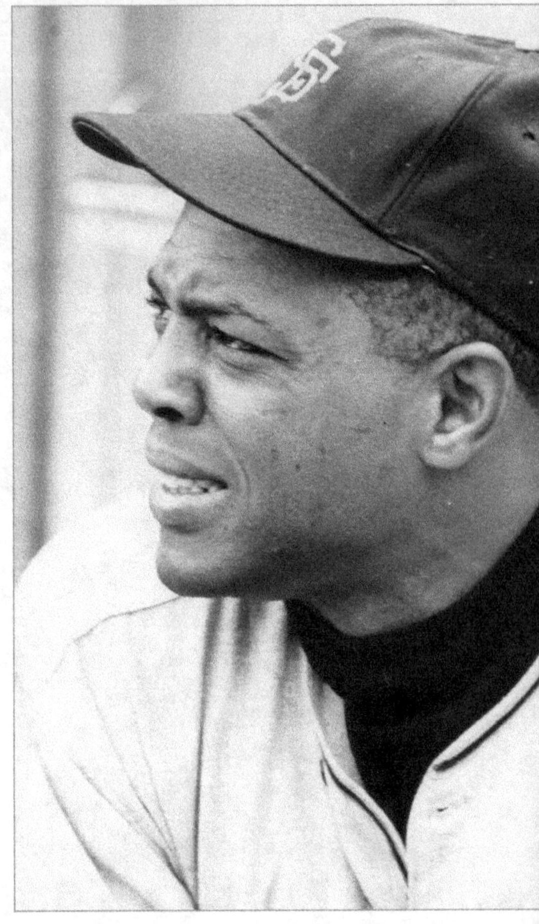

Willie Mays (Bob Martin/ Herald-Examiner Collection)

I grew up listening to Russ Hodges and Lon Simmons call San Francisco Giants games on AM-560. My mother loved to listen to baseball, and I inherited that. My childhood was Willie Mays, Willie McCovey, Juan Marichal. The Giants helped me through childhood. I can never fan-hate them.

Our family never went to see a game together, but our church took a busload of kids to Candlestick Park once a year, often for double-headers. Once we went to a double-header and one of the games went extra innings. We stayed. I think we were gone for around 11 hours. We got our group-rate tickets' worth that day.

When I moved to Los Angeles, I started going to Dodger Stadium—it's the most Los Angeles place in the city. My young adulthood was Fernando Valenzuela, Ron Cey, Don Sutton. My Los Angeles life has the Dodgers as a through-line and Vin Scully as a life coach.

I went to a Fourth of July game once with a fanatic friend from Chicago. He was the happiest clam ever to be able to sit on the outfield grass for fireworks afterwards. Stuck in exit traffic, we watched a hillside go up in flames set off by the fireworks. It was mesmerizing and, weirdly, one of my most indelible memories of the stadium.

I watch on TV and listen on radio. I go to at least a few games every year I've lived here. Despite a few beer showers (when beer was cheap), a lot of man-spreading invasion of my personal space (it's an epidemic), tall/big haired people sitting in front of me (happens everywhere), people skooching up in their seats, and sometimes couples making out and blocking my view (also epidemic), I continue to subject myself to it—'cause, you know, it's baseball. Dodger Baseball.

—Amy Inouye

OPPOSITE TOP: Don Sutton (Paul Chinn/ Herald-Examiner Collection)

OPPOSITE BOTTOM: (Marissa Roth)

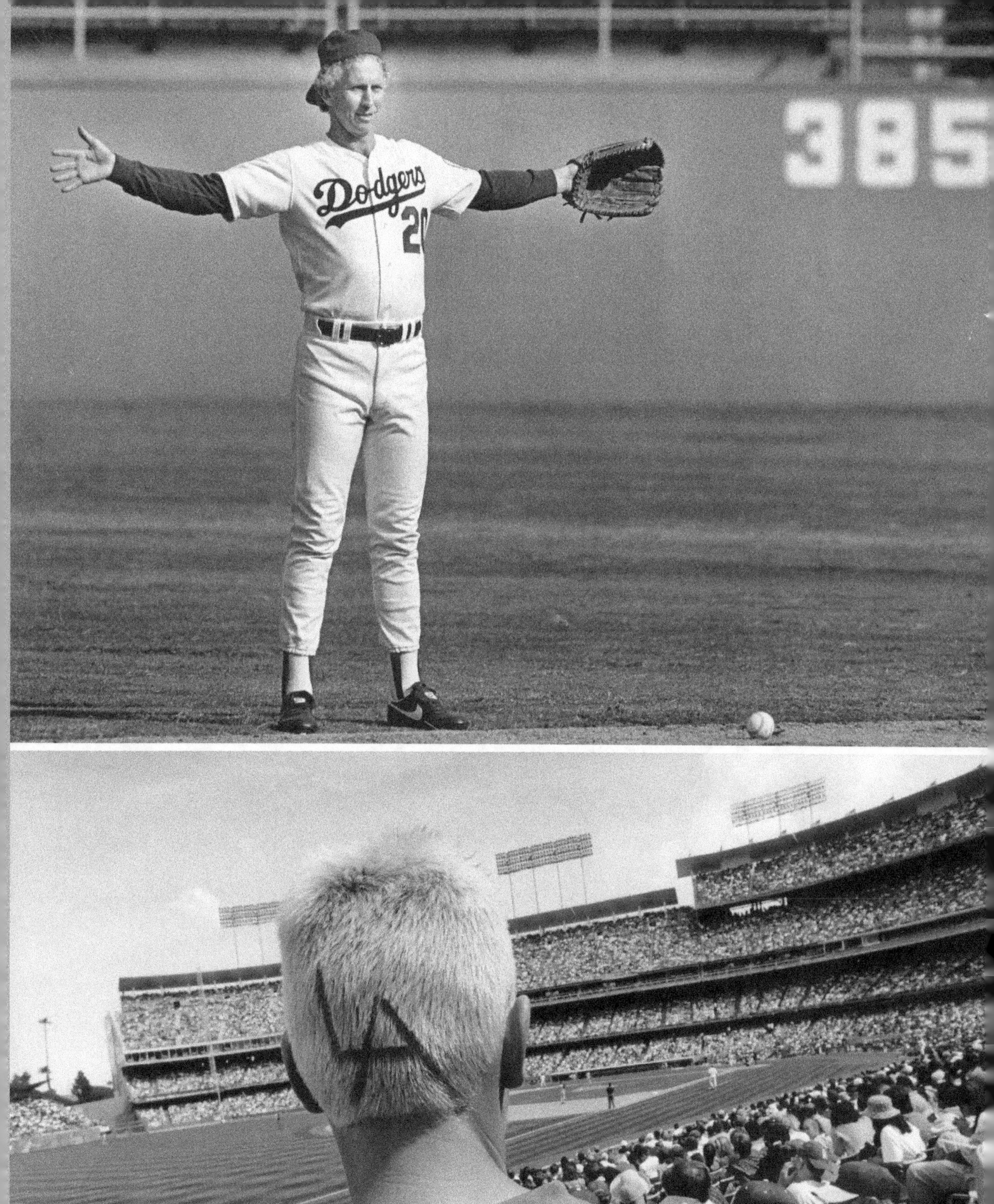
Dodgers
20
385

"Turn It Here, Get It Here"

An art-school buddy was a childhood friend of one of the Arthurs of Arthur Food Services, a former contractor for Dodger Stadium. They needed some simple design work, and as a fledgling graphic designer, I was happy to oblige. The Arthurs were very down-to-earth and kind to me, inviting me many times to the Stadium Club for lunch, and giving me their tickets on many occasions—a couple of rows behind the omnipresent fan, Ethel Bradley.

In 1989, they had me design food coupons. I recently unearthed them. The art was done in pen and ink with press-type headlines, and rubylith overlays, with text type output on a Compugraphic 7200 (*see opposite*).

One of the Arthurs invented a relish- and onion-dispensing machine during the time I worked with them. They are still used at the stadium (and at Costco). I designed the original labels for the machines: minimal for sure—really just a typeface selection (Futura Bold Condensed)—but one of my proudest design moments. The instructional tagline—"Turn It Here, Get It Here"—has become a mantra.

—Amy Inouye

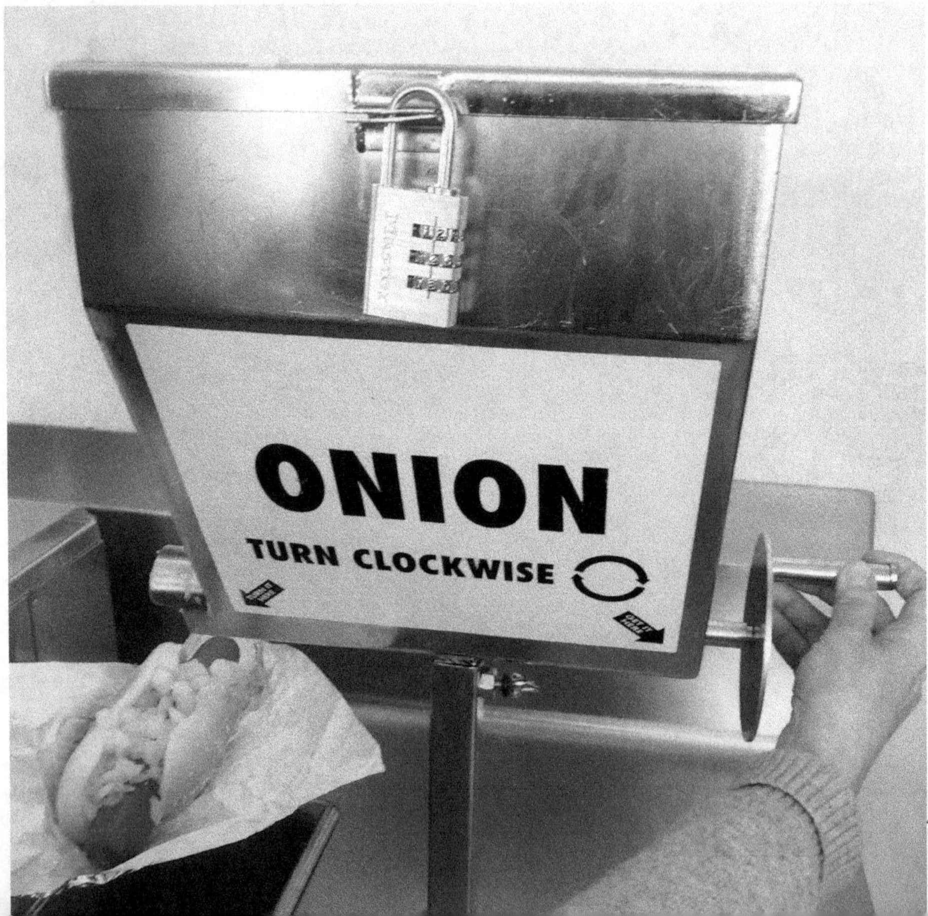

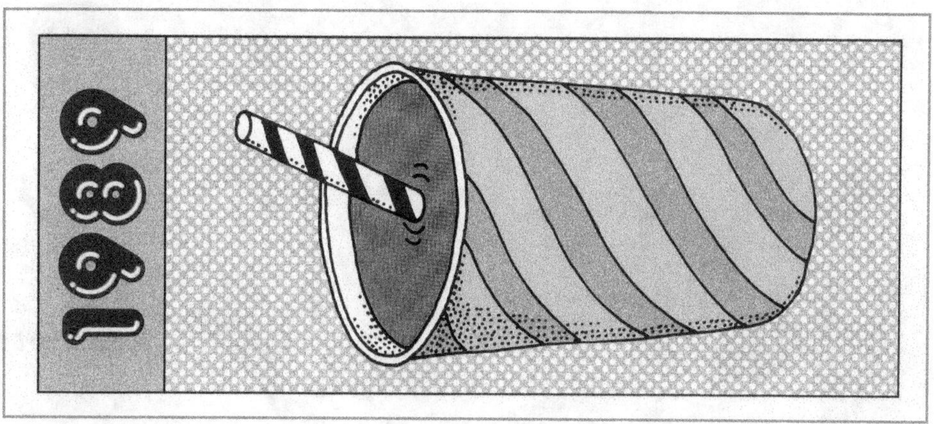
1989

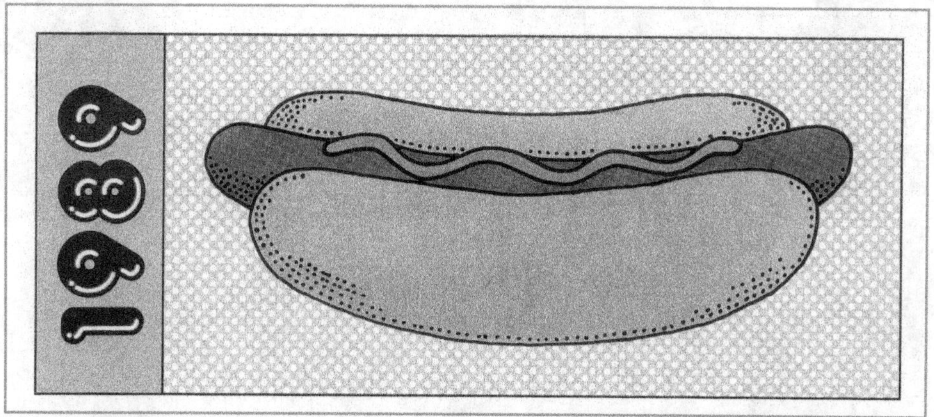
1989

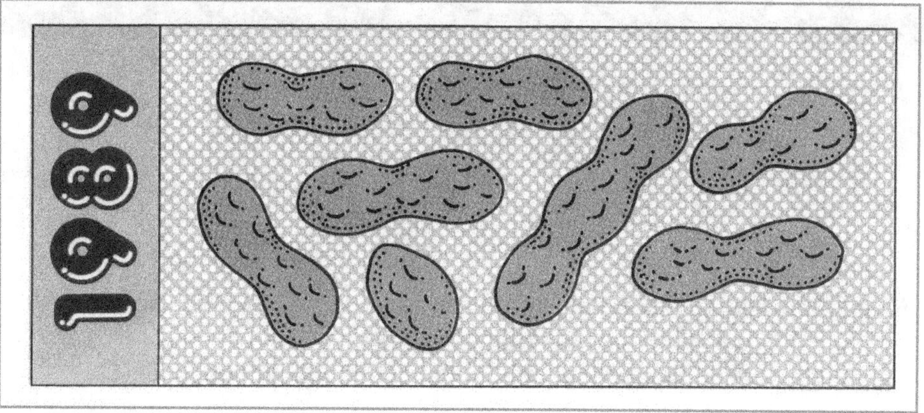
1989

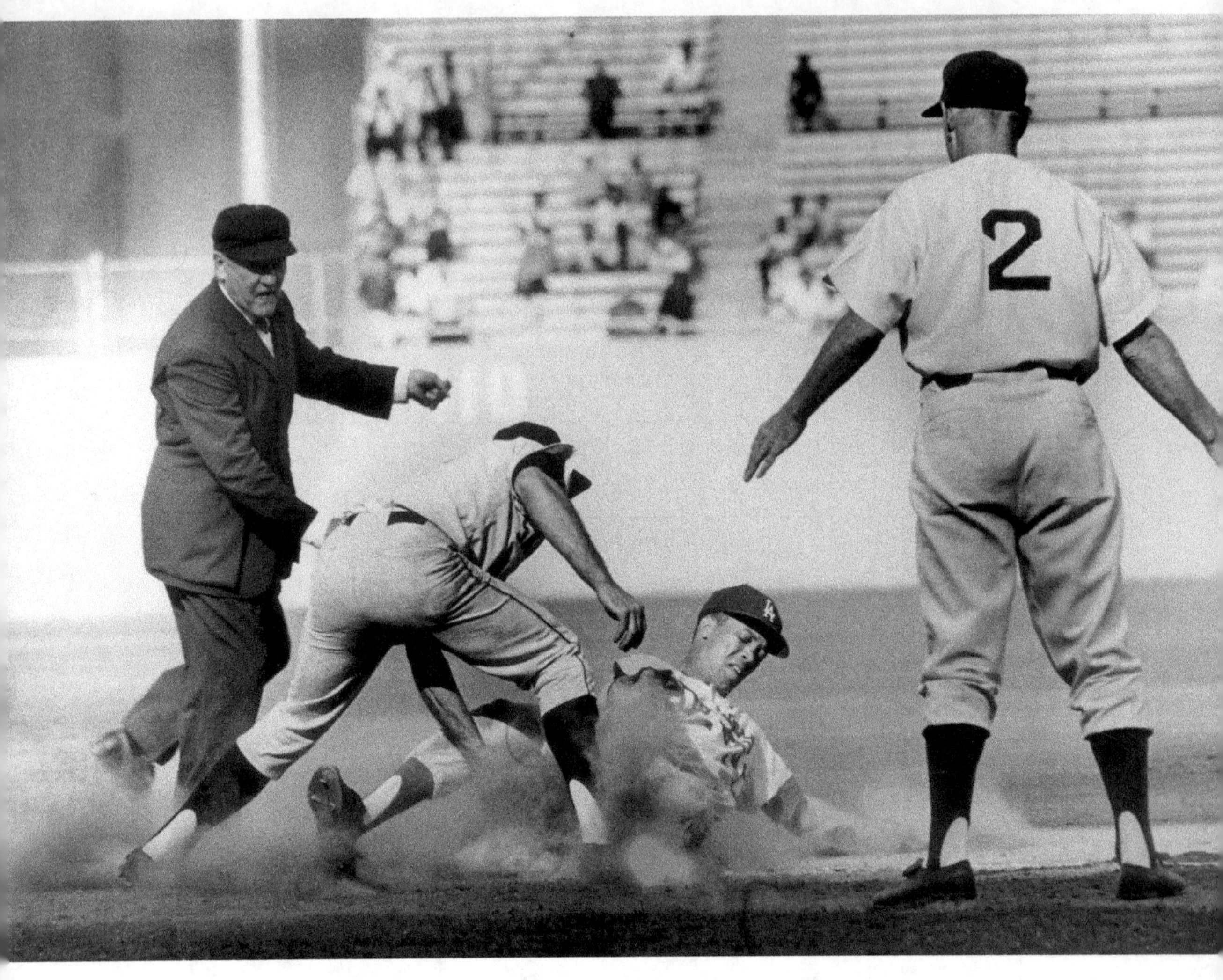

No player was more vital to the Dodgers' success in the early 1960s than shortstop Maury Wills. In 1962, he broke Ty Cobb's stolen-base record, with 104 steals, and won the N.L. MVP award.

ABOVE (George Brich/Valley Times Collection)
& OPPOSITE (Herald-Examiner Collection)

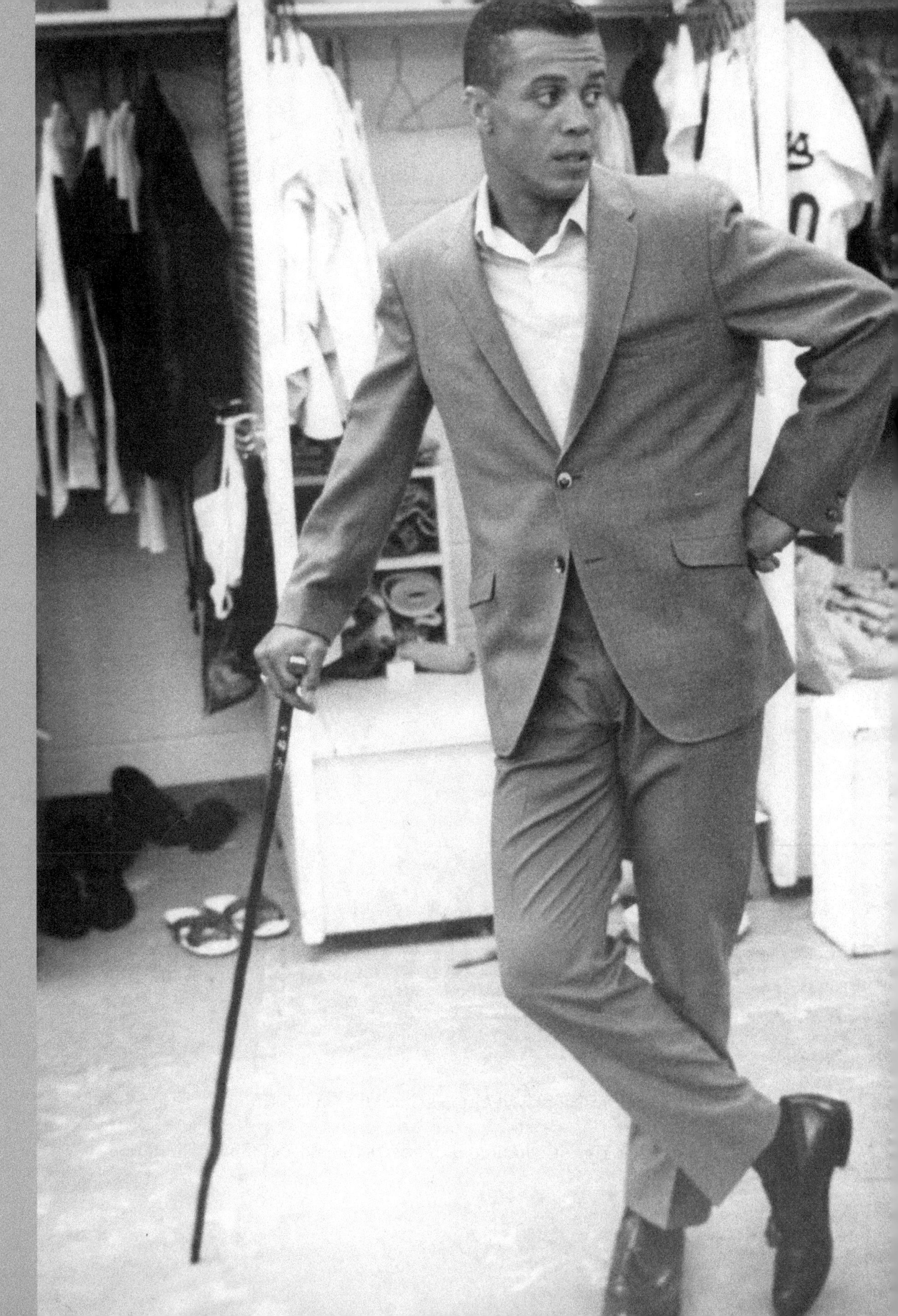

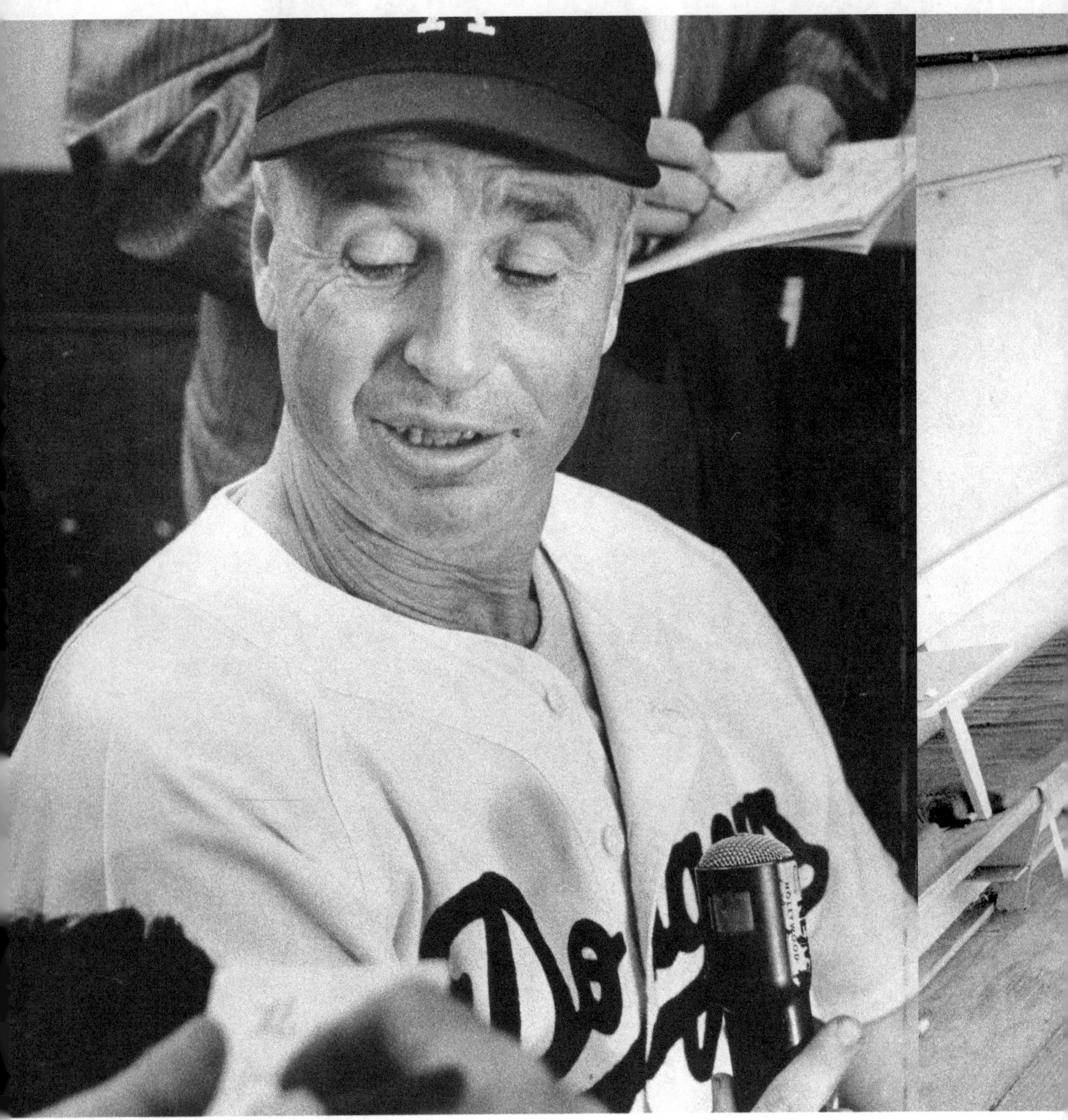

Hall of Fame manager Walt Alston helmed the Dodgers from 1954-1976 and won over 2,000 games.
ABOVE (Valley Times Collection) **& OPPOSITE** (Herald-Examiner Collection)

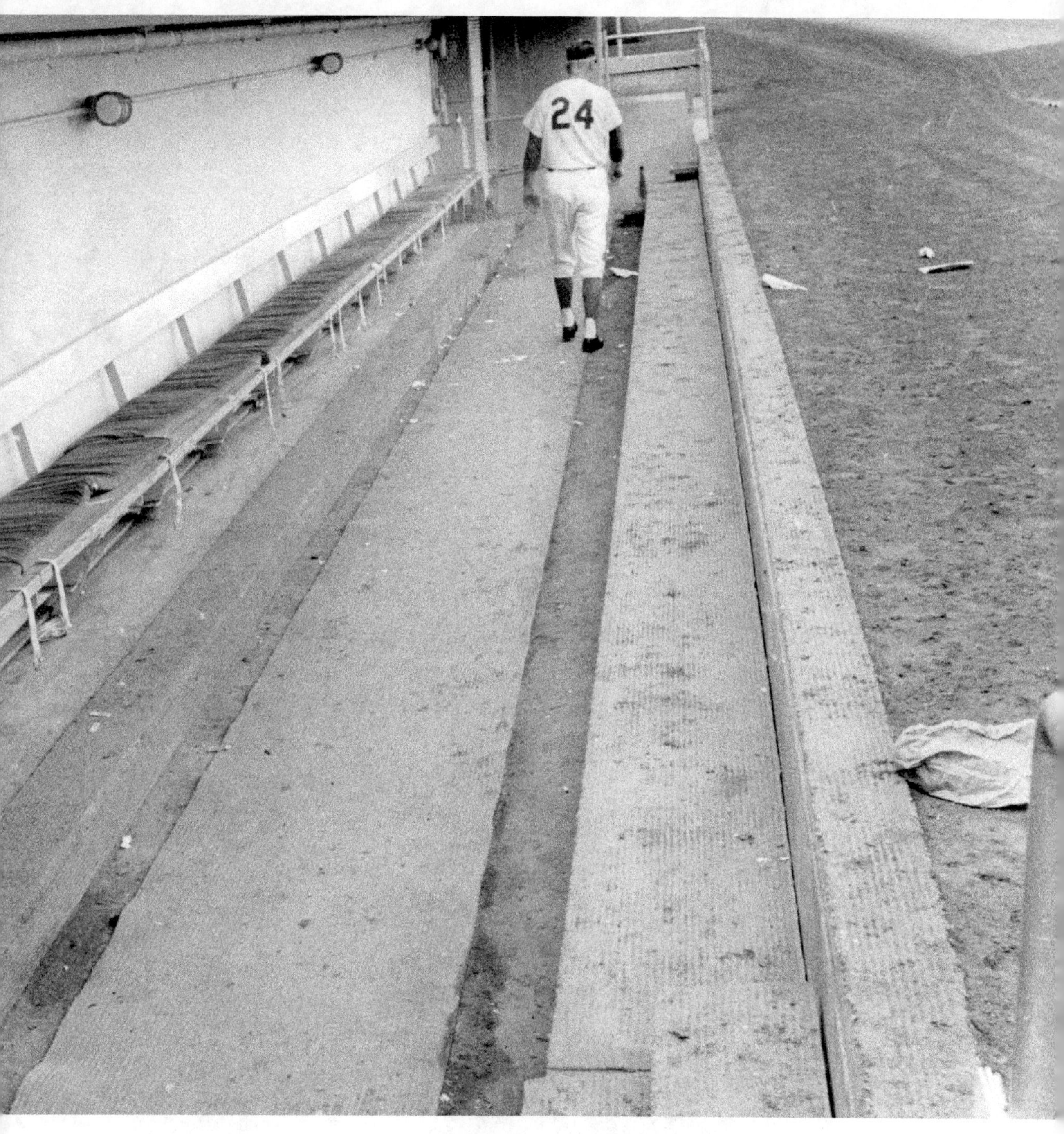
24

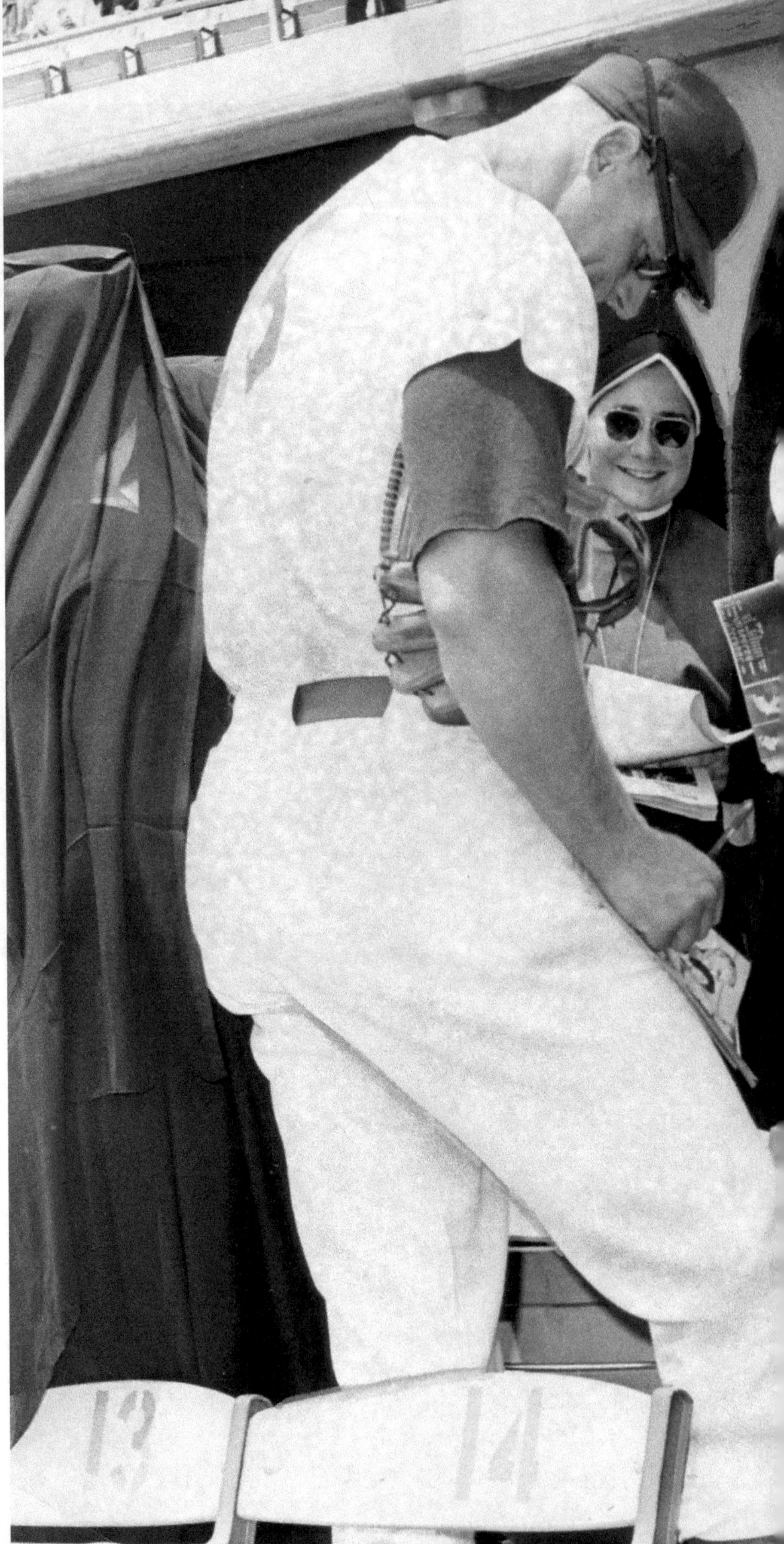

Outfielder Frank Howard signs for the True Blue faithful on Nun's Day. (Tom Courtney/Herald-Examiner Collection)

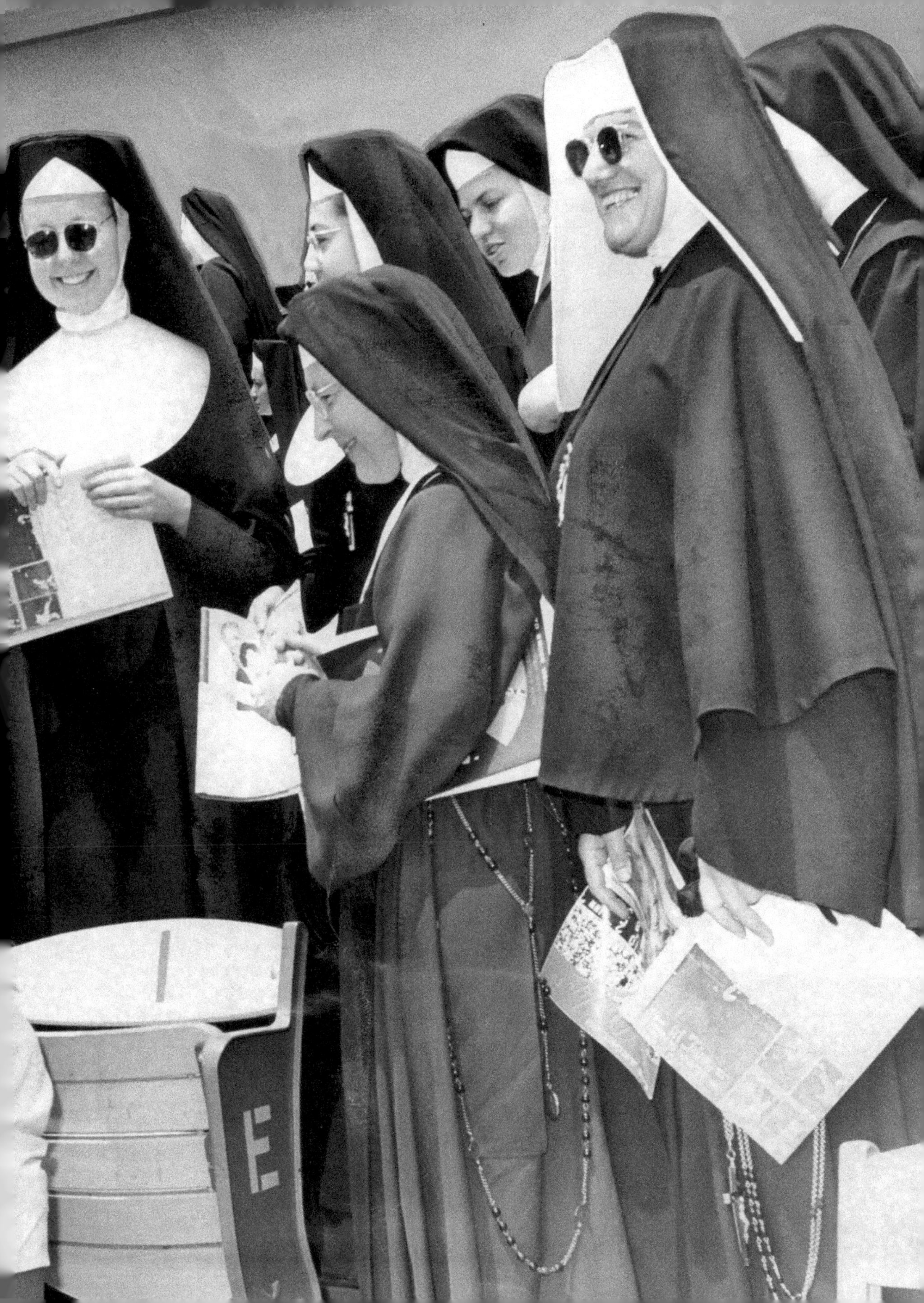

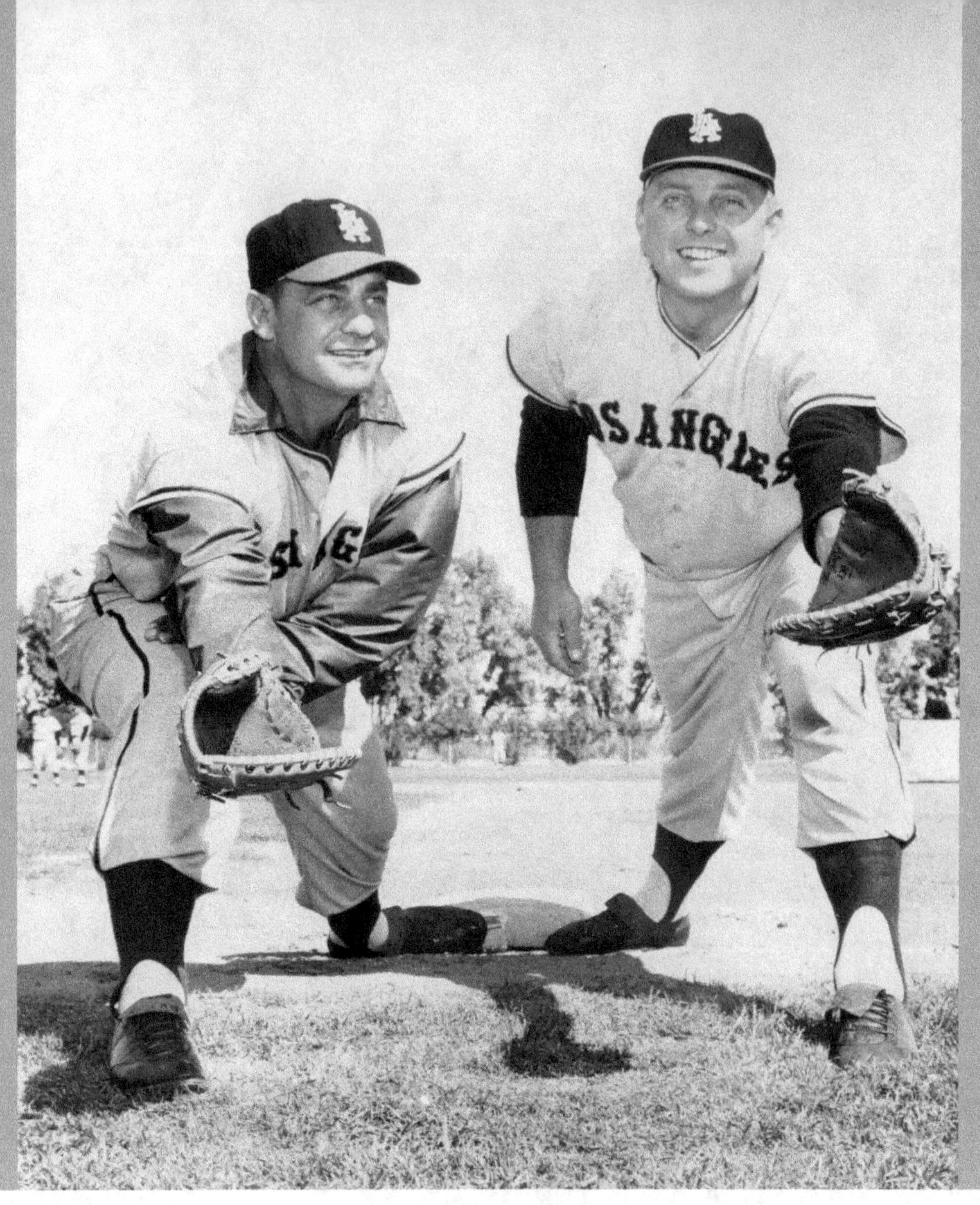

The Los Angeles Angels joined the American League as an expansion team in 1961. They played one year at Wrigley Field, then played at Chavez Ravine for the next three seasons before moving to Anaheim. Here are two slugging first basemen for the 1961 Angels: Ted Kluszewski (*left*) and Steve Bilko. (Valley Times Collection)

OPPOSITE TOP: Angels owner Gene Autry speaks at City Hall ceremony before the 1963 season. (Herald-Examiner Collection)

OPPOSITE BOTTOM: Wrigley Field in disrepair, not long before it was demolished in 1969. (Michael Haering/Herald-Examiner Collection)

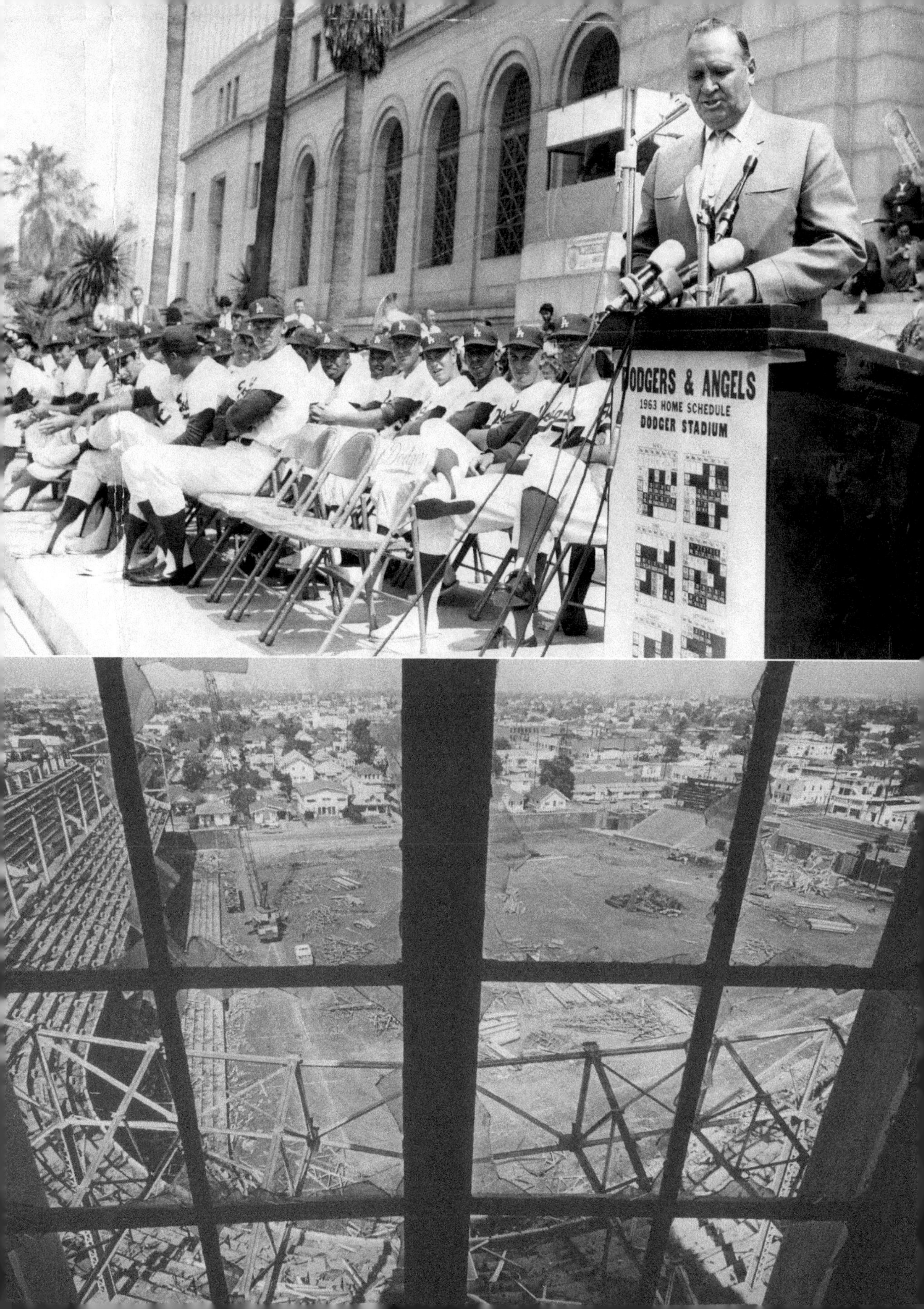
DODGERS & ANGELS
1963 HOME SCHEDULE
DODGER STADIUM

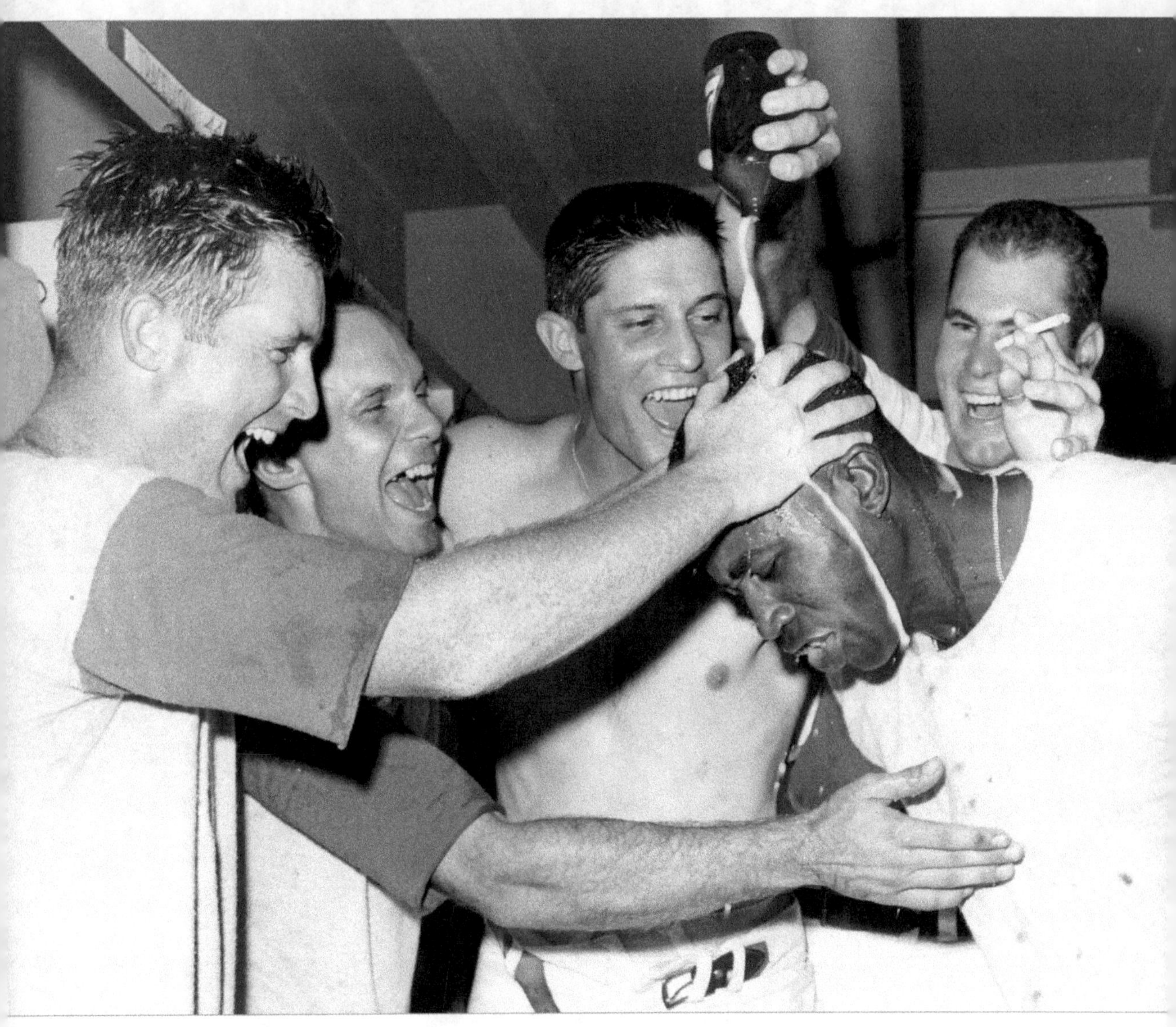

Catcher John Roseboro gets doused with beer after his key homer helped the Dodgers beat the New York Yankees in Game 1 of the 1963 World Series. (Herald-Examiner Collection)

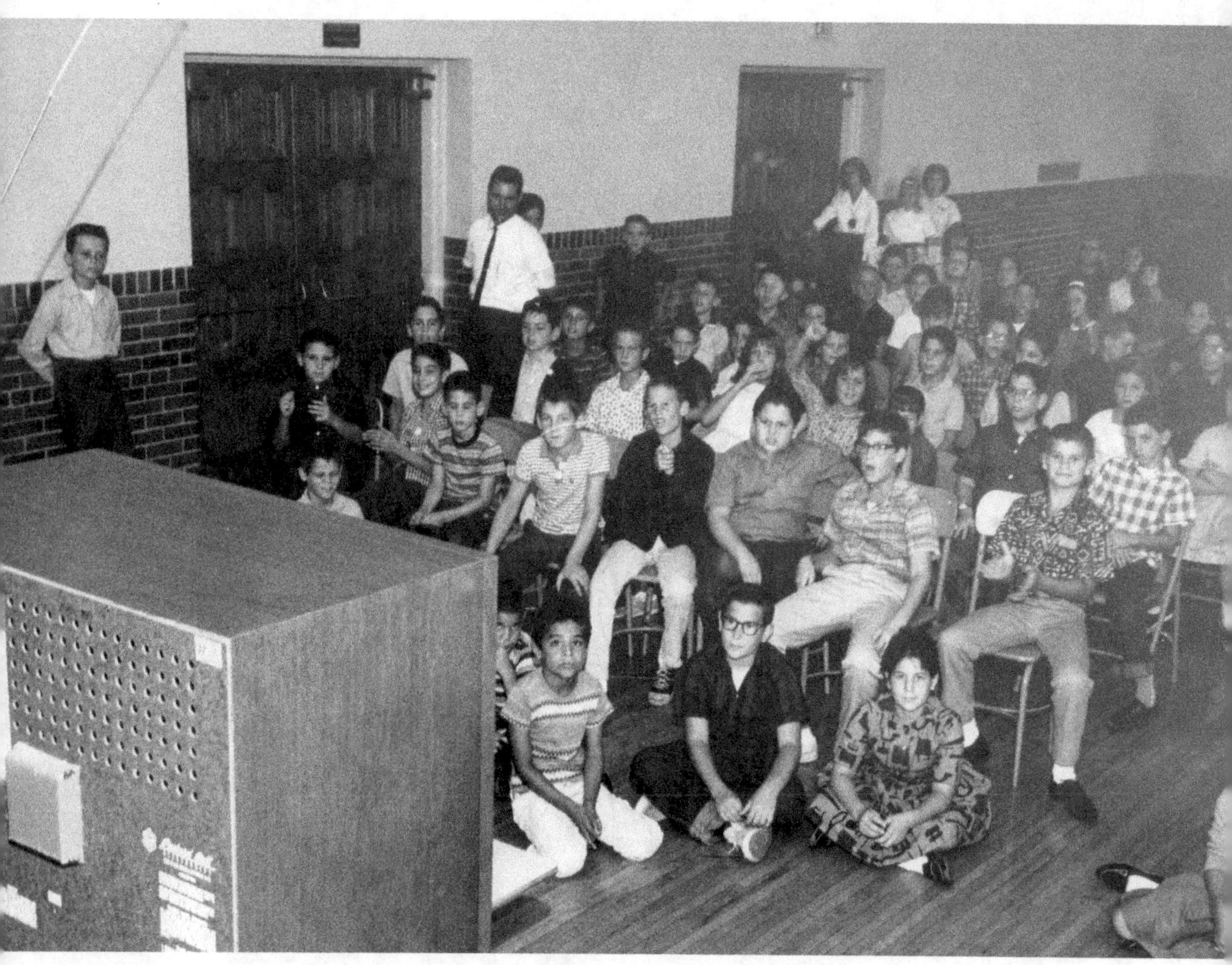

Students at Victory Boulevard School in North Hollywood gather to watch Game 2 in the school auditorium. (Gordon Dean/Valley Times Collection)

PAGES 112-113: Sandy Koufax (*center*) is mobbed by teammates after pitching the Dodgers past the Yankees in a four-game sweep of the 1963 World Series. (Valley Times Collection)

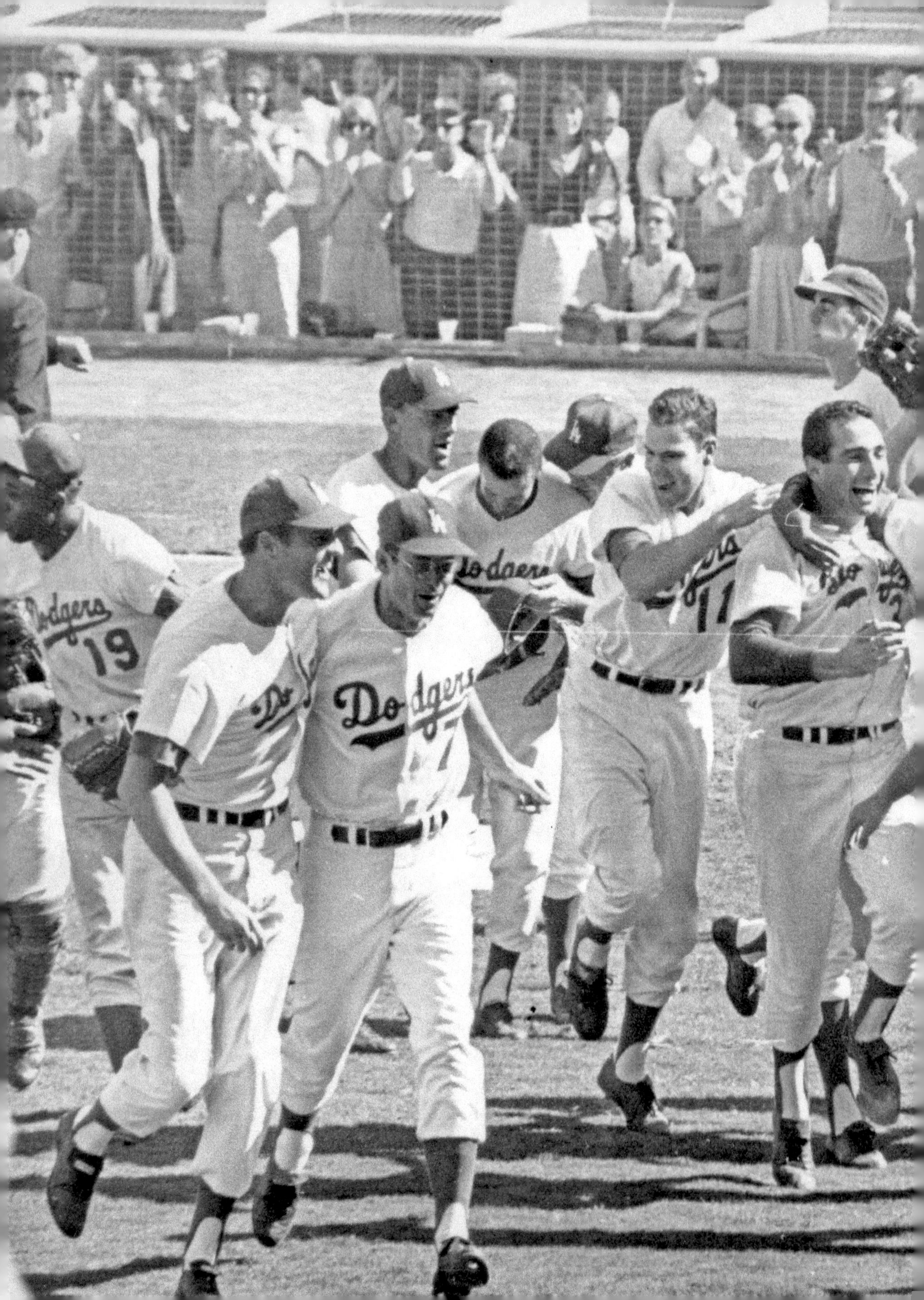
Dodgers
19
Dodgers

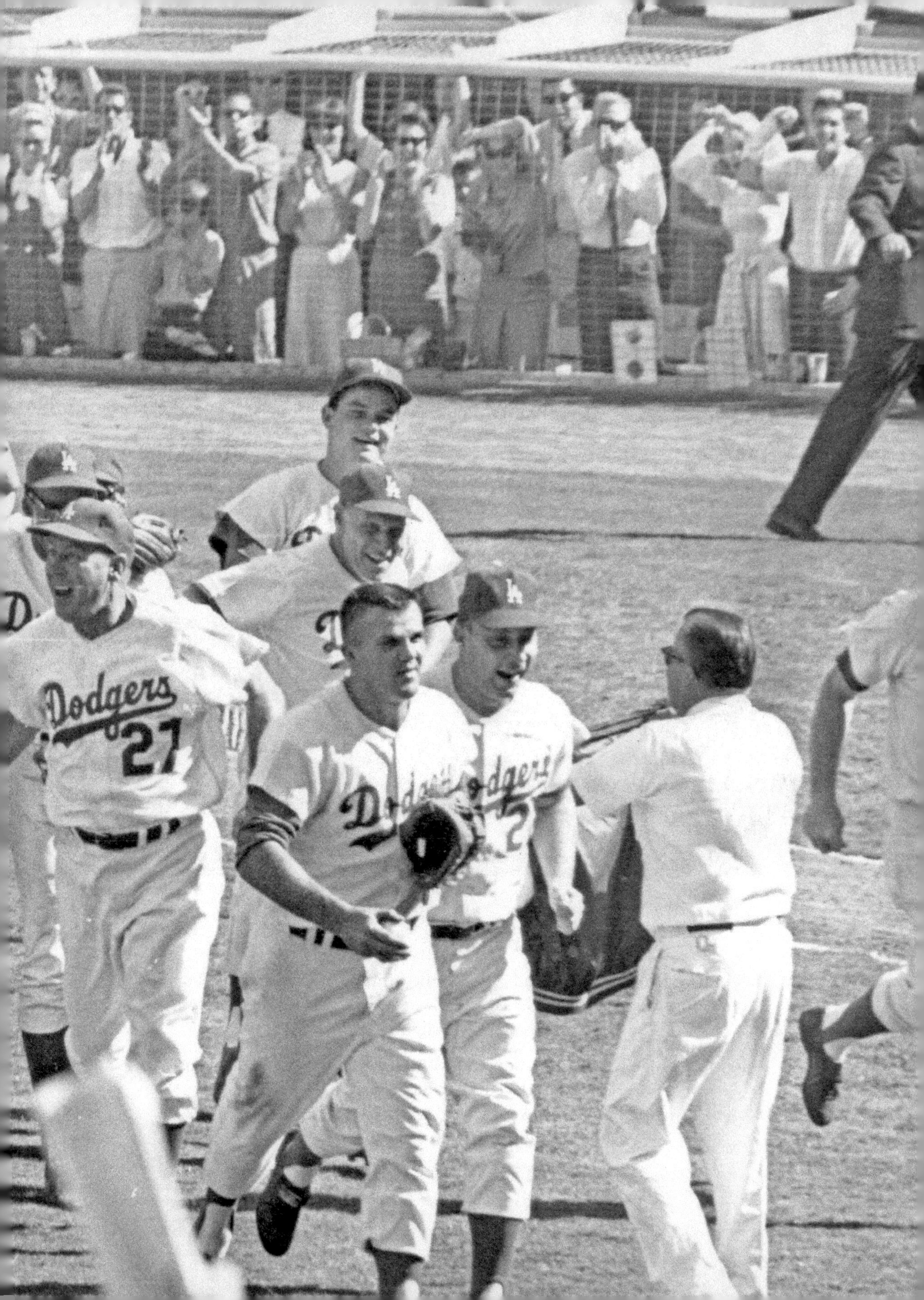
Dodgers
27

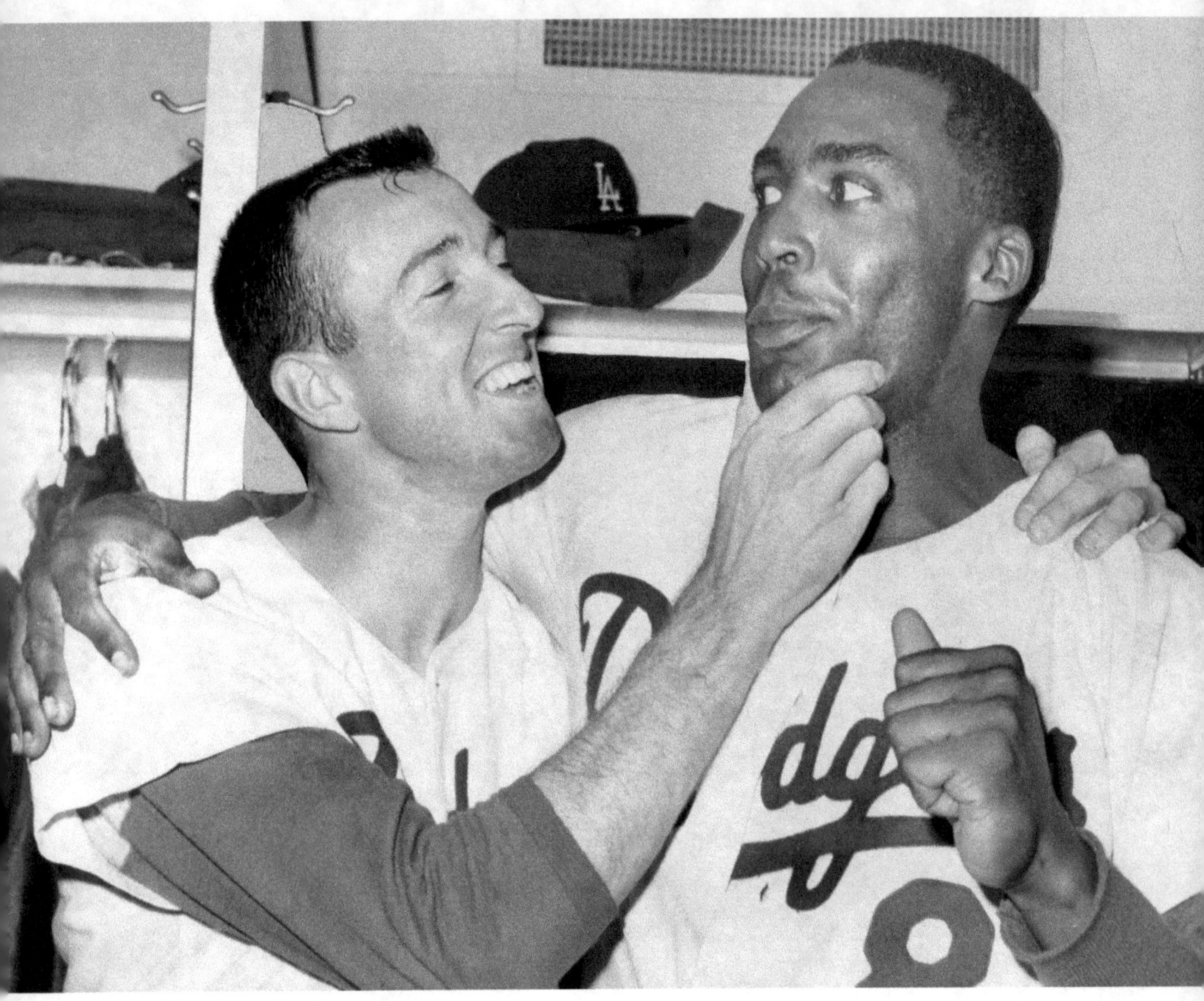

John Roseboro (*right*) and Claude Osteen, the winning battery in Game 3 of the 1965 World Series, won by the Dodgers in seven over the Minnesota Twins. (Dave Cicero/Herald-Examiner Collection)

OPPOSITE: Maury Wills and outfielders Willie Davis (*right*) and Lou Johnson converge after Davis misplayed Andy Etchebarren's pop fly in Game 2 of the 1966 World Series, won by the Baltimore Orioles. (Herald-Examiner Collection)

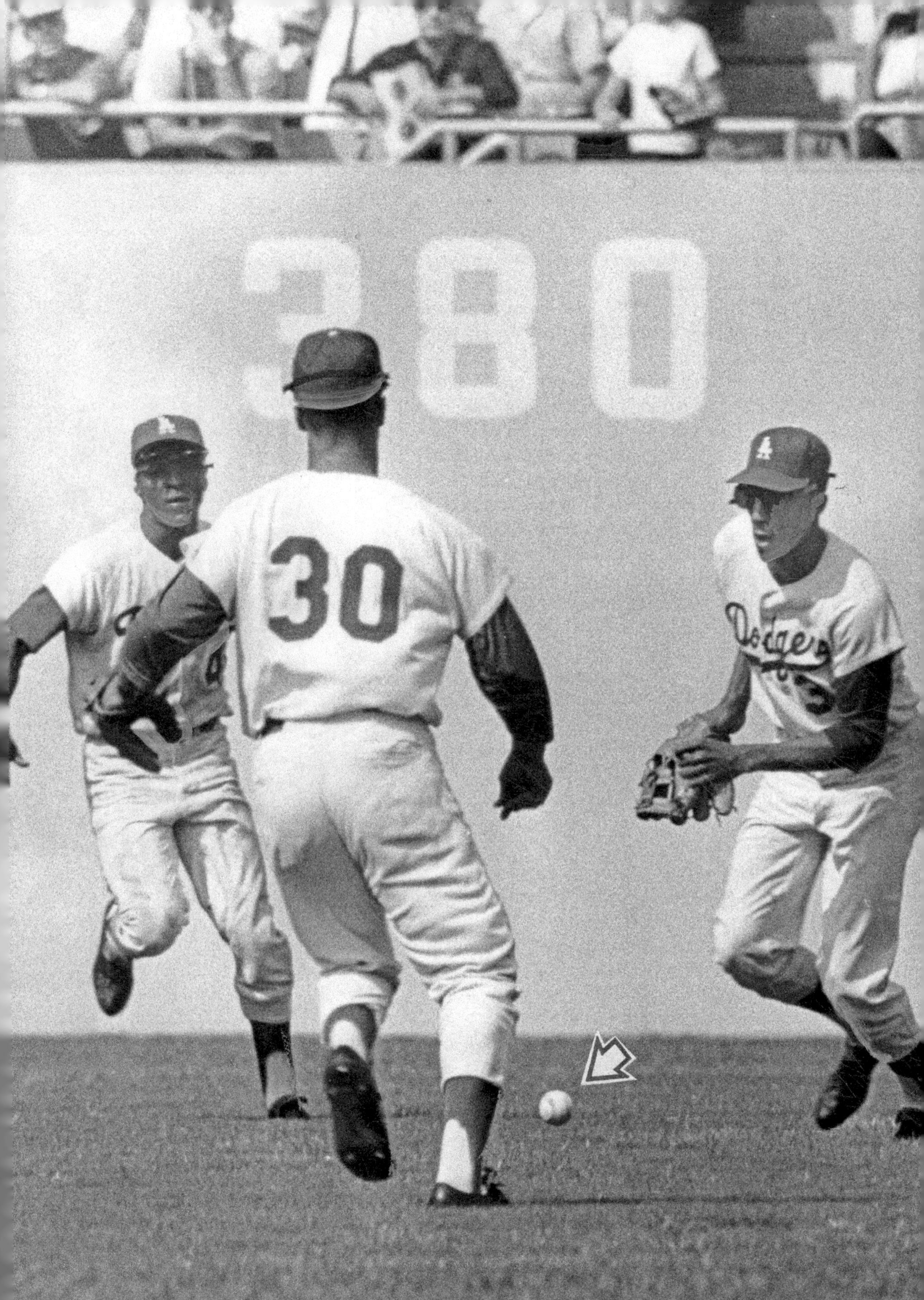
380
30
Dodgers

My First Favorite Dodger: Richie Allen

In 1971 I was five years old. It was the first year I can remember following baseball. I was told by three older brothers and my parents to root for the local team. That was the Dodgers. And the team's best player that year was Richie Allen. So he became my first favorite Dodger. But it wasn't a lasting relationship.

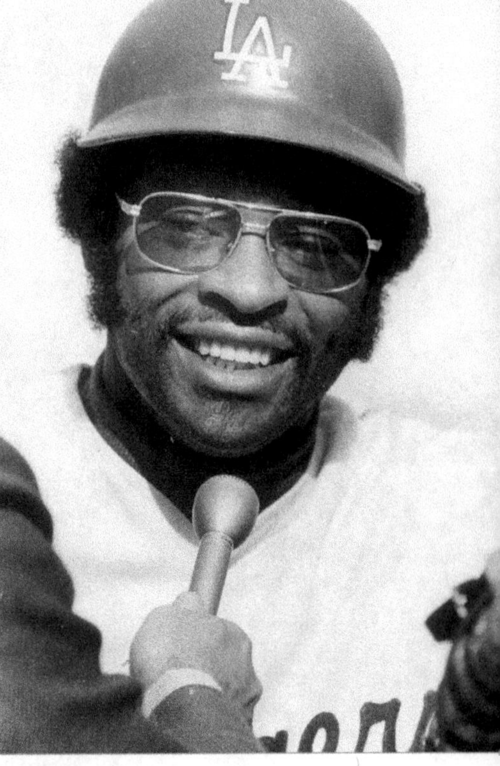
(Gerald Forbes/ Herald-Examiner Collection)

The Dodgers of 1971 were a team in transition. The Koufax-Drysdale squad was gone, although there were still a few holdovers, like Wes Parker, Maury Wills, and Jim Lefebvre. None of them were much to get excited about. They had old relievers who threw trick pitches: Hoyt Wilhelm (knuckleball), Jim Brewer (screwball), Jose Peña (forkball), and Pete Mikkelsen (palm ball). But you didn't see them pitch much because the starters threw so many innings. And the team wasn't on TV much, mostly just games from San Francisco and San Diego and a few Sunday road games tossed in.

When I was able to watch the Dodgers in action, Allen seemed to be the only player doing anything on offense. He was about the only power threat the Dodgers had, leading the team with 23 home runs (second was Lefebvre with 12) and 90 RBIs. He walked a lot (93 times), although when you're 5, you're not thinking a lot about on-base percentage.

Notwithstanding his offensive prowess, I rarely heard Allen getting interviewed on TV or radio. He had arrived in L.A. after a very turbulent stay in Philadelphia and a slightly less bumpy stop in St. Louis, and apparently he didn't care for such matters. Or, for doing community relations around town either. He just wanted to play ball. So that's what he did, even if his defensive skills at third base were, shall we say, limited.

The '71 Dodgers finished one game behind the Giants in the N.L. West standings and decided they needed to retool. Allen was traded to the Chicago White Sox for pitcher Tommy John. To replace Allen's power L.A. traded for 36-year old Frank Robinson. (That didn't work out at all.) The Dodgers also tried top prospect Steve Garvey at third base. (That would be unsuccessful, too.)

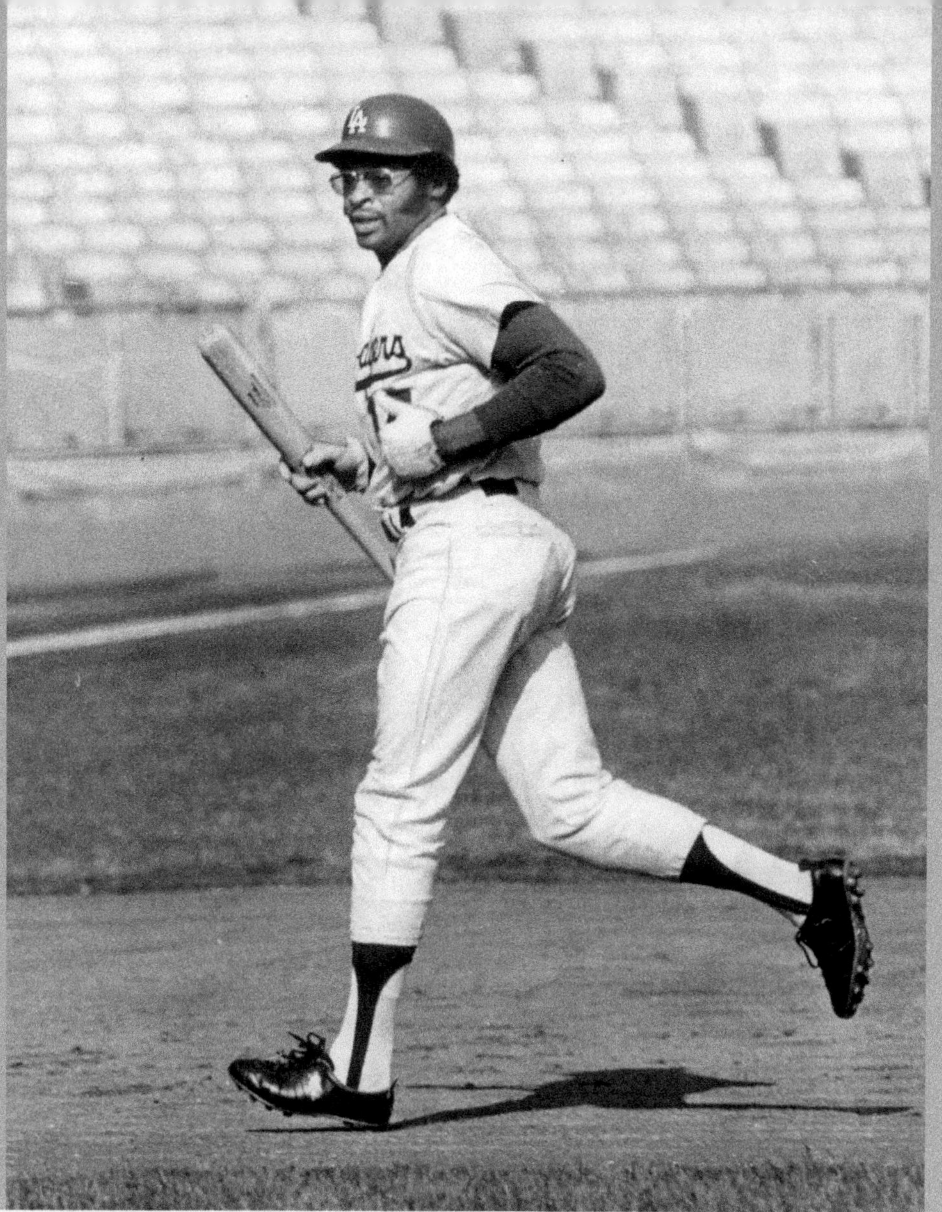

(Herald-Examiner Collection)

As for Allen? The man who became known as Dick Allen in Chicago only won the A.L. MVP in 1972.

When you're five years old, you don't immediately understand why your favorite player is no longer with your favorite team. I don't remember hearing the news about the trade. All I know is that when I bought a pack of baseball cards that spring, there was an odd-looking photo of Allen in profile wearing an odd-looking uniform. He was gone. It was time to find a new favorite player. Which I never did, because I knew that it would always be a temporary thing.

—Bob Timmermann

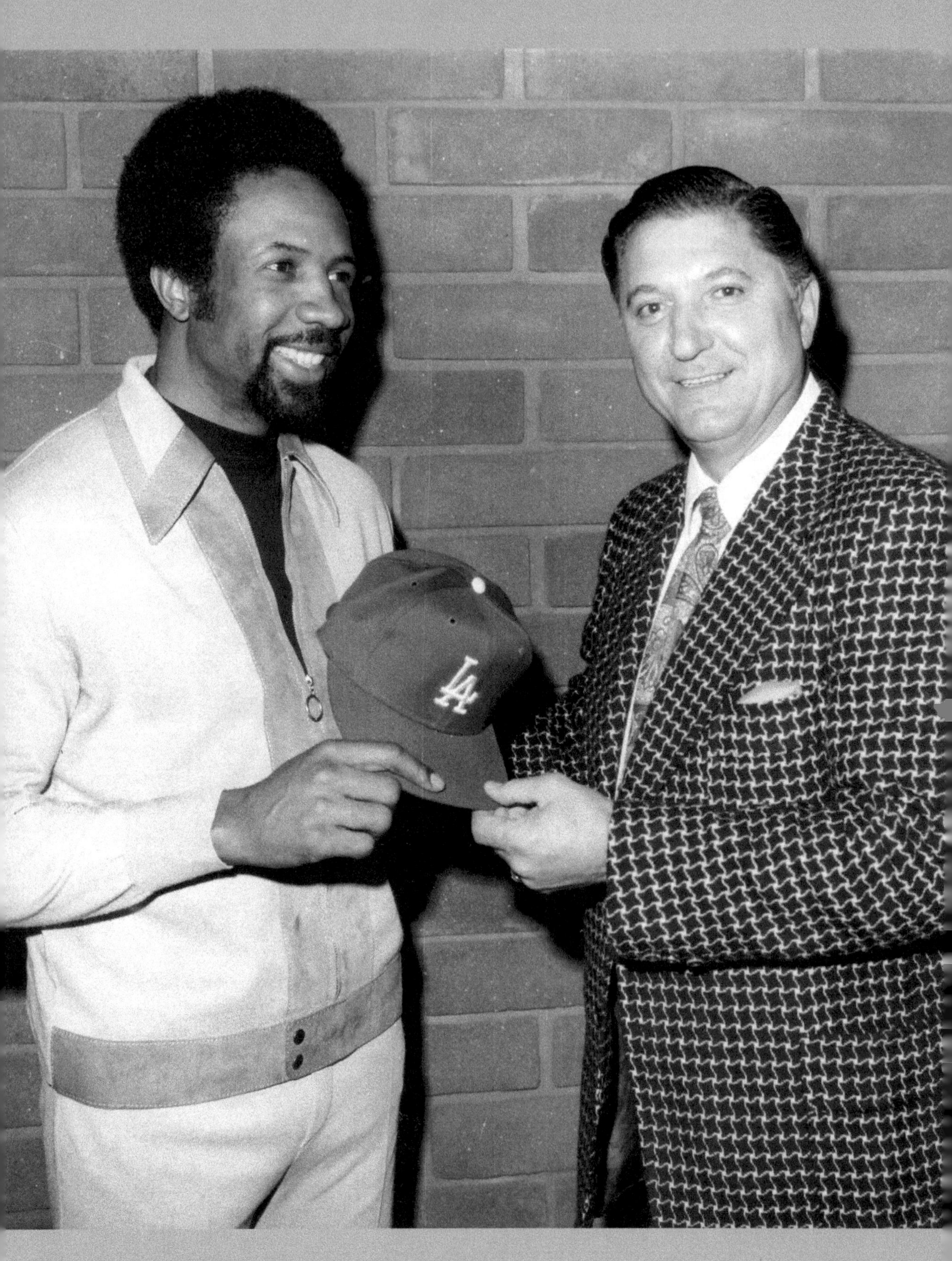
LA

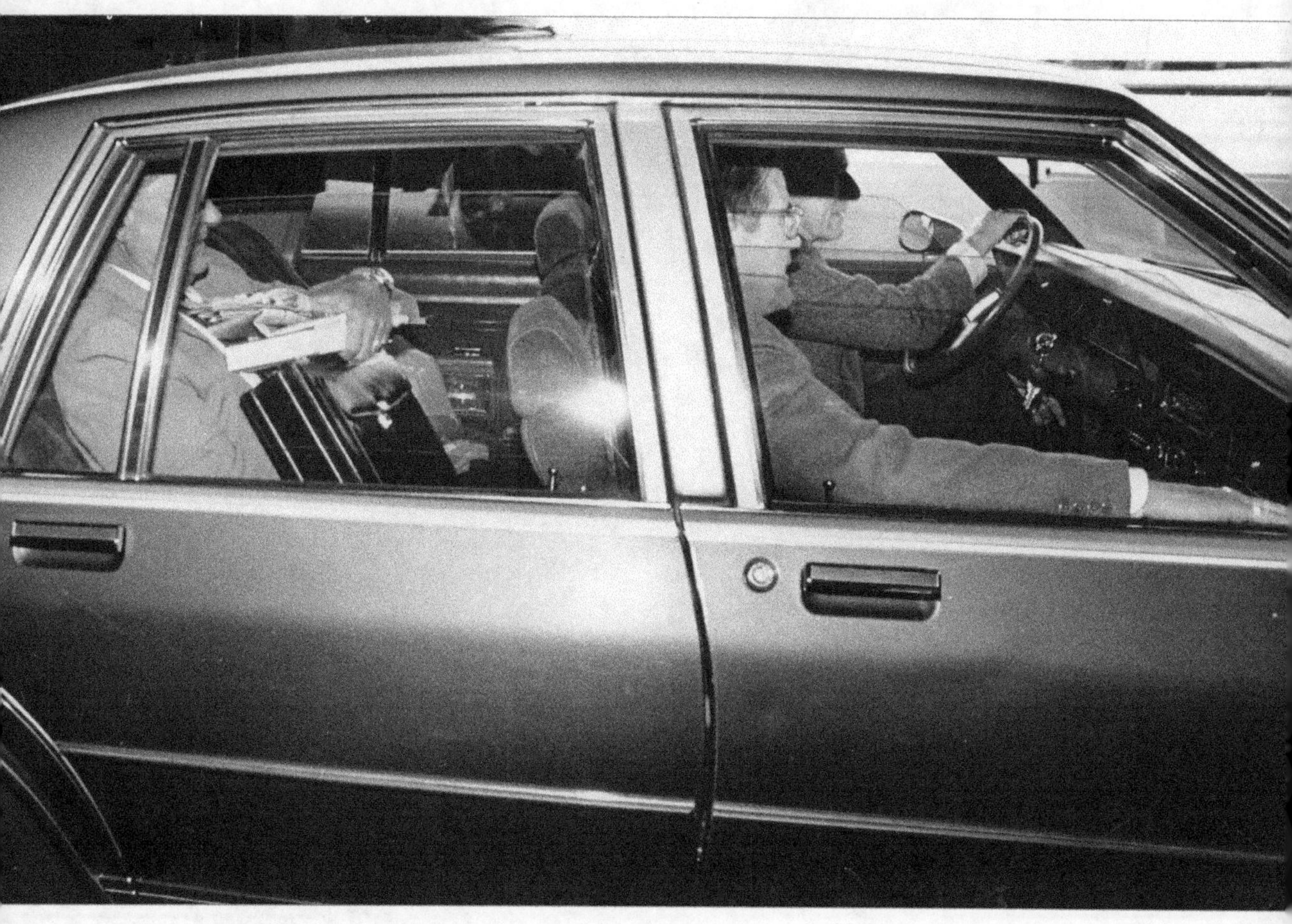

Al Campanis (*back seat*) is whisked away from reporters after his racist remarks that African Americans "may not have some of the necessities to be a field manager or general manager" caused national outrage in 1987. The Dodgers later fired the longtime executive. (Mike Mullen/Herald-Examiner Collection)

OPPOSITE: General manager Al Campanis welcomes veteran outfielder Frank Robinson to L.A. in 1972. Robinson played one season with the Dodgers, and then one with the Angels, before becoming the first African American manager in the Majors with the Cleveland Indians in 1975. (Jim Ober/Herald-Examiner Collection)

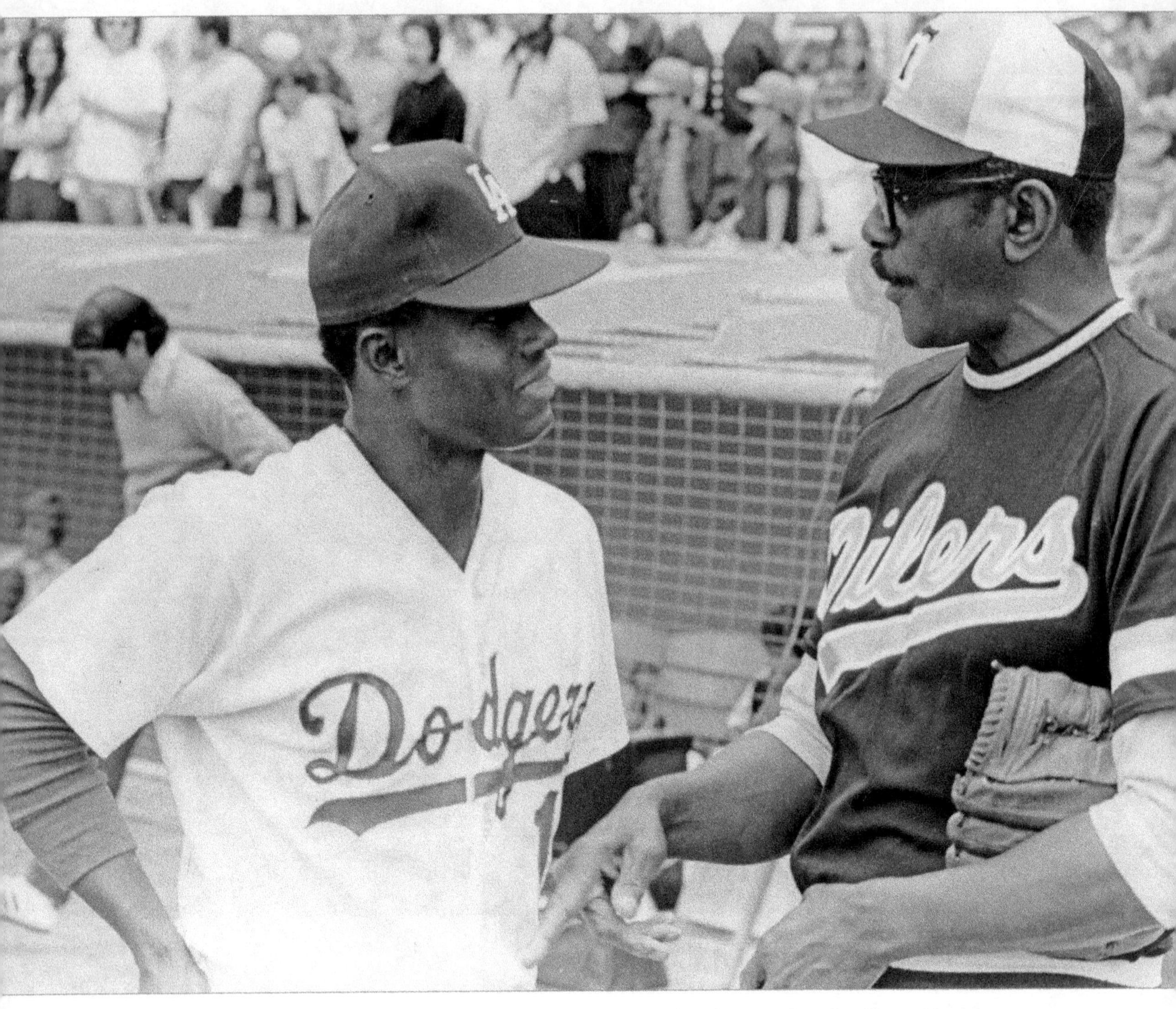

Pinch-hitter extraordinaire and longtime coach Manny Mota (*left*) chats with Negro Leagues legend Satchel Paige before an old-timers' game in 1973. (James Roark/Herald-Examiner Collection)

OPPOSITE: Mike Marshall holds the hardware after becoming the first relief pitcher to win the Cy Young award (1974). (James Roark/Herald-Examiner Collection)

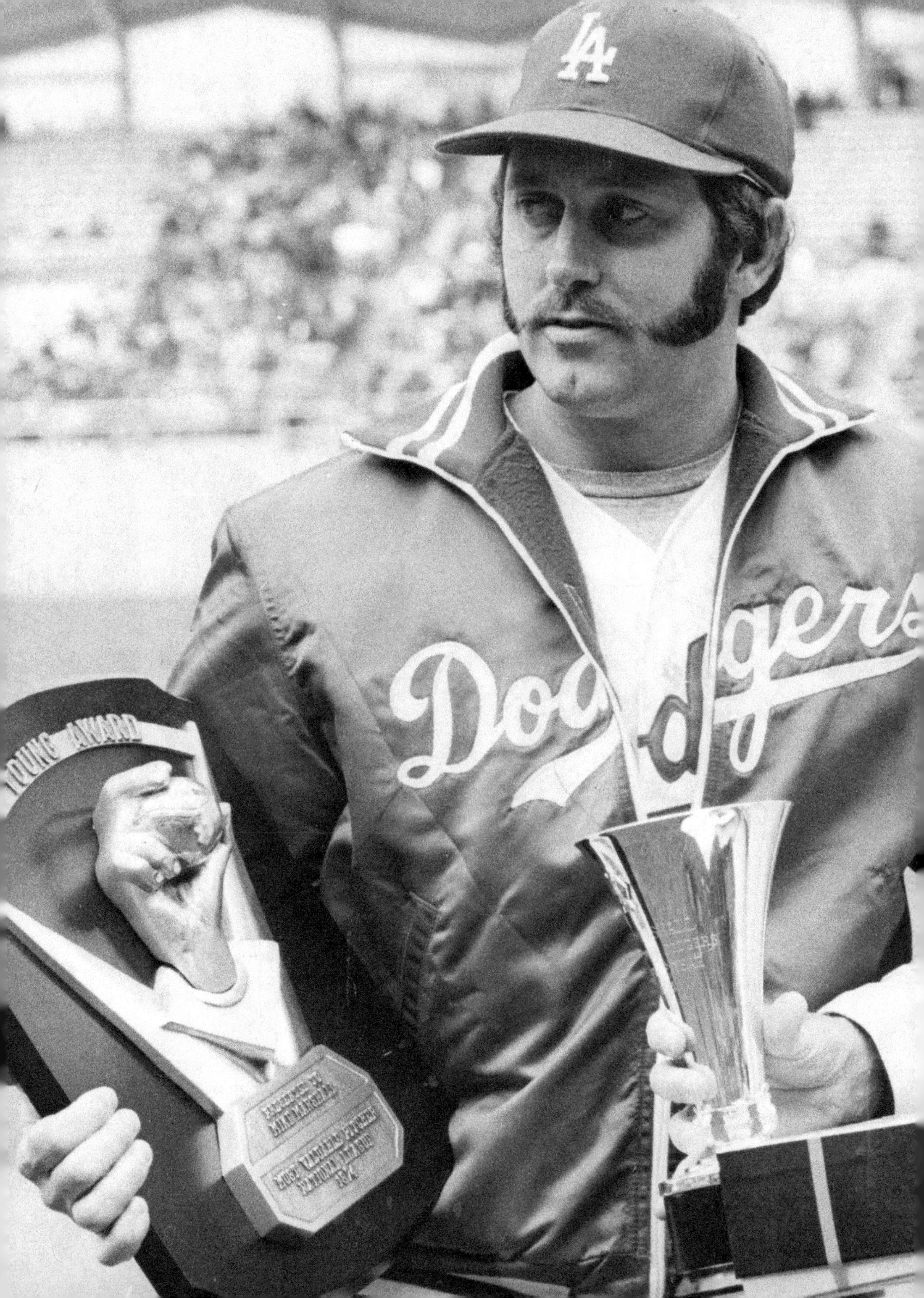
LA
Dod
dgers
YOUNG AWARD

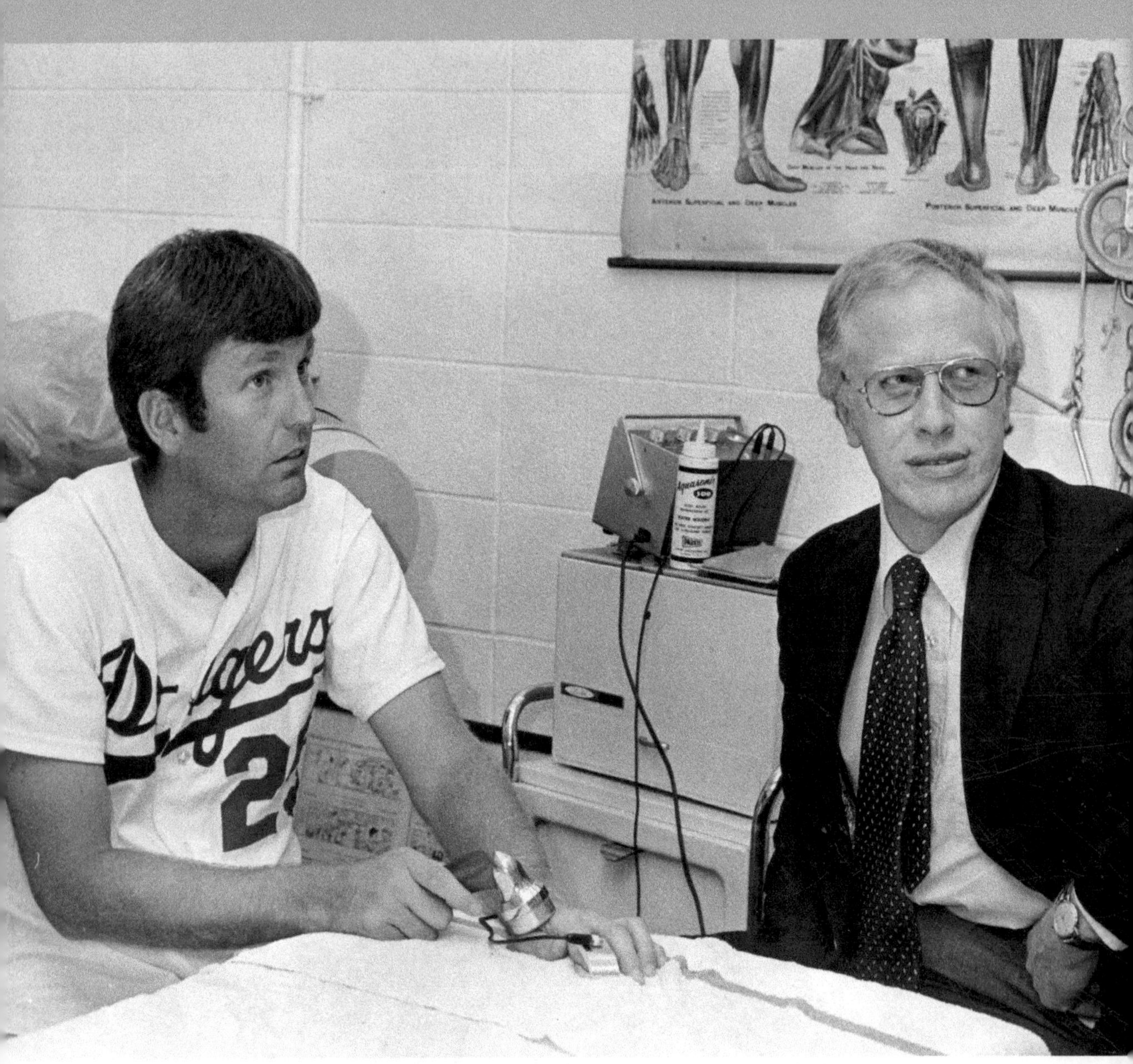

Tommy John discusses the revolutionary elbow surgery performed by Dr. Frank Jobe (*right*) in 1974. "Tommy John Surgery" extended the pitcher's career and has become a routine procedure in sports medicine. (Mark Malone/Herald-Examiner Collection)

OPPOSITE: Pitcher Andy Messersmith challenged baseball's long-standing reserve clause by refusing to sign his contract for the 1975 season. Messersmith's victory in arbitration helped usher in free agency in professional sports. (James Roark/Herald-Examiner Collection)

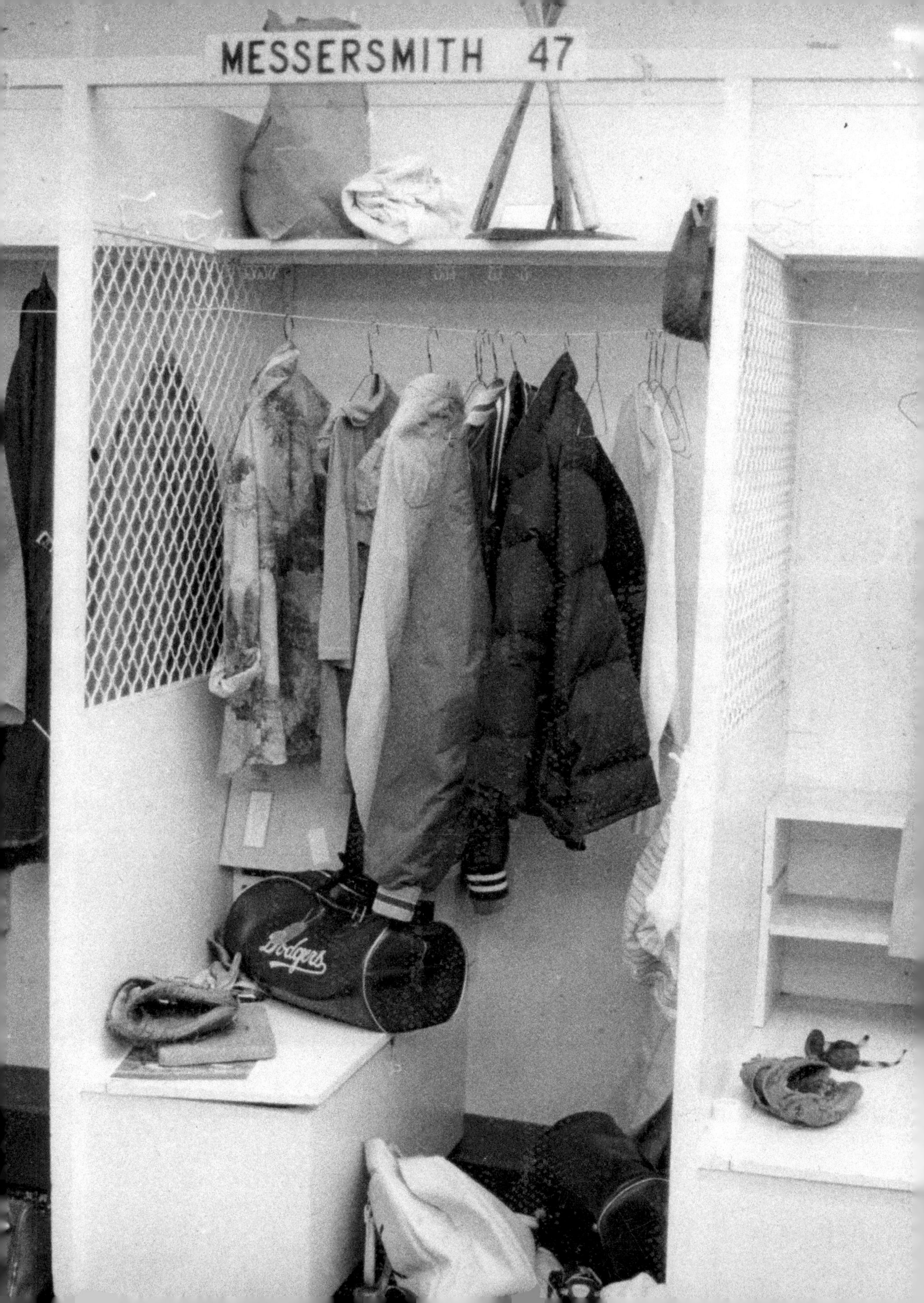

MESSERSMITH 47

Dodgers

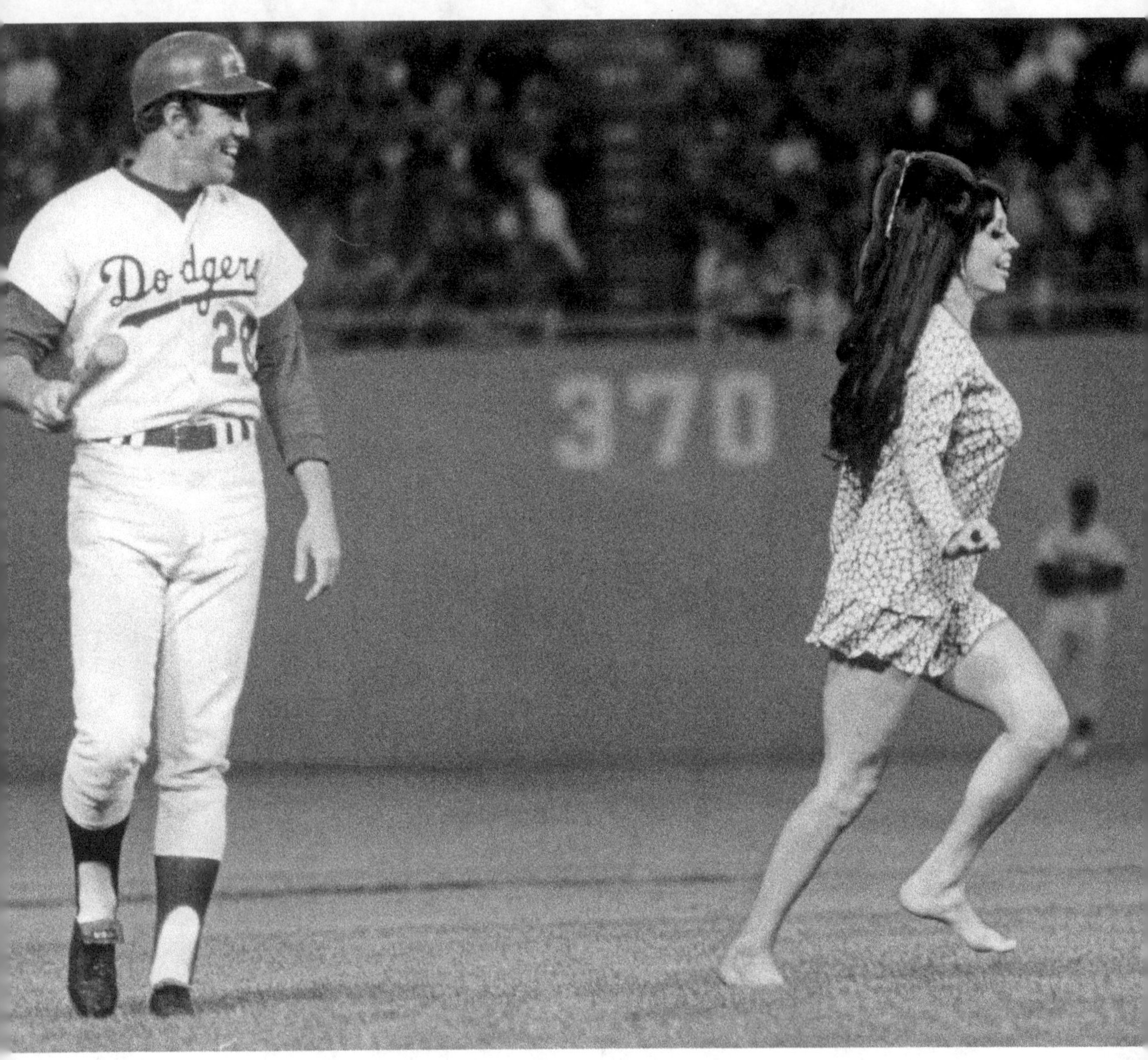

Wes Parker reacts after Morganna, "The Kissing Bandit," strikes again. (Herald-Examiner Collection)

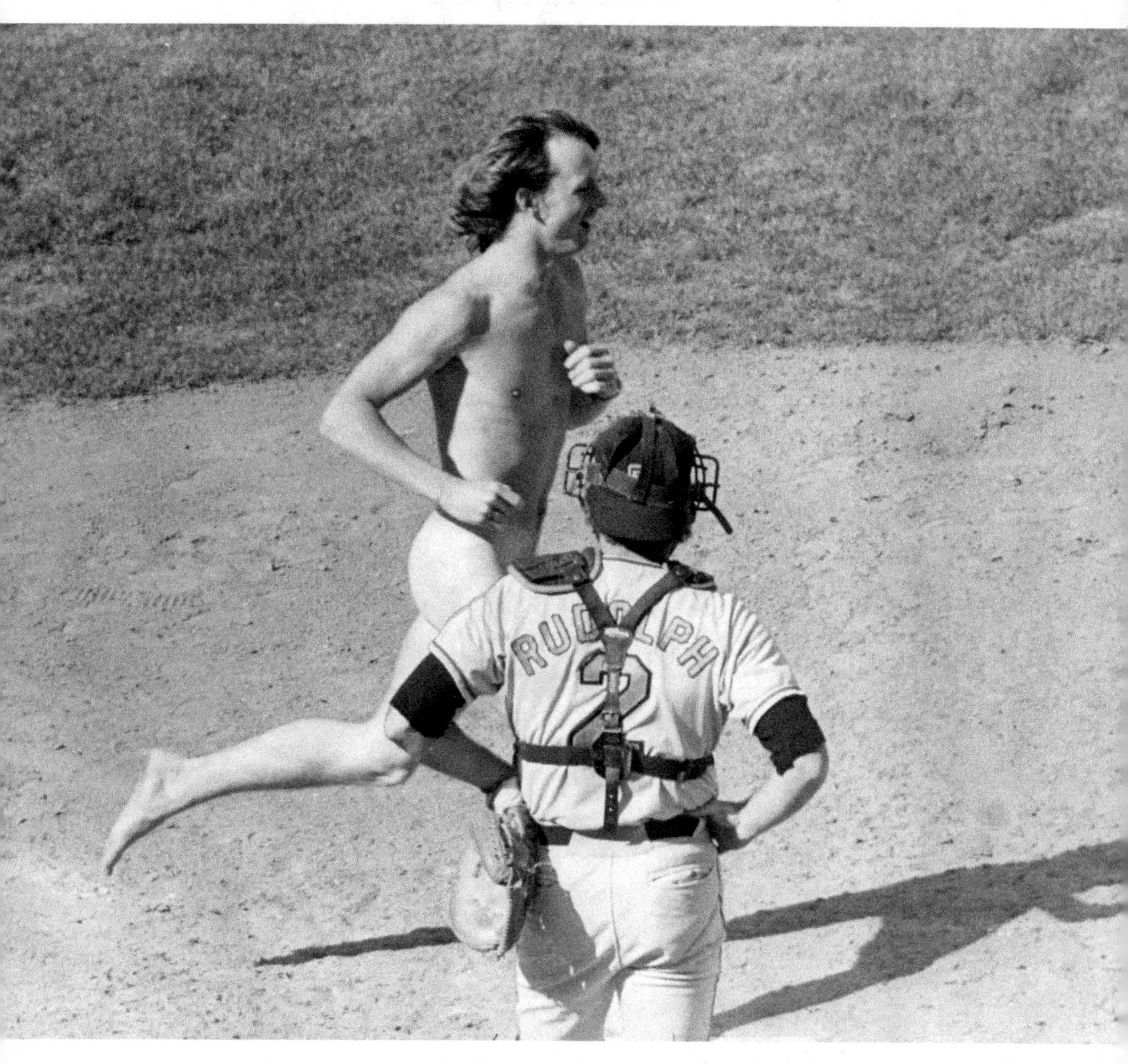

San Francisco Giants catcher Ken Rudolph watches
as a streaker touches home plate.
(Herald-Examiner Collection)

Bicentennial Blues

Rick Monday and the Story of James Roark's "American Flag" Photograph

By David Davis

On April 25, 1976, on a hazy Sunday afternoon, the Los Angeles Dodgers and the Chicago Cubs were playing the final game of a meaningless early-season series at Dodger Stadium. It was the bottom of the fourth inning, and second baseman Ted Sizemore was facing pitcher Ken Crosby, on in relief for injured starter Steve Stone.

Suddenly, a man and a boy ran out from the stands onto the field. They scurried past Cubs leftfielder Jose Cardenal before stopping in shallow left-center. One was carrying an American flag, a not-unfamiliar sight during the country's bicentennial year, which he proceeded to spread on the grass like a picnic blanket.

Cubs centerfielder Rick Monday, playing in his tenth full season in the

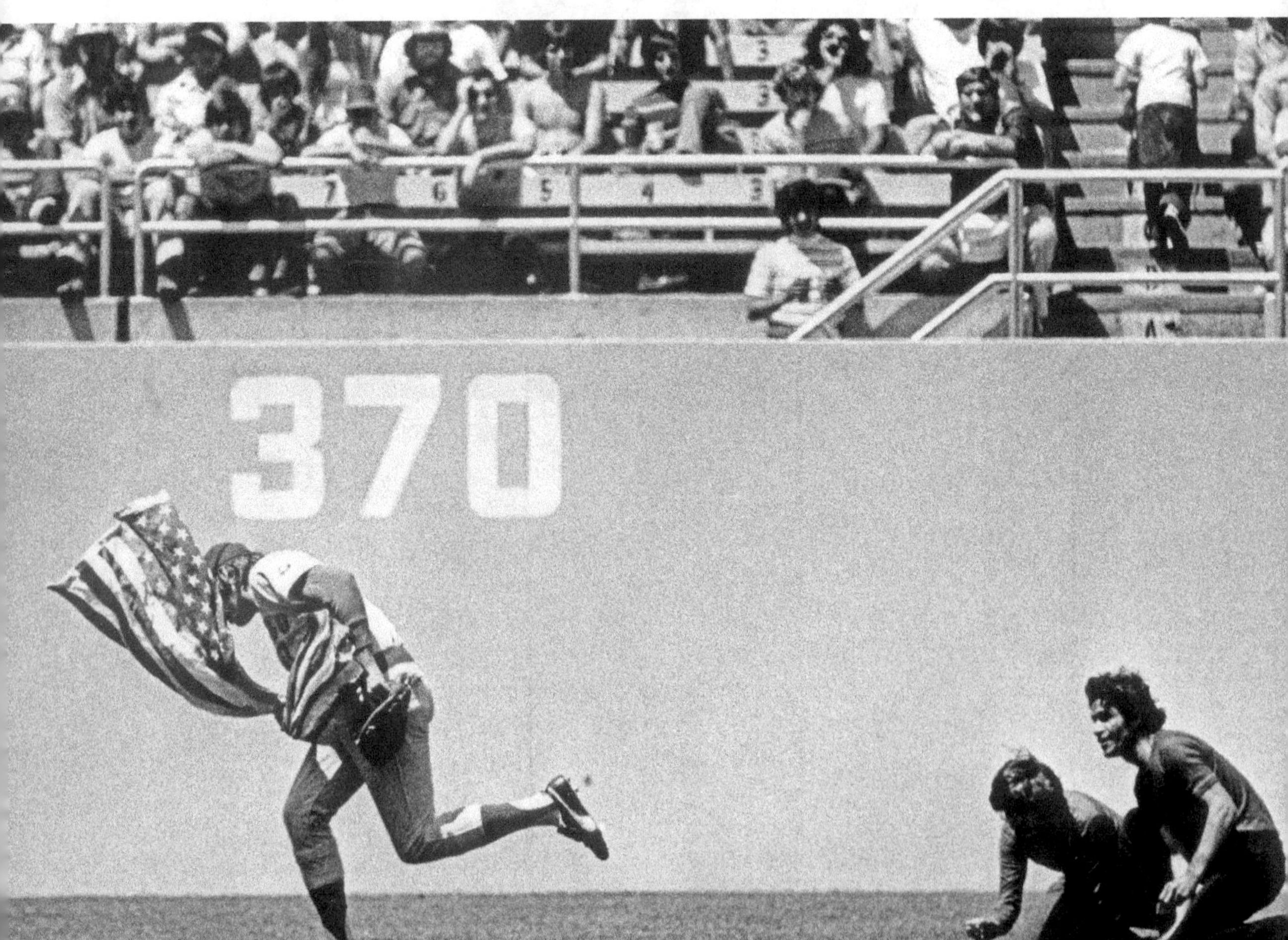

Major Leagues, had plenty of experience dealing with streakers, drunks and other intruders in the outfield. This time he sensed something was different and otherwise awry. The pair just gave off "a vibe," he said.

Then he smelled it: lighter fluid fumes wafting in the air. "I could see the reflection of the sun off of the can that this guy had pulled out," Monday said. "It was a big can of lighter fluid, and they began to douse it, and I was angry. I was angry at them for being on the field, I was angry at them for interrupting the game, and I was really angry at them because now they've got an American flag on the ground and they're not there to celebrate the rights and freedoms that that piece of cloth represents."

A match was lit, which the wind blew out, and then a second match was ignited. "Wait a minute, there's an animal loose," Vin Scully cried out from the broadcast booth. "Two of them. I'm not sure what he's doing out there. It looks like he's going to burn a flag!"

Monday didn't hesitate. He thought about bowling them over, but instead he raced toward the pair, bent down to grab the cloth with his bare right hand, and kept running. One of the would-be immolators hurled the can of lighter fluid at him, but Monday was well beyond his range. Meanwhile, Tommy Lasorda raced over from the third-base coach's box to scream invectives at the thwarted duo.

The crowd of 25,167, many of them reacting to Scully's play-by-play description, gave Monday an impromptu standing ovation that lasted for minutes. Fred Claire, then the Dodgers' vice president of public relations and promotions, instructed the scoreboard operator to type the words, "Rick Monday – You Made a Great Play."

The game resumed with the flag, sodden and smelly, resting safely in the Dodger dugout. Monday returned to his position in center as security escorted the pair off the field. They were summarily handed over to LAPD officers and transported downtown to Parker Center. Oh, and the Dodgers won the game, 5-4, in ten innings.

In the spring of 1976, as the United States prepared to celebrate the bicentennial, the country was profoundly at odds. Reeling from the fallout of the Watergate scandal and the protests over the unpopular Vietnam War, seized by an economic crisis resulting from the Middle East oil embargo, Americans were confronting what author Louis Masur described as "fundamental questions about patriotism and the vitality of the nation."

The difference this time was that the chaotic uncertainty had spilled over onto the green grass of the national pastime.

Initial details about the incident were conflicting and vague. The older man was identified as both William Errol Thomas and William Errol Morris. One

---

OPPOSITE: (James Roark/Herald-Examiner Collection)

newspaper wrote that the protest was "against the treatment of American Indians."

"All Americans are squatters," Thomas/Morris reportedly muttered, according to the *Los Angeles Herald-Examiner* newspaper.

A few facts emerged. William Errol Thomas was indeed the suspect's name. He was 37 years old, unemployed, and from Eldon, Missouri. Several sources mentioned that he was Native American, but provided no further details. The other person on the field was identified as Thomas' son. He was all of 11 years old. According to LAPD investigator George Renty, Thomas wanted to attract "attention to what he claims is his wife's imprisonment against her will in a Missouri mental institution."

Thomas pleaded guilty to trespassing. He was sentenced to three days in jail, with one-year probation. His son, whose name was not divulged because of his age, was held in juvenile hall. Fans and reporters called them every name imaginable: dissidents, clowns, jerks, idiots, animals, nuts, and worse. Two men were reportedly apprehended for trying to physically attack them.

Afterwards, no journalist bothered to interview William Errol Thomas to get his side of the story. No journalist investigated his wife's plight or asked him to explain why he employed his young son as an accomplice. The family did not issue a public statement. By July 4, 1976, as fireworks exploded from Manhattan to Honolulu, William Errol Thomas had disappeared into the red-white-and-blue beyond.

The incident might have escaped notice outside of Los Angeles but for a stark black-and-white picture taken by James Roark, a staff photographer with the *Herald-Examiner*. The image captured the climactic denouement: Monday's balletic snatch of the flag, the stars and stripes clearly visible, juxtaposed against the two field-crashers, on their knees as if in supplication, framed by the outfield wall and the frozen faces of fans in the bleachers. The image was printed in countless newspapers across the country and was nominated for the Pulitzer Prize in photography.

The blink-and-you'll-miss-it moment entwined four unlikely and disparate individuals: a Major League Baseball outfielder who instantaneously became a national hero; a photojournalist whose career was made, seemingly for life, with a single shot; and a father-son duo who faced so much mockery and castigation that they have chosen to remain anonymous.

◆ ◆ ◆

Those who worked with Jim Roark and knew him best were not surprised that he ended up taking the defining image of the flag rescue. He was a fiercely determined individual who willed himself into being, both as a professional photographer and as a person.

Born James Barnas, he grew up in Chicago. His father was a drinker and a gambler, and early on Jim knew that he wanted to leave behind the family strife. He entered the Air Force and worked on helicopters and fighter jets. He served six months in Vietnam on temporary assignment and purchased his first camera while stationed there.

Afterwards, he moved out to California. Another brother, Robert, was an illustrator in the art department at the *Herald-Examiner* newspaper, and he helped Jim land an entry-level post as a copy boy.

The *Her-Ex* had a reputation as a feisty tabloid. A decade-long strike had culled the staff, but its sports section was the best read in town, anchored by crack columnists Bud Furillo, Mel Durslag, and Allan Malamud as well as cartoonist Karl Hubenthal.

Determined to become a photojournalist, Jim took a correspondence course from the Famous Photographer's School in Connecticut, whose faculty included Richard Avedon, Irving Penn, and Bert Stern, and he dutifully studied their instruction manuals. He taped motion pictures directed by Orson Welles to learn more about lighting and composition. His first major credit involved taking photos of famous musicians for a book by Michael Ross titled *Rock Beyond Woodstock*.

Co-workers couldn't help but notice that the Barnas brothers had abandoned their family name. Robert called himself John Galt, after the protagonist from Ayn Rand's novel *Atlas Shrugged*. Jim swapped his last name for that of Howard Roark, the central figure in *The Fountainhead*.

Rand's philosophy of self-empowerment—that individuals control their destiny and are beholden only to themselves—seemed to inspire Jim as he elbowed his way toward his career goal. He made himself ubiquitous: under the basket at the Fabulous Forum, by the 18th green at Riviera, at the Rose Bowl for the Super Bowl, and ringside for title fights at the Olympic Auditorium.

"Jim worked his way up from the literal bottom of the journalism food chain," one former colleague said. "He had this strong drive to succeed."

His hard-charging style won him praise, but also critics. "He thought he knew more than anybody, and everybody who disagreed with him was absolutely wrong," former *Herald-Examiner* photographer Sergio Ortiz said. "He was not a pleasant guy, with an ego as big as the Ritz."

Roark's adopted persona as a take-charge, Olympian figure did not mask his serious drinking habit. "He knew every place in town where you could get a free drink," colleague Leo Jarzomb recalled. "Jim showed me how you could take your press pass to a window at Dodger Stadium and the bartender would give you two drinks."

Her-Ex staffers typically shot baseball action from the Dodger Stadium press box, where they kept a large lens preset to cover the entire diamond. But on the fateful April day of the flag rescue, "Jim decided to go down and make something different," recalled photojournalist Rich Mackson.

Roark stationed himself in the photo well located by the first-base dugout. He was using Tri-X, the black-and-white film of choice, with a Nikon f2 camera and a 300mm f/4.5 lens. When he noticed the commotion in the outfield, he reacted on instinct: he swung the camera up to his face, focused, and fired--snap-snap-snap-snap--with the motor drive. He stuck around for a few more innings before driving to the newspaper's stately offices in downtown L.A.

Even in that pre-digital age, when it took considerable time for the film to be processed and developed in the darkroom, Roark was confident he had captured history. "He came in crowing, 'Hey, I got this great photo,'" fellow staffer Michael Haering said. And, when the shadowy figures emerged from the developer, everyone in the newsroom saw that Roark wasn't blowing smoke. He got the shot.

WGN, the Chicago-based television station that was broadcasting the game, had followed standard protocol and refused to air the interruption of the game. Director Arne Harris said he was worried that the pair rushing onto the field were carrying a bomb. "I just didn't feel like having a close-up of a ballplayer maybe getting his head blown off, not with all those kids watching," he said.

Roark boasted that, without any TV coverage of the incident, he had exclusively captured the moment. He was wrong about this. Mackson himself shot a three-picture sequence from the press box that was published in the *Santa Monica Evening Outlook* newspaper, and a UPI staffer snapped several images, one of which later appeared in *The Sporting News*.

But Roark's dramatic photo was the best of the bunch. A six-foot wide enlargement was hung at the top of the stairs of the second-floor newsroom for the *Her-Ex* staff to admire. The next year, on Flag Day, fans attending the game at Dodger Stadium were given a free, 2×3-foot commemorative poster of the photo. Monday and Roark posed together with a copy of the poster.

The newspaper nominated Roark's work, titled "This Is Our Flag," for the Pulitzer Prize. "I remember thinking, 'That's a cinch to win,'" colleague Jim Ruebsamen said. "It wrapped up the feeling of the period, that everybody was apathetic and nobody gave a crap, and suddenly this hero arises out of nowhere in Rick Monday."

The Pulitzer was awarded to another American flag-themed photograph, published in the *Boston Herald American* newspaper just 20 days before Roark's. Stanley Forman's "The Soiling of Old Glory" was equally powerful. It showed a white teenager using the flag as a lance to attack an African-American attorney during an anti-busing rally in Boston.

Still, the picture boosted Roark's career. He was soon promoted to photo editor by *Her-Ex* editor Jim Bellows. His personal life also was coming together. Divorced from his first wife, Roark met and wooed Catharina Bernström, a Swedish representative in the Scandinavian tourist office. They married in 1979

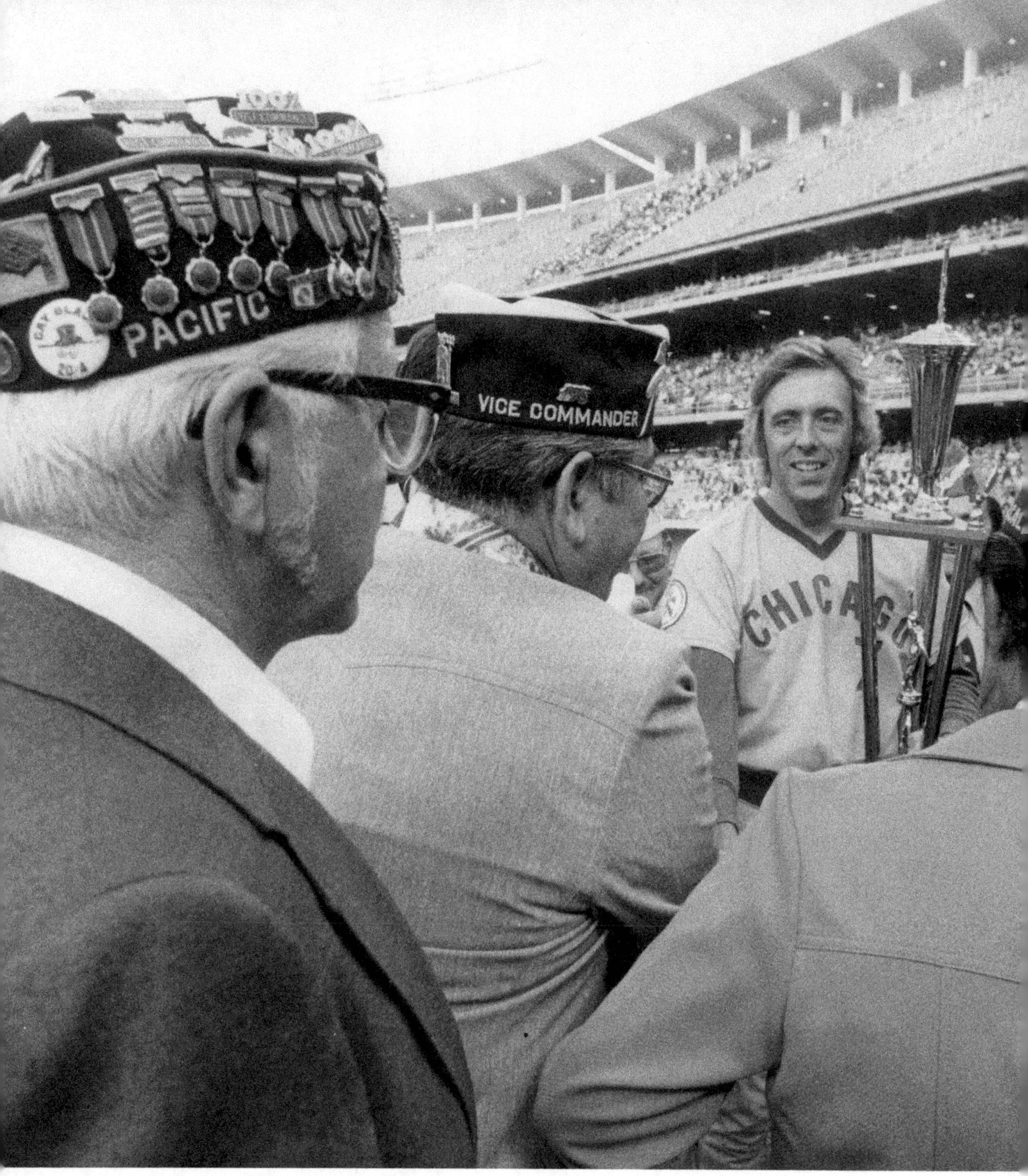

When Monday returned to Dodger Stadium three months later, veterans groups honored his heroic effort. (James Roark /Herald-Examiner Collection)

and moved into a home with a swimming pool in Northridge, where Jim liked to show off his cooking skills. Two sons followed, along with a pair of Rottweiler dogs named Cain and Abel.

"Jim did a lot of freelance work and we met a lot of different people," Catharina said. "I went with him to the opening of clubs and *People* magazine parties. It was exciting."

◆ ◆ ◆

Robert James "Rick" Monday has always prided himself on being a throwback, on playing the game of baseball the way it should be. He learned to play that way under the tutelage of Ruben Navarro, his coach at Santa Monica High School, around the time Major League Baseball was arriving in Los Angeles in 1958. He watched the Dodgers in the Coliseum in their inaugural years and then inside Walter O'Malley's shiny blue bauble in Chavez Ravine.

"I obviously knew the Dodgers very well because I grew up with them in Southern California," he said. "Vin Scully was on my mother's car radio and in our family home and our television."

Tommy Lasorda, then a scout with the club, tempted Monday's mother with offers to sign with the hometown team, but she turned him down in favor of her son getting a college education. He went to Arizona State to play under Bobby Winkles and, along with fellow future big leaguers Sal Bando and Duffy Dyer, led the Sun Devils to their first College World Series title in 1965.

His mother had played her cards well: Monday was now perfectly positioned to be the number-one selection in baseball's inaugural amateur draft. He signed with Charlie Finley's Kansas City Athletics for a reported $104,000 bonus.

Monday returned to California in 1968, when Finley moved the A's to Oakland, and he made the A.L. All-Star team that year. But he missed the club's World Series three-peat (1972-1974) after being traded to Chicago in 1971 for pitcher Ken Holtzman. One bonus about being in the National League was that he got to play in front of family and coach Navarro whenever the Cubs visited L.A.

In 1976, Monday started the season hot. He was hitting over .350 when the Cubs came to Dodger Stadium in late April. Newspapers in Chicago and L.A. were reporting chatter that Dodgers general manager Al Campanis wanted to deal for the left-hand hitting outfielder. "There'd been a lot of talk about it," he recalled, "but what's on your mind is, you go and play. You don't have room for thoughts about trade rumors when you're playing a game."

On the afternoon that he rescued the flag, Monday helped his cause by batting lead-off, going 3-5, and scoring two runs. He was now hitting .365. But few journalists wanted to talk to him about his batting average or the trade talks. All they wanted to know was, what happened out there with the flag?

Monday immediately referenced his own military service. After signing with Kansas City out of Arizona State, he had enlisted in the United States Marine Corps reserve program. He reported for training during the first six years of his professional career, from 1965 through 1971, an annual commitment that required him to leave the club for one weekend a month and two weeks of summer camp during the season. (He recalled being in advanced infantry training alongside fellow ballplayers Dave Duncan and Bob Watson.)

That experience gave Monday a unique perspective about the incident the *Her-Ex* dubbed "A Run for Old Glory," and he refused to hide his feelings to reporters who clamored to interview him. "Those of us in Major League Baseball and those of us American citizens are not going to let people use our flag or the game of baseball to make any type of demonstration as was tried," he said at the time. "If they don't want to do anything constructive to help this country become even a better country to live in and participate in, then also one of the rights that is available to them is that our borders are not guarded and they are free to leave. God bless America."

Monday requested the flag from the Dodgers, but he left L.A. empty-handed because of the ensuing police investigation. By the time the Cubs returned from their road trip to Wrigley Field, he was a national hero, thanks in part to "the most famous picture of its kind since the flag-raising at Iwo Jima," according to *Los Angeles Times* columnist Jim Murray.

It was "Francis Scott Key, Betsy Ross, Verdun and Iwo Jima—all wrapped up on one fleeting instant of patriotism," raved the *Sporting News*, noting that Monday resembled "Paul Revere at full gallop." President Ford awarded him with a Bicentennial Commendation, while Mayor Richard Daley named him the grand marshal of Chicago's "Salute to the American Flag" parade.

The next month, when the Dodgers visited Chicago to play the Cubs, general manager Campanis presented Monday with the now-famous flag. Miss Teenage Illinois Mary Lyn Valkenburg planted a demure kiss on his cheek.

◆ ◆ ◆

Jim Roark relished his job as photo editor of the *Herald-Examiner*, but the stress of the position did not alleviate his drinking problem. That only increased after Bellows, his protector, left the paper. When the Hearst Corporation shuttered the paper in November of 1989, his moods grew darker still. He lost his job and the image he'd constructed for himself as a self-made success.

Even the photograph of the flag rescue—the most famous picture he'd ever taken—lost some of its luster with the surprise discovery, in 1984, of color footage of the incident shot by a spectator from the stands with a handheld, 16-millimeter movie camera. Now Roark's photo wasn't the only visual evidence of Monday's heroics.

Increasingly he spent his days guzzling vodka in front of a television in a darkened room. "He was sad and upset and very worried about his future," his wife recalled. "He applied for photography jobs that he thought, because of his reputation, he was sure he would get. But he didn't, I presume because of his alcoholism. Because everybody knew him."

Roark decided to try another route. He enrolled in a two-year program at the Western Culinary Institute in Portland, Oregon, with the idea of opening his own restaurant. He sold the couple's home in Northridge, cashed in his *Her-Ex* retirement account, and left journalism behind.

His satisfaction was short-lived. He had difficulty finding steady work as a chef. The family's money woes worsened, and Roark's drinking followed suit. He and Catharina fought, then separated. She filed for divorce and returned to Sweden with their children. Roark stopped answering letters from his mother. He told everyone who listened that he didn't miss the news business, but he would often bring scrapbooks filled with yellowing clips of his photographs to show to co-workers.

Late on the evening of October 15, 1995, Roark left work as a night cook at Poor Richard's Restaurant in Portland and walked to a nearby light-rail station. There, he was attacked and beaten by four people in an apparent robbery. He died of head injuries in the hospital the next day at the age of 49. "It was very difficult," Catharina said. "And it was very difficult for the kids."

Roark kept copies of his published and freelance work and filled dozens of scrapbooks. Catharina was able to rescue several of these binders after his death. They represent a small, if significant, visual heirloom she can share with their sons.

"It's a sorrow," former colleague Michael Haering said. "Jim's been dead for over 20 years. His boys and Cat are now deep into their new lives, and he's laying there in the cemetery. It's a tragedy that he had to drink. It lost him his family and his career. He had such potential."

◆ ◆ ◆

The bicentennial season turned out to be Monday's finest in his 19 seasons in the Majors. He posted career bests in home runs (32), runs (107), and RBIs (77) as the Cubs finished fourth in the N.L. East. Trade rumors kept circulating during the off-season until they became fact: the Dodgers paid a steep price to acquire Monday, trading Bill Buckner and Ivan de Jesus to the Cubs for the 33-year-old

---

OPPOSITE: After being traded to the Dodgers for Bill Buckner and Ivan DeJesus, Monday takes batting practice. (James Roark /Herald-Examiner Collection)

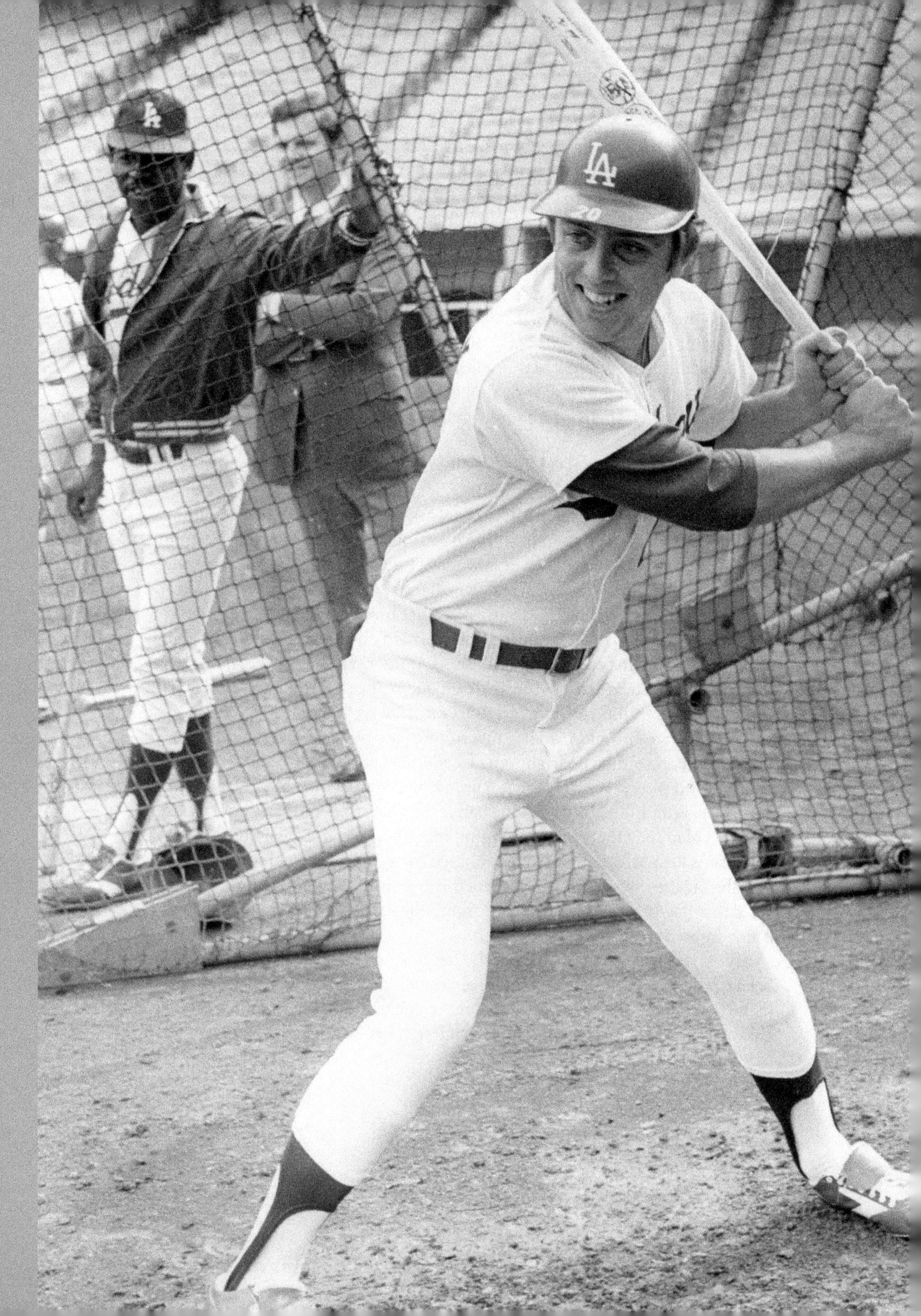
LA
20

centerfielder, and then signing him to a five-year deal worth a reported $1 million. "If he keeps hitting 30 home runs," Jim Murray wrote, "they won't care if he turns Communist."

"Mr. Red, White and Blue," as Campanis called Monday, never came close to reaching that plateau again, but he fit comfortably within a traditionalist organization that preferred to deal away outliers like Dick Allen and Glenn Burke. Monday was a vital cog on L.A.'s pennant-winning teams in 1977-78, and was named to the N.L. All-Star team in '78. His ninth-inning home run in the fifth and deciding game of the 1981 N.L. Championship Series against the Montreal Expos was the decisive blow in propelling the Dodgers to the World Series, and they went on to beat the New York Yankees in six. The momentous homer earned Monday a spot in franchise lore somewhere south of Kirk Gibson's walk-off dinger off Dennis Eckersley in 1988.

Monday retired in 1984 with 241 homers and 1,619 hits. Now in his 70s, he and his carefully calibrated baritone have been part of the Dodgers' broadcast crew for more than two decades. Five years ago, the team held a flag-rescue bobblehead night to commemorate the occasion; the design was based on Jim Roark's photograph, complete with Monday clutching a plastic American flag.

For years, Monday hung the real flag on the wall at his home. He now keeps the tattered and faded relic in a secure place because, he told me, an extremist group tried to take it and destroy it. He has turned down lucrative offers for it.

Monday remains passionate about his actions. "What they were doing was wrong, and I wanted them off the field," he said before a game at the Dodgers' spring-training facility in Glendale, Arizona, in 2016. "I did not want them to be able to desecrate an American flag that some of my buddies lost their lives for [in Vietnam], representing the rights and freedoms that you and I enjoy."

Some 40-plus years after the rescue, the flag has become Monday's identity and cause. With his second wife, Barbaralee, he has used it to raise enormous amounts of money for charity, including veterans groups. He is a board member of Citizens Flag Alliance, which has lobbied for a Constitutional Amendment prohibiting the physical desecration of the flag. (In 1989, the U.S. Supreme Court ruled that flag-burning is considered "symbolic speech protected by the First Amendment.")

When I asked Monday whether the flag rescue and its aftermath have ever been burdensome, he demurred. "If I am remembered only as a guy that stood in the way of two guys trying to desecrate an American flag at a Major League Baseball game, and protect the rights and freedoms that flag represents for all of us, that's not a bad thing to be remembered for," he said.

◆ ◆ ◆

In recent years, usually on the anniversary of the incident, journalists have attempted to contact William Errol Thomas and his son without success. They have never been quoted or interviewed on the record; they have remained hidden from public view even in the age of social media. What befell them has become, according to the Dodgers' longtime historian Mark Langill, "one of the two big mysteries we have: what happened to the Kirk Gibson home-run ball and what happened to the two people who tried to burn the American flag?"

Not long ago I spoke briefly with William Thomas's son. He is now in his early 50s, married, and has a child of his own. His name has never been published; I am respecting his request for privacy.

He was polite during our brief telephone conversation, but he refused to be interviewed. "I'm not interested in reliving that time period," he told me. "I don't see any good from rehashing that situation. I don't feel it necessary to go over this." When I requested to interview his father, whom I'd also located, the younger Thomas declined. Neither returned subsequent phone messages, emails, or letters. Attempts to view LAPD records and the case report from the Superior Court of California, County of Los Angeles, were unsuccessful.

I did learn that William Thomas' wife died from natural causes in 2012. Two of her surviving siblings told me that, growing up, their family moved around often, on account of their father being a Southern Baptist preacher, which made it difficult to make lasting friends. She was tall and dark-haired, intelligent and opinionated, and "never without a book in her hands," according to one sister. One of several family members who attended Moody Bible Institute in Chicago, she married William Thomas when she was 21.

The two left the Midwest for California and rarely returned home. "I didn't see them but maybe one time in all those years," one brother said.

For long stretches, she experienced mental illness. "She was in and out of mental institutions all her life," one sister told me. "Mom and Dad had to go get her several times and put her somewhere. But she never discussed that with me."

There's no way of knowing what hardships she suffered. An acclaimed film in theaters at that time of the incident, *One Flew Over the Cuckoo's Nest*—the film is set in the early 1960s but was released in late 1975—offered moviegoers a glimpse of the harsh and primitive environment that people with mental illness endured in what were then called insane asylums. Her siblings don't recall what occasioned Bill Thomas to react as he did in 1976, or how it related to his wife's institutionalization. One brother told me that he "didn't think she was connected with what Bill Thomas did. I don't know that she knew anything about what he was doing."

The couple eventually divorced. She moved back to Missouri about ten years ago. She died in a nursing home. (Her name has never been publicized; I have chosen not to reveal it.)

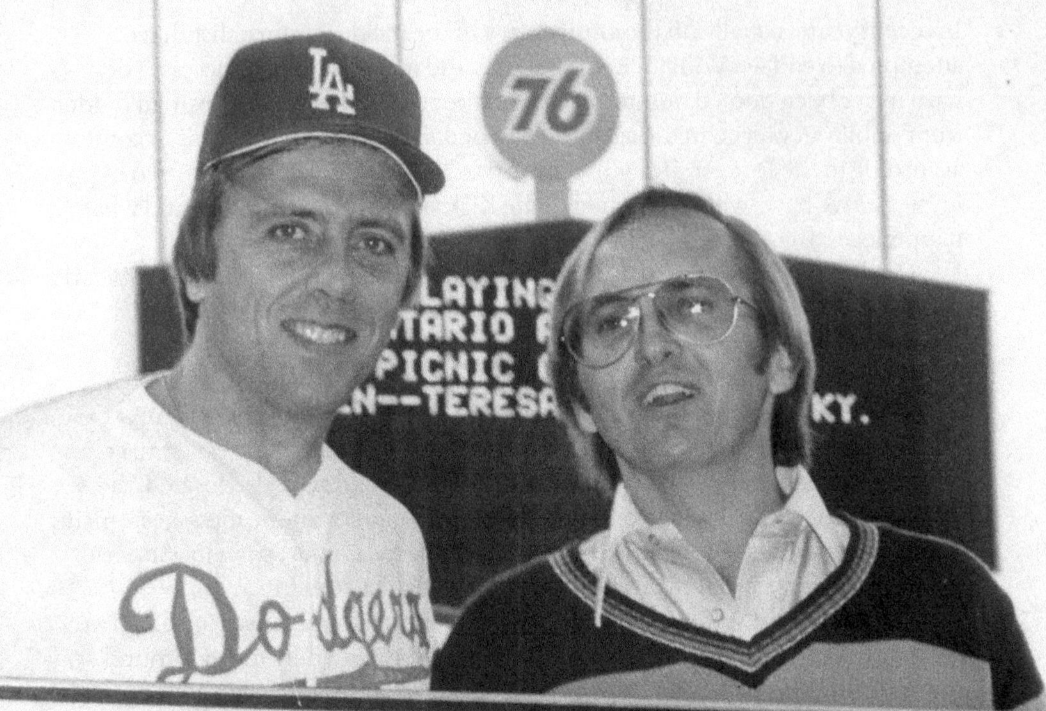
76
LA
PICNIC
Dodgers

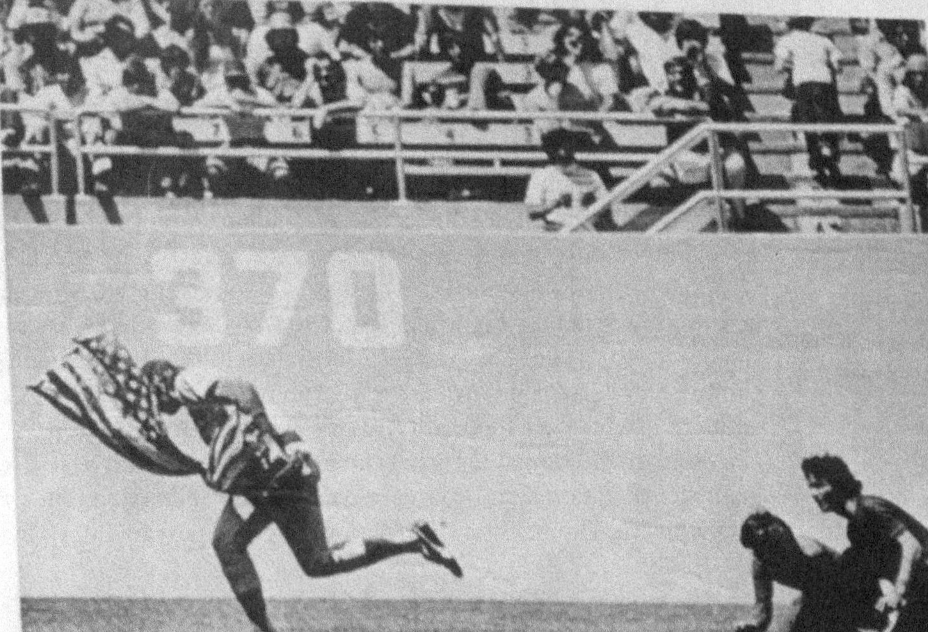
A
RUN FOR
OLD
GLORY
370
Dodgers

It's understandable that the Thomas family prefers silence. Father and son were vilified from the moment they were arrested. Even today, they continue to be publicly chastised and shamed. The comments section below a recent re-telling of the story on one website described them variously as "two scumbags," "possibly illegal aliens," "Muslims," and "war protesters." One commenter facetiously asked: "Were the names of the two perps Bill Ayers and Bernadine Dorn?"

With their disappearance, with their refusal to address the past, they are a frustratingly nebulous void. They can be seen as whatever villain an observer wants them to be or they can be seen as bumbling protesters who failed in their mission to publicize a family calamity.

They leave behind questions that seem likely to remain unanswered. What pain and rage led them to take the field that day, and what did it have to do with a mental institution in Missouri? Why burn an American flag as a method of protest, and why in the outfield at Dodger Stadium of all places? Why did a father choose to use his 11-year-old son as an accomplice? And, surely, there are other questions—questions of regret, questions about what it has been like to live with this memory for decades.

What we're left with is Jim Roark's iconic photo, and its strange and disquieting power, and Rick Monday's proud patriotism. The final element that could complete the story and perhaps bring some resolution remains elusive. In choosing silence, the Thomases have forfeited the opportunity for sympathy or forgiveness or understanding. Their legacy is nothing more than a match blown out by the wind.

Editor's Note: After the Herald-Examiner *closed in 1989, the Hearst Corp. donated the newspaper's photo archives, including the flag-rescue photograph taken by Jim Roark, to the Los Angeles Public Library. A version of this story was originally published in 2016.*

OPPOSITE: Monday and Roark pose together in 1977 with a promotional poster of the now-famous photograph. (Herald-Examiner Collection)

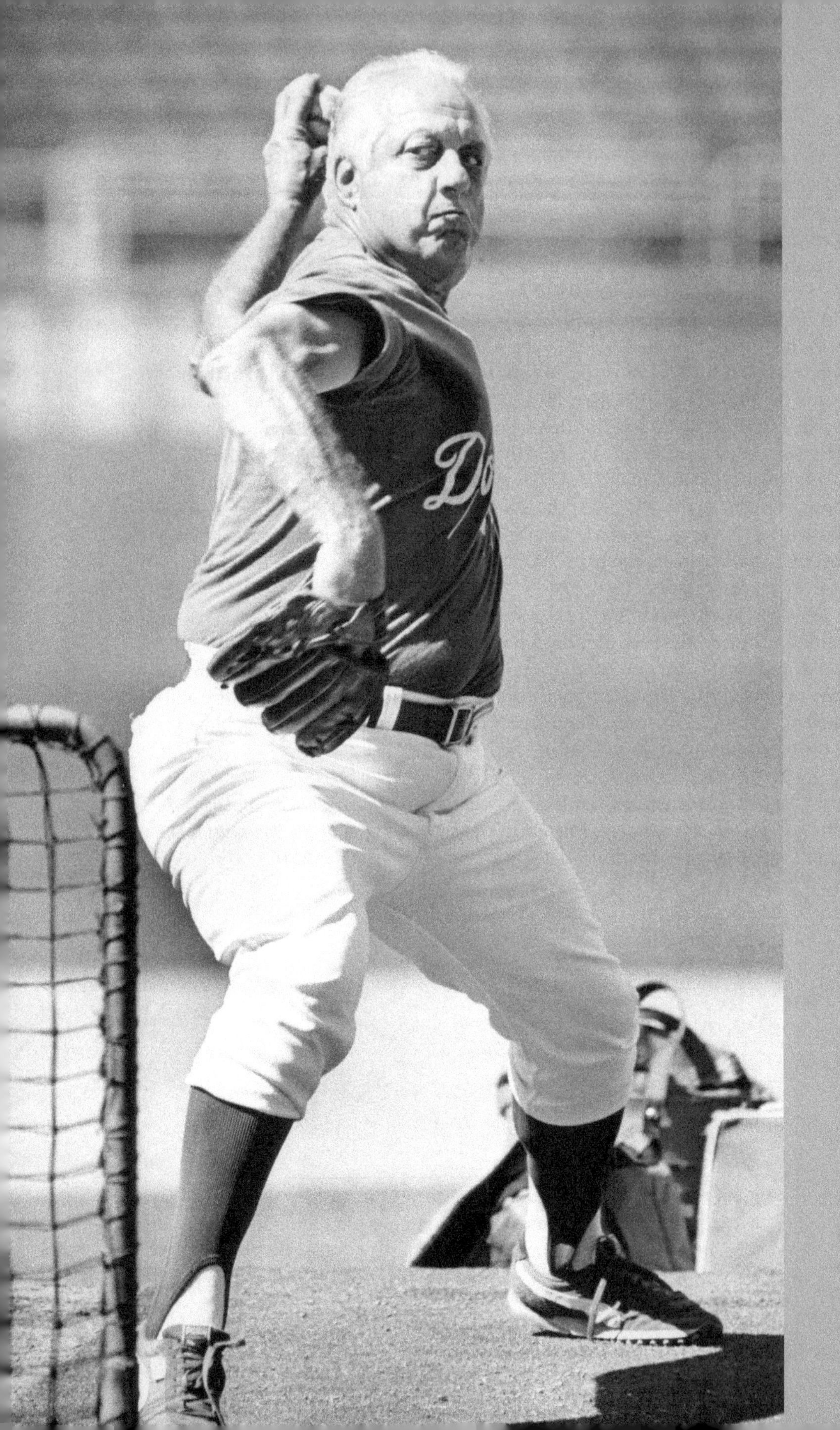

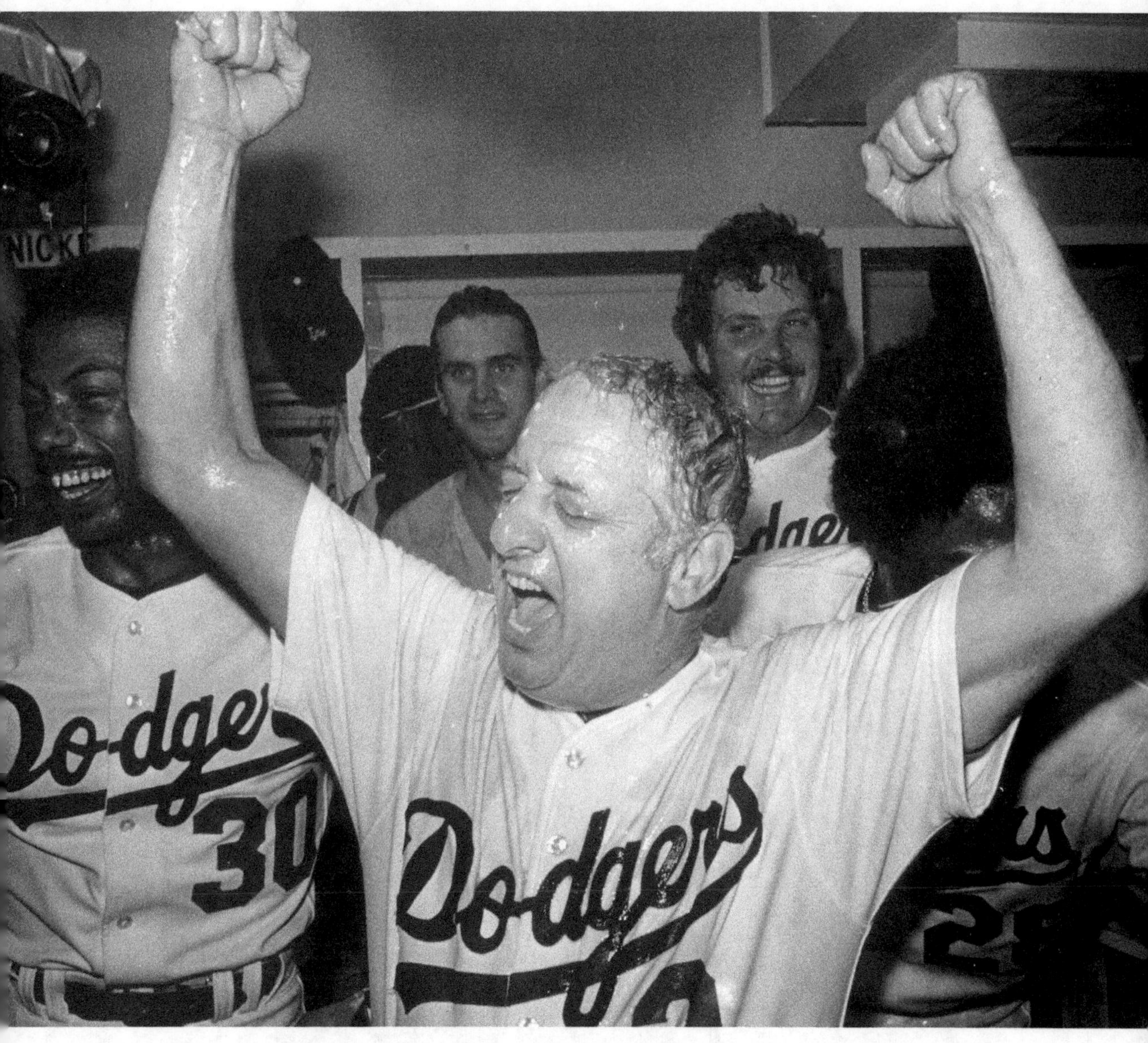

Tom Lasorda celebrating with the team after the Dodgers won the Word Series in 1981. (Rob Brown/Herald-Examiner Collection)

OPPOSITE: Lasorda replaced Walter Alston as manager at the end of the 1976 season. Bleeding Dodger Blue, the irrepressible Lasorda guided L.A. to two World Series titles in his 21-year managerial career. Here, he pitches batting practice. (Leo Jarzomb/Herald-Examiner Collection)

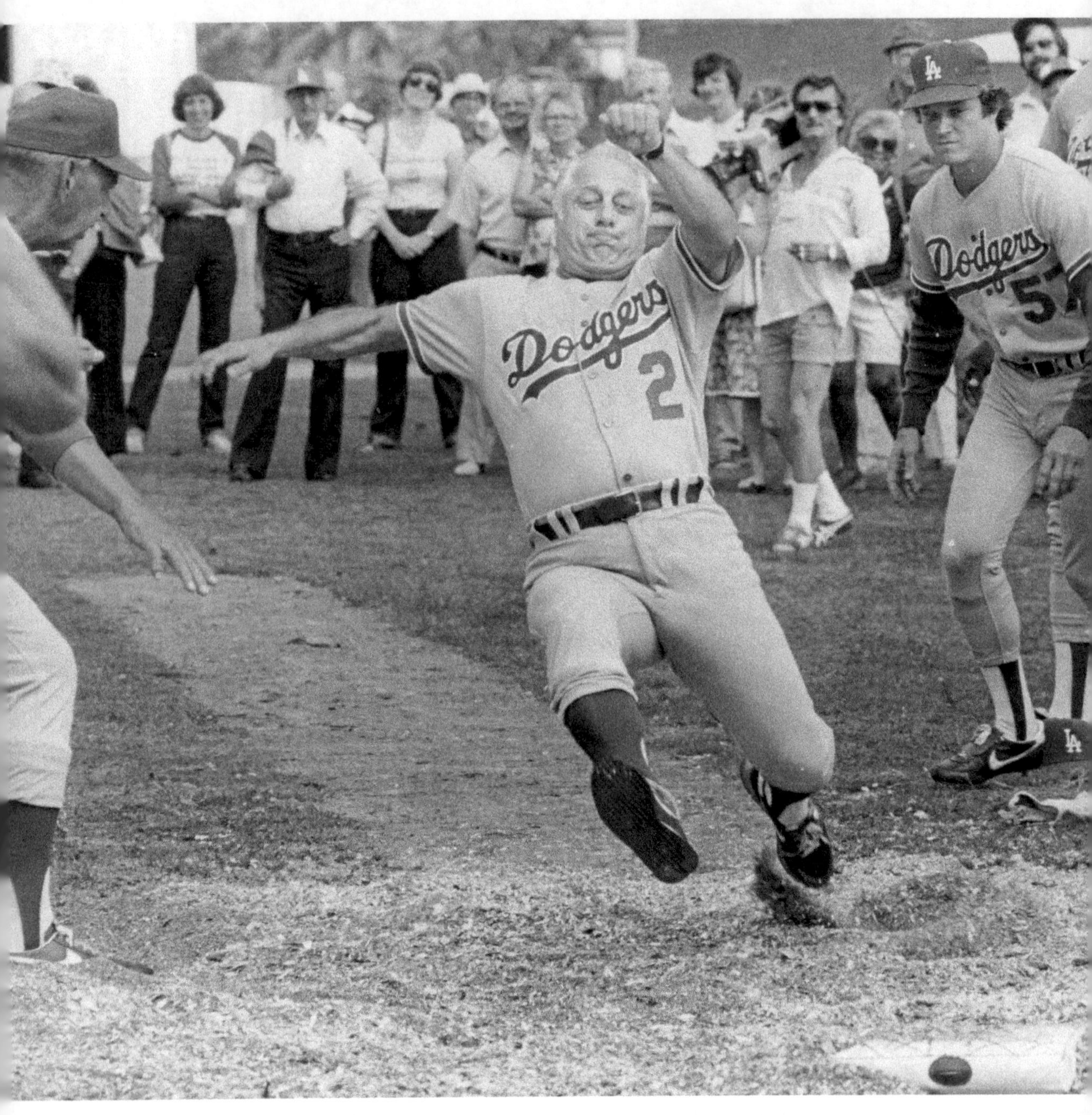

Showing off proper sliding form. (Herald-Examiner Collection)

OPPOSITE: Enjoying a snack. (Anne Knudsen/Herald-Examiner Collection)

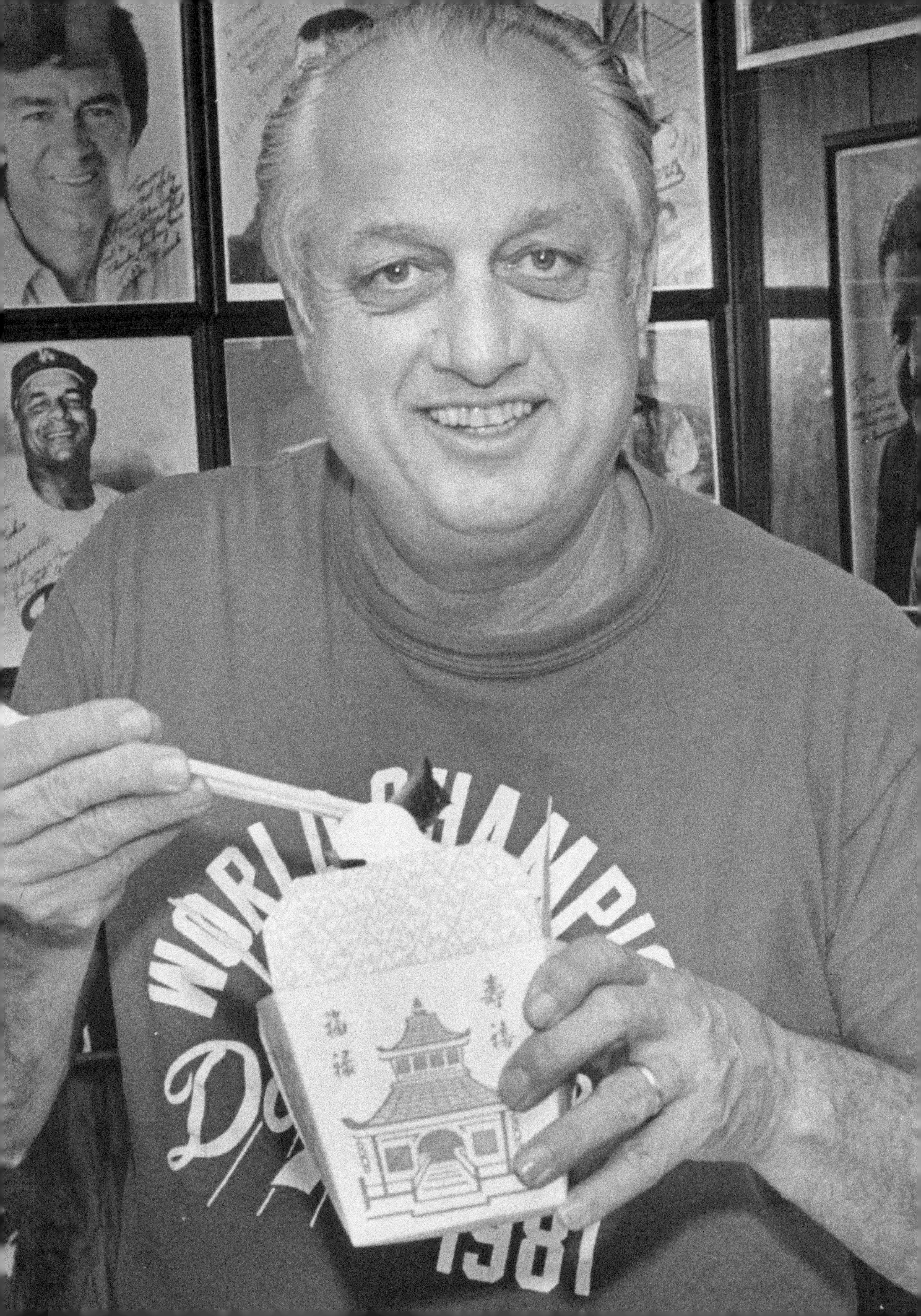
1981

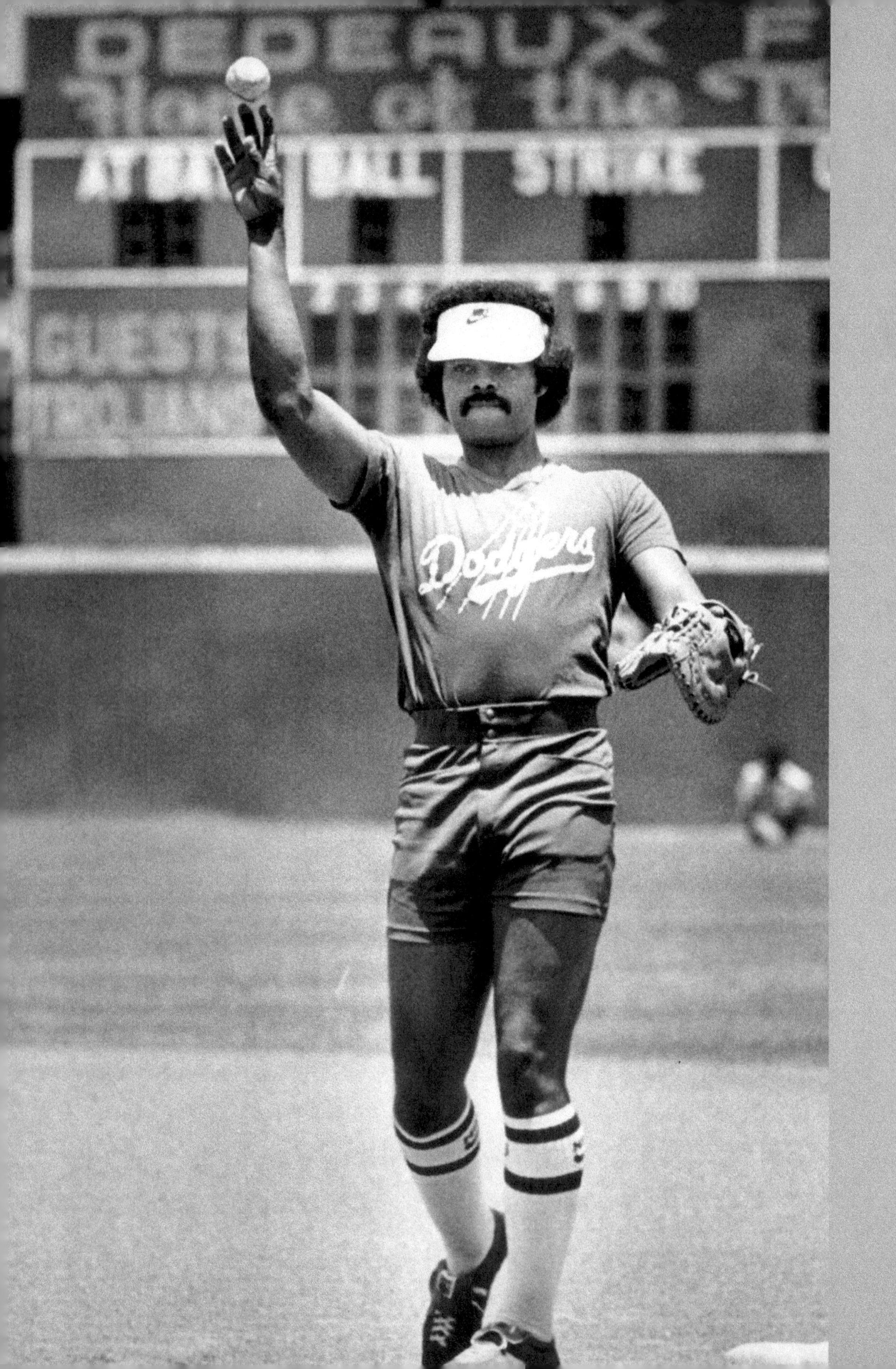
STRIKE
Dodgers

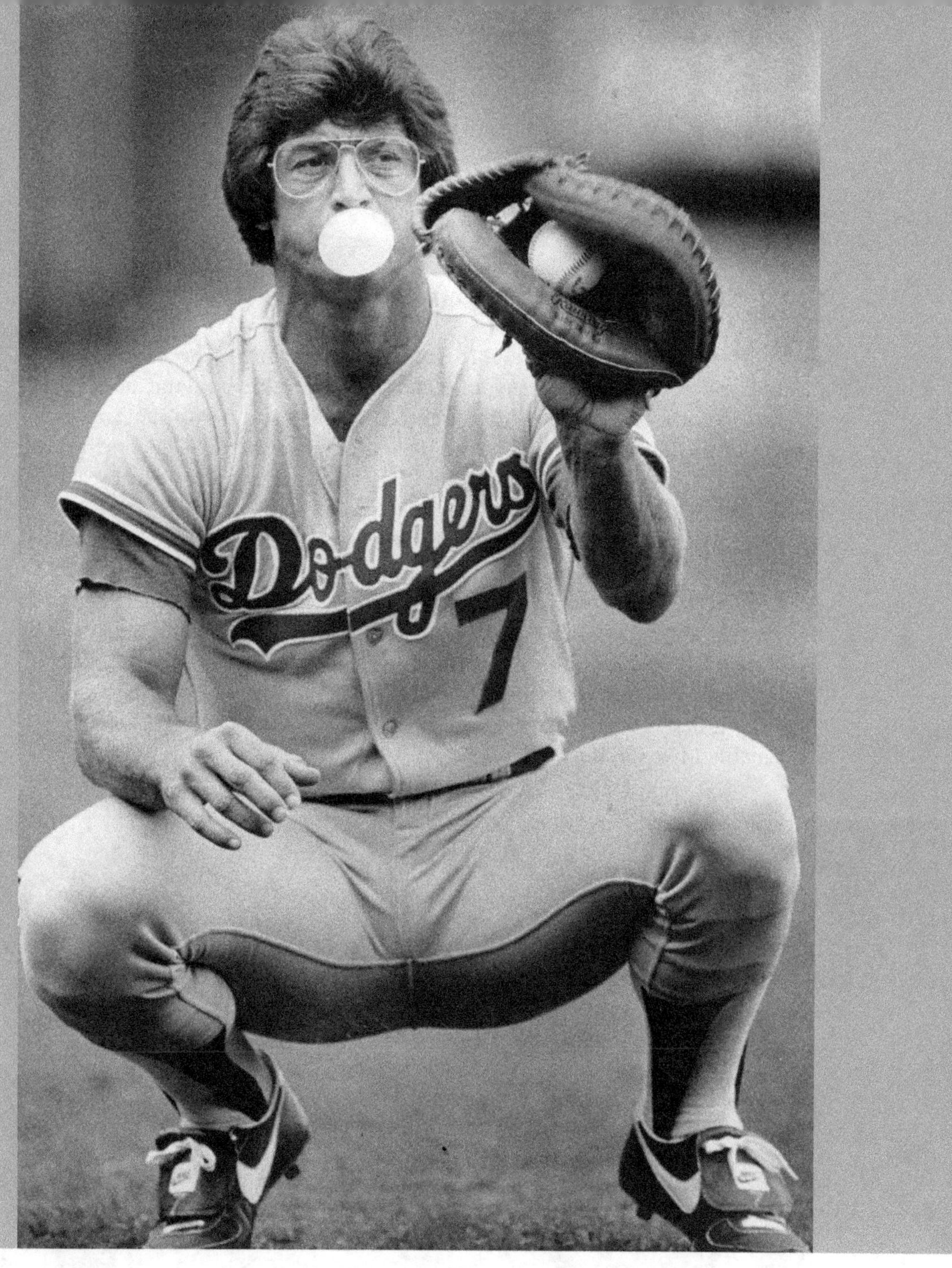

Catcher Steve Yeager practices his bubble-blowing technique.
(Rob Brown/Herald-Examiner Collection)

OPPOSITE: Outfielder Reggie Smith practices his soft-toss.
(Rob Brown/Herald-Examiner Collection)

Dusty Baker: High Five

Major League Baseball brought out greatness in Johnnie B. "Dusty" Baker, then punished him for it.

Recruited straight out of a Sacramento-area high school in 1967 by the Braves, the African American outfielder bore witness to both the racist slurs that rained down on his Atlanta teammate Hank Aaron and Aaron's epic retort of breaking Babe Ruth's home-run record. Baker was traded to the Dodgers for four players in 1975; only after a leg injury and miserable first season did he break out as a slugger in his own right.

In 1977, in the last game of the regular season, L.A. faced the Houston Astros and ace pitcher J.R. Richard. In the sixth inning, with rookie outfielder Glenn Burke on deck, Baker connected with a 395-foot homer that made the Dodgers the first team in Major League Baseball history with four players hitting 30 or more home runs. The exultant raised clap waiting for Baker from Burke was almost instantly returned by Baker after Burke connected off Richard in the very next at-bat with his first career home run.

The high-five was born.

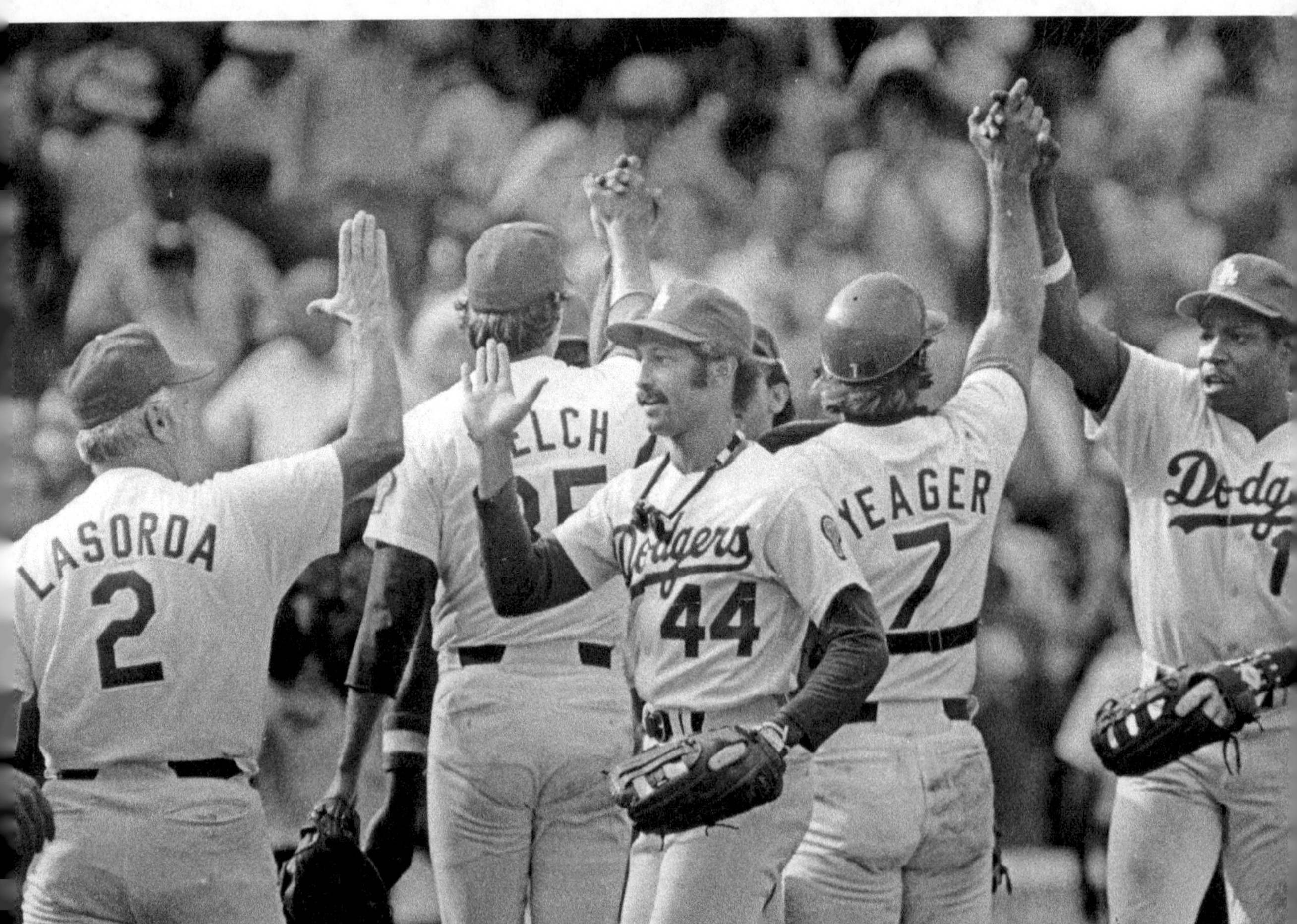

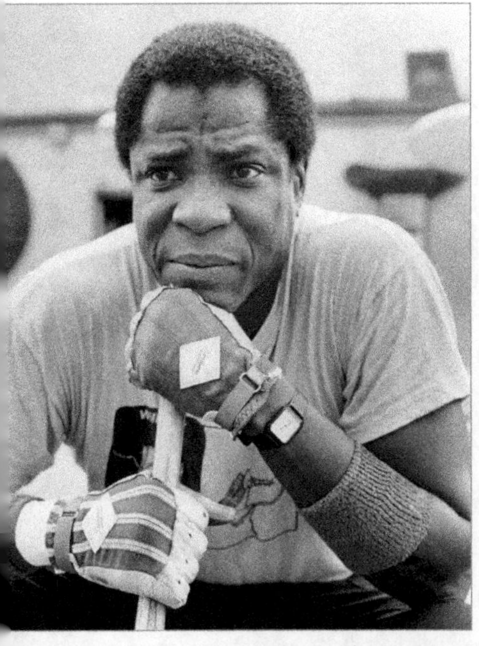

In eight years with Atlanta, another eight with the Dodgers, including the championship '81 season, and another three years split between Oakland and San Francisco, Baker's playing career concluded with 242 home runs, 1,013 RBIs, and 137 stolen bases. Burke was not so fortunate. By the time Baker joined the Giants as a rookie manager in 1993, Burke's brief career was over. The first openly gay player in MLB was homeless in the Castro District and died from AIDS two years later.

If Baker's 22-year managerial career tells us anything about the fickleness of the game of baseball, it's that it's not about how many games you win, but which ones. After taking the Barry Bonds-era Giants to the 2002 World Series before falling to the Angels in Game 7, San Francisco sacked him. Snapped up by the Cubs, Baker took Chicago to the playoffs in 2003 only to be stymied by the Marlins. A stint with Cincinnati was doomed after the Reds squandered a two-game lead over the Giants in the 2012 N.L. Division Series.

The most egregious reward came last. Signed as manager for Washington in 2015 at a fraction of his Cincinnati salary, Baker took over a dysfunctional Nationals franchise that saw closer Jonathan Papelbon try to choke teammate Bryce Harper in the dugout. In two years, Baker's Nationals won two successive division titles. Even Britain's *Guardian* newspaper saluted when, in 2016, Baker and the Dodgers' Dave Roberts became the first two African American managers to face off in the playoffs.

The firing of Baker after the Nationals fell to the Dodgers, then the Cubs, in successive playoff years prompted *Washington Post* columnist Thomas Boswell to wonder aloud about which veteran managers have bettered Baker's career winning percentage of .532? The very short list included three (Joe Torre, Tony La Russa, and Whitey Herzog) who are members of the Baseball Hall of Fame, in large part because they brought home World Series hardware to their team owners.

As trophies and stats fade from memory, the high-five endures. The internationally recognized symbol of jubilation, minted on October 2, 1977, before 46,501 deliriously proud Dodger fans, happened during a game in which Baker and Burke got two of the four hits allowed by Richard—and which the Dodgers lost.

—Emily Green

ABOVE: (Rob Brown/Herald-Examiner Collection)
OPPOSITE: Dusty Baker (*far right*) high-fives catcher Steve Yeager during the 1981 playoffs. (Mike Sergieff/Herald-Examiner Collection)

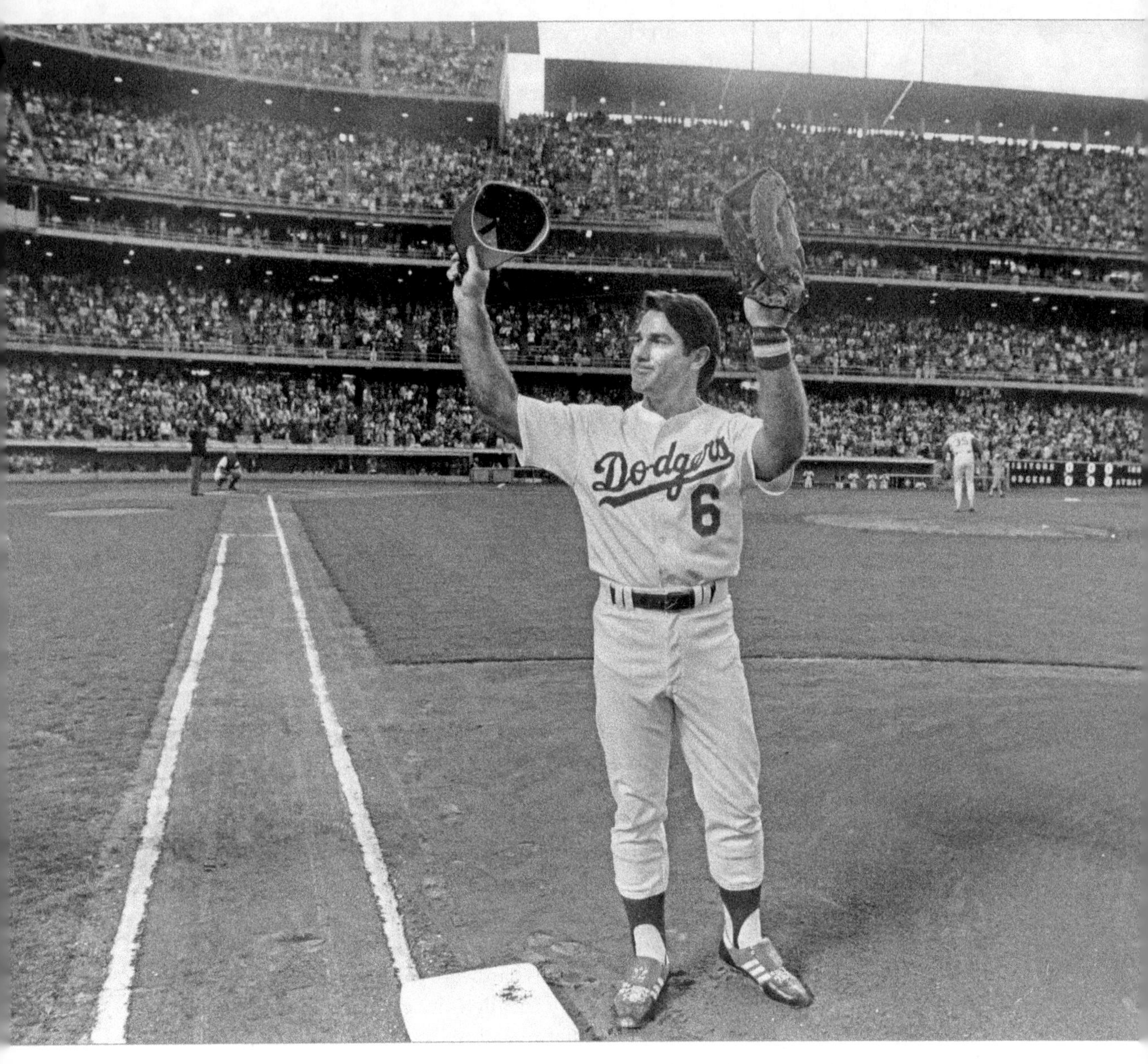

Steve Garvey acknowledges the crowd
as he starts his 1,000th consecutive game in 1982.
(Paul Chinn/Herald-Examiner Collection)

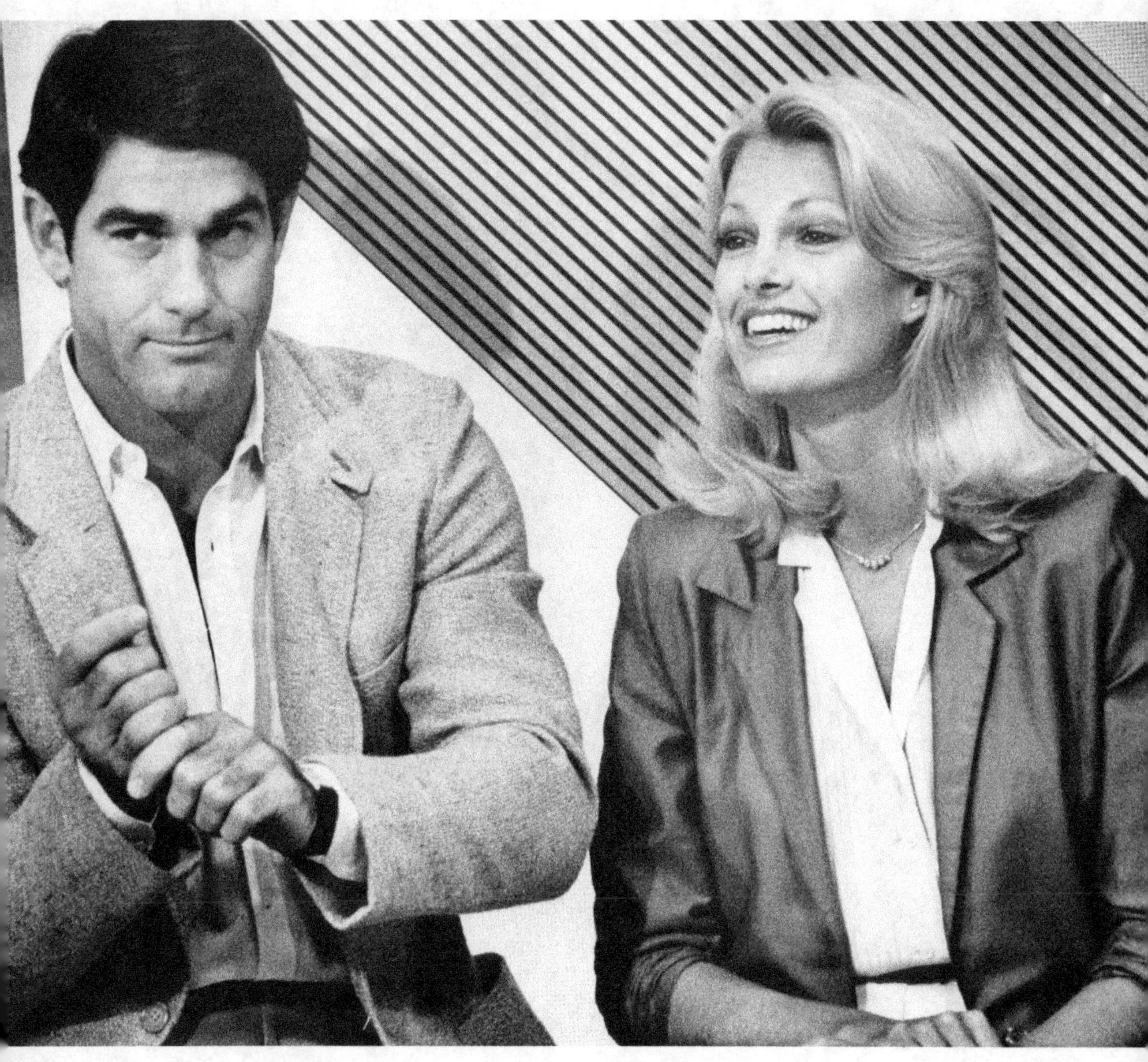

Steve and Cyndy Garvey.
(Mike Sergieff/Herald-Examiner Collection)

PAGE 150 & 151: Second baseman Davey Lopes and shortstop Bill Russell in action during the 1981 World Series.
(Mike Mullen/Herald-Examiner Collection)

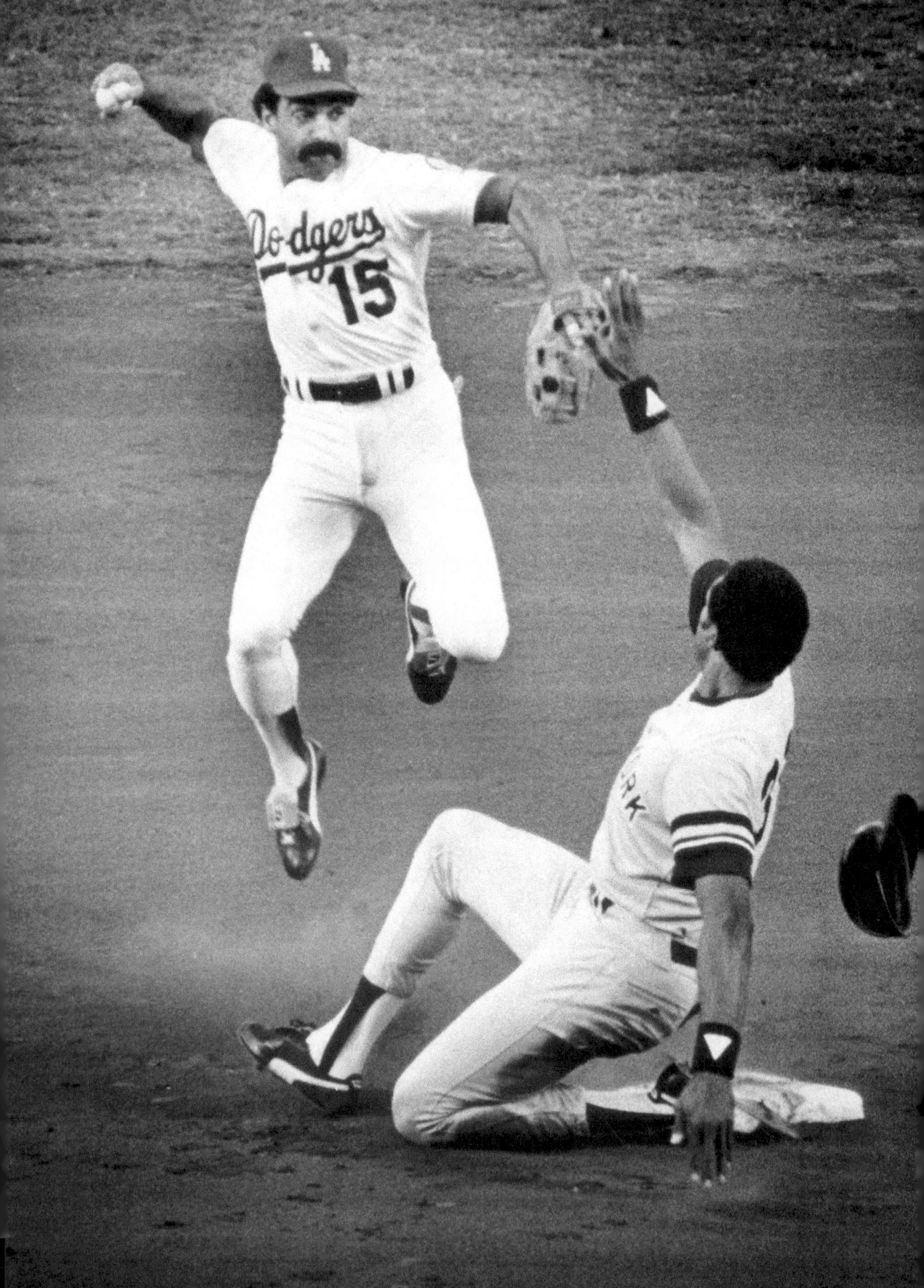
Dodgers
15

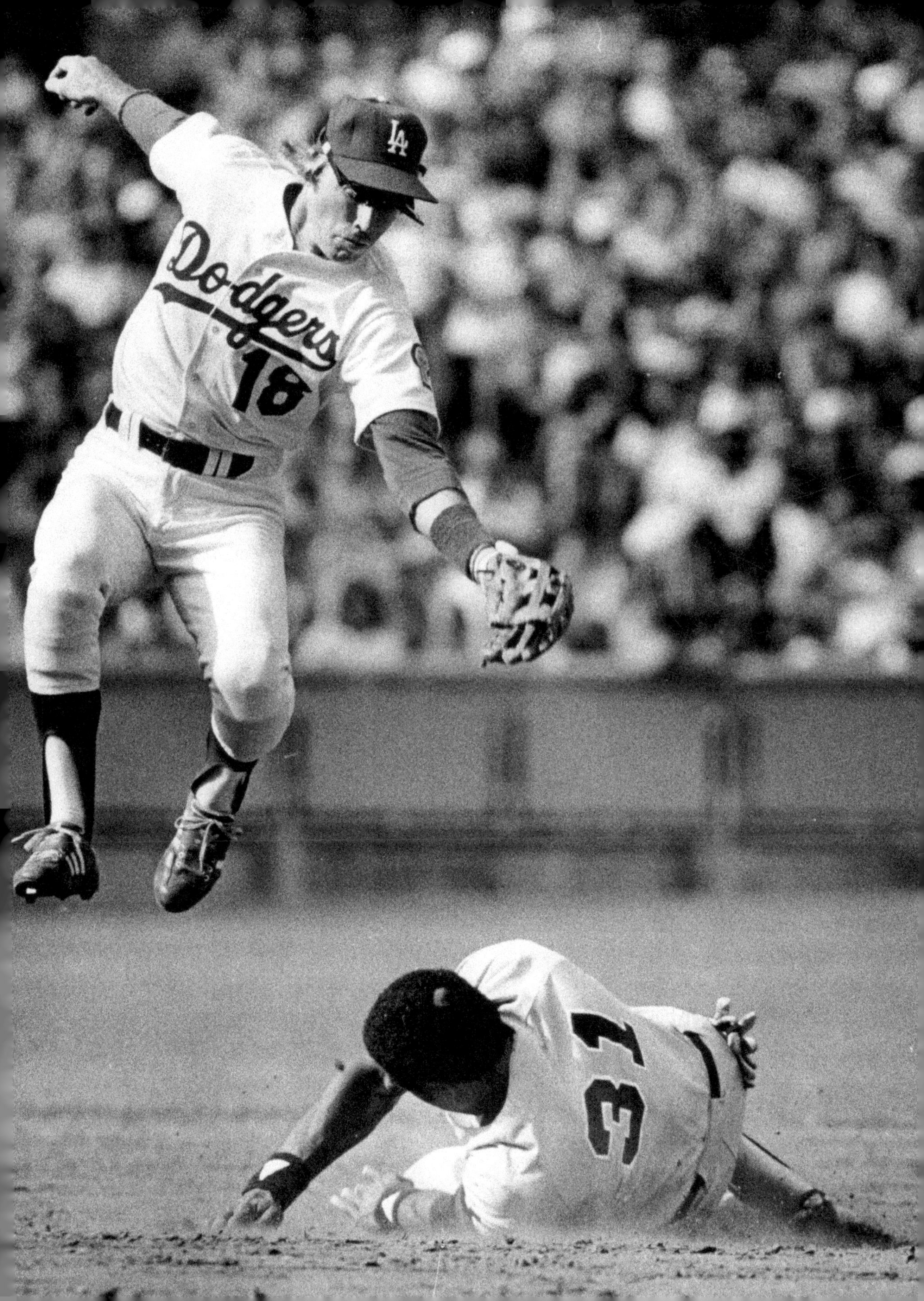
LA
Dodgers
18
31

Ron Cey: El Pinguino

I don't come from a baseball household: the rituals around opening day weren't calendared in; they weren't even on the radar. My father sometimes tuned in to his hometown team, the Pirates, once the playoffs were underway. My brother was more interested in the speed and crush of hockey. My mother tolerated it all as background noise.

I came to baseball on my own, stumbling into it first by way of Vin Scully's voice—thin and tinny over my transistor radio—broadcasting in a leisurely back and forth flow, from a mysterious "Ravine."

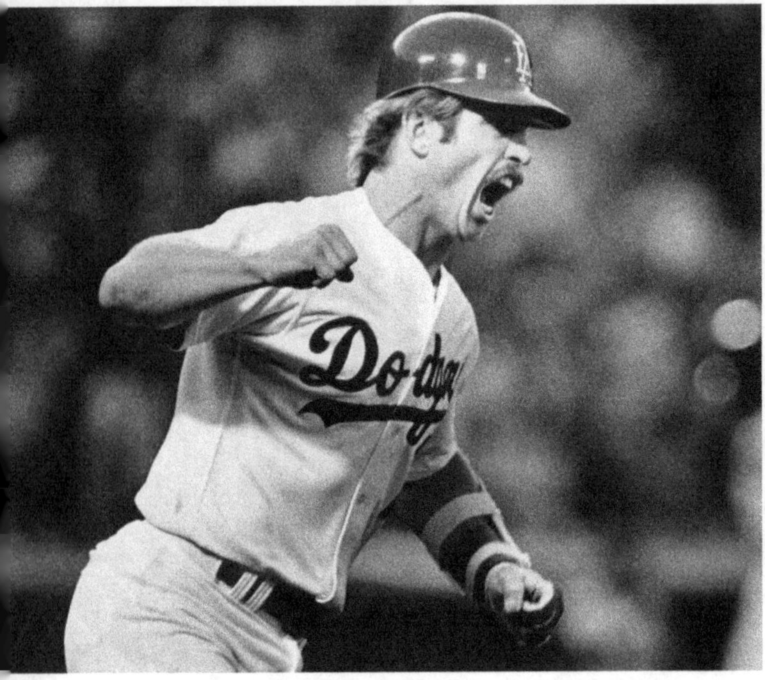

(Rob Brown/Herald-Examiner Collection)

Back then, in the '70s, the Dodgers gifted tickets to Southern California students who maintained a stipulated GPA. You got your name printed in micro-sized type in the newspaper and a pair of tickets. I would finally get to see this storied Ravine. My father ferried the two of us across town to Dodger Stadium. We were perched high over the third-base line with a spectacular crow's-nest view of that green carpet of lawn, the orange-pink blush of the sky as the sun set, and the players drifting back and forth on the field circuiting through wind sprints.

It was my first in-person look at THE infield: Garvey, Lopes, Russell, and Cey. Cey caught my eye because he didn't look like Central Casting's idea of a baseball player. He was sturdy and compact with powerful arms, but he had a poet's gaze. He looked more like the men sitting around me in the stands—men who worked with their hands and were as solid as a tree trunk, their minds on many things, but laser-focused when need be. Seeing Cey move across the field, for the first time I understood the nickname, El Pinguino, that the men behind us bellowed out into the night air at his every at-bat. He had a distinctive lope; a manner in which he shifted his weight as he readied for the pitch. Then too there was the way he gave Dusty Baker a nod, or how, after sending a ball over the wall, he took that leisurely lap home. He wasn't flashy but he was determined. Batting clean-up, he was a bit of a secret weapon. In the clutch, bases loaded, the hometown crowd gathered its force, sent up a chant for El Pinguino.

I became a regular at the Ravine, now conversant in statistics and backstories, sitting amid a diversity of fans rooting for our diverse team, dreaming of a pennant. As seasons passed, I was gifted stuffed and ceramic penguins, which meant my laser-focused curiosity was not just discerned, but deemed official fandom. But the most unexpected keepsake came by way of my "tolerating" mother. A high school teacher, she'd taught Vin Scully's son Michael in her English class and had mentioned in passing that her daughter was a Dodger fan: "She likes that Penguin." The academic year came and went. The next fall, my mother arrived at school to find a large envelope, emblazoned with the Dodger logo, awaiting her in her faculty mailbox. Inside was an 8x10 glossy, a two-paneled portrait and action image of Cey following through on a powerful swing, autographed to me. A generous gift from Mike Scully. I don't know who was more happy to receive this bounty—me or my mother, now newly-christened and invested. Dodger Blue, too.

—Lynell George

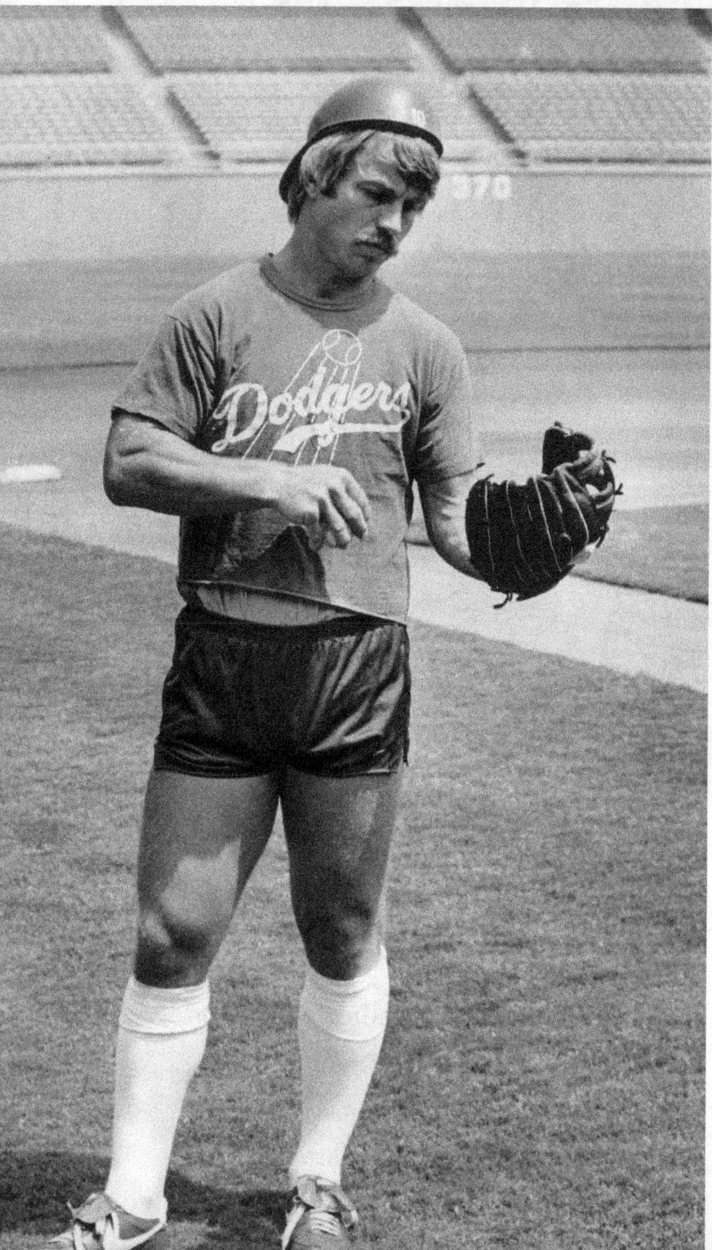

(Mike Sergieff/
Herald-Examiner Collection)

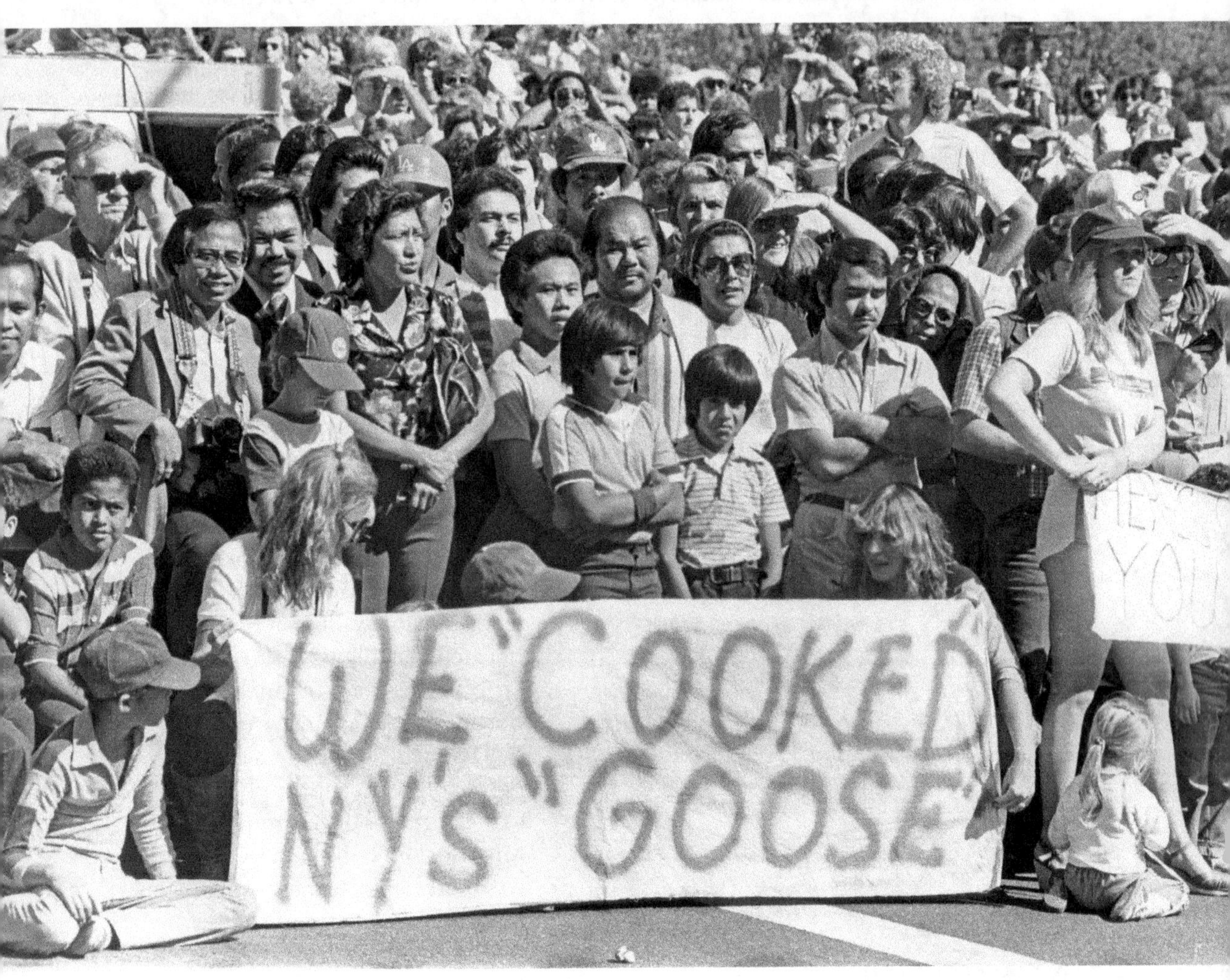

Fans line Broadway at the victory parade after the 1981 World Series. (Mike Mullen/Herald-Examiner Collection)

OPPOSITE: Ron Cey and Steve Garvey wave to the crowd after the Dodgers won the 1981 World Series. (Mike Sergieff/Herald-Examiner Collection)

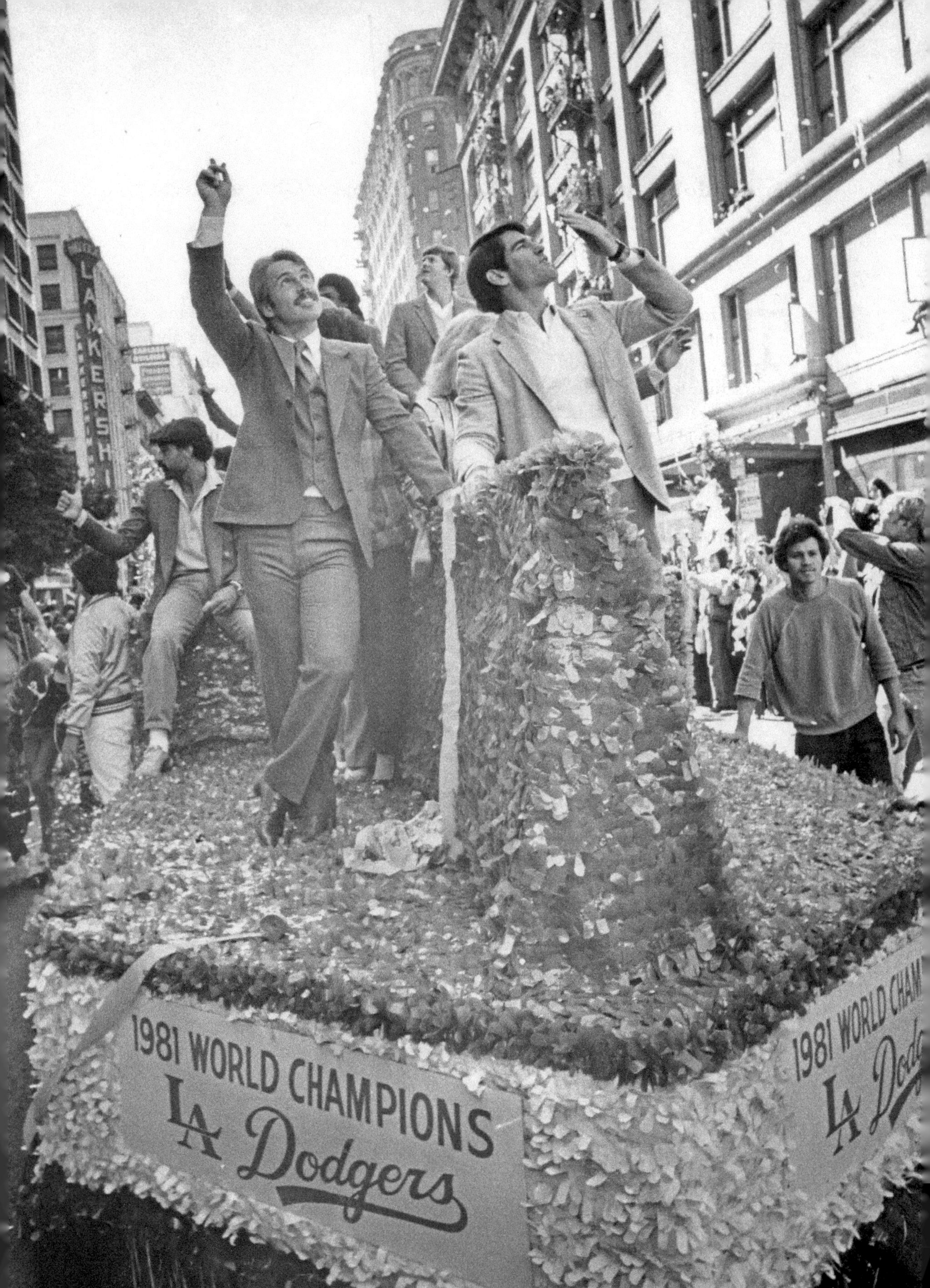
LANKERSHIM
1981 WORLD CHAMPIONS
LA Dodgers
1981 WORLD CHAM
LA Dod

The One

Fernando Valenzuela and the Reconquest of Chavez Ravine

By Tomas J. Benitez

The first game I ever attended at the nearly new Dodger Stadium was Game 4 of the 1963 World Series. Dad surprised me with tickets that morning, and I was so excited I could barely talk. To make it even better, I was going for the first time to see my hero, Sandy Koufax, pitch a game. I grew up in relatively multicultural Boyle Heights. In those days we were already majority Mexican American and Mexicanos, but we still had lots of Jewish and Japanese families, a few whites, including Italians and Russians, some Blacks, and we had a girl on the neighborhood team, the Evergreen Comets, who could throw a ball further and better than any of us! We were all Dodger fans, and we chose our heroes to emulate without regard to race. Larry the Japanese kid wanted to be Willie Davis. Chuck, the Black guy, who we called "Chuck the Black Guy," wanted to be Frank Howard, and Steve Cohen was Junior Gilliam. I was Sandy, and I tried to learn to throw left-handed to make it more so. I ended up playing catcher, but I was Sandy, everybody knew, and no one ever tried to usurp me. Now here I was, sitting in a palace more spectacular than church, watching the World Series, watching legends play, including Mickey Mantle, Yogi Berra, Tommy Davis, Maury Wills, and my beloved Sandy, who won the game and the Series over the Yankees that day.

There were no Latinos on the Dodgers then, and there would not be any for some time to come. As a kid that fact escaped me, but as I got older, especially during the tempestuous late 1960s, when I became a Chicano radical while remaining an avid Dodger fan, it became ever more obvious: there were no Latino—much less Mexican or Chicano—heroes in Dodger Blue. The organization had changed baseball and the nation forever when Jackie Robinson walked onto Ebbets Field in Brooklyn on April 15, 1947, but those of us living in the East L.A. barrio kept asking, seeking, wondering, hoping: Where was OUR Jackie? Where was our #42?

The arrival of the Dodgers in Los Angeles in 1958 essentially signaled the beginning of a new decade and a new metropolis. The world was changing, from Sputnik and television, to a New Frontier led by a young President. Los Angeles was being elevated to big-city status by a matrix of new freeways, the revitalization of Bunker Hill, the expanded harbor, a growing population, and the promise

---

OPPOSITE: Warming up with fans watching every move. (Herald-Examiner Collection)

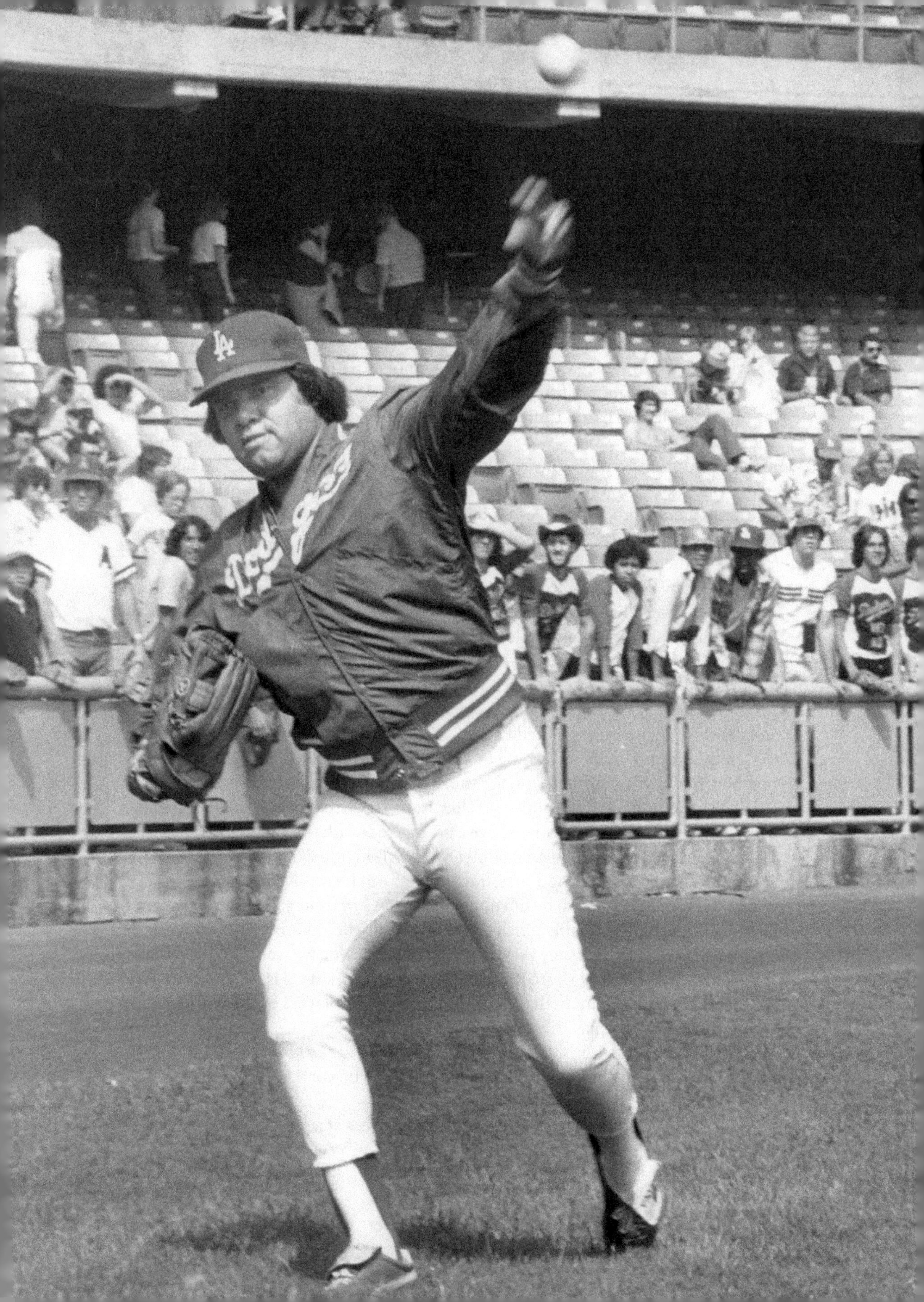

of a new stadium for its new Major League Baseball club. The neighborhood of Chavez Ravine, just north of downtown, had been emptied out under the promise of a huge federal housing project, but the families that lived there were betrayed. The area was in a state of limbo and mostly abandoned. The few families that refused to leave were mostly bought out by the City of Los Angeles, who in turn sold the land to Dodgers owner Walter O'Malley to build the ballpark of his dreams.

Yet, a few stalwarts remained in Chavez Ravine. The ensuing conflict to evacuate those families made national headlines and rallied the Mexican American community, led by City Council member Ed Roybal, who would go on to become a great leader in the U.S. Congress. The Battle for Chavez Ravine was the first important urban skirmish that resonated within the Chicano Movement. The sleeping giant was now "woke," and in the years that followed, the Mexican American/Chicano community would become activated to fight for social justice.

To this day there are still resentments directed at the Dodgers franchise, a sore point among otherwise like-minded comrades and families. But Mexican Americans and Mexicans also love baseball, and thanks to a few World Series victories in their early years, and the wise decision to broadcast the games in Spanish, led by the venerable Jaime Jarrin, the Dodgers became their home team. The wounds over Chavez Ravine left scars, but for most of the burgeoning local community, these eventually healed. Still, Mexicans and Mexican Americans remained for the most part absent on Major League Baseball fields and, more importantly, on home turf at Dodger Stadium.

O'Malley, ever the opportunist, went looking for a "Mexican Sandy Koufax," and the Dodgers early on scouted Latin, Caribbean, and Mexican players. They were at the ground level concerning the Dominican Republic presence that has now become such an influence on the game. But in those days, they managed to overlook a few homegrown ballplayers, like Hank Aguirre, a beanpole from the San Gabriel Valley who went on to have a great career with the Indians and the Tigers. Then there was a kid named Phil Ortega, whom the Dodgers brass hyped as being Hispanic in the early 1960s, but it turned out he was Native American and didn't speak Spanish, and so he did not fit the bill. A few others found their way into the line-up, most notably pinch-hitter extraordinaire Manny Mota from the Dominican Republic, but they were never the one, the one we were looking for, a Mexican or Mexican American. It was not so much a provincial issue, but one of pride and acknowledgement that we had generations of players on both sides of the border who could play this game of baseball.

Then, on the Opening Day of the 1981 season, a chubby kid from rural Mexico walked to the mound at Dodger Stadium and began the Reconquest of Chavez Ravine.

Fernando Valenzuela began his professional career at age 15, pitching for

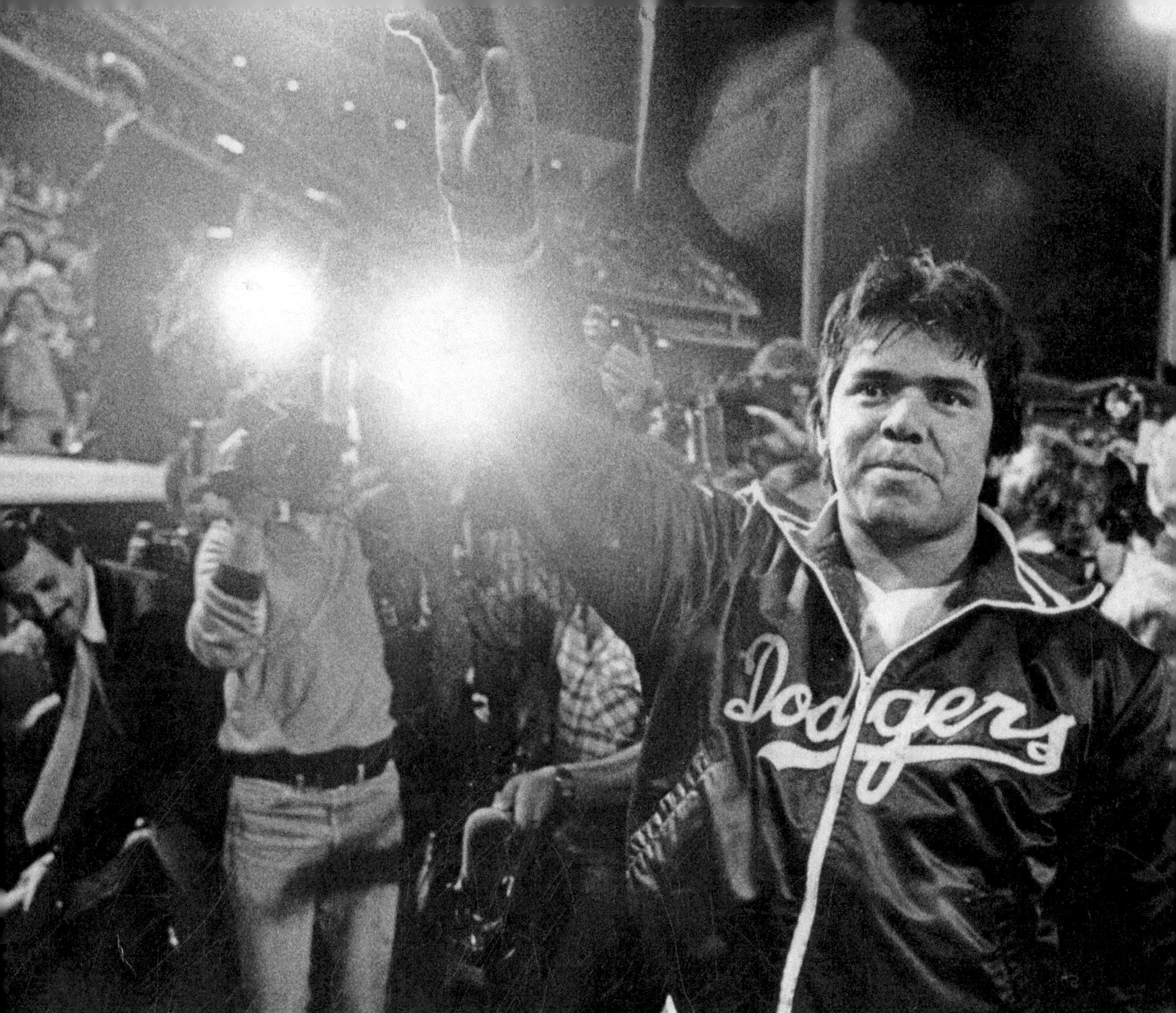

Fernando-mania begins. (Rob Brown/Herald-Examiner Collection)

his hometown of Navojoa, and eventually worked his way up the Mexican professional leagues. The Mexican League had a moment of infamy in the 1940s, when teams drew away a number of star players from Major League Baseball, but for the most part they were a junior circuit and popular only within Mexico itself. By the 1970s, the Dodgers had begun an aggressive campaign to mine talent from South America and the Islands, notably the Dominican Republic and Puerto Rico, and so they had personnel scouring the region. That's where scout Mike Brito found Fernando Valenzuela in 1977.

Brito was impressed by the young southpaw's command and control, his decent fastball and curve, and a few tricks he had learned in five years of knocking around the Mexican leagues. The Dodgers signed Valenzuela in 1979 and brought him into their farm system. That was the same year Fernando met Robert "Babo" Castillo, a local kid from Lincoln Heights who had also been scouted by Brito. It was "Babo" who taught Fernando how to throw a screwball, the pitch that launched his stardom.

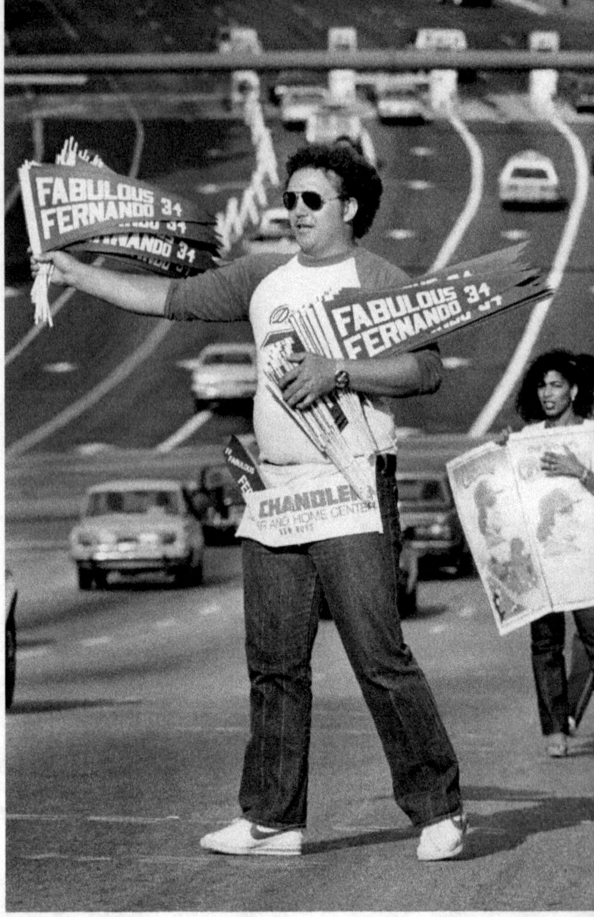

Outside Dodger Stadium.
(Rob Brown/Herald-Examiner Collection)

I remember seeing Castillo walk out to the mound after he had been announced over the p.a. at Dodger Stadium. I figured he was another Latin American player, maybe from Venezuela or Cuba. But when he strode out to the hill, he had "the walk." The walk was everything that told me he was a boy from East Los. A homeboy.

"Babo" will always be a footnote in Dodger history, but he may be the most critical person in the rise of Valenzuela. He befriended the shy kid from Mexico and worked with him to perfect his money pitch. Fernando threw the screwball with such command that he saved ten games in 1980, his rookie season, as the Dodgers fought neck and neck with the Houston Astros for the pennant. For his reward, Babo was exiled to Minnesota, where he had a modicum of success for a couple of years. But not before it happened that a Mexican and a Mexican American joined forces to change the game of baseball.

Beer companies and other American corporations had declared the 1980s as the "Decade of the Hispanic." Little did they know that there would be a public sports figure who lived up to the marketing slogan. When Valenzuela came on the scene, he became the immediate recipient of a series of nicknames. "El Indio" because of his straight black hair flowing out from under his pulled-down baseball cap. "El Torito" ("Little Bull") because of his stocky build. "El Zurdo" because he was left-handed. "El Niño" because of his baby face and shy demeanor. Each one of these nicknames was a love tap, carrying both the implied insult and affection common within Mexican culture. And, he was quickly embraced. As soon as he was discovered to be Mexican, he got long and loud cheers with each appearance as he helped the Dodgers catch the Astros.

He wasn't a star yet. He was just getting to be known. But word was spreading: we had our guy in Dodger Blue at last. The One.

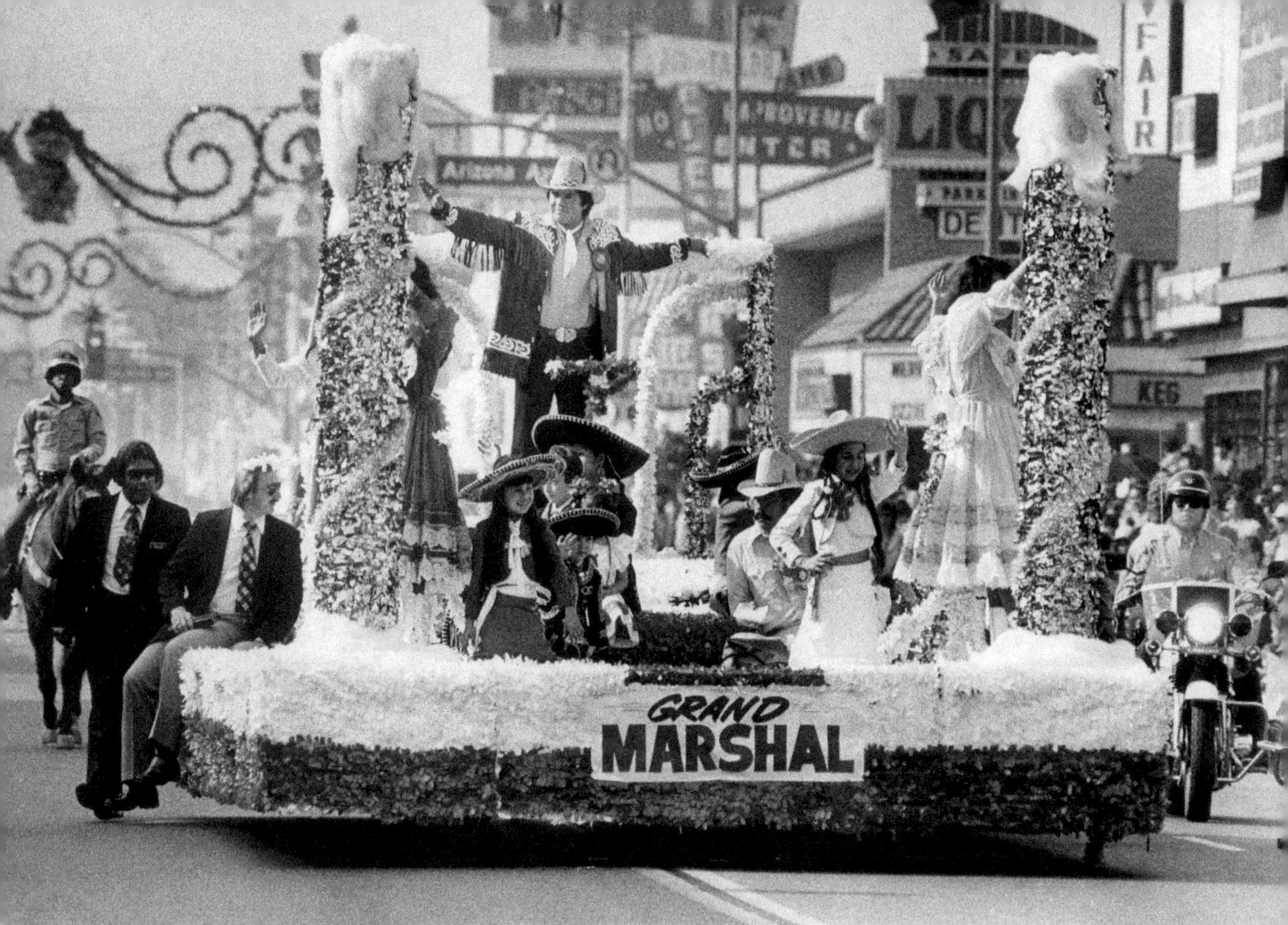

The Grand Marshall of East L.A.'s annual parade, 1981.
(Paul Chinn/Herald-Examiner Collection)

Fernando did himself few favors. He was painfully shy, did not speak any English, and was reticent to utter more than a few words. Ross Porter, one of the Dodgers announcers, complained to Jaime Jarrin that the kid wouldn't open up. "Si, no, si, no, that's all he says!" cried Porter. So Jarrin offered, "Next time you talk to him and he answers with yes or no, ask him 'por que?,' or 'why?' Maybe that will get him to talk a little bit more."

Porter saw his chance a few games later. He asked Fernando a question, to which Valenzuela replied "Si." Porter pounced: "Por que?" Fernando shrugged his shoulders and replied, "Porque si!" ("because"). Porter gave up.

In 1981, Valenzuela's first full season, the Dodgers' starting rotation was anchored by Jerry Reuss, a big, tall, blond Nordic god in a baseball uniform, and a helluva pitcher. Reuss was expected to get the ball on Opening Day. But when he came up lame, manager Tom Lasorda surprised everyone by calling on young Fernando (age 20) to go to the mound in his stead.

Valenzuela had earned accolades from his year-end success in 1980, and had enjoyed a great spring training. But the Dodgers' Latino Nation fan-base had

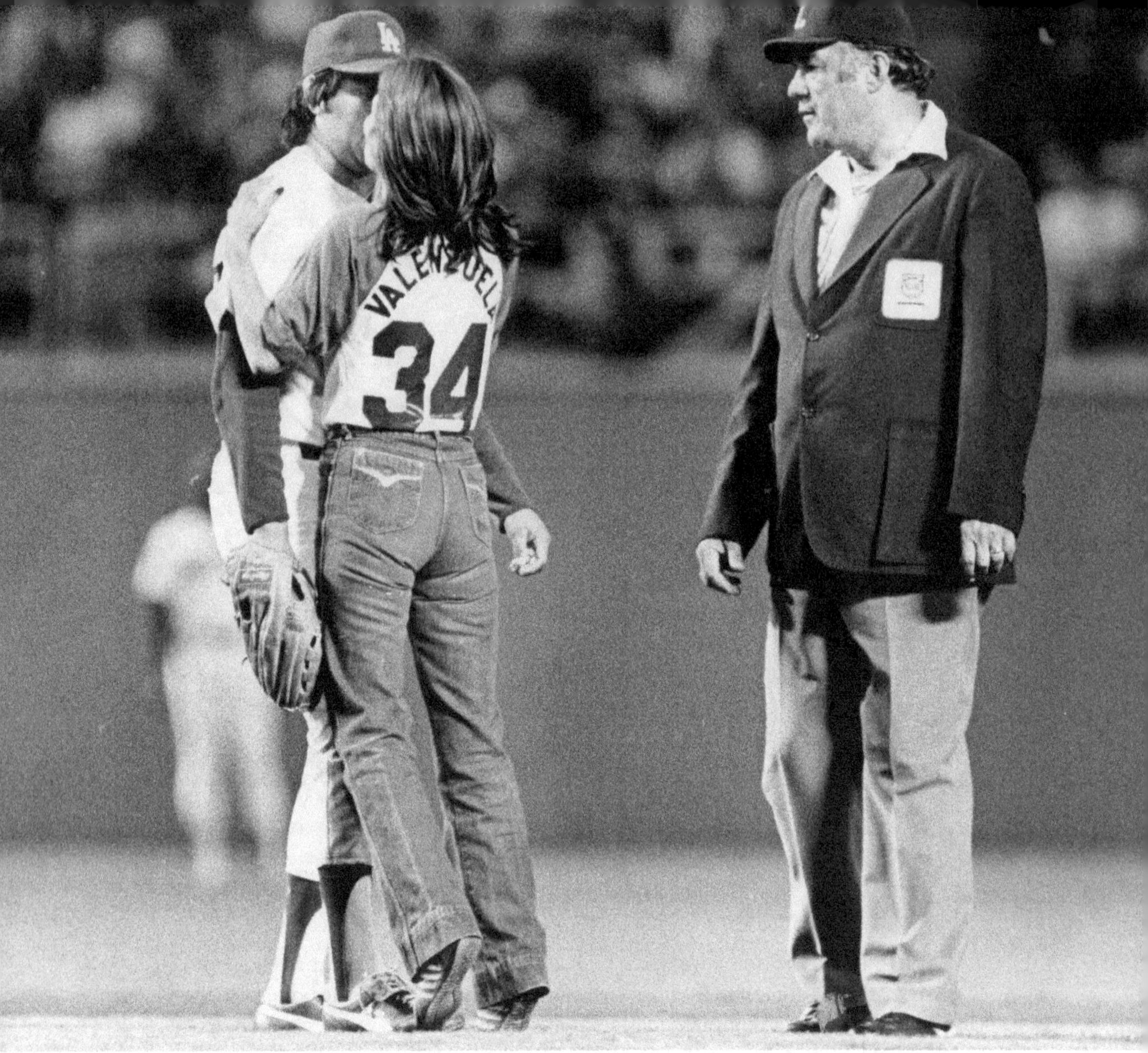

Dodger fan Norma Echevarra ran onto the field to show her appreciation.
(Paul Chinn/Herald-Examiner Collection)

yet to see him in the spotlight. Opening Day was sold out, as usual, but now the scramble for tickets became a frenzy. When I arrived at the stadium there must have been over ten thousand fans running around and trying to buy tickets off the fortunate ticket-holders. I heard English and Spanish pleas and bribes, offers of hundreds of dollars for the two tickets I had purchased for less than ten dollars each.

But I knew I wouldn't be missing this game. It was in the air: something special was about to happen. We got there early, and the place was already packed. In the left-field stands, ground zero for the most rabid, loudest Mexican and

Mexican American fans, the party had already started. I took a free beer offered from a fellow Dodger fan who spoke to me only in Spanish. He quickly uncovered that I was a "pocho," a Mexican American who struggled with the language. But being called a "pocho" that day was not meant as a pejorative; it was a sign of camaraderie. We were cousins that afternoon. We were there for the same reason, to see our boy.

Being a Mexican American sports fan has its own built-in dichotomy. We cheer for the Lakers, but we also cheer for Mexico's national soccer team. We cheer for the USA in the Olympics, but we watch to see if any Mexican athlete might get a medal, any medal, or if there is a Mexican American on any of the teams fielded by the red, white and blue. Fernando wasn't born in East Los, but he was an adopted homeboy, a Mexicano, a close enough relative to be loved by both sides of border brothers. And he was a tubby kid, adorably plain and stoic, a scruffy hairdo, a funny looking body. He was one of us. In baseball, it's not the size of the man that counts. It's his ability to play, it's his heart and skills, it's his talent for the game, period. Fernando had all of that, and he was on the hill, Opening Day.

"Aqui estamos" was what echoed in the stands: "We are here." Even a broken Spanish-speaking "pocho" like myself understood what it meant. He was there, out there, but WE had arrived. WE were here.

Following the pre-game ceremonies, Fernando came out from the bullpen where he had been loosening up and walked to the mound. He took his few last warm-up pitches, and then the home-plate ump cried out, "Play Ball!" A roar went up, and he hadn't tossed a pitch yet. I cried. I felt embarrassed, but when I looked around, other people were cheering and crying, too. He meant that much in that moment. The sun above was beating down on a new day for us.

He settled quickly into the battle like it was any other game, and he proceeded to shut out the hated Astros, 2-0, allowing only five hits. He had an endearing and unorthodox pitching style, rolling his eyes upward during his wind-up. He looked like the angel at the feet of the Virgen de Guadalupe, always looking to the heavens. People in the stands imitated him immediately during the whole game, laughing at each other in celebration. Later, I remember climbing the steps to the top of the bleachers and looking down into the parking lot below—and seeing that the crowd that couldn't get into the stadium had not gone home. In fact, their numbers had grown! There was a fiesta outside, an impromptu tailgate party with lots of beer, and you could hear Vin Scully in the air from all the car radios. Back inside, you could hear Vinny without effort, from all the small transistor radios surrounding us.

Afterwards, people did not leave the stands right away. They lingered and talked to each other, Mexicans and Mexican Americans, hanging out to celebrate their victory, crossing their own borders. When we finally exited the stadium,

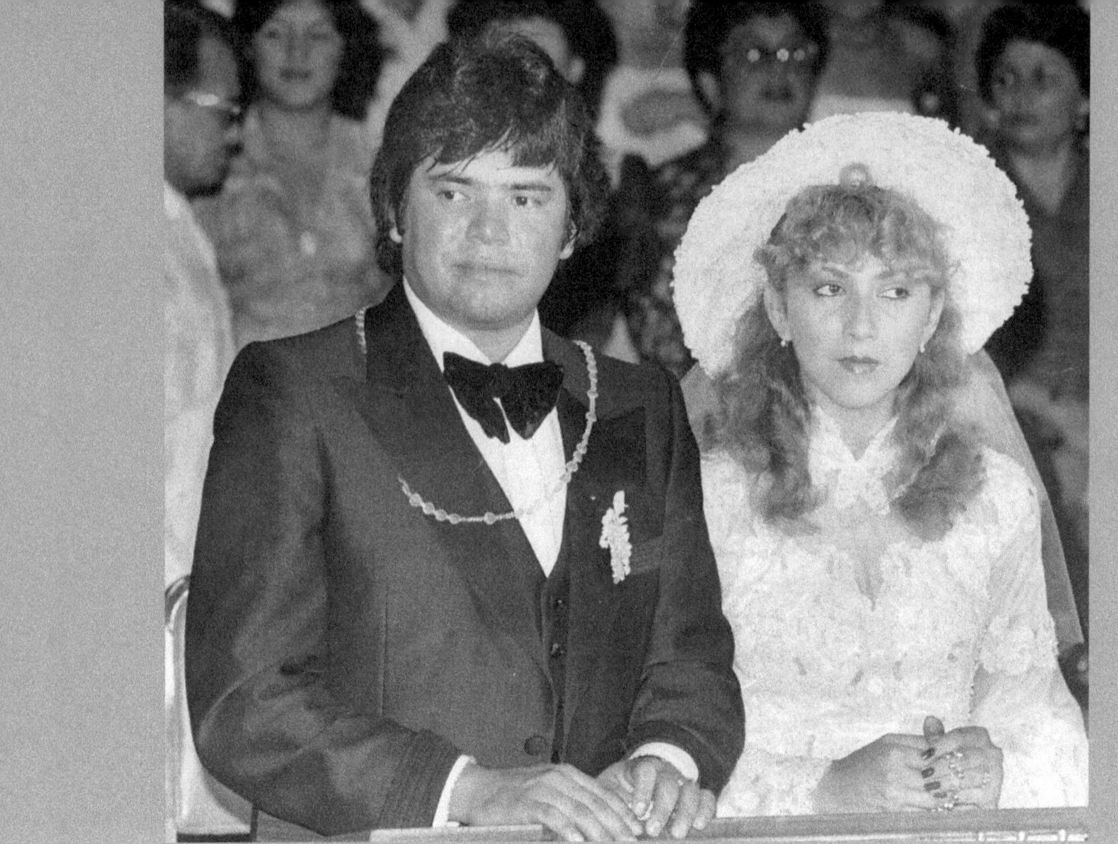

Wedding Day with wife Linda. (Rob Brown/Herald-Examiner Collection)
OPPOSITE: Working hard at working out.
(Rob Brown/Herald-Examiner Collection)

there was another sign that things were different. As if by magic, vendors were in the parking lot, selling Fernando T-shirts and ball caps, merchandise and memorabilia. The Dodgers' heralded marketing machine had been caught flat-footed, while industrious Mexicanos were out there hustling. Everything they sold was contraband, unlicensed, and yet impossible to stop. They all sold out. I got my Fernando Tee and cap, sure. Still have them. And, the ticket stub from that game, which has since been displayed in three museum exhibitions so far. It was a special day at Dodger Stadium. Fernando-mania had begun.

Driving home, the honking horns were a cacophony of jubilation, and irritating as hell, but it was to be expected. Dodger Blue was being flown out of car windows, people were yelling at each other car to car, people were happy. I suspect a few non-Latinos might have been a bit frightened, but everybody got home just fine. At a restaurant on Brooklyn Avenue (now called Cesar Chavez Avenue), the place was as packed and as loud as I ever witnessed. Everybody was wearing Dodger shirts and hats. Blankets, ponchos, and a couple of sombreros were spied above the crowd. How the hell did that happen so fast? It was only the first game of the season!

You'd a-thunk Mexico had won the World Cup, but it was the all-American

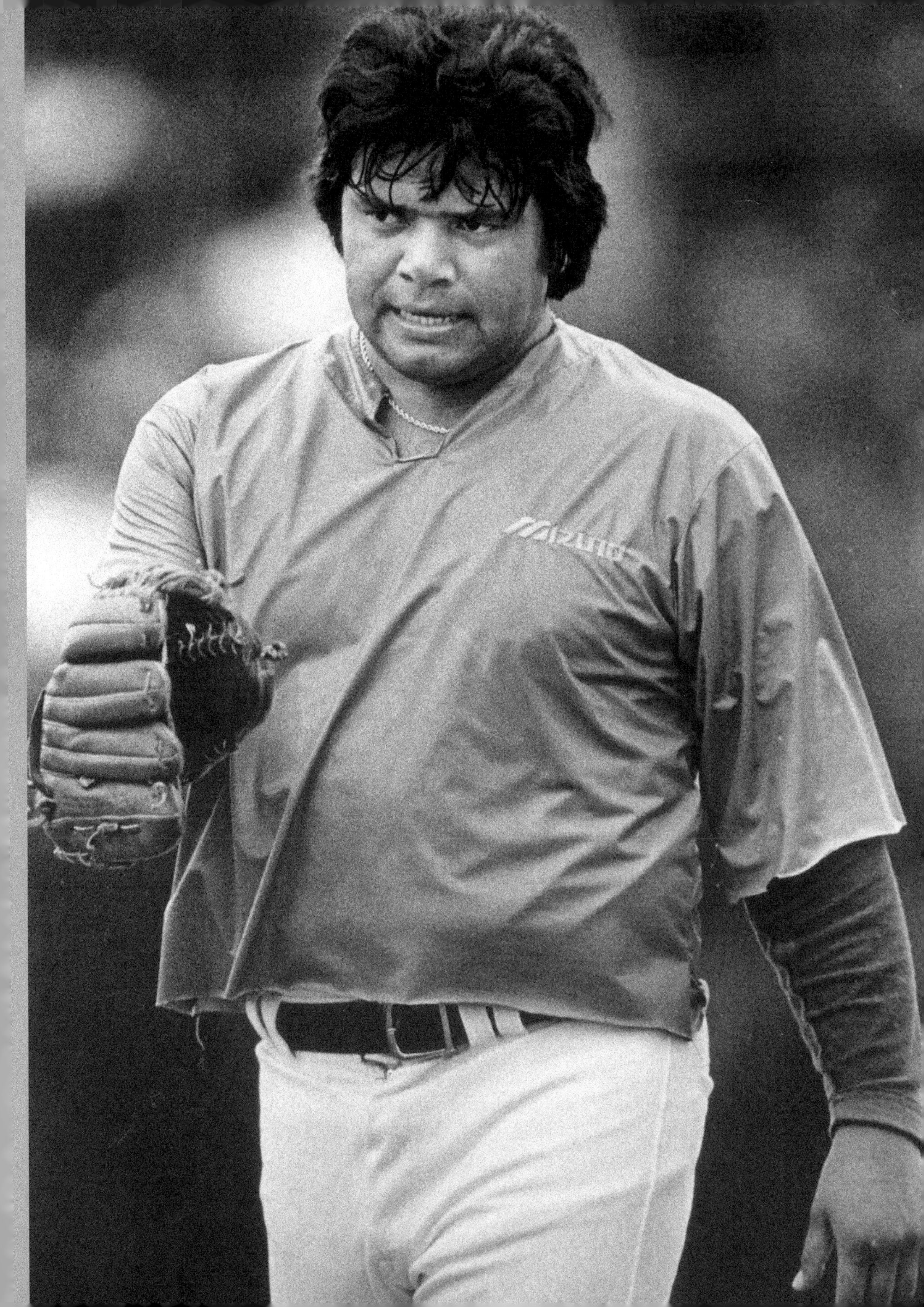

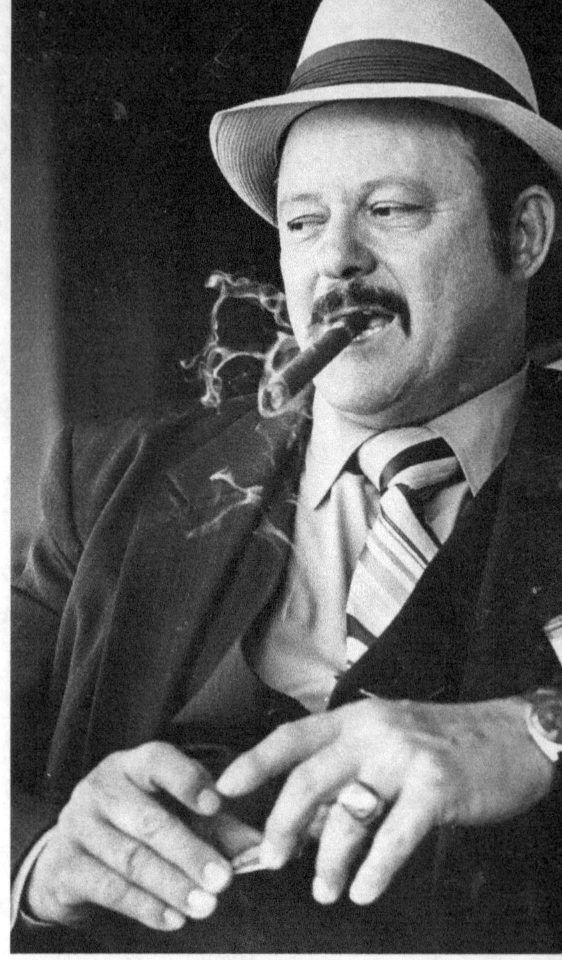

Scout Mike Brito is credited with discovering Valenzuela in the Mexican Leagues. (Rob Brown/Herald-Examiner Collection)

game of baseball being celebrated by Mexicans and Mexican Americans in a way that would signal the rise of a fan-base that is now the largest segment of the Dodgers' audience. Chavez Ravine had been reclaimed.

Over the next few games, Fernando threw a series of shutouts and had some brilliant starts, vaulting him onto the cover of *Sports Illustrated* and becoming a national sensation in the baseball world. When he pitched in cities with large Mexican and Mexican American communities, he filled the house, and it seemed as if the majority seated that day were in Dodger blue cheering him on. I went to a Padres game in San Diego, and that night the majority of the crowd was not only Mexican and Mexican American, but Dodger fans chasing away the hapless locals. Fernando finally proved human and lost a game, but his popularity continued to grow. Spanish-language radio played several tunes immortalizing him that had been quickly recorded, and an unauthorized mural by the East Los Streetscapers went up on a wall on Sunset on the way to the park. Photos of his face appeared in every window up and down Brooklyn Avenue in East L.A.

The 1981 season was one to remember, even though it was shortened by a strike in the middle of the year. When the teams resumed play, Fernando carried on and eventually won not only Rookie of the Year but the Cy Young Award for the best pitcher in baseball. He pitched huge victories in the playoffs, but his most critical and defining moment was in Game 3 of the World Series against the despised Yankees. (Nothing short of irony here.)

New York was up two games to none, and the Dodgers were on the brink of being swept away. When Fernando took the mound in Chavez Ravine, it was clear from the first inning he was struggling with his control. His face was as stoic as it ever had been, but his body language gave away his frustration with his performance. The Dodgers fell behind, but Lasorda kept Fernando in and he just battled. Every pitch was met with bated breath, every swing was dreaded, but he carried on, sweating and grinding, and he inspired his team to come from behind and win the game, 5-4, with a complete-game performance. The Dodgers would

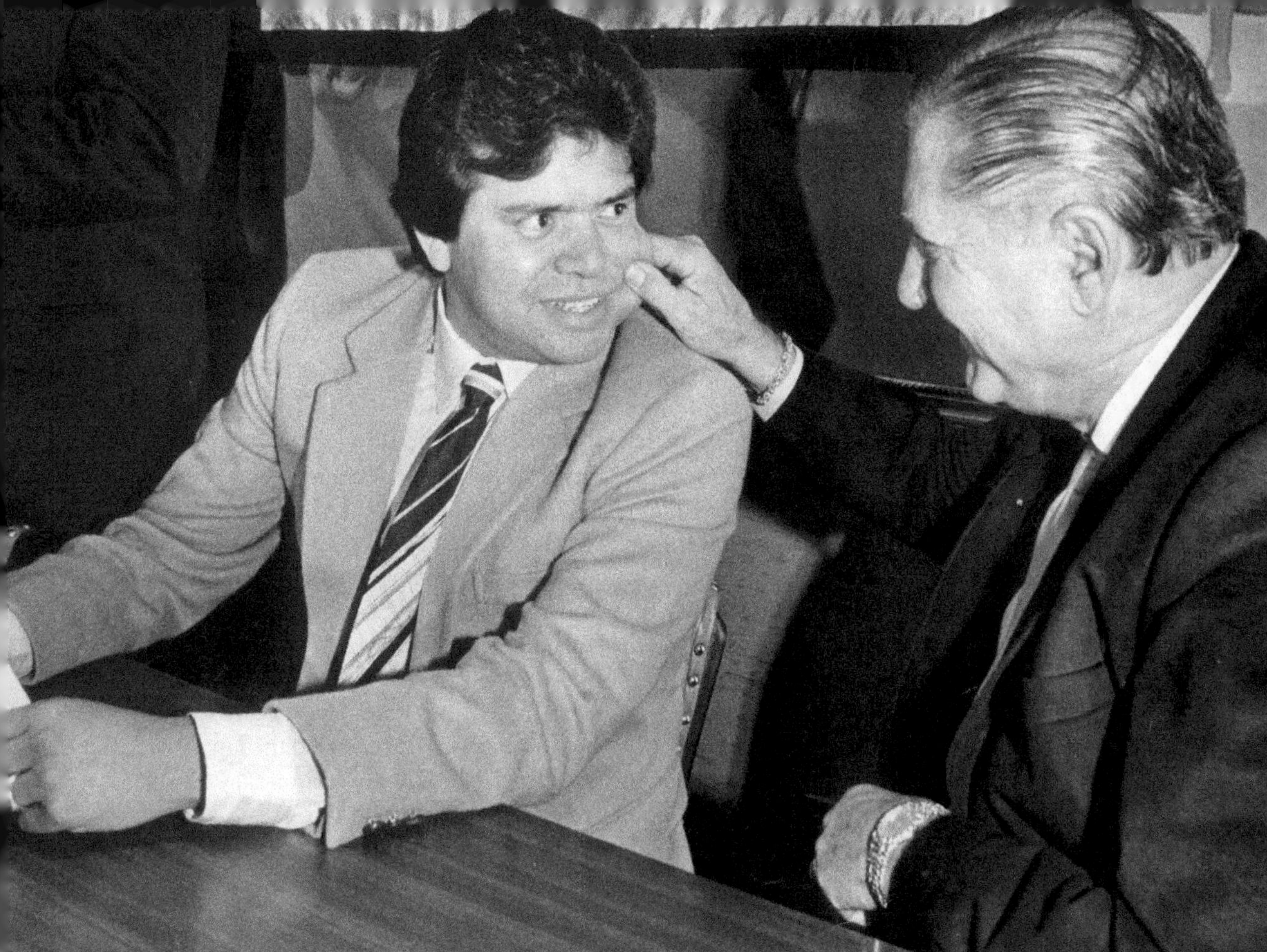

Signing a new contract with general manager Al Campanis.
(James Ruebsamen/Herald-Examiner Collection)

eventually defeat the Yankees and win the World Series. The season had been delivered by "El Niño."

Valenzuela went on to have a stellar career with the Dodgers, including several more winning seasons, league championships, another World Series title in 1988 (although he was injured), and a no hitter, a pitcher's finest individual achievement. His arm was finally pitched out, something Lasorda tended to do with pitching talent, and he was unceremoniously released in 1991, causing a rift with the Dodgers that would last several years. He knocked around the game a few more years, logging short stints for six other teams until his retirement in 1997. He ended up playing for a couple of Mexican teams until he could no longer throw, a box-office draw even in small towns.

Fernando-mania may have been over, but his popularity never waned. He returned to the Dodgers fold after his playing days and, in an ironic twist from those who remembered his "si-no" days, became a radio announcer and a color commentator on Spanish-language TV broadcasts. People who know nothing about baseball know his name. He is still one of the most recognizable and popular icons in the community. He paved the way for new stars, like Nomar Garciaparra and Adrian Gonzalez, to take up the mantle for Latinos wearing Dodger Blue. A young prospect named Alex Verdugo might be next, but whoever it is he will be only the next one, not the first one.

Throughout Valenzuela's career, Major League Baseball also witnessed another phenomenon: the Latinization of the game. More and more players hail from South and Latin America, including Cuba, stars who bring a style and swagger to the game that has not been seen, much less condoned, before. Whether this shift was triggered by Fernando-mania or simply the decision of owners to revitalize the game that had been waning is a matter of debate. But the Latino presence, on the field and in the stands, is undeniable. As that population has grown into an economic force in the nation, and as the impact of the ballyhooed "Hispanic Market" has become a reality, the support from the ever-growing Latino fan-base is undeniable (despite meteoric climbs in ticket prices).

Consider: When Frank McCourt temporarily held the franchise hostage in the aughts, Latinos who were unhappy with the owner's greedy reach led the fan boycott. Around this time the moniker "Los Doyers" took hold as a subliminal protest against this highly unpopular, short-term owner. The initial T-shirt and merchandise brandishing Los Doyers was once again genuine contraband, unlicensed, and readily available; three adult Tees cost $25 on Olvera Street. The Dodgers tried to serve an injunction to cease and desist, only to fail miserably, and then they began to market their own Los Doyers products. If you can't beat 'em, join 'em.

In a world where there are two worlds, Fernando Valenzuela erased the lines between those two worlds—between the Mexican and Mexican American communities—and made it easier for both sides to crossover. His presence made it easier for the outside world, the larger society, to recognize Mexican culture as a viable part of the American landscape, and, most certainly, as a cultural motherboard of contemporary Los Angeles. He changed our city forever and made it a better place to live. That was Fernando Valenzuela. The One.

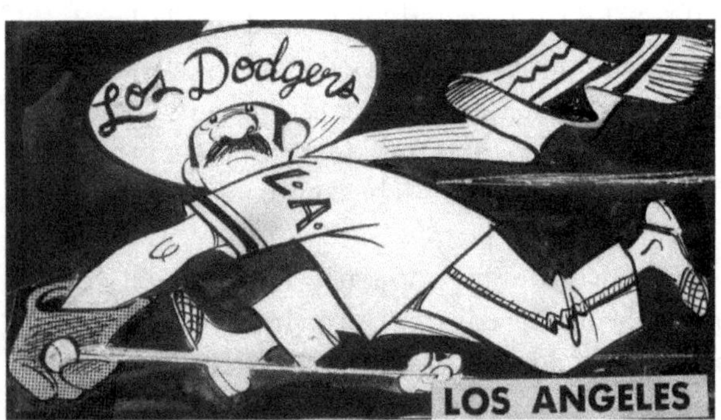

Artist unknown. (Herald-Examiner Collection)

OPPOSITE: (Rob Brown/Herald-Examiner Collection)

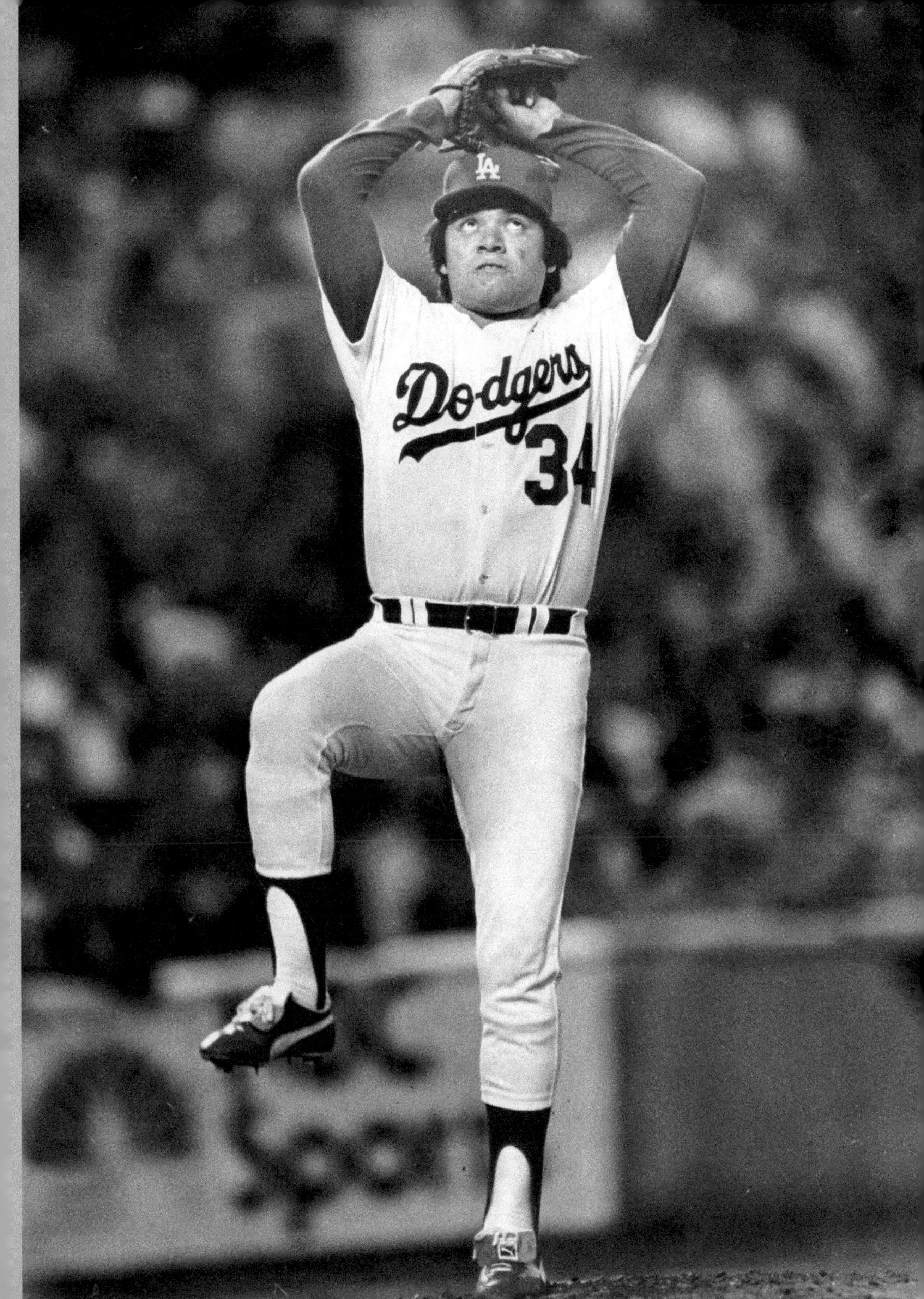
LA
Dodgers
34

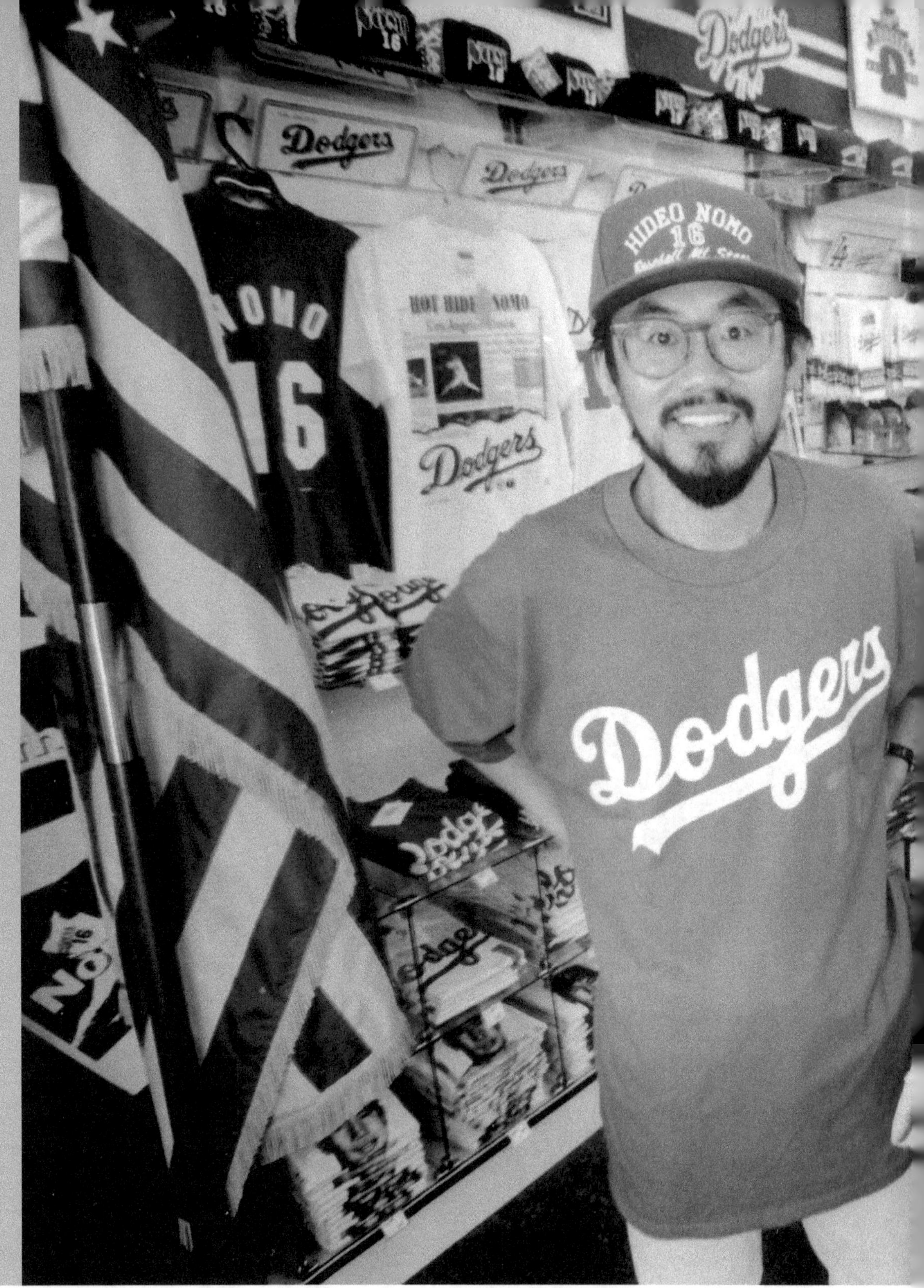

What followed Fernando-mania?

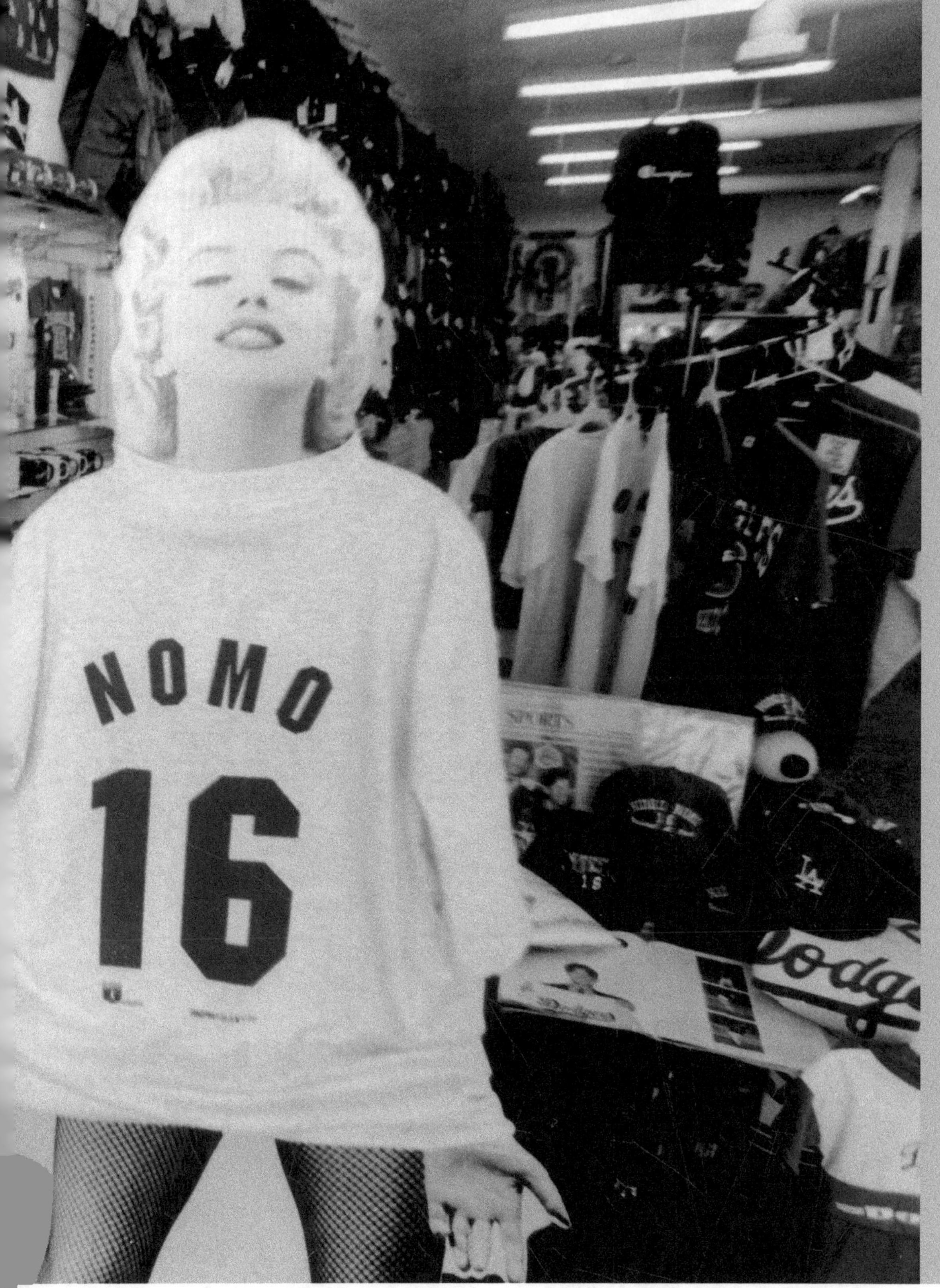

Nomo-mania, for Japanese pitcher Hideo Nomo. (Gary Leonard)

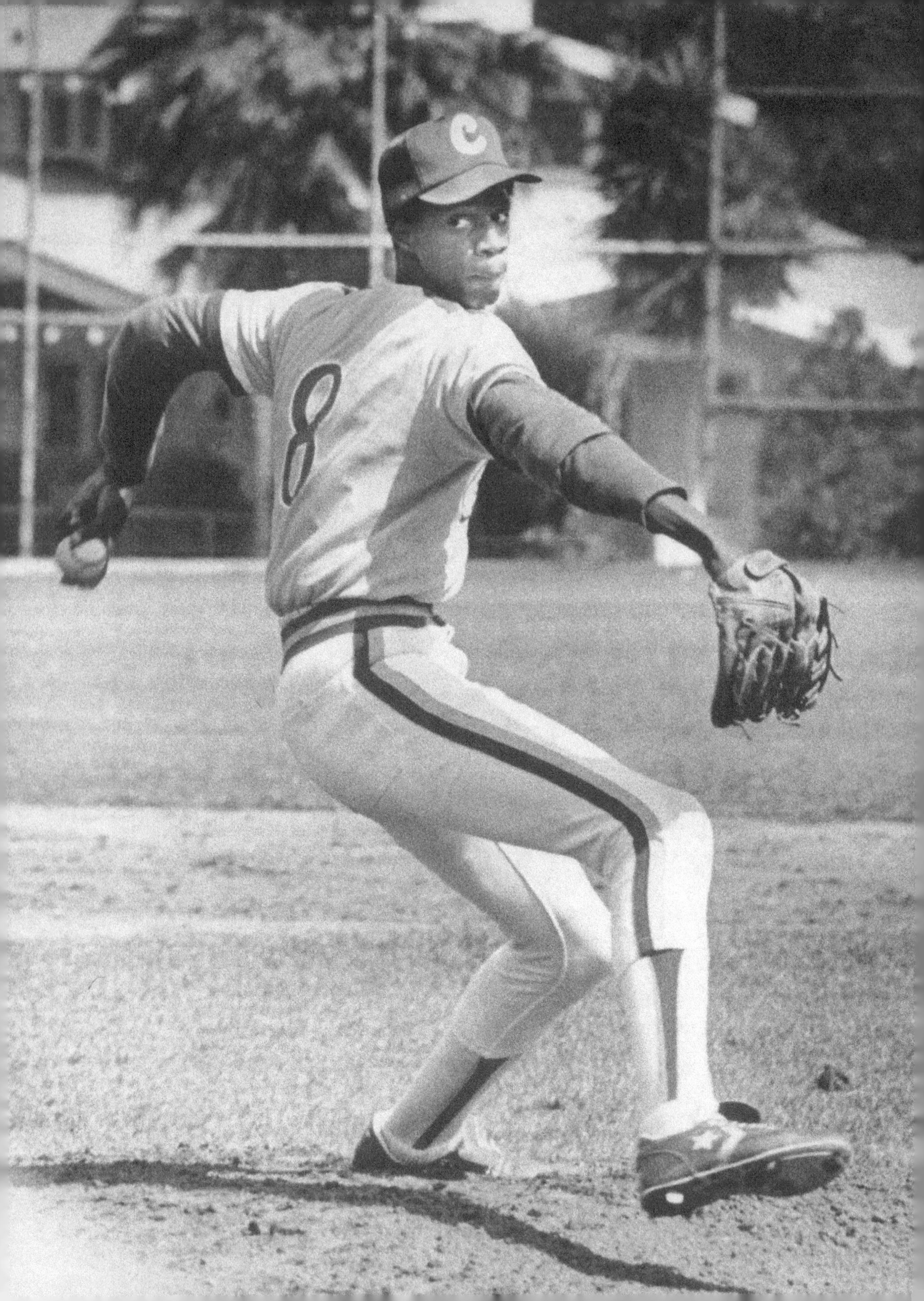

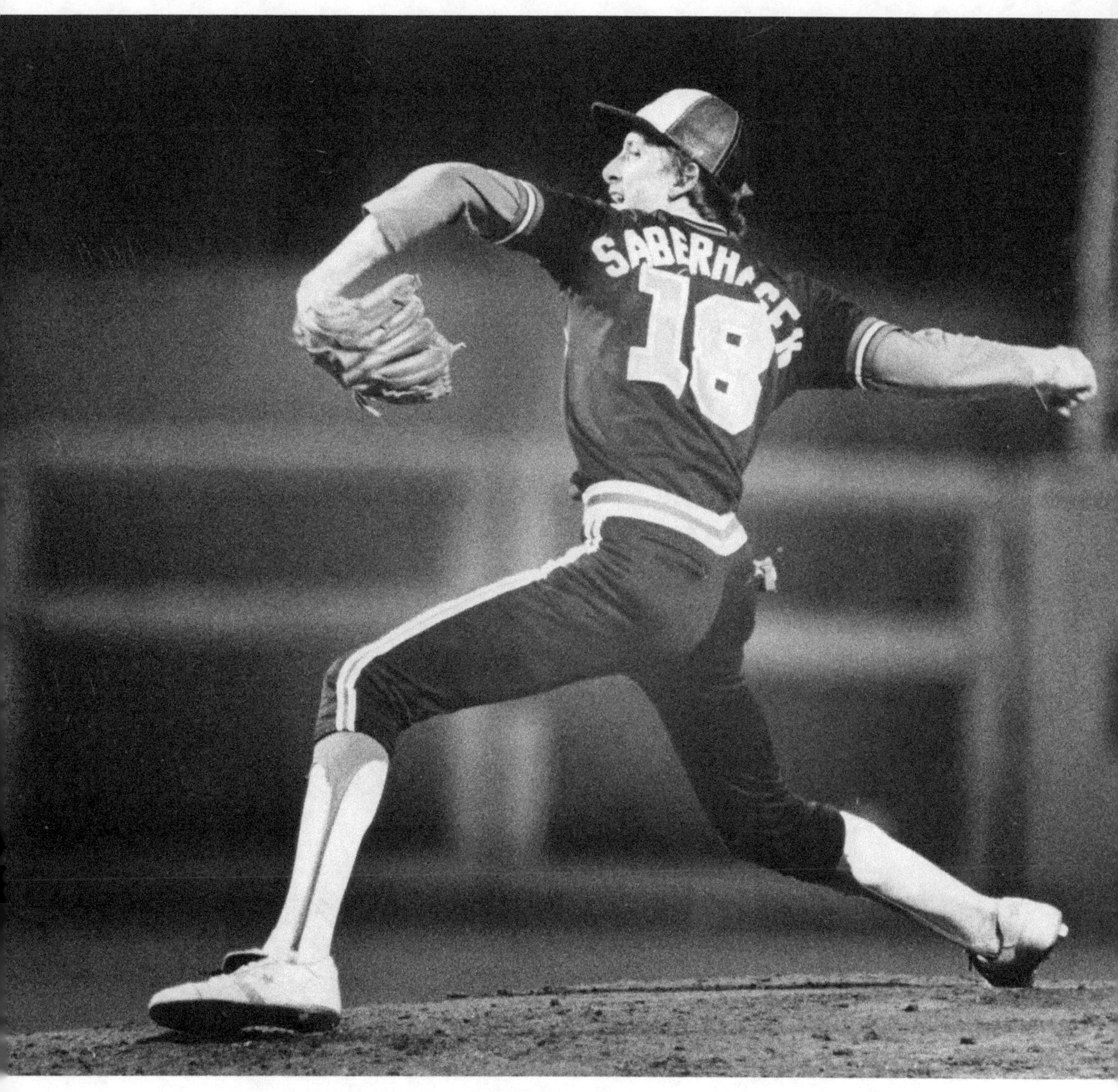

Future Major Leaguers Darryl Strawberry from Crenshaw High (*opposite*) and Bret Saberhagen from Cleveland High (*above*) show off their pitching forms.

ABOVE: (Herald-Examiner Collection)

OPPOSITE: (Mike Mullen/Herald-Examiner Collection)

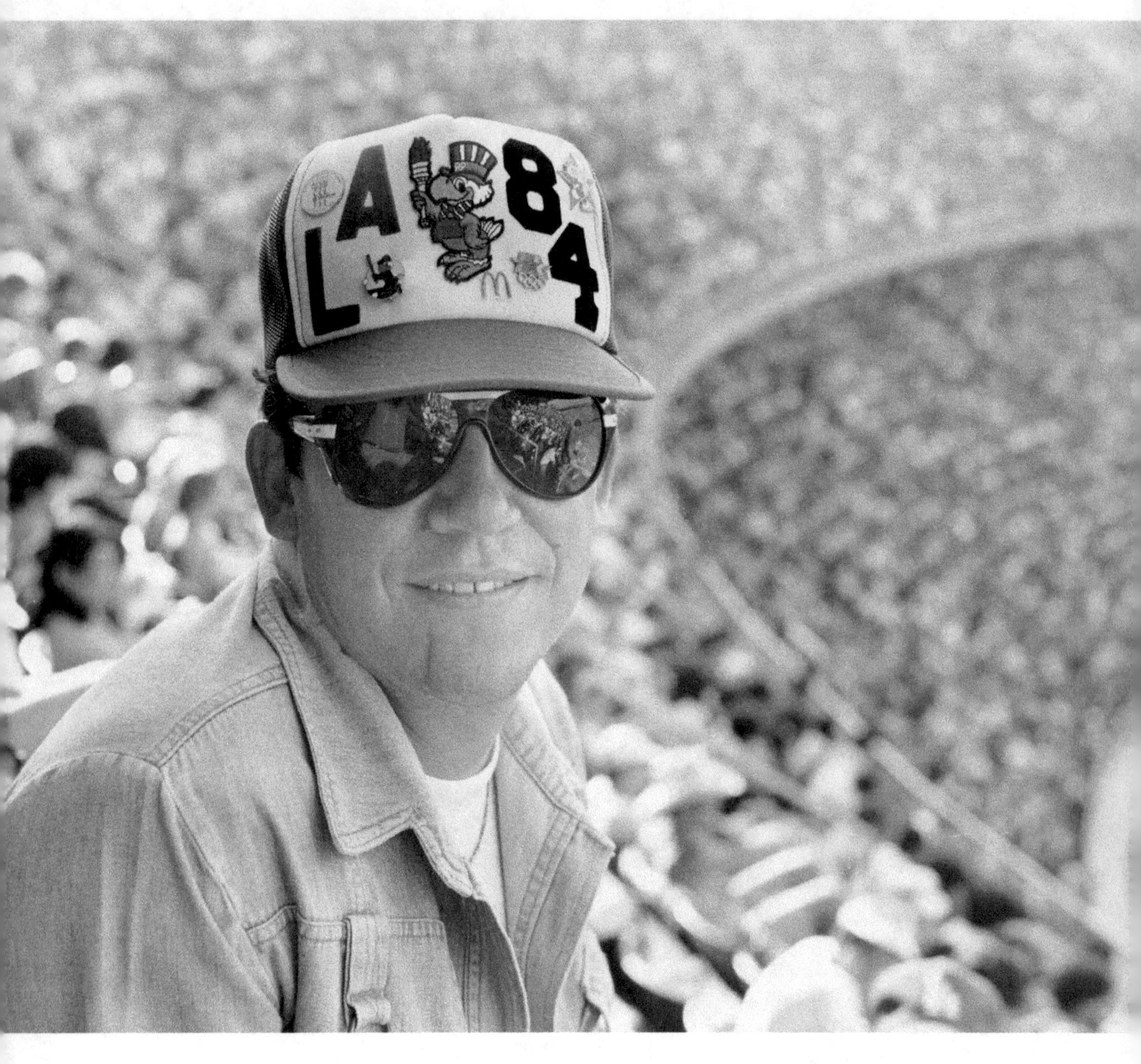

Spectator at a baseball game during the 1984 L.A. Olympics.
(Tom Zimmerman)

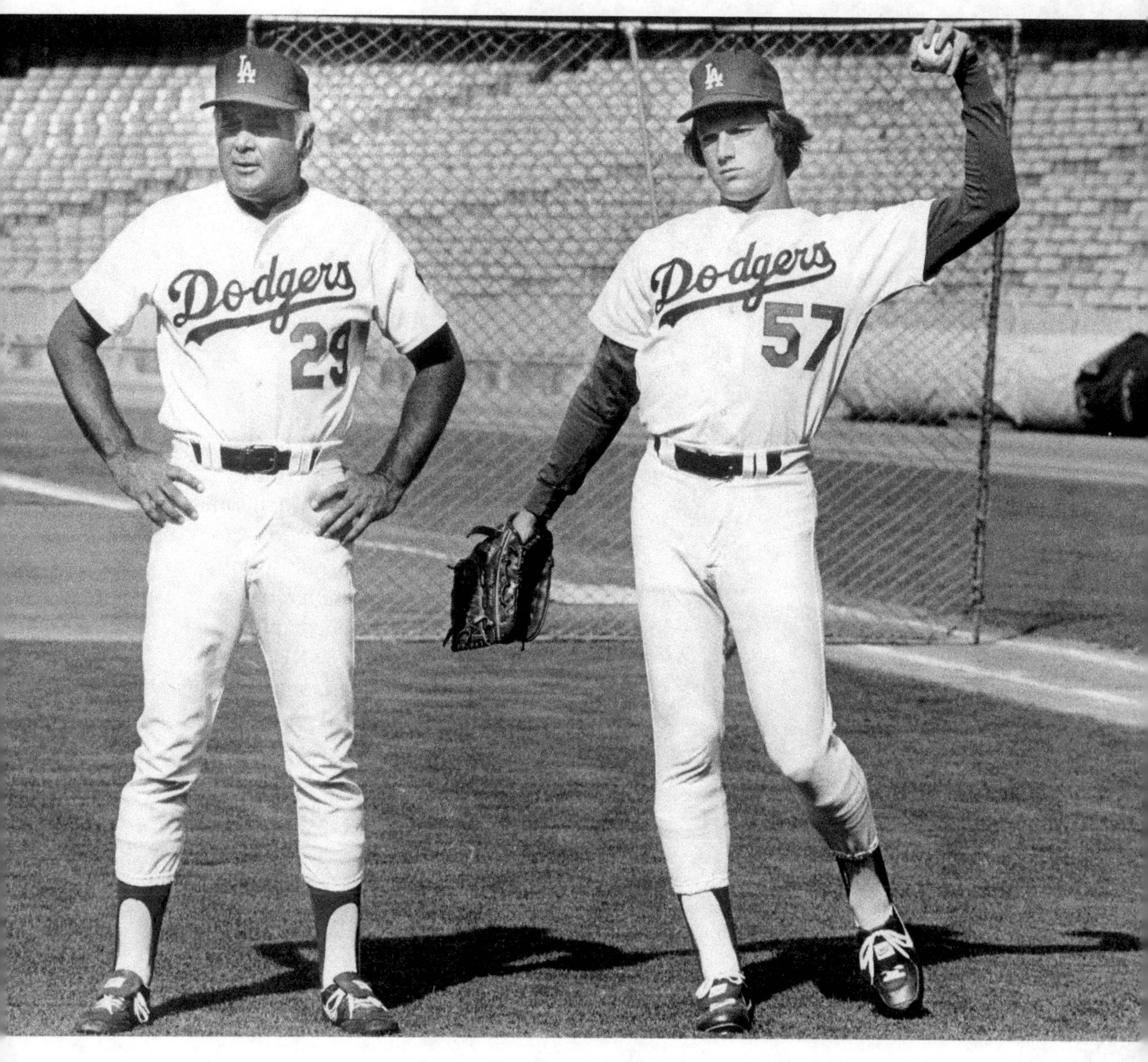

Reliever Steve Howe warms up under the watch of pitching coach (and former reliever) Ron Perranoski.
(James Ruebsamen/Herald-Examiner Collection)

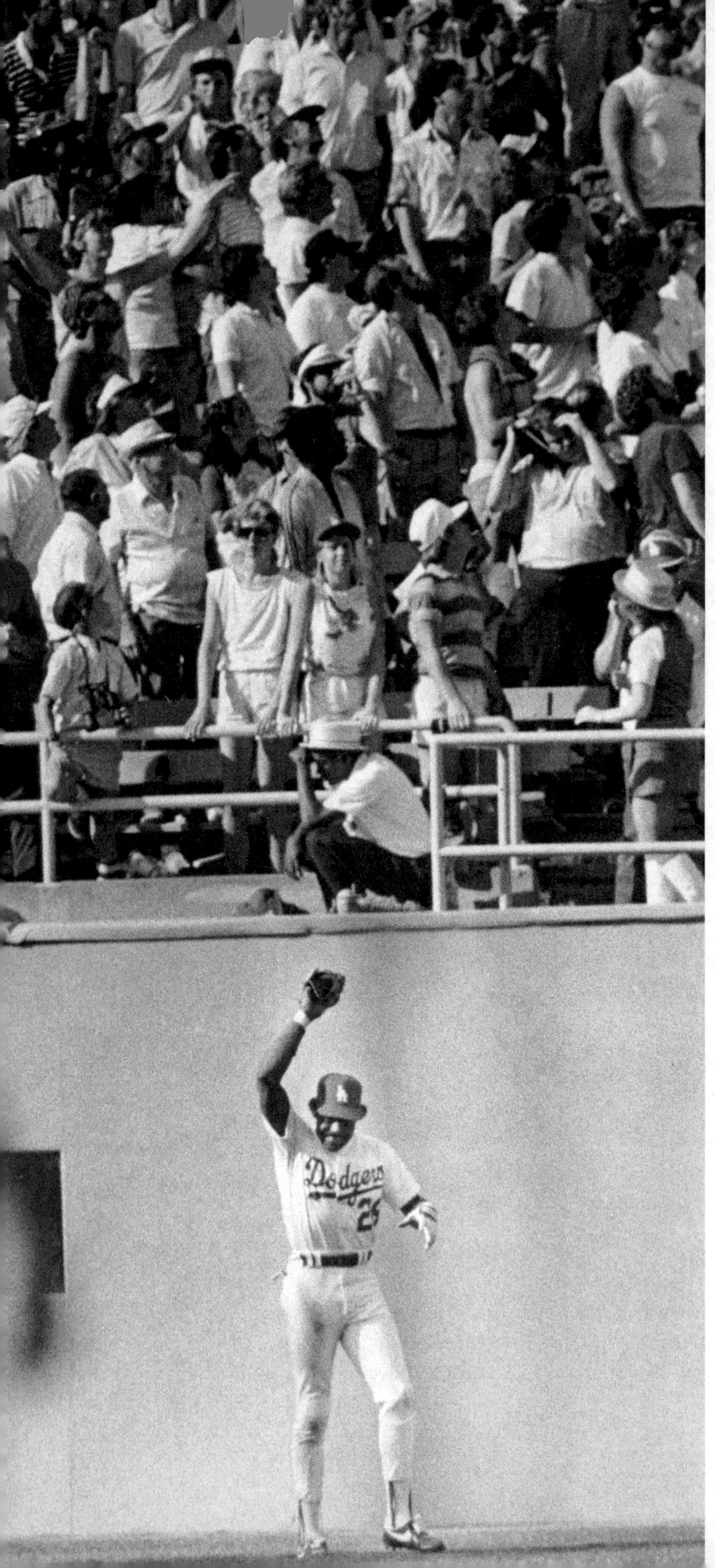

Pedro Guerrero throws down his mitt in disgust after Jack Clark's ninth-inning homer off reliever Tom Niedenfuer in the 1985 NLCS sent the St. Louis Cardinals to the World Series. (James Ruebsamen/ Herald-Examiner Collection)

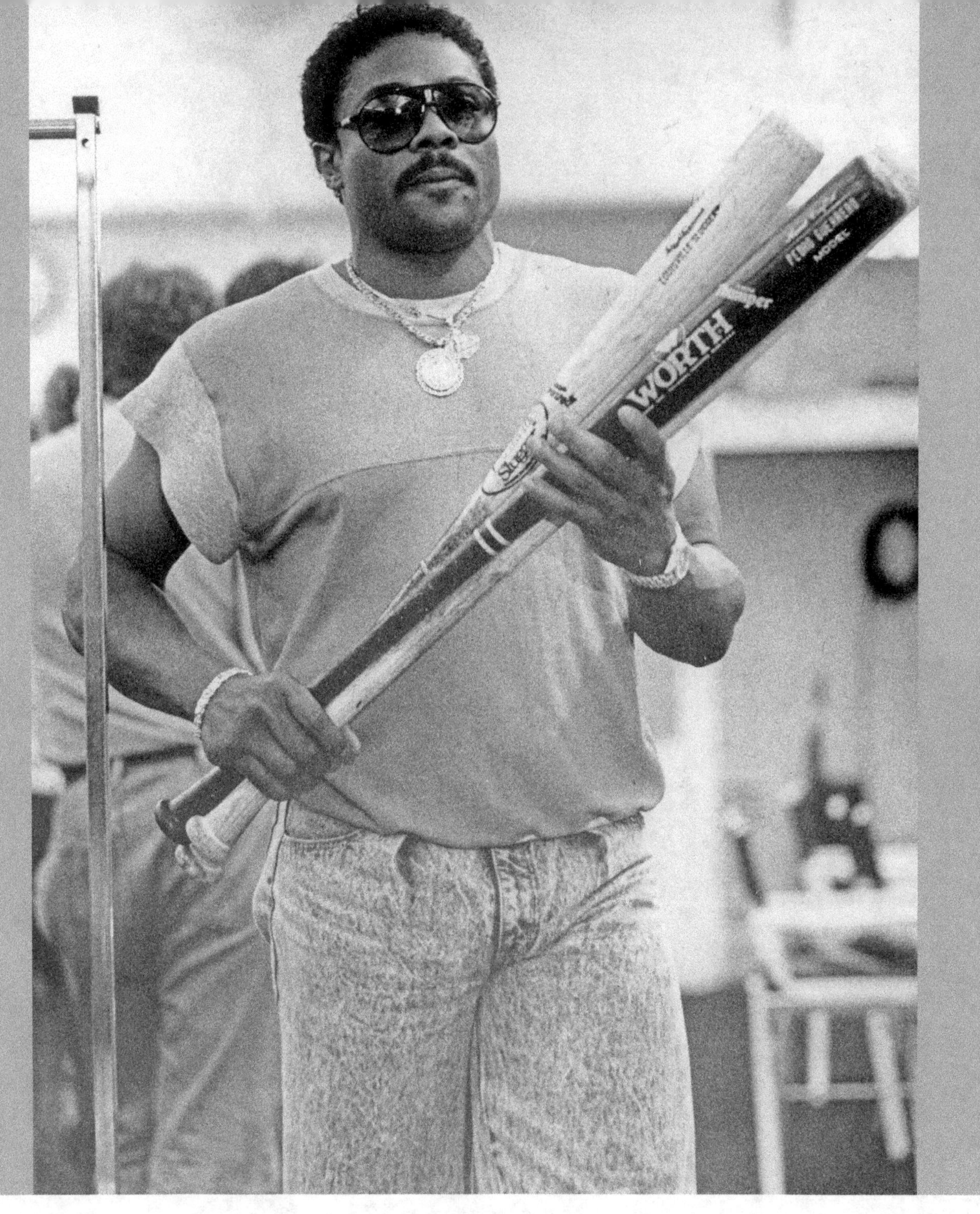

Pedro Guerrero collects his bats after being dealt to the St. Louis Cardinals during the 1988 season. (Mike Sergieff/Herald-Examiner Collection)

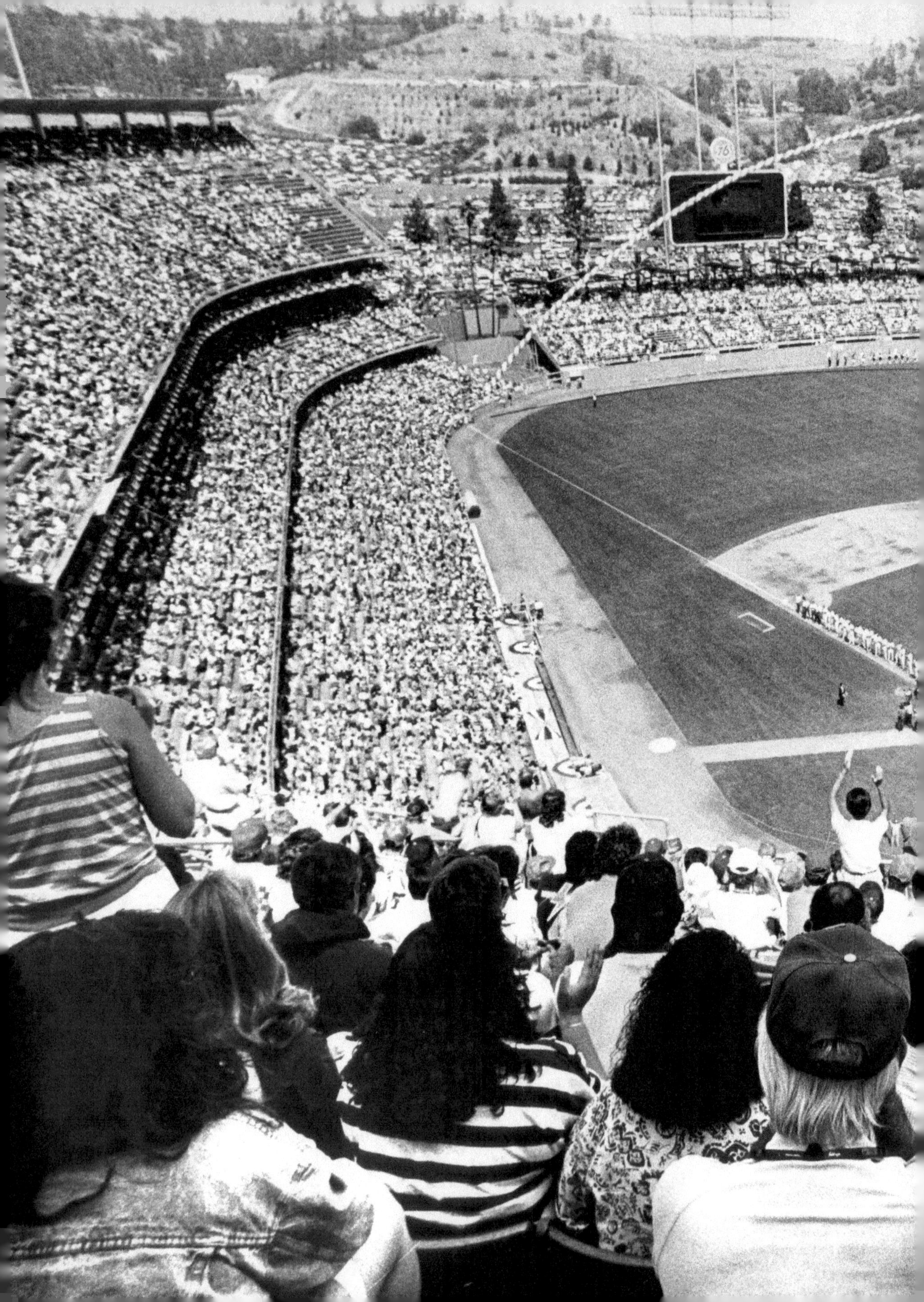

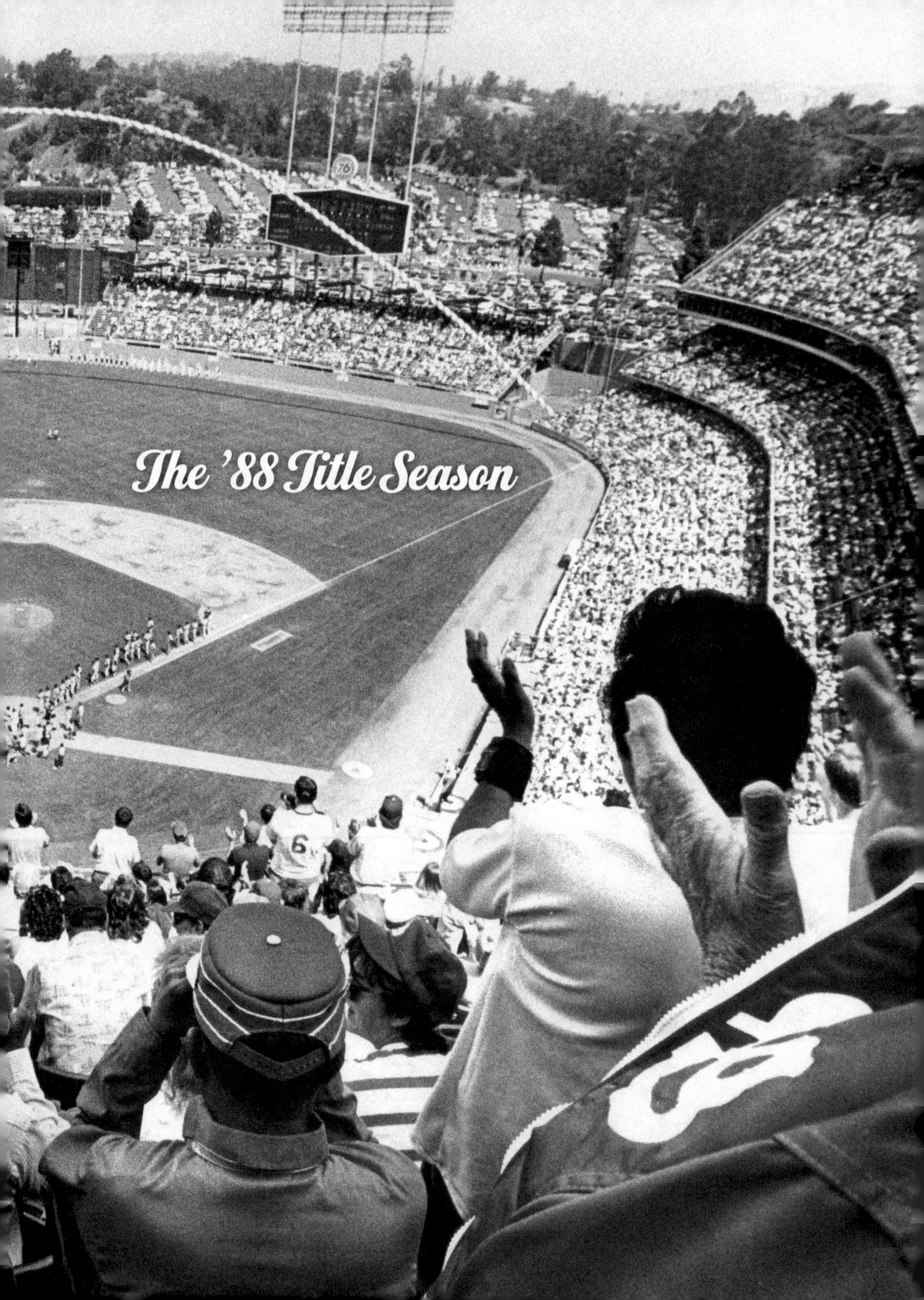

The '88 Title Season

True Blue

So many of us have aspired to make their way onto the sod and clay at Dodger Stadium. It's the dream of scores of young ballplayers who have imagined Vin Scully's broadcast call as they rounded the bases for home. I confess that I was one of those souls.

I was a teen when I received my first invitation to Dodger Stadium. Not as an athlete, mind you. Nope, I was one of many high school journalists who were fortunate to be hosted by the Dodgers for a sports-writing workshop. The sharp green grass was our welcome mat. The field-level seats were our classroom, and the home dugout a brief refuge from the SoCal sun. I learned about media guides, press releases, and photographers' nests.

I opted not to make journalism my career, but I remained an adoring fan. My high-school visit was but one of many enjoyable moments spent at Dodger Stadium. I watched an All-Star game, playoff games, World Series games, and the 1984 Olympics. I attended concerts there and received plenty of police training at the ballpark. Rarely did I turn down an offer to visit. On certain occasions I dug deep into my pockets to fund said visit.

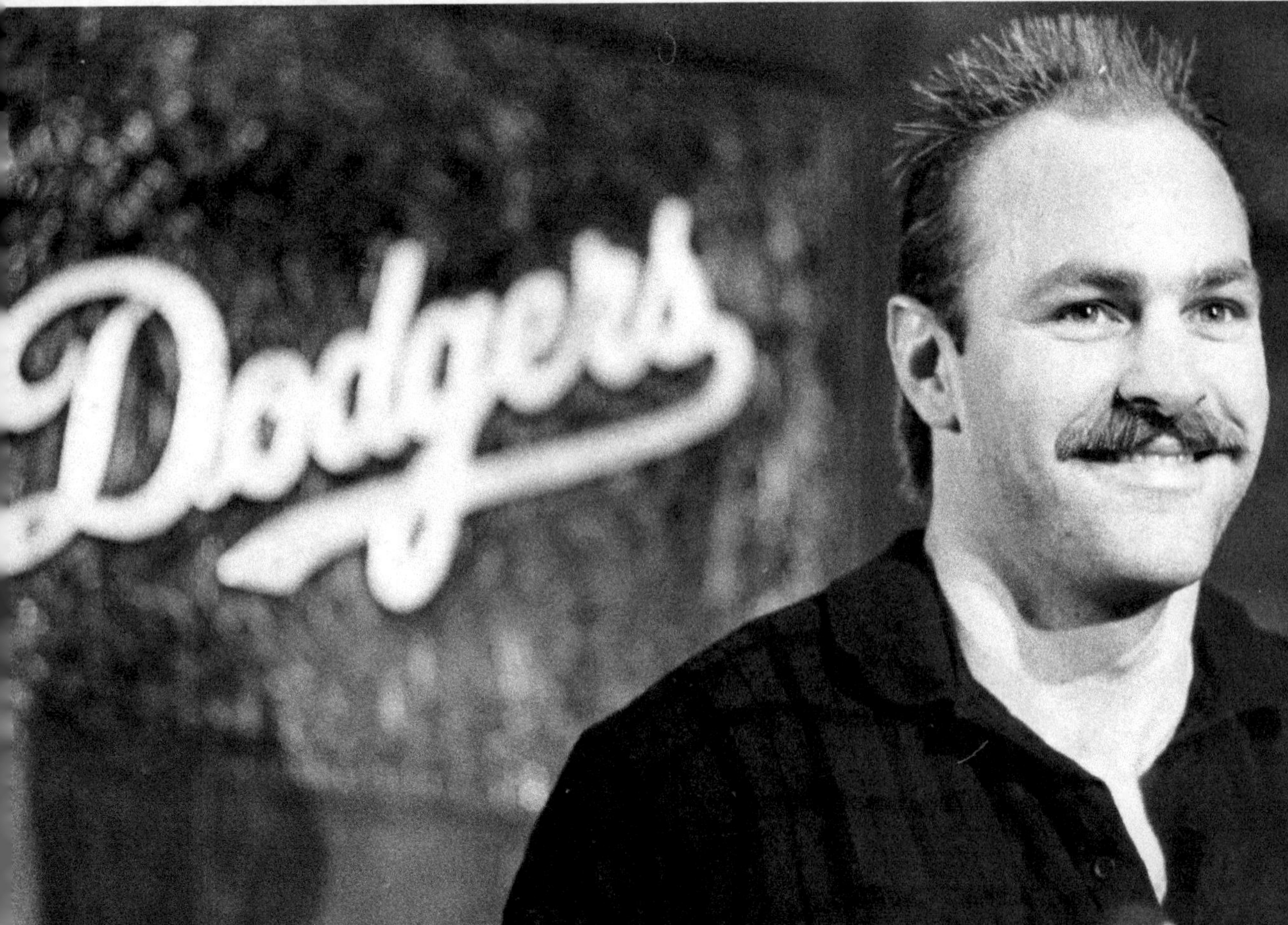

Like, Game 7 of the 1988 NL Championship Series. I was given the opportunity to purchase two tickets to the game, in seats I never figured I could afford. One of my lifelong friends and I sprung for the pair and found ourselves ensconced on the field level, aisle 6, row F. Yup, right behind home plate, just six rows from the turf. Phil Berlioz and I watched Orel Hershiser trim the corners on his way to the pennant-clinching shutout win over mitt-popping Dwight Gooden and the New York Mets.

After the game concluded, the crowd overran the barriers to celebrate on the field. Phil wanted to do the same. I wasn't a bit tempted, however, as I would have had to evade the phalanx of my brothers and sisters in LAPD blue who were guarding the field but were now as much spectators as I was. Watching the game and the after-party on the field was enough for me.

Twenty-plus years later, my daughter made her way inside the stadium thanks to a 5K race to benefit the Dodgers Dream Foundation. Runners trekked through the parking lot, then entered the stadium via the outfield fences. The route coursed the perimeter of the field, with the finish line near home plate. My daughter won her age group and plenty of goodies that went with the honor, including tickets to a game and another trip onto the field. She stood beside the cage during batting practice, and I confess that she was the cutest feature on the message board that night.

She made her way onto the field legitimately, unlike another game-goer I encountered in the final phase of my LAPD career. At that time, I ran the graveyard shift at the LAPD station responsible for Dodger Stadium. Game nights meant ne'er-do-wells from the stadium frequented our holding cells en route to the Parker Center jail. Part of my responsibilities included interviewing the lodgers at the lock-up.

So many of the stories I heard were lies, denials, and false pleas of innocence wrapped in a request for release. But one claim brought me pause and instantly transported me to my own hardball dreams. "I ran across the outfield and slid head first into second base at Dodger Stadium," he told me.

He had my attention and my curiosity, so I asked him a question I frequently posed to prisoners: "Why?"

To which came his response: "It's always been a dream of mine."

Amen.

—Glynn Martin

OPPOSITE: The free-agent signing: Kirk Gibson. (Herald-Examiner Collection)

PAGES 178-179: Opening Day. (Mike Sergieff/Herald-Examiner Collection)

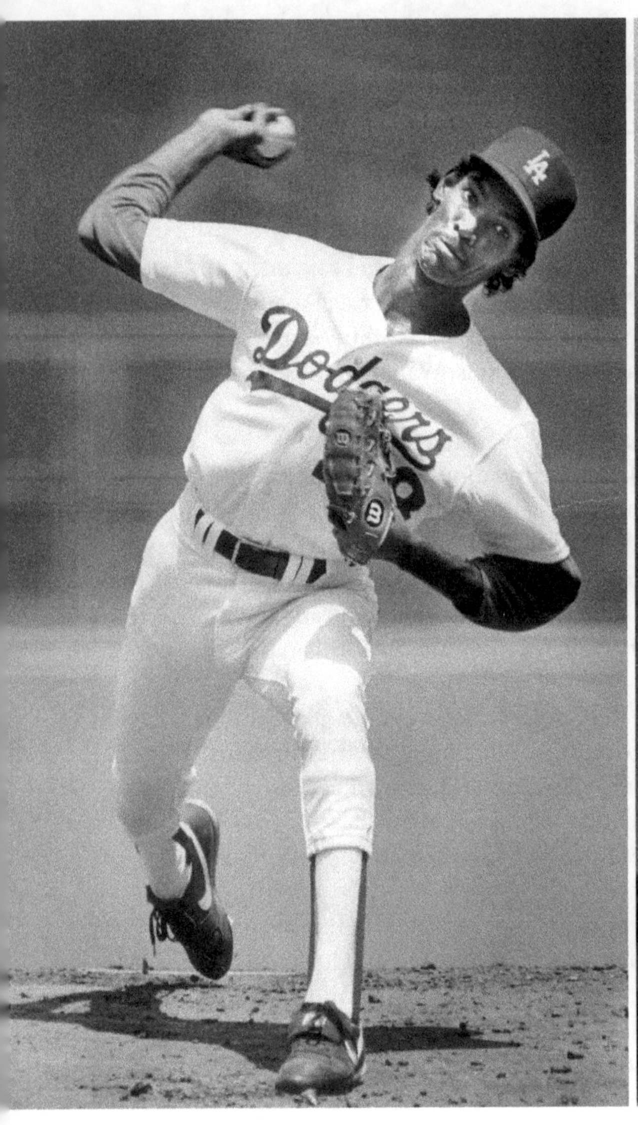

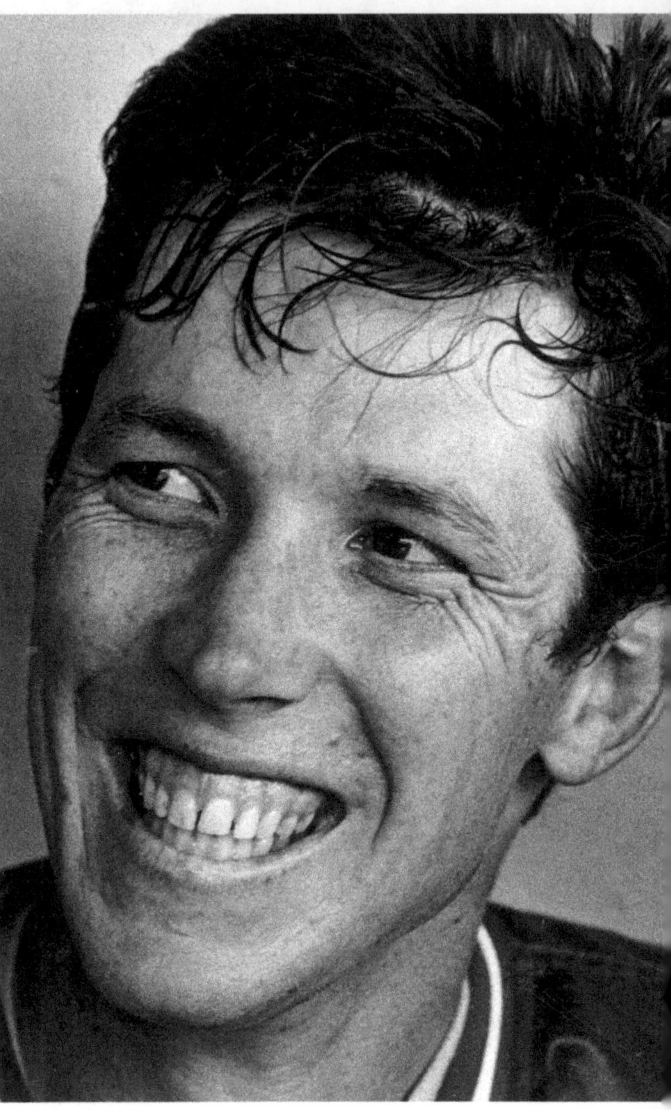

LEFT: The rookie pitcher: Ramon Martinez.
(Javier Mendoza/Herald-Examiner Collection)

RIGHT: The ace: Orel Hershiser.
(Dean Musgrove/Herald-Examiner Collection)

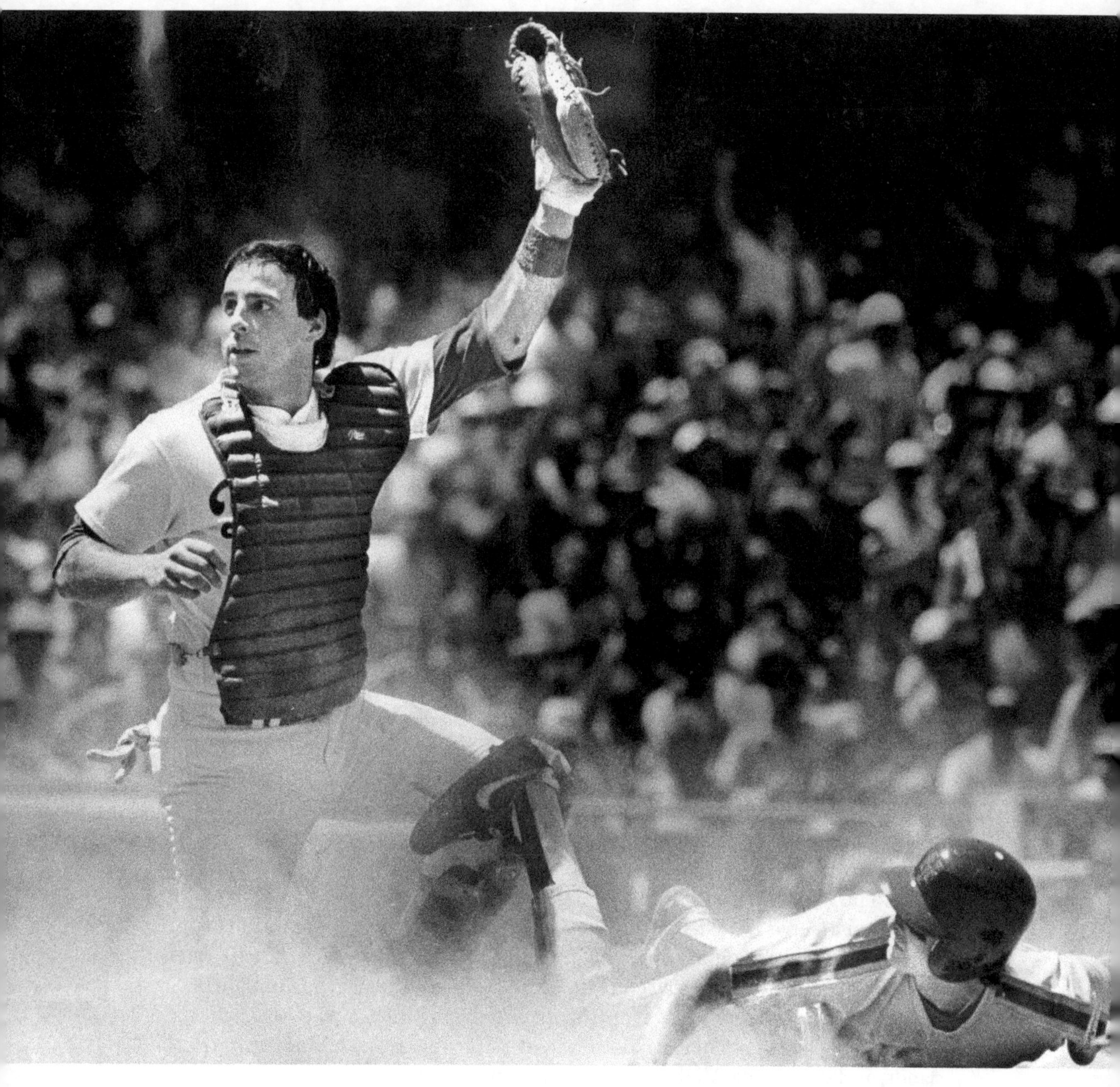

The catcher: Mike Scioscia tags out Tim Teufel of the Mets.
(Javier Mendoza/Herald-Examiner Collection)

Danny Heep: Stuntman Supreme

It's pre-game at Dodger Stadium in the summer of 1988. The pitchers are through in the batting cage. Next to hit are the non-starters. Danny Heep, one of the most intense men on the Dodgers, is part of this group. He's been a role player for the Astros and Mets. This is his second season with the Dodgers and his tenth year in the Major Leagues. The desire and hunger to succeed are palpable when speaking to him. He is one of the Stuntmen, the bench strength the Dodgers have relied on all season. But there isn't a non-pitcher in the Major Leagues who doesn't want to play every day. Heep is no exception.

I once asked Steve Sax if the Major Leagues have been like he expected. "Even better," the starting second baseman said. Not so for Heep. He had been a two-time All-American at St. Mary's in Austin, but he stresses how hard he has to work to stay on the roster. Every spring when he reports, he feels he has to win a place on the team all over again. He never reports for spring training out of shape. The official camp may begin in March, but Heep begins working out with friends and other ballplayers in December near his home in San Antonio. He has never been someone who could coast on his natural ability. Heep has always had to train longer and harder than players with lots of raw talent in order to stay in the big leagues.

What does a man with this much intensity do when he sits on the bench so much? How does he cope with the horror of his June 6th start? Heep, normally an outfielder, was put at an unfamiliar position, first base, and made two errors, only to hear the crowd sarcastically cheer him when he made a routine play. On that occasion, he turned to the crowd along the first-base dugout and doffed his cap. Normally, he just has to keep it to himself because he is a Stuntman, not a starter. He has to practice and stay sharp, and be a supportive teammate. The depth of his burning desire to play and the consequences of his sitting are evident when Heep noted, "What I can never do is take the frustration home. That could ruin my family. The game has to stay at the ballpark."

Danny Heep is not starting today. He will hit b.p. with the other Stuntmen. Then he will shag balls and run in the outfield. Once the game starts, he will watch from the dugout and try to stay mentally alert. He is a role player, and tonight, if he is going to contribute to his team, the role will be to pinch-hit. So he watches the opposing team's pitchers, takes a few cuts at the pitching machine under the stands, and stays ready. All the while the intensity burns.

—Tom Zimmerman

Editor's Note: This piece originally appeared in Zimmerman's book about the 1988 season entitled A Day in the Season of the L.A. Dodgers *(Shapolsky Books).*

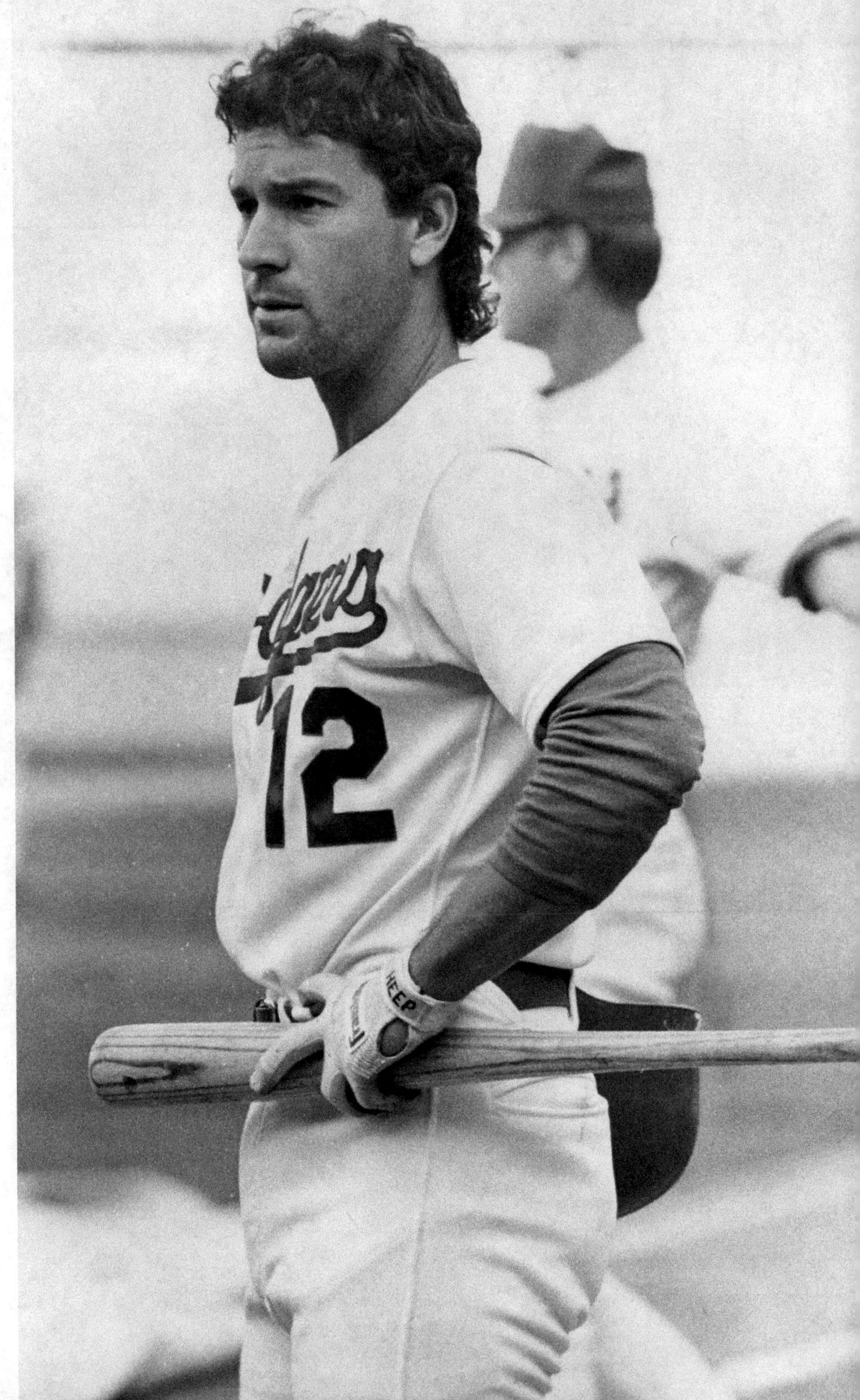

The Stuntman: Danny Heep. (Tom Zimmerman)

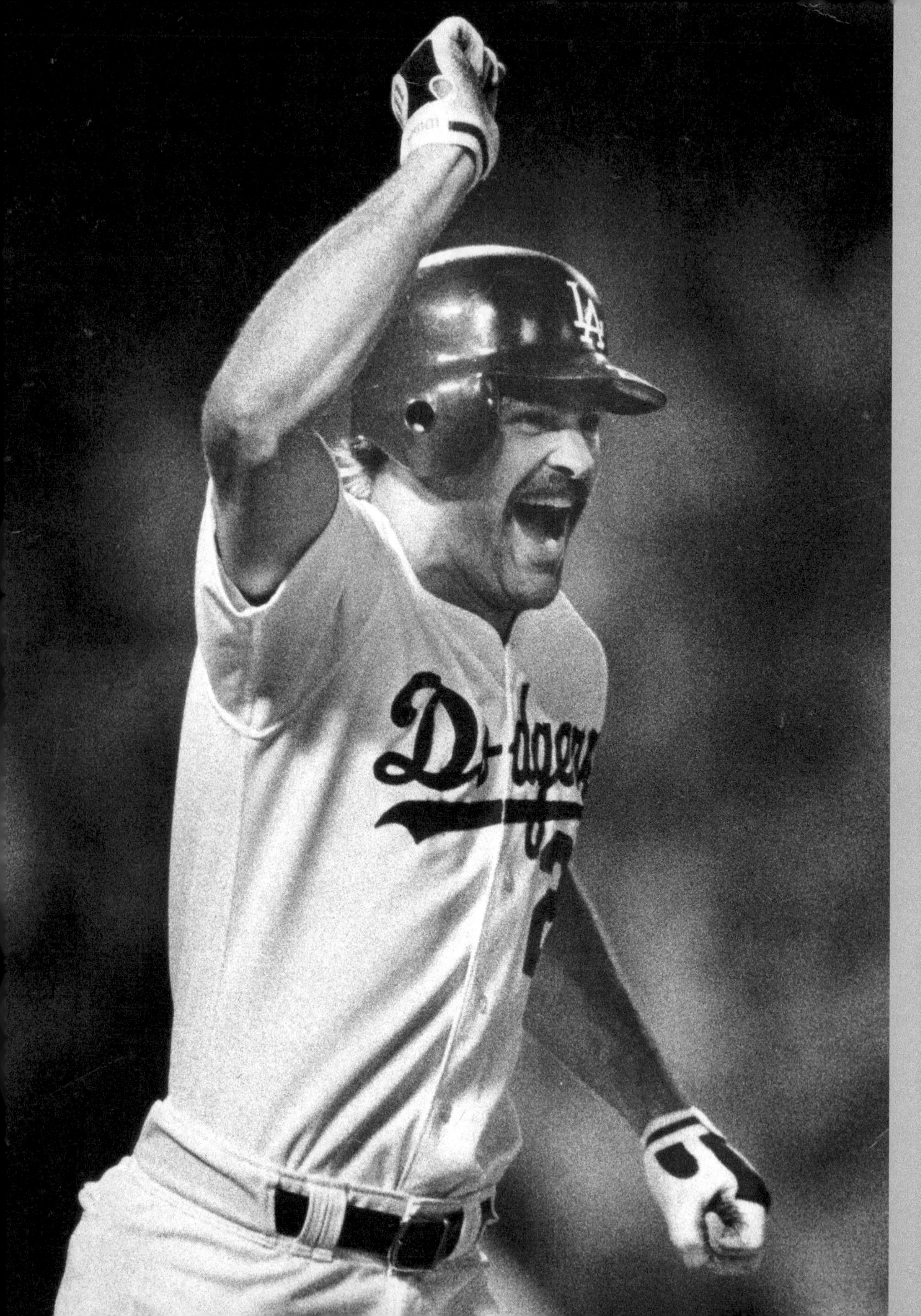

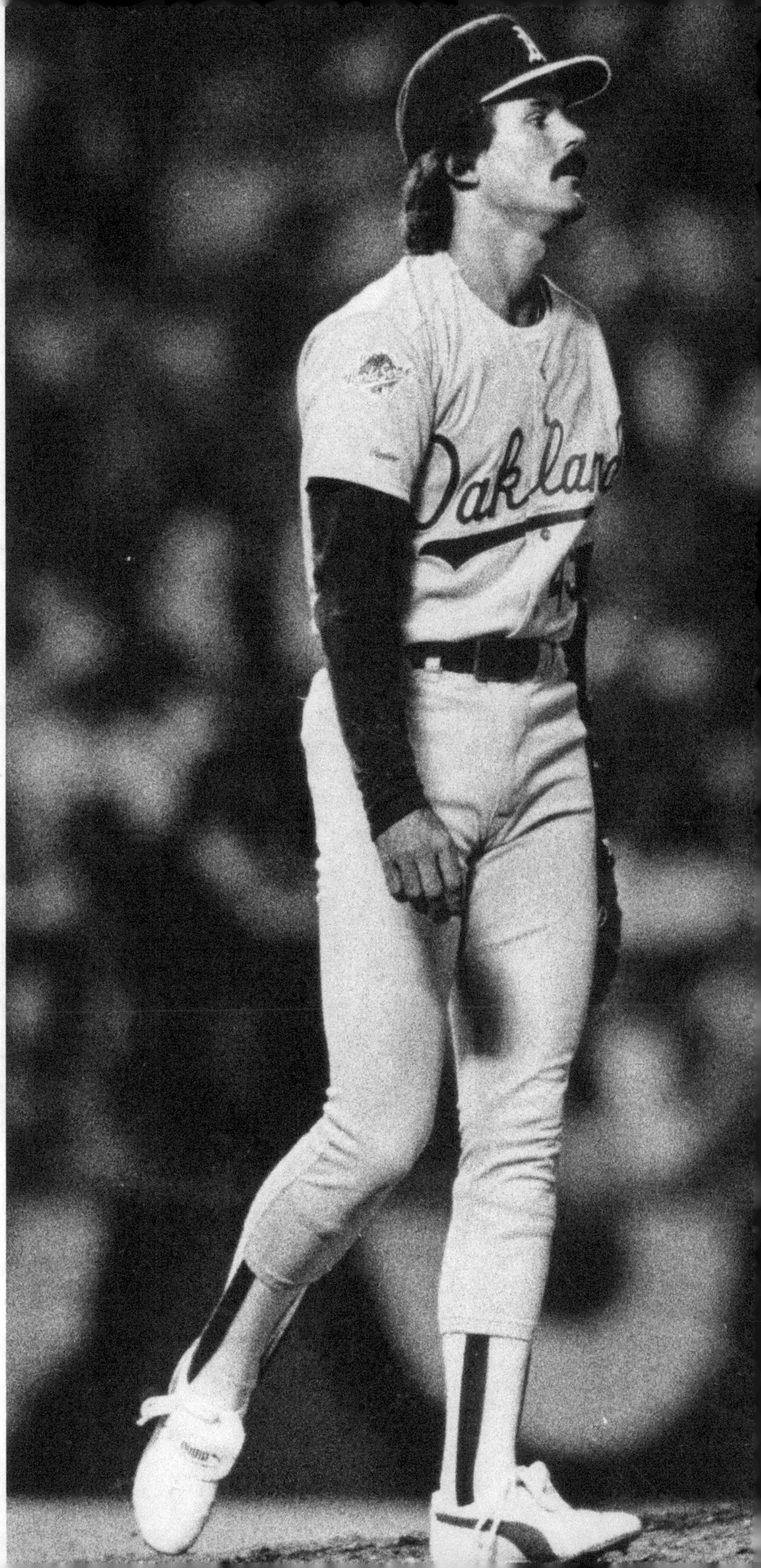

OPPOSITE & RIGHT:
The home run:
Kirk Gibson begins to circle the bases after connecting for the game-winning homer off Oakland A's reliever Dennis Eckersley in Game 1 of the World Series.
(Paul Chinn/Herald-Examiner Collection)

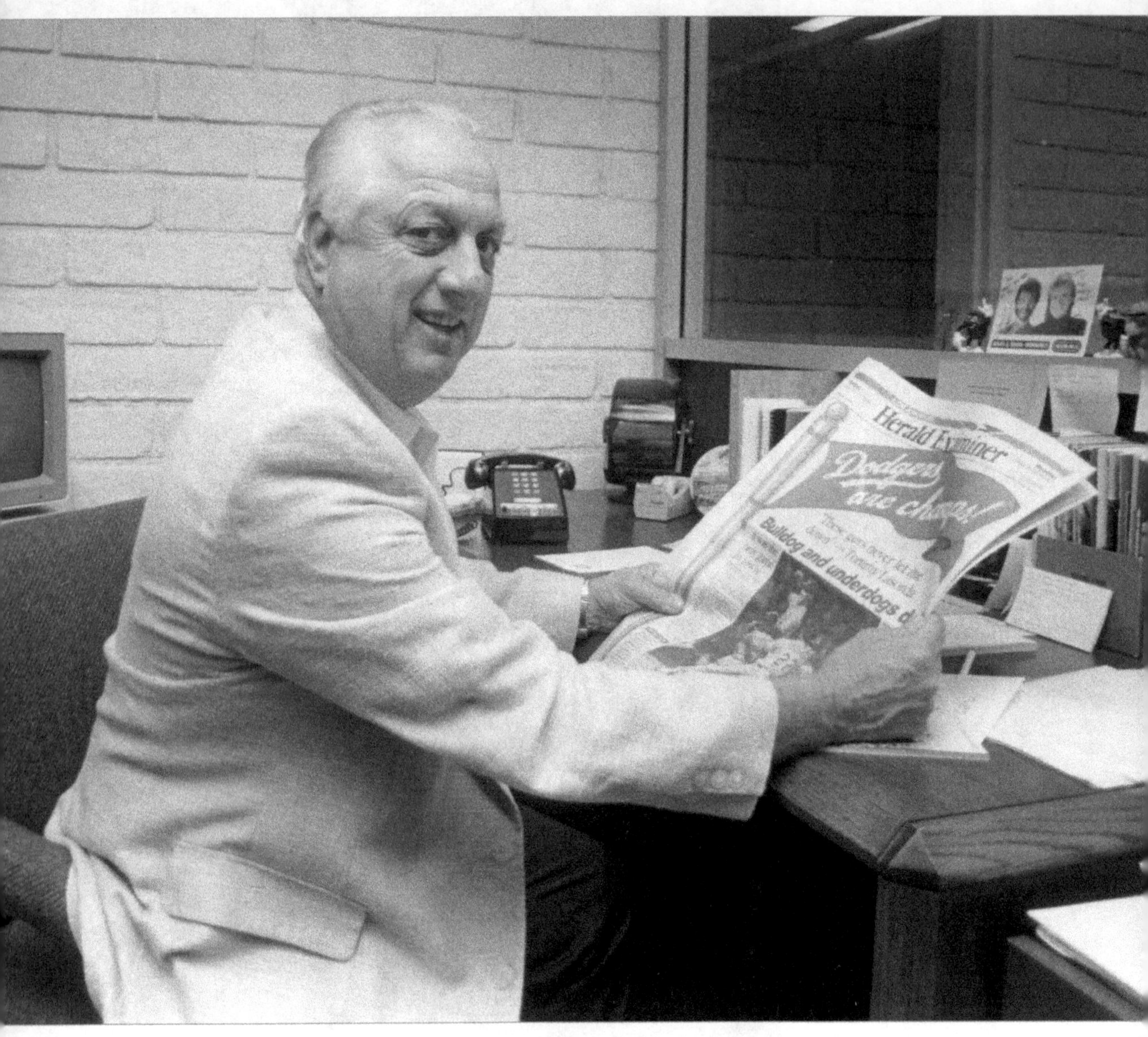

The manager: Tom Lasorda catches up on the news.
(Steve Grayson/Herald-Examiner Collection)

OPPOSITE: The MVP: Orel Hershiser lifts the championship trophy.
(Herald-Examiner Collection)

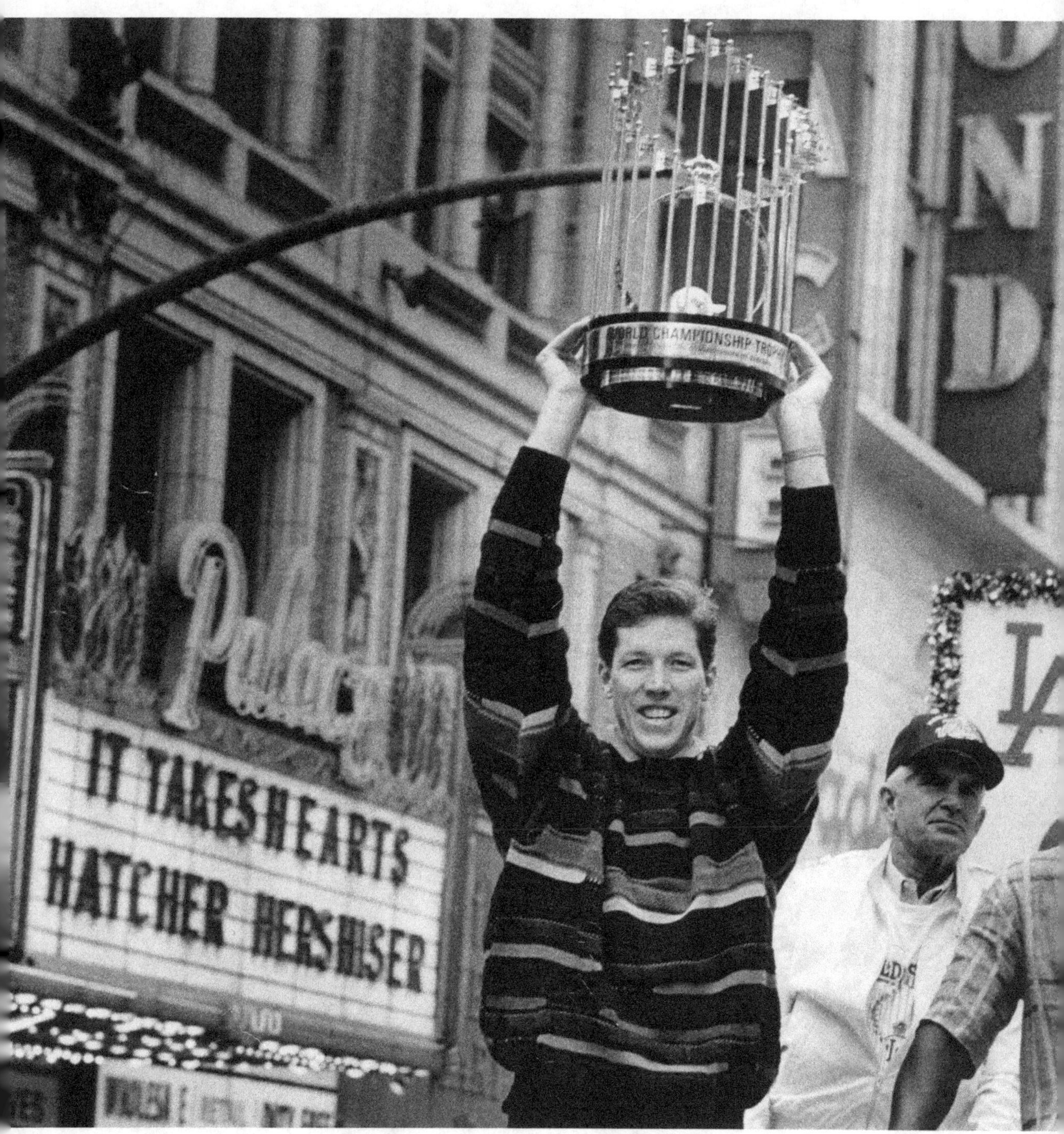
WORLD CHAMPIONSHIP TROPHY
IT TAKES HEARTS
HATCHER HERSHISER
LA

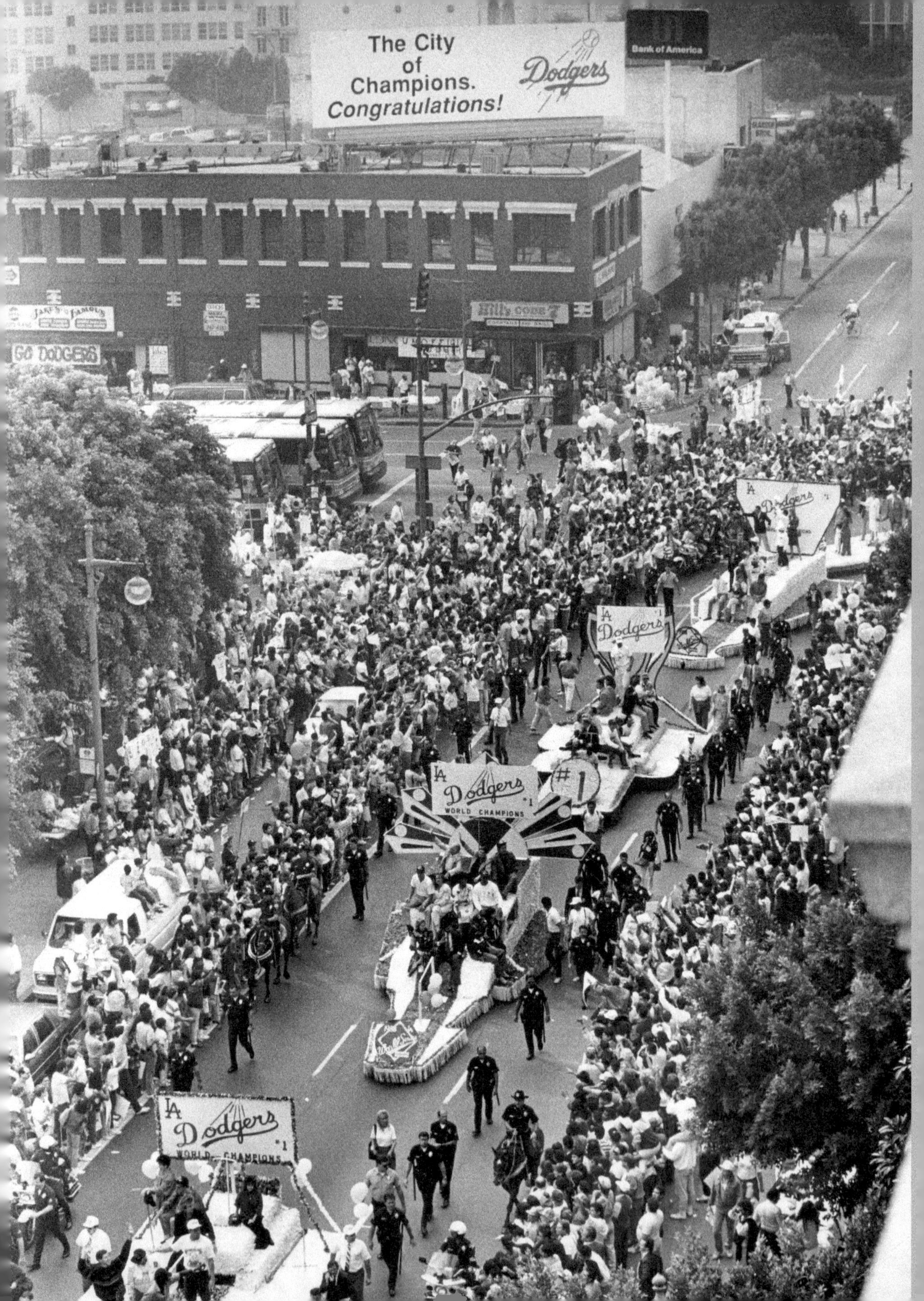
The City
of
Champions.
Congratulations!
Dodgers
Bank of America
GO DODGERS
LA
Dodgers
#1
WORLD CHAMPIONS
#1
LA
Dodgers
LA
Dodgers
#1
WORLD CHAMPIONS

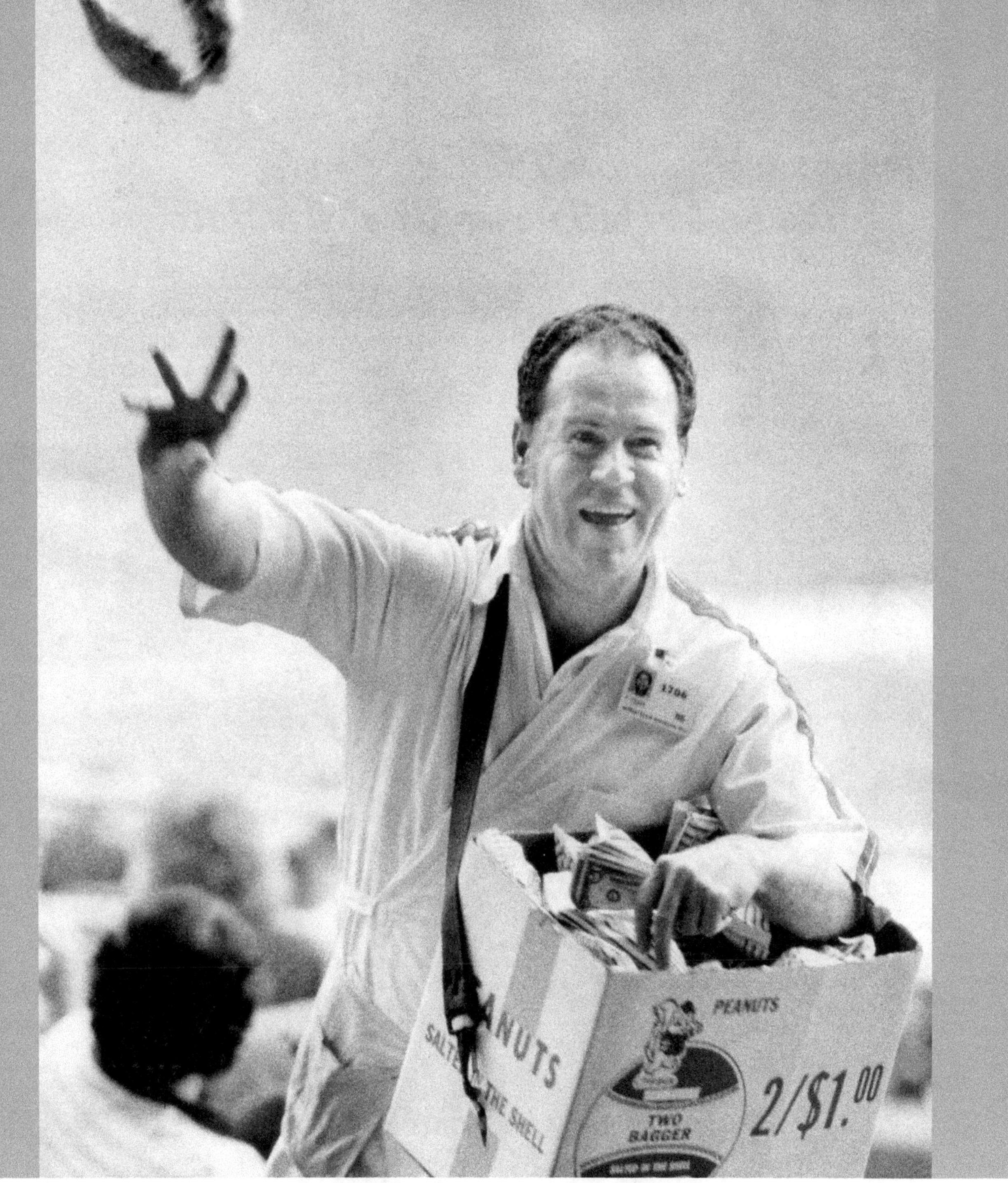

Roger “The Peanut Man” Owens tosses another bag to a fan.
(James Ruebsamen/Herald-Examiner Collection)

OPPOSITE: Victory parade along Broadway.
(Mike Mullen/Herald-Examiner Collection)

Brett Butler: The Batter No Pitcher Wanted to Face

From 1981 to 1997, baseball fans learned never to visit the bathroom when Brett Butler was due at the plate. They would have stayed just to enjoy the skinny centerfielder's offensive destruction—he usually batted around .300, with a high percentage of hair-raising triples. But the greater attraction was

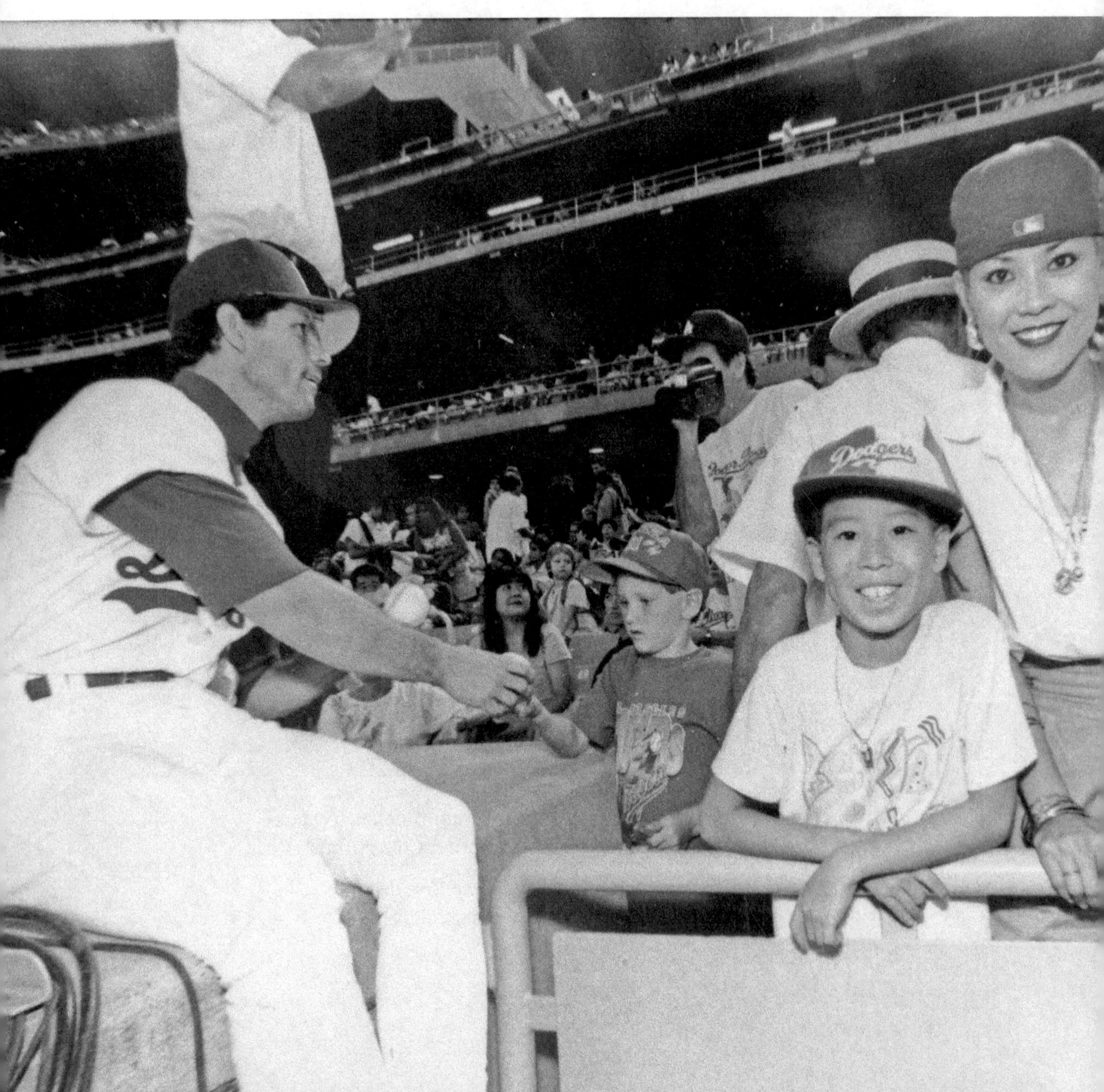

watching the steam pour from opposing pitchers' ears. Butler could foul off 10 pitches at will. Then he'd slap a hit to the opposite field. Or draw a walk. Or reach base with a perfect bunt. Once on base, he upped the torture, stealing more than 30 a dozen times. It's no wonder that Butler scored at least 100 runs in six seasons.

Having suffered sufficient damage from Butler when he served three years with the rival Giants, the Dodgers more than doubled his salary to lure him into their leadoff position in 1991. He immediately became a fan favorite, stepping up to bat left-handed with a focused squint and an enormous cheekful of something. (Gum? Butler has said he used chewing tobacco for less than three years early in his career, and the throat cancer he developed in 1996 has been variously sourced.) Also a canny outfielder, he positioned himself frighteningly shallow but almost never let a drive drop over his head.

Butler weathered 17 seasons for six Major League teams, but the seven he spent in Los Angeles bring special memories. Since retiring in 1997, he has coached and managed several teams; as of 2018, he is a coach with the Miami Marlins.

—Greg Burk

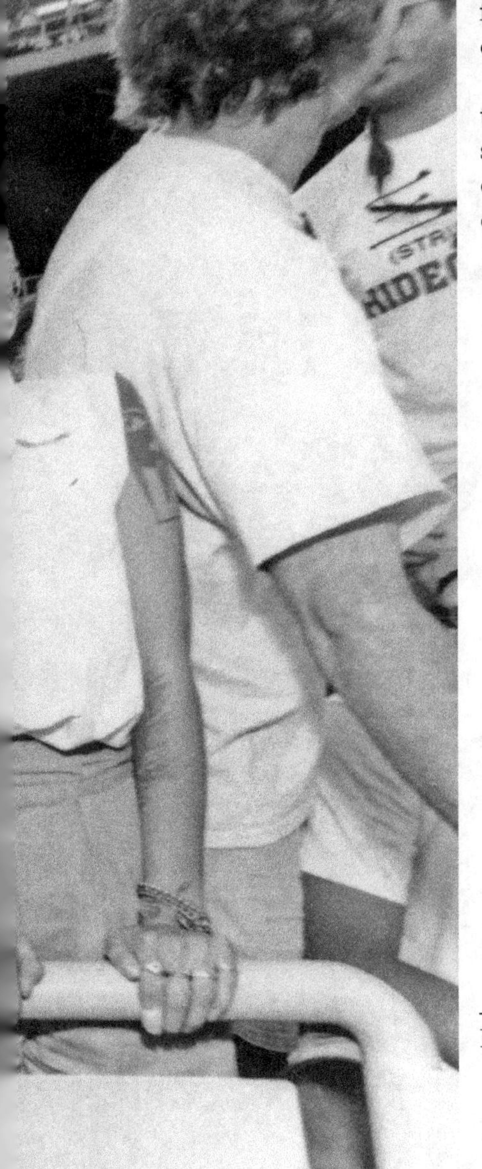

Brett Butler signs another autograph. (Gary Leonard)

Hollywood Hardball

Baseball and Hollywood have long enjoyed a special relationship. Movie studios have produced baseball-themed films since the silent era, and movie stars have flocked to local stadiums to cheer on their favorite teams. It's all entertainment.

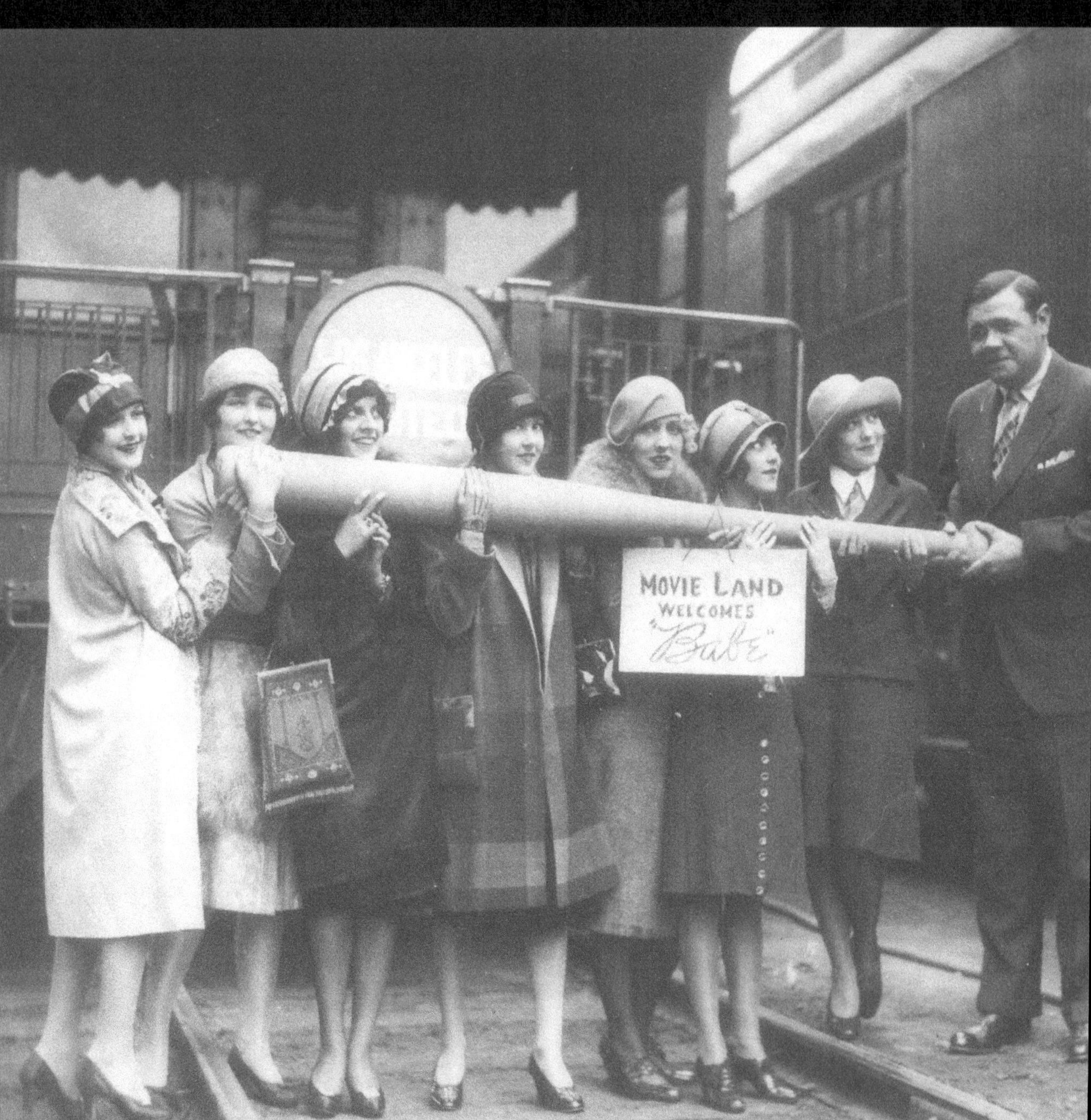

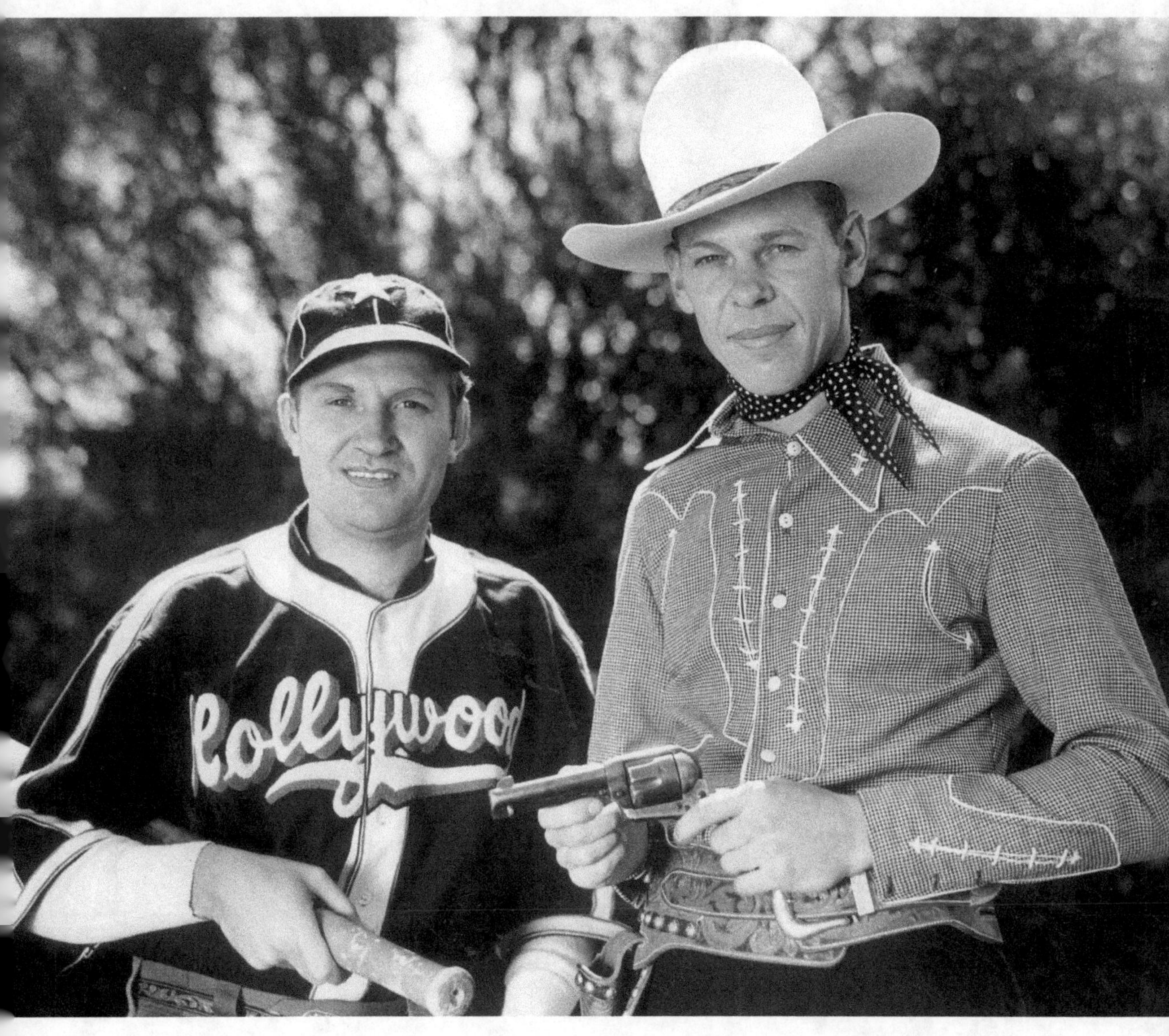

Singing cowboy Gene Autry (*left*) exchanges uniforms with Hollywood Stars outfielder (and Glendale High grad) Babe Herman, circa 1935. (Herald-Examiner Collection)

OPPOSITE: Babe Ruth and his mighty bat come to L.A. to shoot a movie in the off-season. (Security Pacific National Bank Collection)

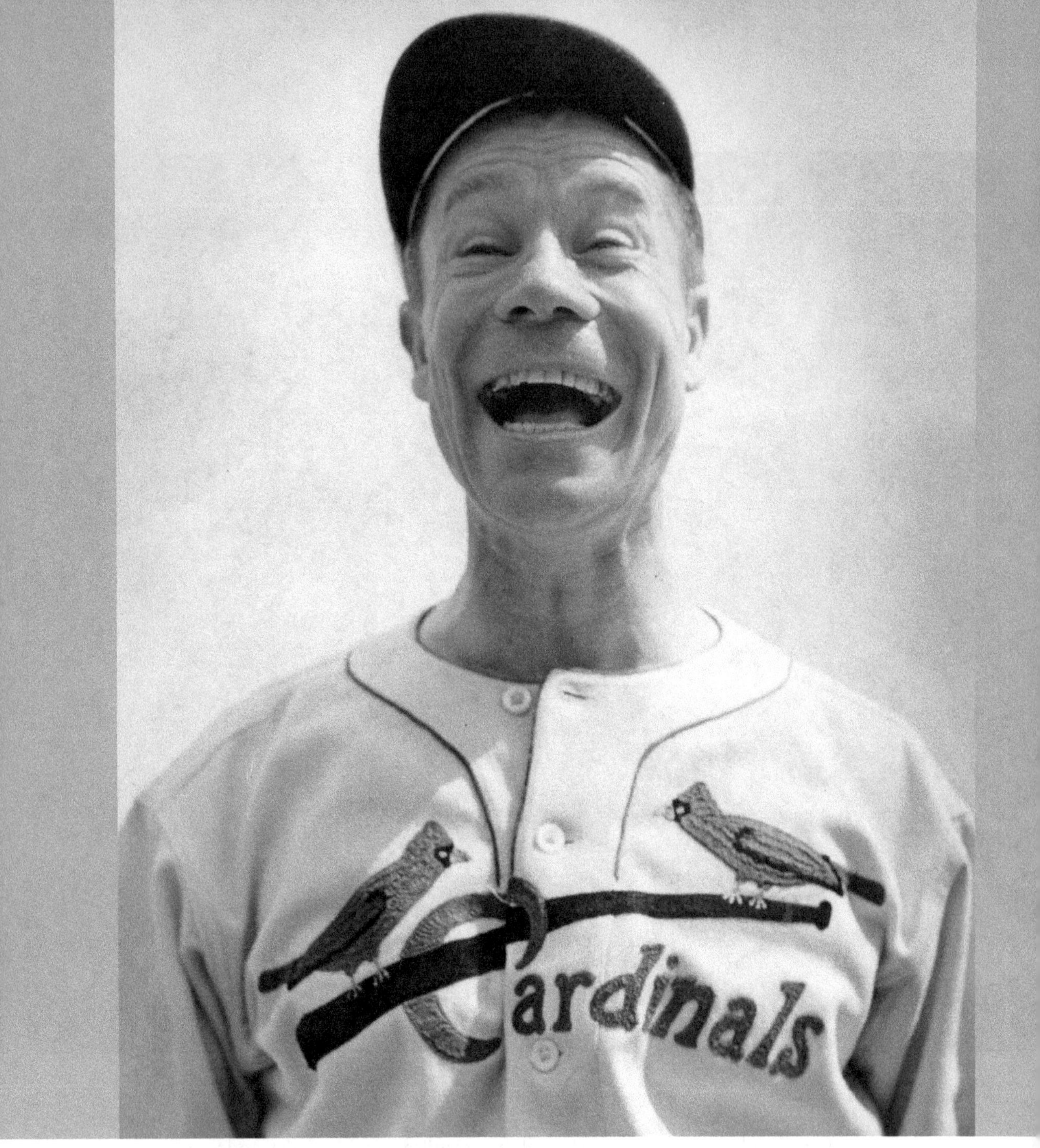

Joe E. Brown prepares to play in an exhibition game at Wrigley Field.
(Herald-Examiner Collection)

OPPOSITE: Katharine Hepburn and L.A. Angels first baseman Chuck Connors (moonlighting as an actor) on the set of *Pat and Mike.*
(Herald-Examiner Collection)

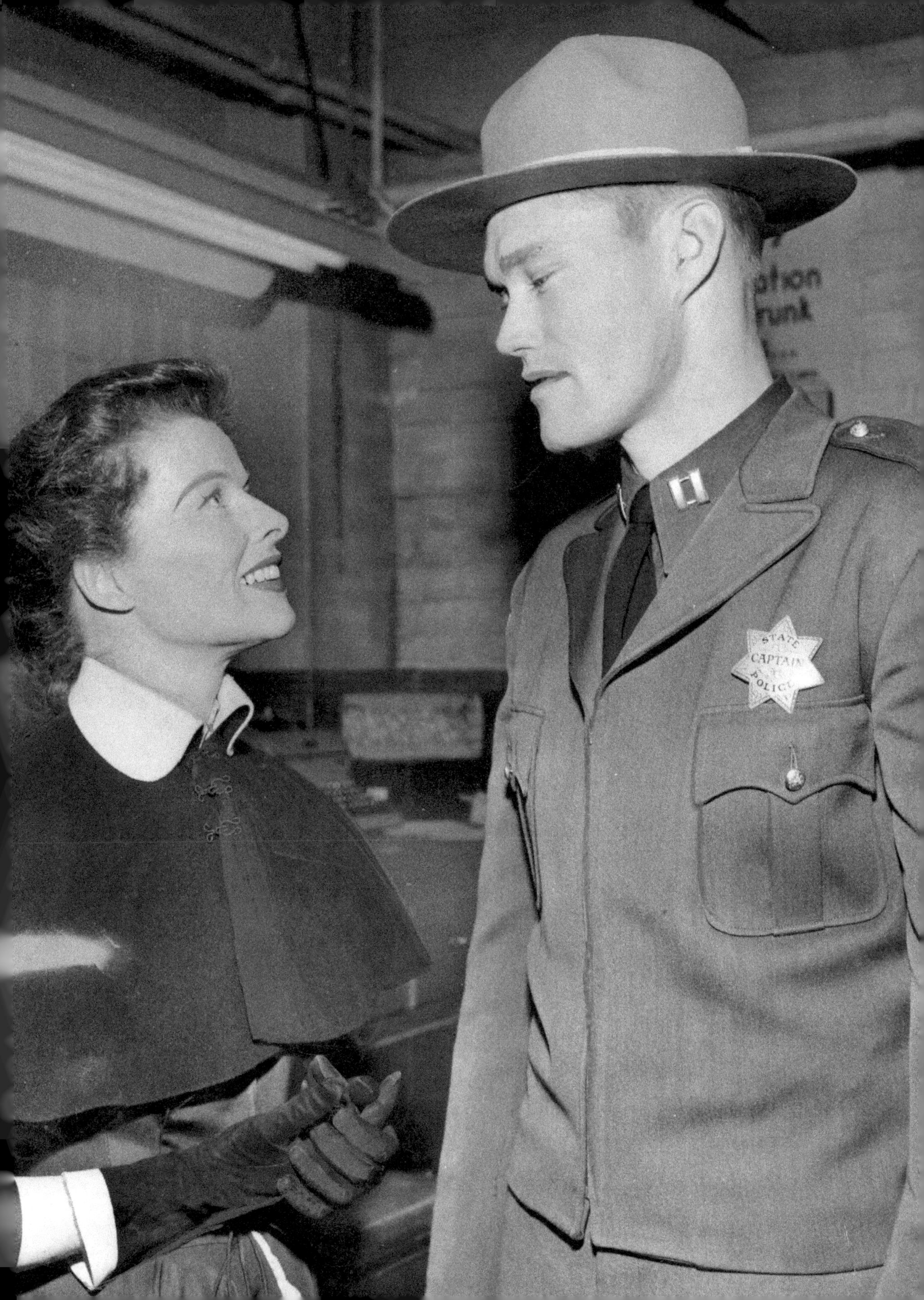
STATE
CAPTAIN
POLICE

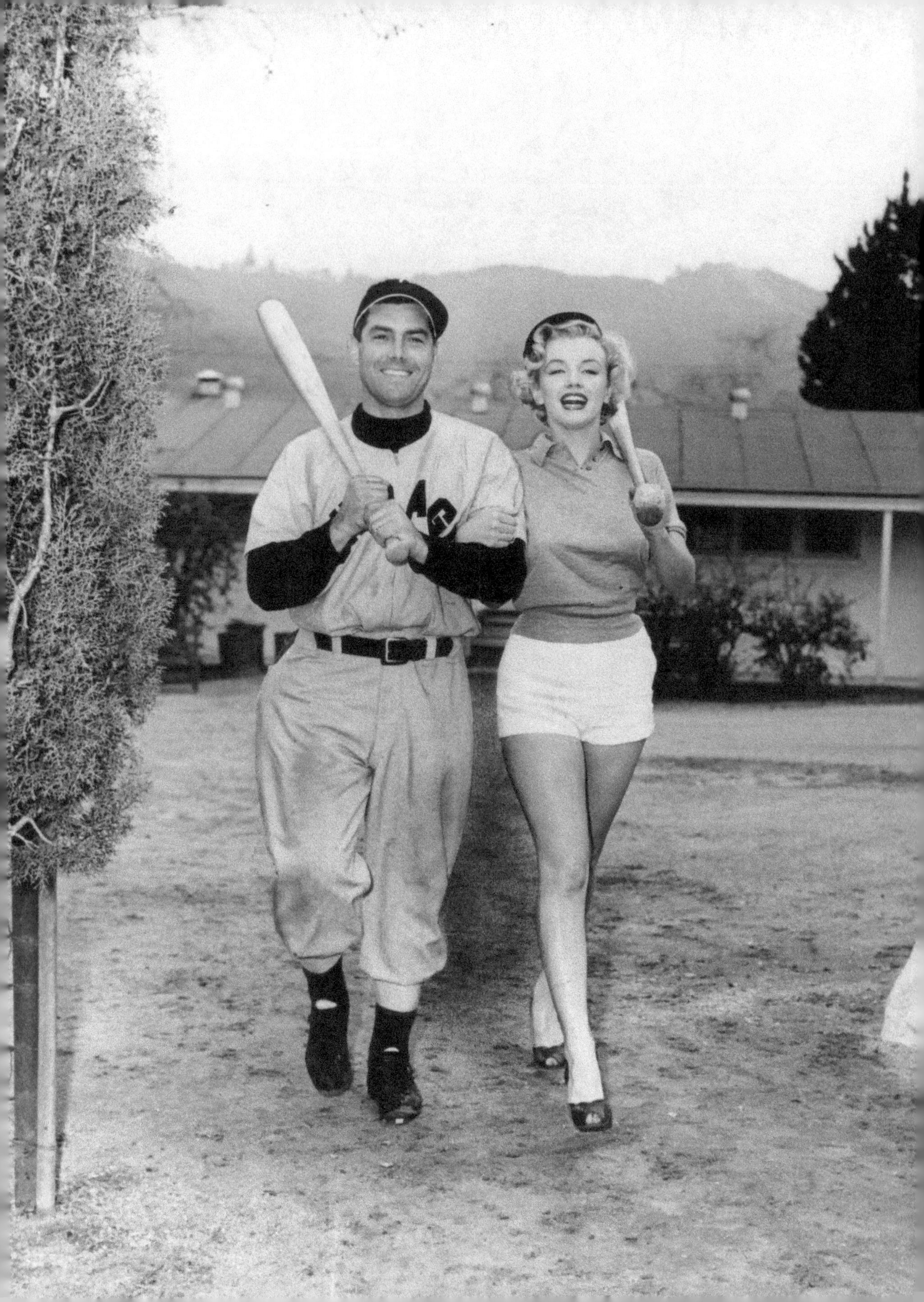

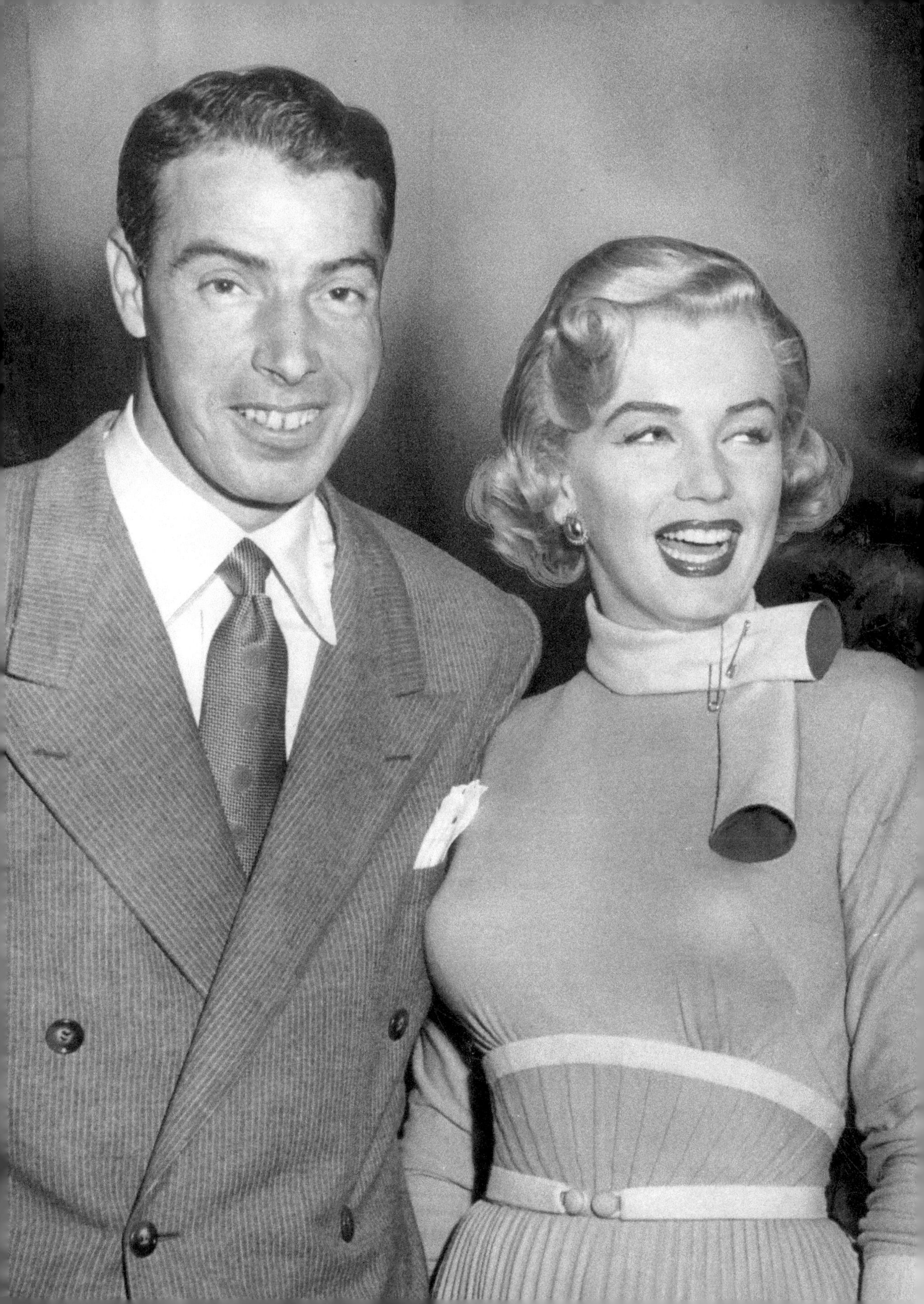

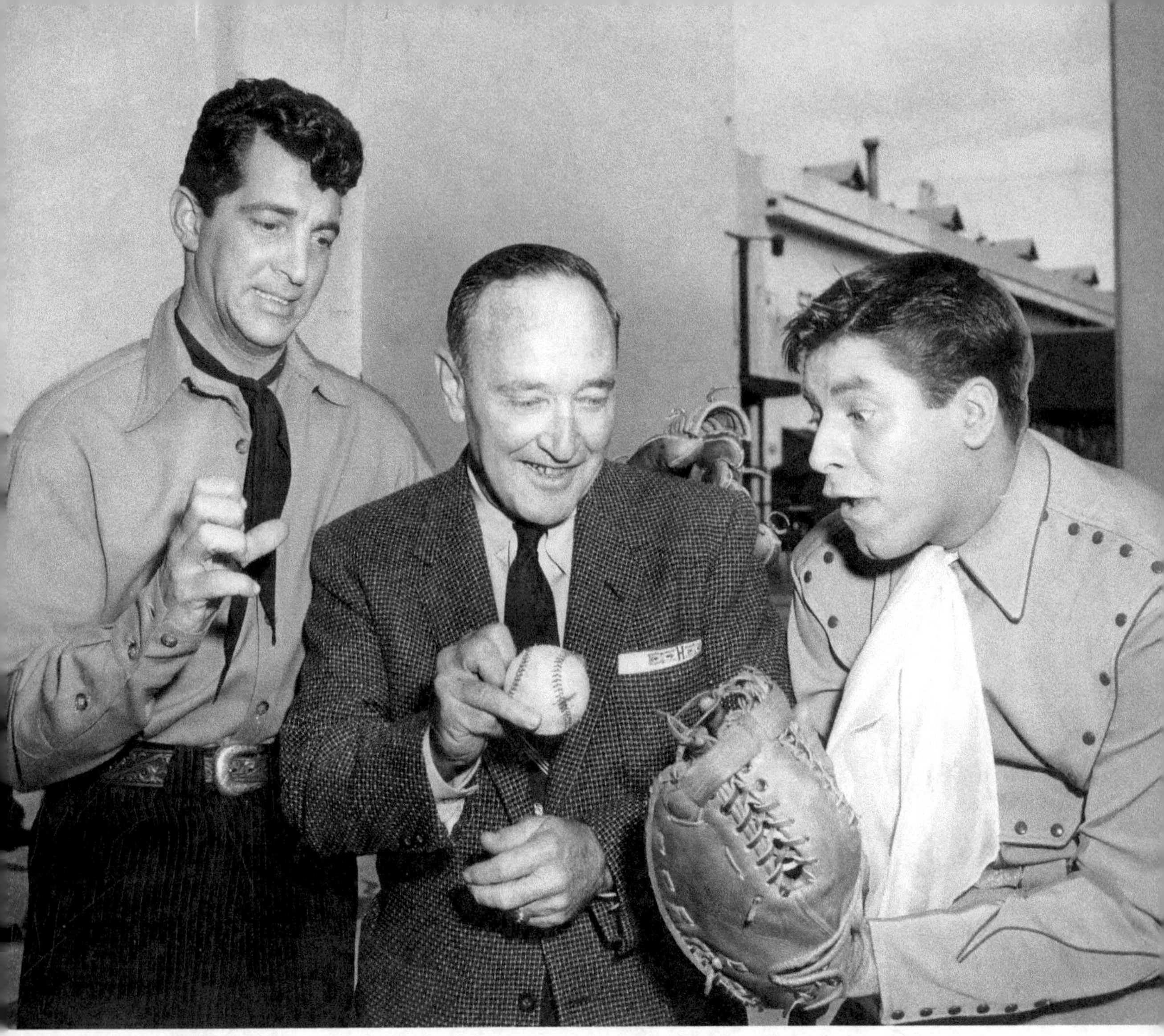

ABOVE: Dean Martin (*left*) and Jerry Lewis clown with Hollywood Stars manager Fred Haney, on the set of *Pardners*. (Valley Times Collection)

OPPOSITE: Dale Evans and Roy Rogers, with members of the "Chilly Willy" Little League team from Sherman Oaks. (Paul Bailey/Valley Times Collection)

PAGE 198: Marilyn Monroe and Chicago White Sox third baseman Hank Majeski at spring training in Pasadena, circa 1950. (Herald-Examiner Collection)

PAGE 199: Marilyn Monroe and retired New York Yankees outfielder Joe DiMaggio, shortly before their wedding. (Herald-Examiner Collection)

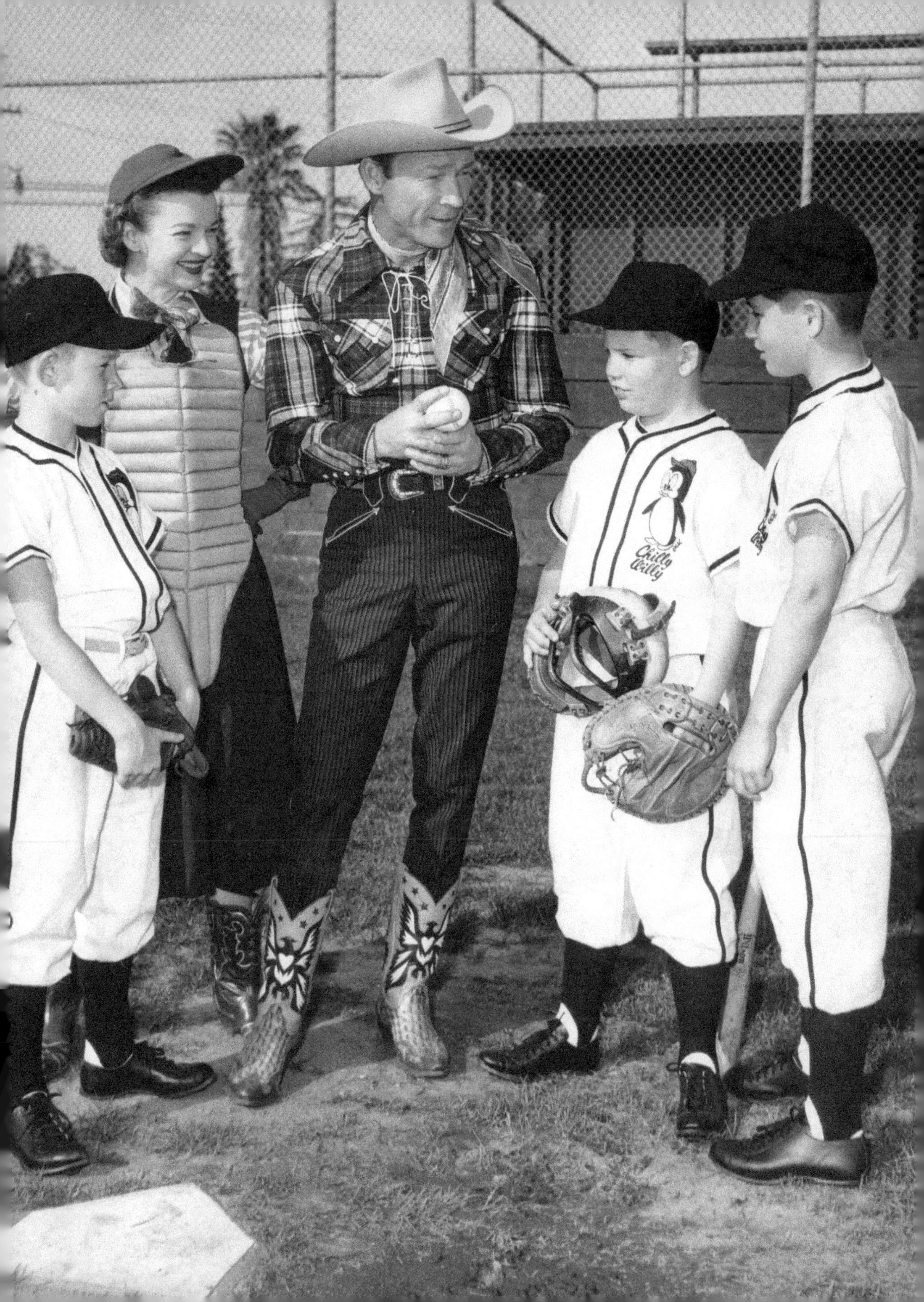
Chilly Willy

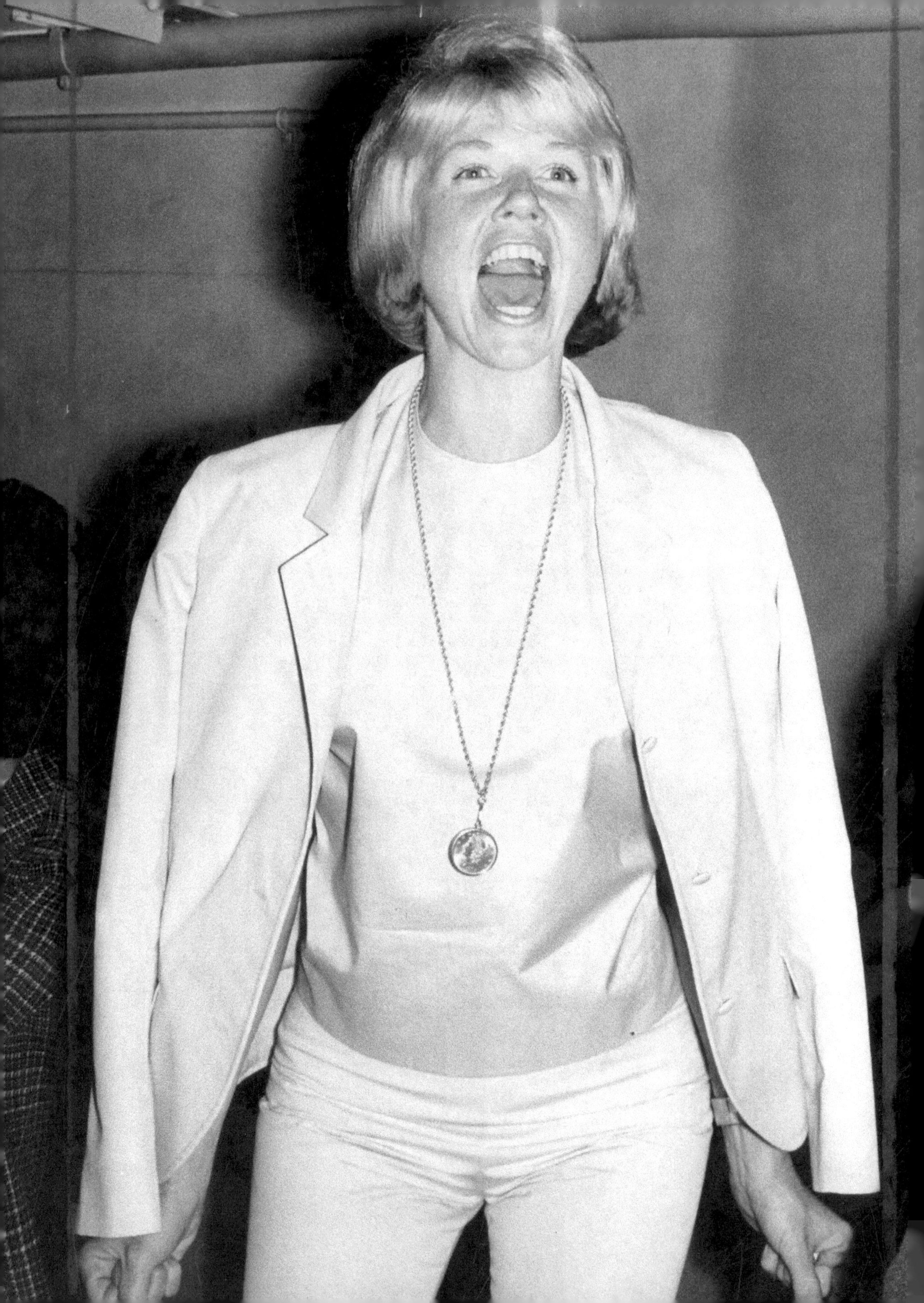

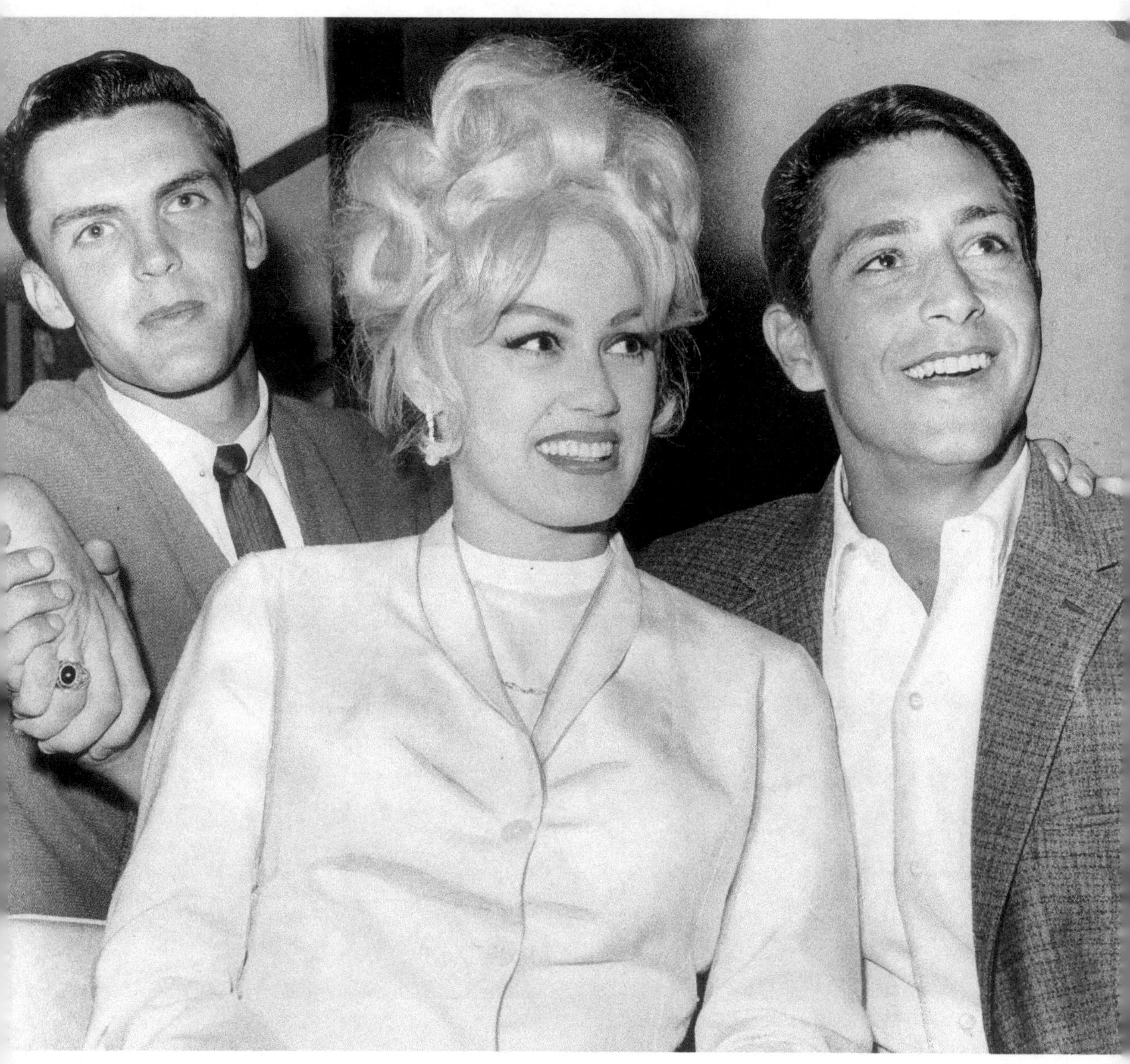

Mamie Van Doren, with Angel pitchers Dean Chance (*left*) and Bo Belinsky.
(Herald-Examiner Collection)

OPPOSITE: Doris Day cheers on the Dodgers.
(Alan Hyde/Valley Times Collection)

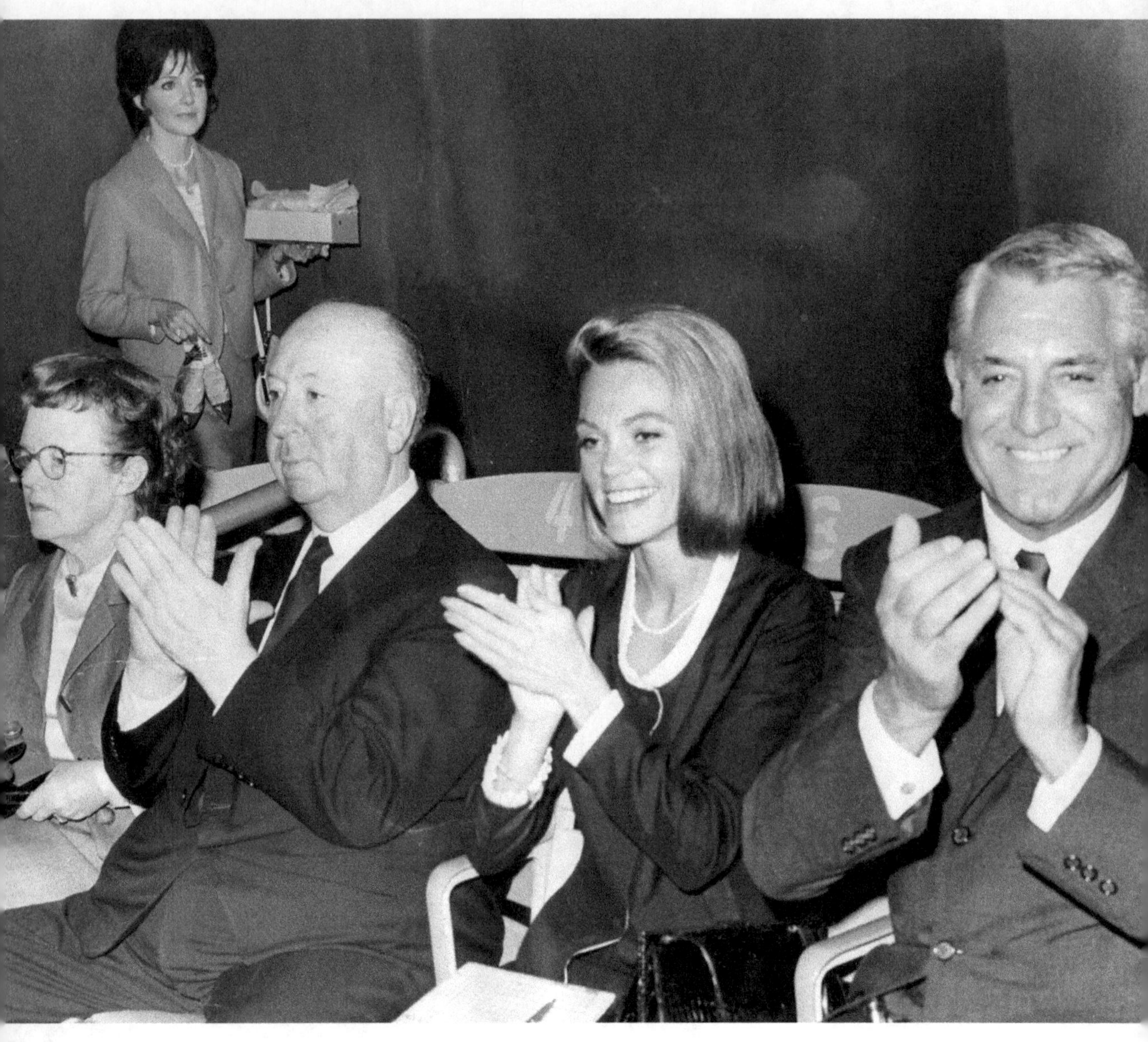

Applause for the Dodgers: (*right to left*) Cary Grant, Dyan Cannon, Alfred Hitchcock, and Alma Reville Hitchcock. (Herald-Examiner Collection)

OPPOSITE: Frank Sinatra and Tom Lasorda in the manager's office. (Rob Brown/Herald-Examiner Collection)

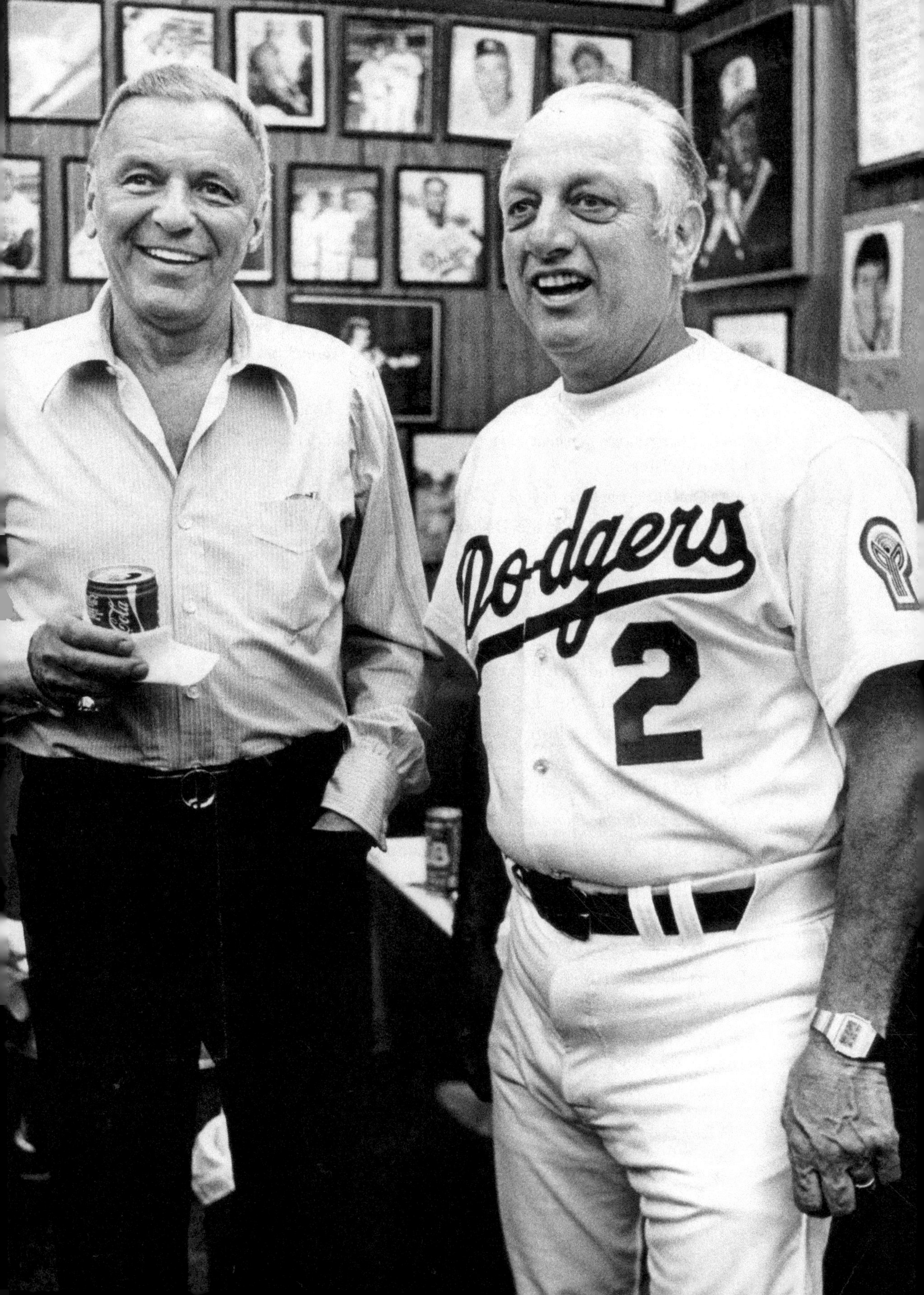
Dodgers
2

Select Bibliography and Resources

Baseball's Greatest Experiment: Jackie Robinson and His Legacy, by Jules Tygiel.

The Best Team Money Can Buy: The Los Angeles Dodgers' Wild Struggle to Build a Baseball Powerhouse, by Molly Knight.

The Bilko Athletic Club: The Story of the 1956 Los Angeles Angels, by Gaylon White.

Black and Blue: Sandy Koufax, the Robinson Brothers, and the World Series That Stunned America, by Tom Adelman.

The Boys of Summer, by Roger Kahn.

Brothers in Arms: Koufax, Kershaw, and the Dodgers' Extraordinary Pitching Tradition, by Jon Weisman.

Bums: An Oral History of the Brooklyn Dodgers, by Peter Golenbock.

Bums No More: The 1959 Los Angeles Dodgers, World Champions of Baseball, by Brian Endsley.

Campy: The Two Lives of Roy Campanella, by Neil Lanctot.

Chavez Ravine, record album by Ry Cooder.

Chavez Ravine: A Los Angeles Story, documentary written and directed by Jordan Mechner for the Independent Lens series.

Chavez Ravine, 1949: A Los Angeles Story, photographs and text by Don Normark.

Chavez Ravine: A Play, by Culture Clash (Richard Montoya, Ric Salinas, Herbert Siguenza).

Cincinnati Red and Dodger Blue: Baseball's Greatest Forgotten Rivalry, by Tom Van Riper.

City of Dreams: Dodger Stadium and the Birth of Modern Los Angeles, by Jerald Podair.

A Day in the Season of the L.A. Dodgers, by Tom Zimmerman.

Dodgerland: Decadent Los Angeles and the 1977-78 Dodgers, by Michael Fallon.

The Dodgers: 60 Years in Los Angeles, by Michael Schiavone.

The Dodgers Encyclopedia, by William McNeil.

The Dodgers Move West, by Neil Sullivan.

The Dodgers: 120 Years of Dodgers Baseball, by Glenn Stout and Richard Johnson.

Forever Blue: The True Story of Walter O'Malley, Baseball's Most Controversial Owner, and the Dodgers of Brooklyn and Los Angeles, by Michael D'Antonio.

The Golden Game: The Story of California Baseball, by Kevin Nelson.

The Greatest Minor League: A History of the Pacific Coast League, 1903-1957, by Dennis Snelling.

High Fives, Pennant Drives, and Fernandomania: A Fan's History of the Los Angeles Dodgers, by Paul Haddad.

The Hollywood Stars, by Richard Beverage.

I Never Had It Made, by Jackie Robinson and Alfred Duckett.

The Integration of the Pacific Coast League: Race and Baseball on the West Coast, by Amy Essington.

It's Good to Be Alive, by Roy Campanella.

Jackie Robinson: A Biography, by Arnold Rampersad.

Jackie Robinson: An Intimate Portrait, by Rachel Robinson.

The Last Good Season: Brooklyn, the Dodgers, and Their Final Pennant Race Together, by Michael Shapiro.

The Last Innocents: The Collision of the Turbulent Sixties and the Los Angeles Dodgers, by Michael Leahy.

The Los Angeles Angels of the Pacific Coast League: A History, 1903-1957, by Richard Beverage.

Los Angeles Coliseum, by Chris Epting.

Los Angeles Dodgers, by Mark Langill.

The Los Angeles Dodgers: The First Quarter Century, by Donald Honig.

Mexican American Baseball in Los Angeles, by Francisco Balderrama and Richard Santillan.

Mexican American Baseball in the San Fernando Valley, by Richard Santillan et al.

Miracle Men: Hershiser, Gibson, and the Improbable 1988 Dodgers, by Josh Suchon.

Mover & Shaker: Walter O'Malley, the Dodgers, & Baseball's Westward Expansion, by Andy McCue.

100 Things Dodgers Fans Should Know & Do Before They Die, by Jon Weisman.

The Pacific Coast League: 1903-1988, by Bill O'Neal.

Play by Play: Los Angeles Sports Photography, 1889-1989, by David Davis.

Runs, Hits, and an Era: The Pacific Coast League, 1903-58, by Paul Zingg and Mark Medeiros.

Sandy Koufax: A Lefty's Legacy, by Jane Leavy.

Shameful Victory: The Los Angeles Dodgers, the Red Scare, and the Hidden History of Chavez Ravine, by John Laslett.

The Ticket Out: Darryl Strawberry and the Boys of Crenshaw, by Michael Sokolove.

Through a Blue Lens: The Brooklyn Dodgers Photographs of Barney Stein, 1937-1957, by Dennis D'Agostino & Bonnie Crosby.

True Blue: The Dramatic History of the Los Angeles Dodgers, Told by the Men Who Lived It, by Steve Delsohn.

walteromalley.com: The Official Website of Walter O'Malley.

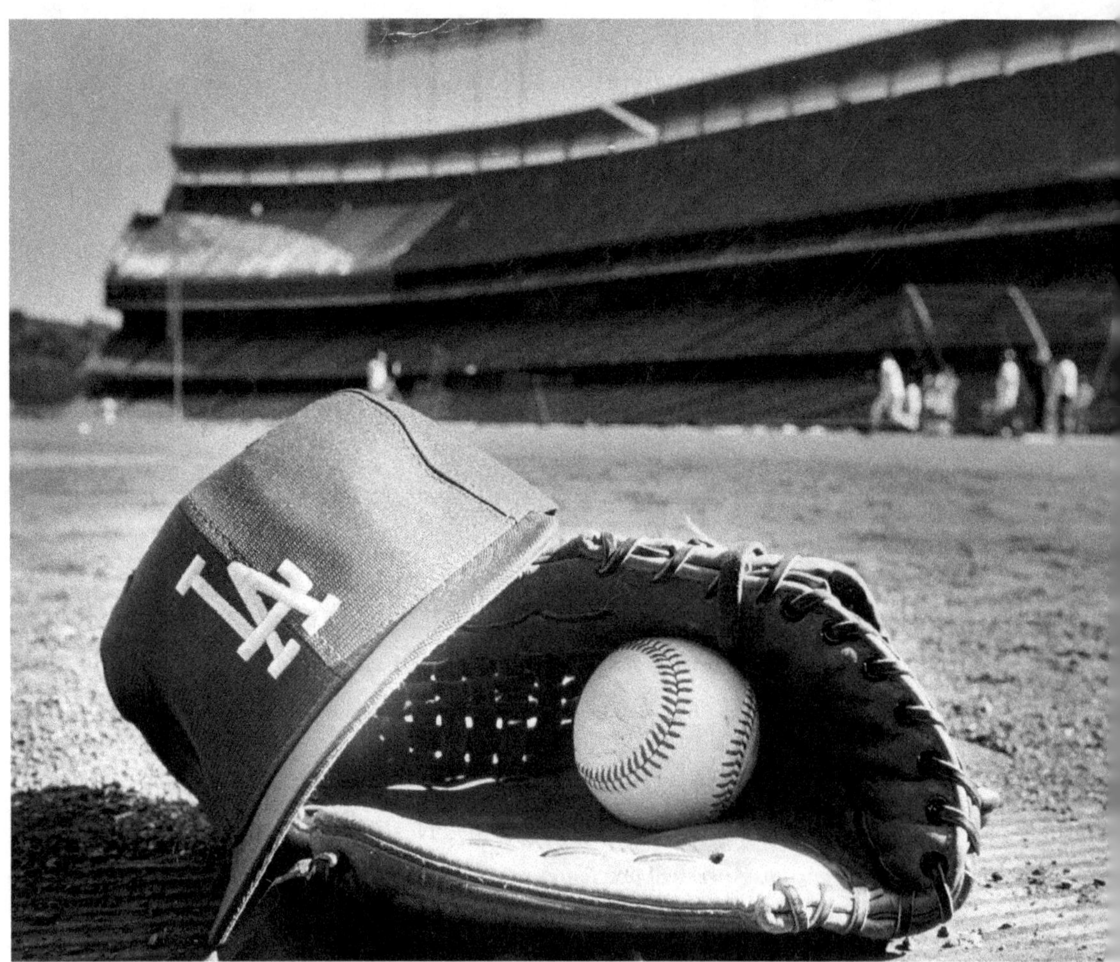

(James Ruebsamen/Herald-Examiner Collection)

About the Editor

Award-winning journalist **David Davis** is the author of four books: *Waterman: The Life and Times of Duke Kahanamoku; Showdown at Shepherd's Bush: The 1908 Olympic Marathon and the Three Runners Who Launched a Sporting Craze*; *Play By Play: Los Angeles Sports Photography, 1889-1989*; and *One Golden Moment: The 1984 Olympics Through the Photographic Lens of the Los Angeles Herald Examiner*; and one eBook: *Marathon Crasher: The Life and Times of Merry Lepper, the First American Woman to Run a Marathon*. His work has appeared in *Sports Illustrated, Smithsonian, New York Times, Wall Street Journal, Los Angeles Magazine* and *Vice*; his writing has been anthologized in *The Best American Sports Writing* series. He has curated two photography exhibitions at the Los Angeles Central Library and has been a board member of Photo Friends since 2004. He lives in Los Angeles.

About the Photo Collection

The Los Angeles Public Library (LAPL) began collecting photographs sometime before World War II and had a collection of about 13,000 images by the late 1950s. In 1981, when Los Angeles celebrated its 200th birthday, Security Pacific National Bank gave its noted collection of historical photographs to the people of Los Angeles to be archived at the Central Library. Since then, LAPL has been fortunate to receive other major collections, making the library a resource worldwide for visual images.

Notable collections include the "photo morgues" of the *Los Angeles Herald Examiner* and *Valley Times* newspapers, the Kelly–Holiday mid-century collection of aerial photographs, the Works Progress Administration/Federal Writers Project collection, the Luther Ingersoll Portrait Collection, and the landmark Shades of L.A., an archive of images representing the contemporary and historic diversity of families in Los Angeles. Images were chosen from family albums and copied in a project sponsored by Photo Friends.

The Los Angeles Public Library Photo Collection also includes the works of individual photographers, including Ansel Adams, Herman Schultheis, William Reagh, Ralph Morris, Lucille Stewart, Gary Leonard, Stone Ishimaru, Carol Westwood, and Rolland Curtis.

Over 120,000 images from these collections have been digitized and are available to view through the LAPL website at http://photos.lapl.org.

About Photo Friends

Formed in 1990, Photo Friends is a nonprofit organization that supports the Los Angeles Public Library's Photograph Collection and History & Genealogy Department. Our goal is to improve access to the collections and promote them through programs, projects, exhibits, and books such as this one.

We are an enthusiastic group of photographers, writers, historians, business people, politicians, academics, and many others, all bonded by our passion for photography, history, and Los Angeles.

Since 1994, Photo Friends has presented a regular series called *The Photographer's Eye*, which spotlights local photographers and their work. In 2011, Photo Friends inaugurated *L.A. in Focus*, a lecture series that features images drawn primarily from the Photo Collection. We have presented programs on L.A. crime, the San Fernando Valley, Kelly–Holiday aerial photographs, and L.A.'s themed environments, among others.

With initial funding from the Ralph M. Parsons Foundation, Photo Friends sponsored the L.A. Neighborhoods Project by commissioning photographers to create a visual record of the neighborhoods of Los Angeles during the early part of the 21st century (all now part of the collection). To ensure the library's collection will continue to reflect such an important part of Los Angeles' history, a generous grant enabled Photo Friends to hire five contemporary photographers to document present-day industrial L.A.; these images have become part of LAPL's permanent collection and are available to view through the library's photo database. Photo Friends also curates photography exhibits on display in the History Department.

Photo Friends is a membership organization. Please consider becoming a member and helping us in our work to preserve and promote L.A.'s rich photographic resource. All proceeds from the sale of this book go to support Photo Friends' programs.

photofriends.org

Thank you to the many photographers whose work fills these pages with indelible images, and thanks to the fine crew of writers who generously contributed to this effort. Thanks especially to Photo Friends president and designer extraordinaire Amy Inouye for her patience, support, and creativity. You are a community gem. Thanks also to Christina Rice, who oversees the Los Angeles Public Library's Photo Collection with skill and aplomb, and thanks to fellow Photo Friends board members for their enthusiasm and wisdom. Finally, thanks to family and friends. See you at the ballpark.
—DD

This catalog was published in conjunction with a photo exhibit
at Los Angeles Central Library's History & Genealogy Department,
curated by David Davis,
on display in the History & Genealogy Department (LL4)
July 19, 2018 - January 13, 2019.

L.A. Baseball
by David Davis

Published by:

Photo Friends of the Los Angeles Public Library
c/o Future Studio
P.O. Box 292000
Los Angeles, CA 90029
www.photofriends.org

Designed by Amy Inouye, Future Studio Los Angeles

Special quantity discounts available when purchased in bulk by corporations, organizations, or groups. Please contact Photo Friends at: photofriendsla@gmail.com

ISBN-13: 978-0-9978251-5-2

Printed in the United States

FRONT COVER: Fernando Valenzuela (James Ruebsamen/Herald-Examiner Collection)
BACK COVER (TOP TO BOTTOM): "Bloomer girls" playing baseball in Echo Park. (Herald-Examiner Collection) • Vin Scully bobblehead night, August 30, 2012. (Gary Leonard) • Babe Ruth and his mighty bat come to L.A. to shoot a movie in the off-season. (Security Pacific National Bank Collection)

www.ingramcontent.com/pod-product-compliance
Lightning Source LLC
LaVergne TN
LVHW081323110826
845149LV00007B/1578

* 9 7 8 0 9 9 7 8 2 5 1 5 2 *